Logistics in
World War II

To a very dear friend. Thank you for the inspiration

Logistics in World War II

1939–1945

John Norris

Pen & Sword
MILITARY

First published in Great Britain in 2020 by
Pen & Sword Military
An imprint of
Pen & Sword Books Ltd
47 Church Street
Barnsley
South Yorkshire
S70 2AS

ISBN 978 1 47385 912 8

Typeset in 11.5/15 point Ehrhardt MT
Printed and bound in India by Replika Press Pvt. Ltd.

Pen & Sword Books Limited incorporates the imprints of Atlas, Archaeology,
Aviation, Discovery, Family History, Fiction, History, Maritime, Military,
Military Classics, Politics, Select, Transport, True Crime, Air World,
Frontline Publishing, Leo Cooper, Remember When, Seaforth Publishing,
The Praetorian Press, Wharncliffe Local History, Wharncliffe Transport,
Wharncliffe True Crime and White Owl.

For a complete list of Pen & Sword titles please contact
PEN & SWORD BOOKS LIMITED
47 Church Street, Barnsley, South Yorkshire, S70 2AS, England
E-mail: enquiries@pen-and-sword.co.uk
Website: www.pen-and-sword.co.uk

Contents

Acknowledgements

I would like to extend my sincere thanks to all the museums where I have conducted research into the subject of logistics, namely the Royal Logistics Corps Museum at Deepcut in Surrey, the Imperial War Museum in London and the Tank Museum at Bovington in Dorset. I am also grateful to the Cobbaton Combat Collection in Devon and the Muckleburgh Collection in Norfolk. I am indebted to all the military historians who gave unstintingly of their time, answered many questions and explained things in detail. Without such assistance I could not have proceeded with this work.

Introduction

It is one thing for a country to mobilise its army and deploy it for battle, but it requires a great deal of support to keep it continuously supplied to levels that allow it to fight to the best of its ability. During the Second World War armies required enormous amounts of ammunition, food, fuel and other supplies to keep them functioning. The war lasted for six years, during which time it drew in fifty-seven countries from five continents.

The fighting affected the largest nations in the world, and it also affected thousands of islands scattered around the world's oceans, such as the islands of Japan and the Philippines, down to the peaceful Channel Islands of Jersey and Guernsey.

In every theatre of war, the armies had to be kept supplied and the wounded evacuated. This required vast resources from civilian labour in factories producing the kit to the non-combatant troops needed to move the supplies forward for distribution. Prisoners of war had to be dealt with by removing them from the fighting area. This involved transportation, either by railway or ships, often over thousands of miles, imposing a further strain on supply lines.

As the size of the armies grew and the fighting spread, commanders in the field realised that in order to conduct their campaigns they needed ever-increasing supplies to function at maximum capacity. Napoleon Bonaparte is famously misquoted as saying, 'An army marches on its stomach.' What he actually said was, 'It is soup which makes the soldier.' If an army is to be effective, and remain so, it has to be able to rely on good and plentiful supplies of food. However, feeding an army is only part of the problem. Pay, ammunition, providing replacement equipment, replacement troops and the evacuation of wounded combine to make up the lines of logistics. During the Second World War, supplies of fuel oil would prove to be the deciding factor in many cases. Without it, tanks could not move and aircraft could not fly.

Countries that became involved in the war were affected by logistics to a greater or lesser degree depending on their geographical position and commitment. Another factor to consider was their allegiance. The Allied countries benefitted from support even from the populations of occupied territories such as France, Belgium and Holland. In the case of Britain, it could count on countries within the British Empire, such as India, along with the Dominions including Canada, Australia and New Zealand, each of which would rally to Britain's aid. The Axis powers of Germany, Italy and Japan would be joined by their own allies such as Hungary, Finland and Korea.

The third side to the conflict were those countries which had declared themselves neutral, such as Sweden, Switzerland and Portugal. These remained neutral throughout the war, and although not engaged in fighting they were inevitably affected by it, both socially and politically. Sweden and Switzerland profited financially by trading with both Allies and Axis forces and in that respect were treading a fine line, which, if crossed too far one way or the other, could see them becoming directly involved. Switzerland, for example, provided Germany with technological and industrial support for payment. By 1941 it had increased its exports of chemicals by 250 per cent from pre-war levels and exports of metals were increased by 500 per cent, all sold for premium prices. Then there were those countries, such as Turkey, Uruguay and Bolivia, which were neutral at the beginning of the war but later joined the Allies. Bolivia benefitted from trade, which in its case was to supply tin to the Allies. Its geographical location meant that, unlike Spain or Sweden, it was beyond the reach of enemy spies or attack by Axis forces.

Almost 250 years earlier, at the start of the eighteenth century, John Churchill, later to become the first Duke of Marlborough, proved himself to be the master of logistics when it came to planning his campaigns. Between 1701 and 1711, during the War of the Spanish Succession, Churchill planned for every possible contingency, applying precise attention to detail from the smallest of matters to the largest. He knew that feeding his army on campaign was of the utmost importance and realised the daily difficulties involved. For example, his army of 62,000 men at the Battle of Ramillies on 23 May 1706 consumed around 90 tons of bread each day which required 60 portable ovens and 200 wagons of fuel for the baking ovens. At one point Churchill's supply line comprised 1,700 horse-drawn wagons, transporting 800 tons of stores. It was his meticulous planning which eventually led to him winning the war.

Two hundred years later, during the First World War, the Russian army was forced to stop fighting in 1917 due a collapse in its lines of logistics. With no food, clothing or ammunition reaching the troops, they became demoralised which affected their ability and willingness to fight. The situation was further compounded by political unrest in Moscow which developed into open revolution.

The situation for the British army could not have been more different. In 1914 Britain went to war with a standing army of some 250,000 men, 27,500 horses and 922 motor vehicles, including 80 trucks, 827 motor cars and 15 motorcycles. By 1918 the army had expanded to 5,363,000 troops, with 900,000 horses for transport and a fleet of motorised vehicles which had multiplied by 132 times to reach nearly 122,000 machines. This figure included 56,000 motor cars and 34,000 motorcycles, the remainder being trucks and armoured fighting vehicles (AFVs) in the form of tanks, armoured cars and the first self-propelled guns. To deal with this huge army, a series of supply depots for the distribution of war materiel was established in France, usually where railways and harbours could handle the bulk of shipments. Between January and October 1915 the supply depot at Calais issued to the British army '11,000 prismatic and magnetic compasses, 7,000 watches, 40,000 miles of electric cable, 40,000 electric torches, 3,600,000 yards of flannelette, 1,260,000 yards of rot-proof canvas, 25,000 tents, 1,600,000 waterproof sheets, 12,800 bicycles, 20,000 wheels, 6,000,000 anti-gas helmets, 4,000,000 pairs of horse and wheel shoes, 447,000 Lewis-gun magazines…' Between 1914 and 1918 the British army issued 137,224,141 pairs of socks to the troops and over 30,000 miles of flannelette cloth used for cleaning rifles and pistols. Administration services recorded everything and the offices had to be supplied with the equipment necessary to keep things moving. This included some 51,000 rubber stamps, so that a soldier's leave could be authorised or an attack confirmed. Rubber stamps were also involved in the issuing of rations, such as the monthly 40,000 tons of bread in 1914, or the 1,600 tons of meat per month which rose to 30,000 tons in 1918.

An additional 6,879 miles of railway track were laid to carry everything. In 1914 the British army had gone to war with a single ammunition train with stocks of several hundred tons in reserve. By the end of the war there were eight massive depots holding

Moving some of the more than five million tons of ammunition supplied to the British army in the First World War.

336,000 tons of ammunition with 120 railheads capable of delivering 9,000 tons of ammunition each day. Railways could only take the materiel so far before it had to be off-loaded and put onto trucks for dispatch to various units at the front.

Recruiting posters went up to encourage men to enlist in specialist units such as the Army Service Corps which needed drivers for the expanding fleet of trucks. As an incentive they were to be paid at the rate of six shillings (30 pence) a day compared to the one shilling a day for the fighting man in the trenches. At its peak the ASC had 10,547 officers and 315,534 men in its ranks, the equivalent of more than twenty divisions or three full-sized armies.

Another specialised unit to expand was the Royal Army Medical Corps, which in 1914 had 20,000 men and by 1918 had increased to 150,000. During that time, they had treated nine million cases of all types from gas poisoning to bayonet wounds, administered 1,088 million doses of various drugs, fitted 1.5 million splints, and used over 108 million bandages and 7,250 tons of cotton wool. All this had to be taken to France and many of the wounded had to be returned to Britain for continued treatment. During the four years of the war the Army Service Corps helped move and distribute for the British army some 3.25 million tons of foodstuffs, 5.25 million tons of ammunition and 5.43 million tons of fodder for the horses and mules. Distribution of petrol rose from approximately 3,800 tons per month in August 1915 to over 58,000 tons by 1918. The Shell oil company was supplying 160,000 gallons of petrol daily to the army, making enormous profits in the process. Lord Curzon said that the defeat of Germany in 1918 had only been possible because 'the Allies [had] floated to victory on a tide of oil.' It would prove to be same again during the Second World War.

Other belligerent nations including Italy, France, Germany, and, later, America, faced the same problem as they laboured to move similar loads of stores for their respective armies. During its advance into France in 1914 the German 1st Army of 320,000 men, commanded by General Alexander von Kluck, had 84,000 horses in its organisation requiring over 890 tons of fodder each day. Ammunition for weapons and food for the men had to be brought forward down the line of supply, which each day became longer and more difficult as they advanced. At the time, the German army had a fleet of only 500 trucks in the area. Each corps involved in the operation required 130 tons of food and fodder each day, 3,900 tons in total daily for the entire force, with the supply lines for each stretching along twenty miles of road and taking a whole day to complete its delivery.

A typical infantry division of the German army comprised around 15,000 men organised into smaller units such as brigades with around 4,000 men and battalions up to 1,000 men. Each man carried his own standard kit weighing sixty pounds, containing ammunition, food, entrenching tools and other sundries. On reaching the point of destination by train, a brigade, for example, would be allocated over three miles of road to assemble ready to march. An entire division with a complement of more than 6,000

Mountains of boxes full of stores were sited in depots like this along the Western Front on both sides during the First World War.

horses and over 1,000 wagons, for transport of supplies and stores, would be stretched out along fifteen miles of road and could take up to five hours to pass any one point. Every day there were hundreds of thousands of troops from both sides on the move at any given time as reinforcements arrived and units were redeployed to other areas or simply moved into reserve positions.

In the first months of the war in 1914 the French army was faced with a crisis concerning the lack of troops arriving at the front. In an inspired response General Joseph Gallieni, military governor of Paris, ordered all available taxis from the city to transport troops to the front. The French army tested the capacity of its supply lines to its limit eighteen months later, when, at the beginning of 1916, commanders became aware that the city of Verdun, straddling the river Meuse, was being threatened by the Germans. The city was of no particular strategic value, but the French saw its defence as essential for national pride. They resolved to defend it whatever the cost. The French moved thousands of troops into its defence. The main supply route to the city was the 45-mile stretch of road leading to the depots at Souilly and Bar-le-Duc. It was the main artery for moving supplies and reinforcements and the term 'Voie Sacrée' (Sacred Way) was conferred on it by the French author and politician Maurice Barrès. An average of 3,900 trucks passed along the route each day. Motorised trucks were faster than horse-drawn wagons and on 21 February all horse-drawn transport was ordered off the road to make way for the untiring motorised trucks. In one week from 28 February some 190,000 troops and 25,000 tons of supplies were moved along the Voie Sacrée to bolster the defences of Verdun. The city was held but at a terrible cost to both sides. During the ten months of fighting the French lost almost 380,000 men and the Germans 340,000. In that time, it is estimated that between them the two sides fired over 37 million artillery shells of all calibres.

America declared war on Germany on 6 April 1917 and the first American troops landed in France in June that year. By November 1918 the American Expeditionary Force had 1.98 million men in France of which more than 688,000 were engaged in the Services of Supply (SOS). These men were comparable to the British ASC and operated a fleet of 30,000 trucks. In the first seven months of service in France the Americans received 484,000 tons of supplies directly from America. This level gradually increased so that by the end of the war an average of 426,000 tons was arriving every month. This included 1.2 million weapons, including rifles, pistols and machine guns, along with other ancillary items such as 425,000 axes and 1.3 million sets of cutlery. The war in Europe, until April 1917, had not been America's affair, but once the country became fully committed it lost no time in catching up. Its troops fought hard and many lessons were learned, not the least of which was how vital good supplies were in keeping an army operational on the battlefield.

Then, on 11 November 1918, it was finally over. All the hard work to keep the armies fighting was made redundant at a stroke when the Armistice was signed and the fighting stopped. Movement of all war materiel suddenly stopped, leaving the belligerents with massive stockpiles of supplies, weapons and ammunition.

During the war, all armies had learned many lessons, especially the importance of supplies. The war had been the first great conflict to be decided as much by the power of motorised transport and the need for fuel oil as by any strategy or weapon. It also demonstrated to armies around the world what scale of resources they would need to fight any prolonged war in the future.

A word came into common use to describe the duties of supplying an army with all its necessary equipment – logistics. It comes from the ancient Greek λογιστικὸς, meaning 'accounting and financial organisation'. In Roman and Byzantine military societies officers would be appointed to serve as 'logistikas' and were responsible for the financial and supply distribution affairs of the army.

In recent times it has been suggested that logistics accounts for '90 per cent of the business of war' and considering the amount of war materiel absorbed on campaigns this may well be the case. Unfortunately, the role of the troops serving in the units handling supplies has never been fully understood by those serving in the front line. They appreciated the supplies when they arrived, but not knowing the difficulties involved developed a belief that those in the rear areas were having an easy time of things.

Consequently they were referred to in derogatory terms, such as *Ettappenschweine* (lines of communication pigs), an expression used by the German fighting man in the First World War. This was rather unfair because the support troops faced dangers from artillery as they moved forward and suffered casualties as they did so.

By 1918 there were over 325,000 men in the ASC and so vital was their role the regiment was granted the prefix Royal. The units in which these men serve have come to be referred to as 'tail' arms as opposed to 'teeth' arms.

The Prussian officer and military theorist Carl Philipp Gottfried von Clauswitz (1780-1831) wrote extensively on the conduct of war, his most famous work being *Vom Kriege (On War)*. In this he states, 'Everything is very simple in war, but the simplest thing is difficult.' On the matter of logistics, he wrote, 'There is nothing more common than to find considerations of supply affecting the strategic line of a campaign and a war.'

He was not the first person to put down on paper his thoughts concerning the importance of logistics to keeping an army fighting fit. In the fourth century, during the late period of the Roman Empire, the military thinker Flavius Renatus Vegetius wrote *De Re Militari*. It became influential in the Middle Ages and contained some opinions which held true to the armies in the Second World War. One of his thoughts was that an army which was not properly supported with logistics would not succeed. Another opinion concerned the destruction of an enemy's resources such as food and shelter, that, in the event they should counter-attack, they would find nothing to support them. This, in effect, was 'scorched earth' in reverse.

The French had their equivalent to Clauswitz in Swiss-born Antoine-Henri Jomini (1779-1869). He famously wrote that 'Logistics comprises the means and arrangements which work out the plans of strategy and tactics. Strategy decides where to act; logistics brings the troops to this point.' Both theorists had written in a time before the motor vehicle when draught animals such as oxen, mules and horses were the only means of moving supplies either in wagons or as pack loads, but even so their comments are still valid today.

The British military historian and theorist Major General J.F.C. Fuller wrote, 'Surely one of the strangest things in military history is the complete silence about the problems of supplies. In ten thousand books written on war not one is to be found on the subject, yet it forms the basis on which rests the whole structure of war: it is the very foundation of tactics and strategy.'

Without logistics none of the amphibious landings undertaken by the Allies during the war – Normandy, Salerno, Anzio, Sicily, North Africa – or the entire island-hopping campaign in the Pacific against the Japanese, would have been possible. For the Axis powers, they would experience the difficulties of supplying armies in the field. The German army would become a victim of its own success as it pushed ever-deeper into Russia. For the Japanese it would face the problems of supplying the many isolated island garrisons spread across the Pacific Ocean, as well as the great distances in China.

Chapter 1

A New Kind of Warfare

In 1939 General Archibald Wavell presented the Lees Knowles Lecture to Trinity College in Cambridge in which he expressed the importance of logistics by stating to his assembled audience, 'I should like you to always bear in mind when you study military history or military events the importance of this administrative factor, because it is where most critics and many generals go wrong.' Wavell had served in the First World War, losing an eye and winning the Military Cross. He was one of the few more progressive post-war military thinkers who grasped the fundamentals of this new form of supplying an army. On the other side of the Atlantic, the American General Brehon B. Somervell held the same opinion, perhaps more strongly, stating that 'Good logistics alone can win a war. Bad logistics alone can lose it.' He knew from experience how vital it was to keep an army on the move. Somervell had seen service against Pancho Villa in 1916 before proving himself a capable organiser in Europe in the First World War where he earned a reputation for getting things done.

Several years after presenting his lecture to Trinity College, Field Marshal Wavell, as he was by then, took up writing and toured giving lectures. He had served with distinction during the Second World War, seeing action in North Africa, where Rommel was impressed by him, and then later in Burma. Six years of war had strengthened his belief in the importance of logistics. It became the subject of some of his talks and his writings, such as *Speaking Generally* (1946) in which he paid tribute to the troops engaged in bringing up the supplies: 'The more I have seen of war, the more I realise how it all depends on administration and transportation (what our American allies call logistics). It takes little skill or imagination to see where you would like your army and when; it takes much knowledge and hard work to know where you can place your forces and whether you can maintain them there. A real knowledge of supply and movement factors must be the basis of every leader's plan; only then can he know how and when to take the risks with these factors; and battles and wars are won by taking risks.' Wavell referred to such administration as the 'crux of generalship'.

At the time Wavell was delivering his Lees Knowle's Lecture Europe was on the brink of war. It was a situation which had been approaching for four or five years. There were so-called 'hot spots', such as the Spanish Civil War which had erupted in 1939, and a handful of countries were flexing their military muscles in overseas territories. One of these was Italy, which had been under the Fascist leadership of Benito Mussolini, since his appointment as Prime Minister in 1922. Three years later, in 1925, he became virtual dictator, known as *Il Duce* (the leader) and set about destroying any political opposition, crushing the labour unions and abolishing strikes by workers. In October 1935 Italian troops invaded Ethiopia in North Africa where the ill-equipped and inexperienced local troops stood no chance against aerial bombing and the use of poison gas. The following year Italian troops marched into East Somalia. Despite this, Mussolini was not seen as a potential threat. If anything, he became a popular figure, with his picture appearing several times on the front cover of *Time* magazine.

The same could not be said about the situation in Germany, where the actions of Adolf Hitler, who had been appointed the country's Chancellor in 1933, were being viewed with deep suspicion.

The German army had quit the battlefield in November 1918 and, although battered and weakened, it was not a defeated army. Several months later on 28 June 1919 in the French town of Versailles, the League of Nations, which had been formed only two months earlier in April that year, delegates from the Allied nations gathered to debate the future political and economic position of Germany and impose the size and state of the country's armed forces. The Treaty of Versailles imposed strict levels concerning German armed forces. Their army was limited to 100,000 men without conscription. Anti-tank guns, anti-aircraft guns and heavy field artillery were forbidden, nor was Germany allowed tanks, aircraft or submarines. Naval vessels had to be under a size of 10,000 tons and no general staff was permitted.

They were harsh terms, intended to prevent Germany from posing a threat to Europe in the future, and, with no option, the Weimar Republic reluctantly agreed. But resentment ran deep and secret negotiations were conducted between German representatives and agents from countries such as Sweden and Russia to help the reconstruction of the German military. One of those involved in these discussions was General Hans von Seeckt who had served on the general staff during the war. He was serving as the commander-in-chief of the Reichswehr army, while at the same time engaging in secret negotiations with Soviet Russia to acquire weapons, vehicles and access to training for troops.

German weapons designers from companies such as Krupp moved abroad to take up 'temporary' residency in countries, particularly Sweden, where they were able to work on the design and development of weapons in secret. One of these was Joseph Vollmer, who had been behind the design of the A7V tank, Germany's only operational tank of the entire war. During his voluntary exile he helped design the LK I and LK II tanks used by Sweden. Another German weapon which benefitted from Swedish cooperation was the 8.8cm anti-aircraft gun, based on a design going back to the end of the First World War. German armaments technicians, who worked in Sweden between 1920 and 1930, took with them the developed plans for this gun which Germany was forbidden to possess under the terms of the Treaty of Versailles. Numbers of these new guns were used in Spain in their intended role, but it was against tanks that they really showed what they were capable of. During the war the 88mm anti-tank gun would come to be feared by Allied tanks crews from France to Russia.

Outwardly, Germany was seen as observing the limits of the Treaty of Versailles. France, Britain and Belgium began to relax and even to scale down their armed forces. In 1922 the Committee on National Expenditure, headed by Sir Eric Geddes, sliced into Britain's armed forces and implemented huge reductions in size in a move known as the 'Geddes Axe'. Twenty-two infantry battalions were dissolved, along with eight regiments of cavalry, and several battalions were withdrawn from overseas service. In 1926 the strength of the British army stood at 184,161 and the budget for the purchase of armaments was capped at £2 million.

The budgets for research and development into new weapons were cut back in most countries as the effects of the 'Great Depression' hit the economies around the world. Britain's budget for the design, development and building of tanks was only £357,000 in 1932. It was not until 1937 that this allocation would be substantially increased to £3,625,000, by which time Europe had weathered several crises, all of Germany's making. Some countries began rearmament programmes, but, as in Britain, it would prove too little too late. In America, a policy of isolationism was adopted and the military budget was slashed. Disarmament talks were held in 1933 but they broke down when France refused to disarm and the German delegation walked out of the proceedings and left the League of Nations in October.

Hitler made his first move in January 1935 by ordering troops to enter the region of the Saar on the border between France and Germany. This was a French-administered zone but when France and Britain did not react Hitler knew he could go further without any repercussions. Two months later, on 1 March, Hitler announced the reintroduction of conscription for the army and repudiated the Treaty of Versailles. A year later, no doubt encouraged by the inactions of the League of Nations against Italy's invasion of Ethiopia, he ordered troops to enter the Rhineland, which, under the terms of the Treaty of Versailles, had been declared a 'demilitarised zone'. These moves returned to Germany the coalfields and industrial resources necessary for Hitler to complete his planned rearmament programme. Yet still Britain and France did nothing.

With the small army Germany was allowed under the Treaty of Versailles it was not such a problem to reorganise its structure. It served as a framework on which to build a modern army and introduce new weapons. This included Panzer I light tanks, which were really armoured machine gun carriers, introduced into service in 1934, but they were new and modern. Troops were trained in modern tactics which combined all arms. They were introduced to the new weapons and, without any prior instruction to influence them, they learned only those skills required to operate those weapons currently in service. Emphasis was placed on training NCOs. Communications were improved and the supply lines that would keep the army on the move were also strengthened and reorganised with better structure. Unlike the armies of France and Britain, which were set in their ways, the new German army was willing to embrace innovations.

In June 1935 Stanley Baldwin became Prime Minister. Apart from a brief foray into military service as a volunteer lieutenant, he was a career politician. He knew that rearmament was a contentious point among the people and understood that it would not be a popular policy, stating, 'Supposing I had gone to the country and said that Germany was rearming and that we must rearm, does anybody think that this pacific democracy would have rallied to that cry at that moment? I cannot think of anything that would have made the loss of the election from my point of view more certain.' Baldwin was replaced by Neville Chamberlain, another career politician but with no military experience at all, in May 1937. MPs who had resisted rearmament now changed their minds following the start of the Spanish Civil War and seeing the

Armies across Europe prepared for war in the mid-1930s. Here, a unit of the Territorial Army in Eltham, London, train with a searchlight in 1937.

Vickers Medium Tanks were used in limited numbers by the British Army during the rearmament period.

aggressive moves on the part Germany. Sixteen new factories for war production were immediately established and a further twenty-nine were sanctioned. The defence budget was massively increased to £580 million for aircraft, tanks, artillery and warships. The British government was trying to play catch-up with Germany but the country was a couple of years behind. Still, better late than never, and British industry began to mobilise, weapons were produced and hundreds of factories turned to the production of uniforms, kit and equipment.

France had started its rearmament programme in 1936 and one of the first projects it undertook was the building of new tank designs such as the Renault R-35 Light Tank for the specific role of supporting the infantry.

Up to this point all the military manoeuvres by German army had been localised and required minimal support in the way of logistics. The Italian invasion of Ethiopia went unopposed and Mussolini's troops could transport their supplies unimpeded. The League of Nations had threatened sanctions which, in the end, were never implemented. One of these had been the threat of an oil embargo. Mussolini later admitted that had such an embargo been instituted he would have been left with no option than to withdraw his forces within a week because their position would have become impossible to maintain.

In mid-July 1936, events developed in Spain, on the western edge of Continental Europe, leading to civil war between the Republican troops under men such as Manuel Azaña and Julián Besteiro fighting Nationalists led by General Franco, who harboured Fascist ideals. One of the earliest demonstrations of military power during this bloody war took place when 10,000 troops for Franco were airlifted from Morocco to Spain. Mussolini and Hitler, who had signed the Berlin-Rome alliance in October, readily offered military support to a fellow Fascist leader. They sent troops, artillery and tanks to support Franco. France and Britain did nothing beyond criticising them.

Soviet Russia then sent 700 tanks, mainly old-fashioned Christie and Vickers types, to support the Republicans.

The Spanish Civil War has since come to be described as a 'live firing rehearsal' for the total war that was to erupt five months after the fighting in Spain had ended. This not entirely correct because, although Hitler sent some 16,000 troops to aid Franco, this left the greater proportion of the German army, more than three million men, without combat experience. What these men did achieve, along with the crews of the tanks Hitler sent, was to use their weapons, such as the 88mm anti-aircraft gun, in actual battle conditions, and refine drills. When these men returned to Germany they were able to pass on what they had learned by forming training cadres for other troops. Hitler sent 600 aircraft and the pilots were able to pass on their combat skills at training centres. Mussolini made a greater contribution by sending 50,000 troops between 1936 and 1939, along with 660 aircraft, 150 tanks, 800 pieces of artillery, 1,500 mortars, 10,000 machine guns and 240,000 rifles.

All of this materiel had to be transported along with the troops which formed the logistics lines between Germany and Italy as they dispatched it to Spain. Germany could airlift the equipment or send it by sea without having to cross France. For Italy, everything could be loaded onto ships and sailed directly to ports in Spain. Soviet Russia could do the same in sending supplies to the Republican forces. Volunteers from around the world, including France, Britain, Canada and America, travelled to Spain to fight for the Republicans in so-called 'International Brigades'.

While the eyes of the world were focused on events in Spain, Hitler made his next move. On 12 March 1938 German troops crossed into Austria to complete the *Anschluss*, which annexed the country to create the 'Greater German Reich'. This move gave Hitler access to even more manufacturing capabilities for weaponry, vehicles and the potential resources of troops to operate them.

The year of 1938 was to prove a time of decisions which would show weaknesses and flaws in some and strengths in others. The growing military state in Germany was causing consternation, added to which the involvement in Spain along with Italy was deeply concerning. Every day there was increasing talk of war, despite reassurances from politicians. Across Europe, countries began to rearm and take measures to prepare for what many saw as inevitable war. Switzerland was a neutral state and Holland, which had been neutral in the first war, retained this status. Belgium, which had been invaded by Germany in 1914 even though it had been neutral at the time, had returned to its state of neutrality after 1918. In 1938 its army consisted of only twenty-two divisions with no armoured support. France had a large army and reserve force, and had recently completed work on the Maginot Line, a series of defences designed to protect its eastern border in the event of an attack by Germany. The French had an unwavering faith in the line which stretched for eighty-seven miles and was heavily armed with subterranean fortresses served by 250,000 men.

Between 1930 and 1938 the number of trucks produced for the French army had been halved and those designs it did take into service were based on civilian models. In 1936 the French Defence Minister, Edouard Daladier, ordered a rearmament programme calling for 3,200 modern tanks and 5,000 other tracked vehicles at a cost of 14 million Francs. It was too little too late. Combined with the building of the Maginot Line, defence spending was spiralling. France had one of the most powerful armies in Europe, yet within a year it still found itself going to war equipped with a mixture of modern designs and ageing vehicles such as FT17 tanks and Berliet CBA trucks both of First World War vintage. The main truck production companies of Renault, Citroën, Panhard and others such as Berliet produced vehicles which could carry troops and equipment but they were still essentially based on civilian models.

France began to rearm and its reservist forces were mobilised in 1939.

Some countries began to prepare their civilian populations in the event of war and built public air raid shelters. In Britain, the government issued family air raid shelters, which could be erected in gardens, known as 'Anderson Shelters' named after Sir John Anderson, Lord Privy Seal, whose duties included the preparation of air raid precautions. These structures were issued free of charge to families with an income of less than £5 per week, and could be purchased at a cost of £7 by those with a higher income, if they wished. During the war, some three million of these shelters were built. The government also issued 38 million gas masks, including 1.5 million special 'gas helmets' for new-born infants, in the event of an attack by poison gas. But with a population of 48 million, this meant a shortfall of around ten million gas masks. Troops in the armed forces were issued with their own service respirators, but even so, that still left millions without gas masks. In June 1939 the Women's Land Army (WLA), which had been formed in the First World War to help agricultural workers on farms to produce more food, was reformed by Lady Denman in preparation to once again serve in the same role. At its peak it would have 90,000 women working on arable and dairy farms across the country. The Timber Corps branch of the WLA had several thousand women workers who felled trees to produce the wood for ammunition boxes, railway sleepers, panelling for vehicles and a range of many other products requiring timber for the war effort. This was another aspect which would become part of the 'Home Front' when war broke out.

As early as 1937 plans for rationing in the event of war had been put in place in Germany. The German diet was almost opposite to that in Britain. For example, while British farmers had four million pigs, Germany had 23 million, and while Britain had 25 million sheep, Germany had 4 million. As for tractors, Britain had one for every 300 acres of farmland, Germany had one for every 1,000 acres, with animal power machinery accounting for the rest. When war was declared Britain and France implemented a blockade on imports entering Germany. At first the country, with its millions of farms, was virtually self-sufficient in food production. The blockade hit in other ways by cutting off Germany's supply of cotton, essential for clothing and uniforms. Later, feeding did become a problem, even when taking foodstuffs from the occupied territories. Rationing was introduced and so-called *ersatz* or replacement commodities formed part of the diet, not only for the civilian population but also the armed forces.

Joseph Goebbels, the German Minister of Propaganda, addressed an assemblage on 17 January 1936 stating, 'We can do without butter, but, despite all our love of peace, not without arms. One cannot shoot with butter, but with guns.' Herman Goering, the commander-in-chief of the Luftwaffe, continued in the same vein by declaring, 'Guns will make us powerful; butter will only make us fat.'

Winston Churchill, the veteran soldier-statesman, continually issued warnings about Germany's intentions. Few bothered to listen to the one man who, almost alone, had the singular vision to realise what the situation in Germany would lead to.

Tens of thousands of women served in the Women's Land Army to support the farmers after the men went off to war.

Two years later, in September 1938, Hitler ordered his troops to occupy the Sudetenland region which stretched in an arc along the border between Czechoslovakia and Germany. It seemed as though Hitler had gone too far. The British Prime Minister, Neville Chamberlain, and the French Prime Minister, Edouard Daladier, met with Hitler in Munich and terms were discussed. Between them they reached a compromise, which Chamberlain declared meant 'Peace in our time'. Hitler had got away with it and in doing so gained a further 11,500 square miles of territory. More importantly, he gained a sympathetic population of German-speaking people, who would be potential manpower for his growing army and the workforce for the armaments factories and the coalmines to produce the fuel to power them. Observing on these developments, Churchill commented, 'England has been offered a choice between war and shame. She has chosen shame – and will get war.' One of those who recognised the situation was the former Prime Minister, Stanley Baldwin, who after Chamberlain's return had commented, 'Can't we turn Hitler East? Napoleon broke himself against the Russians. Hitler might do the same.' It would be three years later that the words would echo with a strange familiarity and Baldwin himself must have mused over his prediction.

Six months later in March 1939 Hitler followed up his takeover of the Sudetenland, his troops marched into the rest of Czechoslovakia and he gave it the title Bohemia-Moravia. This move gave Germany further access to armaments manufacturing capability such as the important Brno factory which produced small arms including rifles and machine guns, and the Skoda Works, which was already manufacturing tanks, vehicles and artillery and which the German military seized with relish. Czechoslovakia was now a nominal ally of Germany and would come to suffer as badly as any other occupied country during the war.

Hitler could not believe his luck. He had acquired even more armaments manufacturers, including the CKD (Praga) factory which was producing also armoured vehicles and tanks. Two Czechoslovakian tank designs in particular, the LT-35 and the LT-38, were to prove vitally important to the German army in the opening months of the war. They were taken into service with the designations Panzerkampfwagen 35(t) and 38(t). These would form the core of the German armoured divisions between 1939 and 1941. Indeed, these two tank designs alone made up at least one quarter of the German army's armoured forces at the beginning of the war. Of the two designs, it was the 38 (t) which proved to be the more versatile, with more than 1,600 being produced in eight different models during the war. The basic chassis was also used for thousands of other types of vehicle operating in roles from reconnaissance to tank destroyers, such as the SdKfz 138 Hetzer tank destroyer. The 35 (t) was classed as a light tank but it proved just as versatile as the 38 (t) and the chassis was adapted to serve in a variety of roles, including ammunition carriers and artillery tractors.

As Führer – leader and head of the armed forces – Hitler took a keen interest in military developments, while at the same time continuing his political manoeuvrings. During meetings with military commanders he made much about his experiences as a soldier in the First World War and constantly reminded all around him of it. Hitler was not a master tactician and had never attended a military academy, but it did not take a genius to realise what would be a decisive weapon on the battlefield. It was during a tour to observe military manoeuvres at Kummersdorf in 1934, in the company of General Heinz Guderian, that he saw the first German tanks engaged in field exercises. Impressed, he turned to Guderian saying, 'That's what I need. That's what I want to have.' Indeed in his book *Der Kampfwagenkreig* (*Tank Warfare*) published in 1934 Guderian had recommended the creation of armoured divisions. He had been joined in this opinion by General Ludwig Ritter von Eimannsberger, who advocated ideas such as attacking on a narrow front, to bring weight of force to bear on a target, which would later evolve into the Blitzkrieg strategy.

In 1939 the French army was one of the largest in Europe, with a tank force larger than any other European country and a fleet of trucks to support it. When war was declared in September 1939 Winston Churchill, who had been appointed to the post of First Sea Lord, stated, 'Thank God for the French Army.' The French had a standing army of 900,000 men with a further five million trained reservists, and a tank force of 3,500 vehicles comprising 2,700 light tanks, 500 medium and 300 heavy tanks, along with a strong artillery force for support. By comparison Britain had an armoured force of 600 light and medium tanks, along with some 100,000 vehicles, including around 21,500 motorcycles, and several thousand trailers for carrying stores and equipment.

In 1938 it had been decided that in the event of war, Britain would send two divisions to deploy to France. It was not much, but at least it was something. In reality, the army was not prepared for war. Sir Thomas Inskip, 1st Viscount Caldecote and Minister for the Co-ordination of Defence, pointed out how gravely lacking such a force would be in the event it should be sent to France. Among the deficiencies he highlighted was the fact that they would have only 10% of their allocation of modern machine guns, 15% of the ammunition required for mortars, and would be lacking entirely in infantry tanks. It was a hard-hitting admission and Inskip concluded that these points should be redressed with the utmost urgency. At the time, the British army had troops posted in garrisons around the world. There were 55,000 in India, making up 47 battalions of infantry; 18 battalions with 21,000 troops in the Middle East where they were deployed to protect British interests, such as the oil fields and Suez Canal; 1,800 in the West Indies; and 12,000 in the Far East. This represented over 90,000 men in garrisons abroad while the Home Army consisted of 107,000 men in 64 infantry battalions.

Against this, the German army had an armoured force of 3,400 light and medium tanks, which had been built up from nothing, and an army of 51 divisions, including five panzer or tank divisions. In the space of five years, it had been transformed from General Seeckt's Reichswehr force to Adolf Hitler's Wehrmacht. The Luftwaffe, air force, had been formed in 1935 and from nothing it had been built up to 1,500,000 men by 1939. This included 900,000 men designated for anti-aircraft duties, 25,000 in administrative duties and 80,000 engaged in maintenance and supply. In the 1930s the German aero industry was employing more than 250,000 men who annually produced 10,000 aircraft of all types. The army and the air force would work closely together in the coming campaigns. In addition to its own engineer and supply units, the army benefitted from the organisation of the German Labour Service (Reichsarbeitsdienst) which kept open the lines of supply by undertaking the repair of bridges and roads under army supervision.

Bolstered by weapons and vehicles from its own armaments manufacturers and the factories in Czechoslovakia, Hitler believed the German army was in a strong enough position to make its next move. He had in mind the reunification of East Prussia with Germany proper. The only problem with this was that the two areas were separated by the so-called Danzig Corridor which was Polish territory. This narrow strip of land gave Poland its only access to the Baltic Sea through the port of Gdynia and, as such, was vital for its trade routes. On 21 March Hitler demanded that Danzig be turned over to Germany in order that road and rail links could be built to connect the two for commerce. Ten days later the Polish government replied that if Germany forced access across Danzig it would lead to war. The British government stepped in to say it would stand by Poland in such an eventuality.

Throughout all this Italy had not been idle. Since October 1935 Italian troops had been engaged in a ruthless war to suppress Ethiopia in east Africa, which included the use of poison gas, as well as remaining committed to providing military aid to Franco in Spain. The war against Ethiopia was concluded on 9 May 1936 and the country annexed. Mussolini made his next major military move on 7 April 1939 when he sent 100,000 troops into Albania which was also annexed to Italy. The invasion was a one-sided affair with Italian troops being supported by air cover and a fleet of vehicles. Several weeks later, on 22 May 1939, Hitler and Mussolini signed an agreement called the 'Pact of Steel' which bound them as allies in the event of war.

At the time, Italy was producing few armaments and the country was far from being prepared for conducting operations in the event of a full-scale war. This was something of which Mussolini was acutely aware and he went to great pains to make Italy's position clear to Hitler during a meeting in August. Like Hitler, Mussolini had fought in the First World War, achieving the rank of corporal, and like him had never attended a military staff college. However he had the common sense to realise that it was one thing to subdue an ill-prepared country like Ethiopia or Albania, but waging a war against a well-equipped European army like France was something entirely different.

Massed rallies, such as this in Nuremberg, should have alerted European countries as to what was about to happen. But politicians, such as the British Prime Minister, Neville Chamberlain, chose to ignore the signs.

Manpower was plentiful in the German army in the early stages of the war, but it was to become a problem later, especially on the Eastern Front.

Villages and towns across Germany, such as this one, would be affected by the war.

There was one last step Hitler had to take before he was prepared to make a move to seize Danzig, which was to discover what Soviet Russia would do in the event that such blatant provocation should lead to war. After negotiations, the German Foreign Minister Joachim von Ribbentrop and Vyacheslav Molotov for the Soviet Union signed a non-aggression pact between their respective countries on the evening of 23/24 August. The signatories also agreed to share between them the partition of Poland. The two countries continued to trade, with Russia supplying wheat and oil to Germany, and in return Hitler would not intervene in Stalin's attack against the Baltic states of Latvia, Lithuania and Estonia, or Finland. This was not the first time the two countries had cooperated. Seventeen years earlier, on 16 April 1922, Germany and the Soviet Union had signed an agreement at Rapallo in Italy, under the terms of which the two countries promised mutual aid. Although it never amounted to a great deal it had allowed Germany to send troops to Russia in order to train in secret.

The German army began moving things into place with the deployment of three million men, 200,000 vehicles and 400,000 horses transported towards the Polish frontier by 5,000 trains. To move this amount of men and materiel took time and the build-up was gradual and had to be concealed, in order not to arouse suspicion, but once everything was ready Hitler could make his next move. On 1 September German troops crossed the Danzig border and, although Britain and France had pledged their support to Poland in the event of war, there was little they could do other than issue an ultimatum calling for the immediate withdrawal of troops. Hitler chose to ignore the French and British demands and on 3 September Chamberlain made a radio broadcast to announce that the country was at war with Germany. The French declared war on Germany the same day. Two days earlier Britain had introduced a mass evacuation of children and pregnant women from the cities to less vulnerable locations, ideally the countryside, to protect them from air raids. Within three days, more than 1.5 million children had been sent from the cities in the largest voluntary mass movement ever managed.

On the same day a nationwide blackout scheme was implemented, designed to prevent unnecessary lights from shining which could give away the location of towns and cities in the event of air raids. The speed limit for driving vehicles in urban centres was reduced to 20mph, mainly to prevent accidents in the darkness as the vehicles had to dim their headlights. Despite safety precautions, over 4,000 civilians were killed and injured in road accidents between September and December. By February the following year a further 1,100 civilians had been killed on the roads, without a single military casualty. Petrol rationing was introduced on 16 September and a special scheme known as the 'Car Pool Scheme' was created, whereby drivers volunteered their services to drive vehicles for deliveries of emergency supplies for hospitals, such as blood. In one month alone volunteer drivers used over 20,700 vehicles to transport a variety of cargo. They logged almost 3,576,000 miles using more than 107,000 gallons of fuel.

The Car Pool worked well and volunteer drivers delivered essential supplies to hospitals such as blood for transfusions.

In 1939, private car ownership in Britain was one vehicle on average to every 14 people of its almost 48 million head of population. In Germany, with its population of 79 million, car ownership was also one to every 14. In France the figure was one to every 28, while in America, with a population of 132 million, ownership was one vehicle to every three head of the population. When war broke out, with severe petrol shortages, these figures changed dramatically, except in America where oil and petrol were plentiful.

The German army attacked Poland at 4.45am on the morning of 1 September 1939 supported by over 2,300 aircraft from the Luftwaffe. Around 1.5 million German troops were committed to the attack comprising 60 divisions supported by 9,000 pieces of artillery and 2,750 tanks. Although the early hour of the attack took the Polish military by surprise it was not altogether unexpected. For several months Polish military intelligence had sensed a growing threat and as early as March the Polish government had ordered partial mobilisation of reserve troops which was increased to general mobilisation on 30 August as tensions increased. German planning was meticulous and the support with supplies was the best any army could hope for. Three days after the launch of the attack, German tanks were fifty miles into Polish territory.

The Polish army of 1,500,000 men was the fourth largest in Europe and it fought as gallantly as any army could, but under the circumstances it was no match against the German army which outnumbered them and, being supported with modern tanks and aircraft, they smashed anything the Poles sent against them. The Pomeranian Division lost 2,000 horses out of 3,000 mounts in only thirty minutes. The Polish army fought stubbornly and bravely, but on 27 September Warsaw surrendered. At one point the city was the target of 1,000 pieces of artillery firing 30,000 shells each day into the streets. The Polish army had consisted of 30 infantry divisions, 12 cavalry divisions and 10 reserve divisions, a large number of which were mounted on horses. Indeed, the total number of horses in the Polish army at the time was around 37,250 with a further 49,000 used as draught to haul artillery and pull wagons of supplies. Poland had gone to war with over 900 tanks, mostly small, light 'tankette' designs except for 95 larger 7TPjw tanks equipped with 47mm guns, but there was little these and the armoured cars could do against 60 German divisions with thousands of tanks and vehicles. The Germans suffered 40,000 casualties killed, wounded and missing, with 217 tanks destroyed or damaged. Much of the Polish weaponry captured by the Germans would later be pressed into service and the surviving vehicles used for transport and supply duties. This move to absorb captured weaponry would become standard practice for the Germans with all beaten armies.

Heinz Guderian commanded XIX Corps during the Polish campaign, which included a Panzer Division and two divisions of motorised infantry. In 1918 he had served in France with the quartermaster of the XXXVIII Reserve Corps as part of Operation Michael, the German spring offensive. The Corps had kept the German army supplied as it advanced up to fourteen miles a day on foot. This experience allowed him to understand the importance of good supply lines probably better than any other German officer. Fuel was a prime consideration and he would have realised that, but at this early stage in the war not even he could not have foreseen just how much would be needed.

The Polish army was still fighting the German invasion, when, on 17 September, the country's suffering was added to when it was unexpectedly attacked by the Soviet Red Army. This attack from the east allowed Russia to consolidate the eastern portion of Poland under the terms of the agreement signed between Germany and the Soviet Union only weeks earlier. This sudden move, coming only two weeks after Germany's attack, while the bulk of the Polish army was still engaged against the German army in the west, allowed the Soviet Union to take advantage of the weakened state of the Polish army. The attack was launched with at least 800,000 troops supported by artillery, tanks and aircraft. By 6 October the fighting was ended with the Red Army having sustained perhaps 3,000 killed and 10,000 wounded. The Polish army had lost a further 7,000 killed, 20,000 wounded and around 230,000 taken prisoner. As far as Hitler and Stalin were concerned, such was their contempt for the country, the state of Poland ceased to exist on 25 September 1939, even as the fighting was still raging around Warsaw.

The German army took 694,000 Polish troops prisoner and these would have to be fed, kept in camps and guarded. This put pressure on supply lines and took soldiers away from other duties. While Germany incarcerated the prisoners the Soviet regime preferred to deal with them in a brutal manner. In March 1940, the chief of Soviet security, Lavrenti Beria, suggested they be executed. Stalin agreed and between April and May 1940 some 22,000 to 25,000 were summarily shot, prisoners mainly from the Kalinin and Kharkiv camps, executed in the Katyn forest in Russia. A further 350,000 were allowed to starve to death in camps over the months. Some Polish troops managed to escape and fled to France. By 1940 around 30,000 Poles had reached Britain where they served with distinction in Polish squadrons of the Royal Air Force, and were formed into Polish divisions, such as the 1st Armoured Division (Poland), later taking part in the Normandy campaign from June 1944.

Blitzkrieg was an all arms tactic using infantry supported by artillery and armour, which in turn was supported by aircraft to attack strategic points. The Blitzkrieg tactic was broken down into phases or elements and was essentially an expression of combined operations using land and air forces working in close cooperation. They were basic principles put into practice on a large scale and it was perhaps this which the Allies could not fully comprehend.

The first phase involved the commander deciding on the axis or line of advance to be taken by the attacking units of infantry and armour. The route had been carefully reconnoitred by advance vehicles such as armoured cars and motorcycles scouting ahead and reporting back. Under cover of artillery bombardment, supported by ground attack aircraft such as the Ju 87 Sturzkampfflugzeug, the 'Stuka', which had been developed in Sweden in secret and became the most dreaded of all dive-bomber types, the infantry moved forward following the tanks. While the defending enemy was still reeling from the shock of the artillery and aerial assault the armoured units attacked in strength and pushed their way through the defences. Next, having smashed through the enemy positions the armoured units moved out to encircle any points of resistance which were left for the follow-on infantry units to deal with. These armoured thrusts pushed forward to cut lines of communication and supply routes. In the fourth and last phase, the armoured thrusts continued to advance with air support from ground attack aircraft, leaving isolated pockets of resistance to be dealt with by the infantry.

All the lessons concerning the tactics the German army would come to use in combat had been freely available to read in books such as *Infanterie Greift* (*Infantry Attack*) by Rommel and *Achtung-Panzer!* (*Attention Armour!*) by Guderian. Both these works were published in 1937, but, along with Guderian's *Tank Warfare,* they went largely overlooked. Guderian's books contained all the elements for modern armoured warfare, combined operations and support and were possibly influenced by *Taschenbuch der Tanks* (*Pocketbook of Tanks*) by Fritz Heigl who had served as a major in the First

World War. If senior officers in other armies had paid attention they would have seen the blueprint for the innovative tactics which would become known as Blitzkrieg. (This word was almost certainly not coined by the Germans. Indeed, it is believed the term may have been written by a journalist to describe the swiftness of the Polish Campaign in 1939. Heinz Guderian confirmed this when he later stated that '… our enemies coined the word Blitzkrieg.')

The armies around the world had been given a demonstration of Germany's new Blitzkrieg tactics during the Polish Campaign, but those in positions to instigate changes, did little, if anything, to introduce any form of strategy to counter them. In fairness though, it is unlikely that any European army could have formulated anything, given the time and resources available to them.

Before the war a handful of British officers *had* taken notice of the writings of Rommel and Guderian. One was Captain Basil Liddell Hart, whose own writings on tank warfare had, in turn, influenced a number of German officers, one of whom was Guderian. Indeed, the two men corresponded and Guderian sent Captain Hart a signed photograph of himself, which he personalised with the inscription, 'To Captain B.L. Hart from one of his disciples in tank affairs.' Another German officer to be impressed by Hart's writing was General Hasso von Manteuffell, who also sent Hart a personal photograph signed to 'the creator of modern tank strategy'.

The German tank force, like the air force, had been built up from nothing, and with a blank canvas to work with, visionary men such as Guderian and Manteuffel could forge the nascent tank force into their ideal. In October 1935 Manteuffel was appointed to command a battalion in Guderian's 2nd Panzer Division. In 1936 he became the training officer, a role he continued to serve in until May 1941 when he was reassigned to the 7th Panzer Division, in preparation to take part in the attack against Russia. Between them Guderian and Manteuffel, along with other capable officers, developed further the Blitzkrieg tactics to deal with the large numbers of Soviet tanks they judged to be waiting for them. The conditions of terrain in the Soviet Union and the huge distances were unknown quantities as they planned how to overwhelm enemy defences.

There were some British officers, such as General Wavell and General O'Connor, who learnt from these tactics, adapted them and put them to use against the Italians in North Africa. Later in the war, the Americans would learn similar lessons, and even the Russians would develop 'tank armies' which would overwhelm the Germans in battles such as Kursk in 1943.

Above all, Guderian was adamant the tank had to be used as a concentrated force in order to maximise its use as a mobile weapon of protected firepower. The tank crews were taught to halt and fire, which produced better results in accuracy. Other armies, including the French and British, continued to use the method of firing on the move, which was inaccurate. The German tactic did leave them vulnerable to anti-tank fire but in 1940 the British army's main anti-tank gun was only a 2-pounder, a variant of which was fitted to many of the British tanks. The French army was equipped with the Canon léger de 25 anti-char SA-L mle 1934 and the Canon de 47 anti-char SA mle 1937, with 25mm and 47mm calibres respectively. Of these three designs only the French 47mm, with its penetration capability of up to 80mm of armour, was of any use against the Panzer. The British 2-pounder had been introduced into service in 1938 and by 1940 was widely regarded as obsolete.

Chapter 2

The Storm Breaks – the Allies Face Blitzkrieg

With the conclusion of the Polish campaign the British and French facing the Germans in the west could only wonder as to what the next move would be. In late September Britain finally sent the British Expeditionary Force (BEF) to France. It would eventually comprise ten divisions amounting to some 160,000 men under the command of General Lord Gort VC, with orders to take up positions close to the Franco-German border. They had a motorised fleet of 22,000 vehicles to transport all the supplies of food, 36,000 tons of ammunition and 25,000 tons of fuel. The force, which included 10,000 men from the RAF, did not encounter any major problems and went into prepared defensive positions by the River Dyle east of Brussels, from where patrols were undertaken. There was not much else which could be done under the circumstances as the opposing sides became locked down in a period of inactivity. Several months later they were still in their trenches and bunkers, staring at one another along the Franco-German border. The American Senator William Borah referred to it as the 'Phoney War', a term adopted by the British press. Chamberlain called it the 'twilight war' and claimed that Hitler had 'missed the bus'. The French called it 'drôle de guerre' (funny or peculiar war) and the Germans knew it as 'Sitzkreig' (sitting war). Whatever term one used, everybody knew the next move depended on the Germans.

Although there was no shooting these troops still had to be fed and supplied with fuel and those falling sick had to be treated. Because they did nothing positive to prepare for what they knew must eventually come, they would suffer the consequences of their indecisions, which would lead to catastrophe for the French and the neutral countries of Holland and Belgium with their small armies. Had they used this time more wisely to prepare better defences, build up reserves and train the troops, things might have been different. The British army would suffer but it would survive, if only just, following a severe mauling. As the period of inactivity stretched on without air raids, many of those who had been evacuated from the cities began to return. Indeed, by Christmas 1939, around 700,000 of the evacuees had returned to their city homes.

The next phase in the war took the world by surprise. Everybody had been expecting Hitler to attack west, it seemed the most logical move in his agenda, but what happened next could not have been anticipated. Eight weeks after the surrender of the Polish army to the Russians, it was Stalin and not Hitler who made the next move, attacking

Finland on 30 November. How would Britain and France react? Given the distances involved, there was little they could do. Indeed, in the end, there was nothing they did do, except watch events as they unfolded.

At the time the Soviet army had around 1.8 million men under arms and an estimated reserve of eleven million which could be mobilised. The attack was made using some one million men supported by 1,500 tanks and 3,000 aircraft. Such a weight of numbers looked set to easily crush the Finnish army, with its strength of only 200,000 men and very few tanks. The Russo-Finnish War of 1939-40, or Winter War as it is also known, is often overlooked in the wider history of the Second World War, but it revealed weaknesses within the Russian military which Hitler later sought to exploit. It also showed how wrong it was to prejudge a smaller country's fighting ability when attacked by a larger force.

As well as having enormous levels of manpower, the Russians had an estimated 24,000 tanks from which force they could bring up more reserves such as the massive KV-1 tank. More importantly they had supplies in abundance and unlimited reserves of fuel oil. At the time, Russia was producing more oil than the Middle East. The country's annual oil production in 1938 was around 35 million tons, making it the fourth largest producer in the world at the time, easily outstripping the combined efforts of Iraq and Iran, which, between them, produced 14.6 million tons. This meant that Russian tanks could rely on home-produced fuel to keep them operational.

Germany, on the other hand, was unable to produce its own oil and had to rely on imports from several sources such as Romania; 34% came from Russia. At the beginning of 1940 it was not only oil that Germany was dependent on Russia to supply; it also imported 74% of its animal feeds from there along with 65% of its chrome ore, 55% of its manganese and 40% of its nickel, metals which were all vital for Germany's war effort. When Germany did eventually seize the Russian oil refinery at Maikop and Baku, which had supplied up to 90% of the Russian army's oil, it was found to be destroyed. To bring it back into production the Germans sent in a specialist unit of 6,500 engineers called the Petroleum Technical Brigade.

Despite the odds being stacked against them, the Finns turned out to be a competent adversary. The fighting lasted almost four months and when the war ended in March 1940 the Finnish armed forces had killed or wounded some 200,000 Russians and destroyed 1,600 tanks. The Red Army had killed only 25,000 Finns but Russia gained all the territorial demands it made. Finland had hoped that Britain and France would send support, but in the end nothing materialised. On 7 March, just a week before the end of the war, General Sir Edmund Ironside, Chief of the Imperial General Staff, announced to Finland that it was prepared to send 57,000 men to help in the fight. He promised that the first division of 15,000 men would arrive by the end of the month. As events turned out, the war had finished by the time the force set sail. As events would later show, those 57,000 men would be needed by Britain for its own defence.

Finland, under Marshal Carl Gustaf Mannerheim, would later re-enter the war on 26 June 1941 as Germany's ally, to once more fight against Russia in what is generally referred to as the 'Continuation War'. The campaign lasted for more than three years until 20 September 1944, when the Finns sought peace negotiations with Russia and then, in an about-turn, took up arms against Germany on 1 October 1944. During the time they had fought as Germany's ally Finnish volunteers were formed into the Nordost-Bataillon of the Waffen SS and the SS Wiking Division, both units of which required its own armoured support and trucks for supply and transport. Not being able to supply all of its own equipment most of the burden was carried by Germany. The sub-zero temperatures and harsh terrain meant that motor vehicles were not suited to such conditions. To help ease the transportation problems the Finns, uniquely, used reindeer as pack animals to pull sleighs in the deep snow. Being indigenous to the region these animals were better suited to the conditions than horses, which suffered terribly from the cold.

The BEF had gone to France with just four divisions in 1939 and the period of quiet had allowed the build-up of forces so that by early 1940 it had increased its strength to ten divisions.

The BEF deployed a range of tanks, including the A11 or Matilda Mk I, Vickers light tanks, A9 'Cruiser' tanks and the heavier Matilda Mk II. These were 'Infantry' tanks,

Tanks such as this Matilda Mk I had been used in France in 1940. Although the crews were brave, the tank was no match against the heavier, more modern tanks of the German army.

The Matilda Mk II was better armoured but lacked a heavy gun. Nevertheless, the type served in North Africa.

so-called because they were specifically designed to support the infantry as opposed to engaging enemy tanks.

The Matilda Mk I had armour protection between 10 and 60mm in thickness which was proof against small arms fire and the lighter anti-tank guns. In 1940 the Germans used the 3.7cm calibre PaK35/36 anti-tank gun which could penetrate this level of armour at close range (later in the war, as tanks became heavier, German soldiers nicknamed the gun the 'Heeresanklopfgerät' (the doorknocker) because it was no longer effective). The main weaknesses of the Mk I Matilda tank lay in the almost skeletal quality of its chassis and the exposed track, suspension and drive mechanism. Operated by two men and armed with a single Vickers machine gun in its turret and a top speed of 8mph on roads, the vehicle was little more than an armoured, mobile machine gun post. It looked obsolete compared to either French or German tanks, but when put to the test in battle the crews of these Mk I Matildas did not go down without a fight.

With regards to motorised truck transport one design at the time was the Leyland Retriever, dating from the early 1930s. The fleet had been declared obsolete, but the coming of war provided a reprieve and the trucks were kept in use for the duration to transport supplies. It was a classic case of better to use something rather than nothing. Examples of the Retriever were also fitted out to serve in the role of field workshops, breakdown recovery vehicles and some were equipped to serve as searchlight pontoon

During the rearmament period in the mid–1930s, the German army demonstrated the new weaponry in its armoury such as this 7.5cm field gun.

During the rearmament process the German army introduced many new weapons into service, including the PaK 36 3.7cm anti-tank gun, a type of weapon forbidden under the terms of the Treaty of Versailles.

Heavy pre-war vehicles, such as this example of a refurbished original vehicle known as a 'Retriever', were used as command vehicles because they could be fitted with office facilities for maps and radios.

trucks. One Retriever gained fame when it was fitted as a field caravan and used by Field Marshal Montgomery for campaign service, being spacious enough for his maps and for conducting meetings with officers.

On 9 April 1940, when three German troopships sailed into the harbour at Copenhagen, the invasion of Denmark had begun. The reason given by Hitler this time for yet another unprovoked attack was to prevent an attack by Britain. At the same time the newly created German 1st Parachute Regiment landed in company strength at Aalborg and Vordinborg to seize bridges and airfields. The tiny Danish army, numbering fewer than 10,000 men at the time of the attack, was no match and after a brief exchange of fire eleven Danish soldiers and three frontier guards were killed along with twelve Danish airmen. The country capitulated later the same day.

On the same day Germany also attacked Norway, taking the fighting to the borders of neutral Sweden. With the fall of Norway the country would be surrounded by German occupied countries. Sweden annually exported ten million tons of iron ore to Germany, sent out through the port of Narvik in the north. German parachute troops captured the capital Oslo on 9 April and further landings by airborne troops took place at Stavanger and Dombas. Fighting broke out and German supplies being brought in by aircraft were delayed by bad weather. It showed how vulnerable troops could be, even on a small scale, when relying on supply by air.

Well supplied with boats, German troops could negotiate the Norwegian fjords and other waterways.

Almost 9,000 troops of the invasion force were transported by the German navy with a further 8,000 troops being flown in by Fliegerkorps X, an air fleet of 500 Ju52 transport aircraft supported by 345 bombers and protected by fighters. The Norwegian army had a strength of 100,000 on mobilisation and Hitler believed that around half this number could be deployed against the invasion force. To assuage any argument there may have been about German forces being outnumbered he declared that 'numerical weakness must be compensated for by astute handling and the use of surprise.' Certainly, the rapidity of the attack gave Hitler the edge but being over a thousand miles away at the end of a supply line from Germany rendered his troops vulnerable. If it was any consolation, the Allies were also at the end of a very long and weak supply line dependent on shipping.

To meet the increased level of military activity Hitler had to find the manpower from somewhere which came at a cost to the country's labour force. Germany's population of 79 million had a workforce of 24.5 million and to boost the armed forces around four million workers were enlisted. This led to a drop in industrial output, especially in steel production, ammunition and weapons. The shortfall would eventually be compensated for by bringing in foreign labour from occupied territories, such as France, Holland and Belgium, who were either forced or came voluntarily.

German warships supporting the attack against Norway suffered casualties from the start of the campaign. On 9 April the cruiser *Karlsruhe* was sunk by HM Submarine

Truant, and the cruiser *Konigsberg* was sunk the next day. The *Lutzow* was sunk on 11 April and ships of the Royal Navy wrought havoc and destruction among several other German warships supporting the operation. To support the Norwegians, Britain and France sent 15,000 troops, but it was obvious that the force was too small to do anything substantial. Besides, they lacked the proper training and equipment for winter operations in the snow. The British commander, Major General Sir Adrian Carton de Wiart, reported the situation as hopeless. The Norwegian army put up strong resistance in Oslo, but the Germans, using air support, were able to fly in more troops and supplies.

On 1 and 2 May the first British troops were issued with orders to begin evacuation, even while fighting still continued around Narvik and Trondheim. Eight days later events in France and the Low Countries changed the campaign situation and hastened the withdrawal of the Anglo-French force from Norway. By the end of May, the last troops had been withdrawn. The Norwegians continued to fight on alone until the 10 June, the same day that Italy declared war against Britain and France.

The campaign had been costly to all sides. The two-month long campaign had cost the Germans 21 transport and merchant ships lost in addition to their warships. The British and French had lost 20 warships and, together with Norwegian losses, had suffered 70 transport and merchant ships sunk as they supported the operation.

Neutral Sweden, being bounded to the west by Norway, found itself cut off from the Norwegian Sea due to the German occupation, leaving only the Baltic open for maritime trade through its ports. The country's geographical position meant that it served to act as a barrier against seaborne invasion, thereby further assisting with its historical position of neutrality. This status had been reaffirmed before the outbreak of hostilities and was acknowledged by the Allies and Germany alike. Even so, Sweden felt it only prudent, especially with the fighting right on its border, to maintain a state of 'armed neutrality'. Sweden now found itself in a unique position of being able to continue to trade with both sides throughout the war, but favouring the Allies.

Alarmed at developments as early as 1936, Sweden had increased its defence budget almost eightfold by 1939. Three years later this had increased by another sixty per cent. During the war the country served as a route for Danish and Norwegian soldiers and civilians to escape German occupation. Around 50,000 Norwegians fled to Sweden, many of whom made their way to England to fight as part of the Utefronten (Forces Abroad). In 1939, several thousand Swedish nationals had volunteered to fight for Finland against the Soviet invasion and, as in the Spanish Civil War, other nationals joined them. These came mainly from other Scandinavian countries, but the numbers probably never amounted to more than 11,500 volunteers.

Sweden went a stage further in helping Finland by supplying stocks of weapons, including 135,000 rifles and 800 machine guns along with 50 million rounds of ammunition. A total of 144 pieces of field artillery were sent, 100 anti-aircraft guns, 92 anti-tank guns and 300,000 rounds of ammunition which, technically, contravened its neutral status. Swedish aircraft were flown by Swedish pilots and nearly 9,000 men fought as volunteers in the Finnish army. Because of its position, Sweden was forced to maintain border guard posts along its frontier with German-occupied Norway to the west and Finland to the east. In 1940 the country had a standing army of 100,000 men and plans were in place to mobilise a further 320,000 troops in the event of an attack. The Swedish army had a few armoured vehicles, such as the Pansarbil m/39 Armoured Car, equipped with a Bofors 20mm cannon and 8mm machine gun, which had entered service in 1939. It also had heavier vehicles including the Stridsvagn m/40 Light Tank, based on a German design, and the Stridsvagn m/41 based on a Czechoslovakian design with a self-propelled gun variant known as the Stormartillerivagn m/43 armed with a 105mm gun.

Sweden had been used as a base for research by German armaments designers in the 1920s and 1930s as a way of getting around the embargo governing the development of specialist weapons. Swedish armaments manufacturers such as Landsverk, Bofors and Volvo had the engineering facilities necessary to undertake research and design to produce armoured vehicles. Just before the outbreak of hostilities the Swedish armaments company of Jungner obtained a licence to build fifty Czech-designed AN-IV-S tanks which entered service with the Swedish army as the Stridsvagn m/37. The company of Scania-Vabis was also granted a licence to produce armoured vehicles, one of which was the Stridsvagn m/41, a light tank of conventional design, armed with a 37mm calibre main gun mounted in a fully traversing turret. In 1940 a new Swedish tank entered service known as the m/40L from which an improved version was developed.

Swedish troops continued to patrol frontier posts along the border with Norway to ensure there was no breach of neutrality protocol. Throughout the war both the Allies and Germany conducted trade with the country, either buying directly from the factories or seeking to procure licences to produce weapons from the country's armaments manufacturers such as Bofors, which produced the 40mm anti-aircraft gun that was unarguably one of the finest weapons of the war. These guns were exported or built under licence and used by armies around the world including Britain and America. The Germans had their own comparable weapon in the form of the Flugabwehrkanone or FlaK 36/37 but still used captured Bofors guns. Even with the outbreak of war and the German occupation of Norway, Sweden was still annually exporting ten million tons of iron ore to Germany to make steel for armaments production. Sweden also traded openly with Britain by supplying essential war material such as ball bearings for vehicles from trucks to tanks.

As war approached, Germany and Britain sent out agents to buy up stocks of metals essential for war production. One of the leading figures in the intriguing move to gain the monopoly for Britain was Oliver Lyttleton, chairman of the British Metal Corporation. He had dealings with his opposite numbers in Germany, and was able to pre-empt them.

In 1938 Germany had imported 22 million tons of iron ore to make steel. In December 1939, Germany was using 400,000 tons of steel each month just to produce ammunition. When war broke out the British blockade reduced this amount to half its pre-war level, leaving only Sweden open as a supplier of iron ore to Germany, which in 1940 guaranteed to supply at least ten million tons in that year alone.

By March Germany was facing an 80% drop in its imports and suffering a critical shortage in certain other metals. One of these was copper of which Germany asked Italy to supply 3,500 tons. This was beyond Italy's capacity and to meet the demand Mussolini appealed to the nation to supply their pots and pans for the cause. He was advised against stripping the churches because of the ill-feeling it would create, but he went ahead anyway in his anxiety to please Hitler. After 1940, Germany would anyway strip everything it needed from the occupied territories. In 1943 Germany was obtaining 37% of its tin, 27% of its iron ore, 24% of its bauxite (for aluminium), 24% of its copper, 16% of its alumina and lead and 10% of its nickel from occupied countries.

The military situation in Europe changed again when, on 10 May 1940, Hitler ended the guessing and made his long-anticipated move westwards launching Operation Fall Gelb (Case Yellow). For eight long months the British and French had been waiting and preparing to meet the German attack and now, at last, here it was. The German attack stretched from the Dutch border, and included several points along the Belgian and French borders. It was a decisive moment in England, because that same day Neville Chamberlain resigned from office and Winston Churchill was invited to form a government. Chamberlain, with his appeasement policies, had lost support and faith in his ability to conduct the war. Churchill was made of sterner stuff and would prove himself tireless in his efforts to win the war.

Within days the Germans claimed their first victim when the Dutch army of 114,000 men surrendered on 14 May after the city of Rotterdam had been bombed resulting in the deaths of 980 civilians and wounding of 29,000. In the five days of fighting the army of neutral Holland had sustained 9,779 casualties and the few armoured cars it had, such as the M39 Pantserwagen, had proved no match for the German tanks or anti-tank guns. Those vehicles and weapons of the Dutch army not destroyed in the fighting would later be taken into service by the German army, the suffix letter 'h' denoting Holland. For example, the M39 would be known as the Pz SpWg L202(h). The intensity of the German attack, spearheaded by parachute landings, columns of tanks, armoured cars and fast-moving motorcycle units was beyond anything they could have prepared for. Hitler later wrote an assessment of the Dutch army: 'They put up a stronger resistance than we expected. Many of their units fought very bravely. But

Even captured vehicles from the defeated Dutch army, such as this M39 Panserwagen armoured car, were taken into service by the German army which designated it as the Pz SpWg L202 (h).

they had neither appropriate training nor experience of war. For this reason they were usually overcome by German forces which were often numerically very inferior.'

The speed at which the Germans advanced startled even their own commanders. Guderian, commanding the XIX Corps, found himself covering the distance of 151 miles from the point of his initial attack to the Channel coast in eight days, an average rate of 19 miles per day advancing with a best performance of 56 miles in one day. This led to Guderian being nicknamed 'Der Schnelle Heinz' (Fast Heinz). Fuel consumption was a problem, with an armoured division requiring 1,000 gallons for every mile on roads and as much as double that when operating cross-country. German tanks were fuelled by petrol which meant that they could, in theory, refuel from commercial garages. Trucks carried extra fuel in specially-designed, heavy-duty cans made from pressed steel. In addition, there were tankers carrying bulk fuel following behind with the supply column.

Speaking much later about the campaign in France, Guderian explained, 'After regulating the fuel stocks in the hands of the troops it proved possible to continue the advance. One must always distrust the report of troop commanders [who say] "We have no fuel". Generally they have. But if they become tired, they have no fuel. This is a common experience of war with forward troops. During the campaign in France there was no lack of fuel; good staff work can avoid this calamity.' He went on: 'Later in the war we often had a real scarcity of fuel because of the destruction of our industry. But in 1940 it was only a question of transport and easy to solve.'

This was Guderian changing his mind with hindsight because he knew it could be, and indeed was, vastly different from the pre-war manoeuvres he had watched in 1938 when he was commanding a Panzer division during the Anschluss between Germany and Austria. On that occasion his tanks had covered 400 miles in two days, proving what could be achieved when they were pushed to their extreme. On average, there was a 30% mechanical breakdown among the tanks and he noted at the time the 'inefficiency of maintenance facilities, particularly for the tanks'. The exercise taught the German army much about specialist support and recovery vehicles, supplies of fuel and maintenance problems. In combat during the Polish campaign in 1939 and in the attacks against France, Belgium and Holland, levels of mechanical failure among the tanks were higher, with some units reporting a 50% failure rate. This was only to be expected because the stresses in combat are greater than peacetime manoeuvres. Even among lorries the mechanical failure rate was higher than pre-war exercises had shown. In ordinary operational use before the outbreak of hostilities, the army could lose 10,000 vehicles a year just through breakdowns. If the tanks were to be kept supplied, then more supply lorries and specialist recovery vehicles had to be made available to the Panzer divisions.

The other exponent of modern warfare involved in the campaign in France that summer of 1940 was Rommel, commanding 7th Panzer Division. He too pushed his men and vehicles to their extremes, covering a distance of 110 miles at an average rate of 13.75 miles per day, leading to the unit being nicknamed the 'Ghost Division'. Rommel and Guderian had given written warnings of what could be expected in future wars and here they were now proving it in practice on the battlefield.

A typical column of an armoured division, including troops, supporting artillery and horses, could stretch along 70 miles of roadway and in some cases crawl forward at only 2.5 miles per hour, causing long tailbacks and bottleneck jams at junctions. The tanks could move across country but the supply lorries were restricted to roads. Roads did not always run parallel to the axis of advance and they had to keep up as best they could. The supply trucks had to be fuelled themselves in order to remain operational.

The German army had six standardised types of supply unit called Kolonne or 'columns' to provide support. The first was the Fahrkolonne which was a horse-drawn unit with the capacity to transport 30 tonnes. The second was the Leichte Farhkolonne which was identical to the Fahrkolonne but could only transport 17 tonnes. The Leichte Kraftwagen Kolonne was a motorised column capable of transporting 30 tonnes. The Schweres Kraftwagen Kolonne was the heavyweight unit capable of transporting 60 tonnes. The Leichte Kraftwagen Kolonne für Betriebstoff was the motor transport column responsible for fuel and had the capacity to move 5,500 gallons. Lastly was the

Schweres Kraftwagen Kolonne für Betriebstoff which could transport 11,000 gallons of fuel. These transport columns would move supplies as close as possible to wherever they were required to minimise handling.

The strength of armoured divisions would vary during the war but it would always remain autonomous and this was the same in all armies. In 1941 a German Panzer division was made up of a tank regiment with 150 to 200 tanks, a regiment of artillery with 24 guns of 150mm calibre, 30 guns of 105mm calibre, 30 88mm guns which served in the dual role of anti-tank and anti-aircraft, and a battalion of light FlaK anti-aircraft equipped with 2cm guns, a brigade of four battalions of Panzergrenadiers, a battalion of motorcycle and sidecar combinations, and support units such as signals, reconnaissance, army air corps and supply detachments. In all, such a formation amounted to some 14,000 men and 4,200 vehicles.

One of the units within the British Expeditionary Force which would face the Germans in France was the 1st Army Tank Brigade, which at the time of its deployment had a complement of 139 Matilda Mk I tanks. The brigade had taken up its position and showed its presence by engaging in exercises and conducting reconnaissance patrols. Apart from these activities there was little to do in the way of real operational duties. All this changed with the German attack and the British Tank Brigade would find itself having to provide rearguard actions to cover the retreat to Dunkirk. During the campaign the brigade would lose all 139 of its Matildas, either in fighting or abandoned because they were unable to cope with the mechanical strain placed on them. Indeed, it has been estimated that 75% of British tank losses were due to mechanical failure. The crews put up a valiant fight, but German armour and anti-tank guns were just too powerful and ripped into the flimsy design of the Matildas.

The BEF had some larger, more powerful A12 Matilda Mk IIs, armed with a 40mm gun firing a projectile weighing two pounds. Weighing 26.5 tons it was one of a series of new, heavier tanks beginning to enter service with the British army and followed the same direction in design as those used by other armies which were re-equipped at the time. It was intended to support the infantry and a General Staff policy of the British army at the time stated, 'If tanks are to survive at infantry pace while supporting men on foot, they must [be able to] resist the fire of current anti-tank guns, and yet retain the ability to destroy hostile men and weapons, including enemy tanks.'

At the time the Mk II Matilda was being planned, no account had been taken of the fact that Britain lacked the heavy industrial capacity to produce the large castings required for the design. This shortcoming was due to the simple fact that there had previously never been any demand for large castings. Many of the British tank designs at the time, such as the Mark II Medium Tank, Vickers Light Tank and Cruiser Tank, along with several other types including the Mk I Matilda, were built using welding and riveting techniques. Other countries such as France, but especially Germany, had advanced manufacturing processes to develop heavy casting techniques and welding processes to produce machinery for larger tanks. The Mk II Matilda was far from being an easy machine to put into mass production, because the size of the castings and other features had fine tolerances which allowed little margin for error. For example, the side skirts over the tracks were cast as a single unit and the turret with a thickness of 78mm was also a single casting. It has been calculated that it took some 2,000 man hours to assemble all the components for the Mk II Matilda on the production line.

When Britain went to war in September 1939, there were just two of these new tanks in service. Six months later there were enough to equip one battalion of the 7th Royal Tank Regiment with some left over for other units.

There were a number of tank engagements during the campaign, but the only really credible attempt was made using armour to spearhead a counter-attack mounted on the 21 May. After eleven days of constant battle, the 4th and 7th battalions of the 7th Royal Tank Regiment were reduced to 16 Mk II Matildas and 58 other types of tank including Mk Is. They were supported by three battalions of Durham Light Infantry. The unit was known as Frankforce after Major General Harold Franklyn who had assembled it to mount an attack against the Germans approaching the town of Arras. It was supported by elements of the French 3rd Light Mechanised Division.

Their line of attack took them directly towards positions held by 7th Panzer Division, which included the 5th Panzer and 25th Panzer Regiment commanded by Rommel. The ensuing battle continued throughout the day and, while it was well-intentioned, it did little in the long run to prevent the inevitable over-running of France. The action gave Rommel a foretaste of fighting British tanks. He recorded: 'We now directed our fire against the other group of tanks attacking from the direction of the Bac du Nord, and succeeded in keeping the tanks off, setting fire to some, halting others and forcing the rest to retreat…' In fact, the British attack went in so determinedly that Rommel believed he was being assaulted by five divisions. Major Fernie instructed Warrant Officer 3 Armit of the 4th RTR to attack the German guns. The NCO drove towards the German positions and later recalled: 'The guns were not camouflaged, and their only cover was a fold in the ground. I got two of them before they realised I was into them – the range was about 200 yards. The survivors turned on me and one hit the gun housing.' The action was close range and some of the Germans including the highly-trained SS were seen withdrawing. Armit continued: 'I got my gun going and returned to the attack. They must have thought I was finished for I caught the guns limbering up, and revenge was sweet.' The attack had been planned quickly and the cost was high with the RTR losing forty-six tanks, but it inflicted 700 casualties on the Germans and destroyed 20 tanks. It made the Germans more wary of their adversary in the future and show more concern for their flanks.

In addition to their tanks the Germans had large numbers of Panzerabwehrkanone (PaK) anti-tank guns, including some 2,800 of the powerful 88mm calibre (known simply as '88') such as the PaK 18 and 36 from which there was little chance of survival if hit. The German army had another 7,700 pieces of field artillery but the French army had around 11,000 pieces of artillery of various calibres which was taken to over 14,000 when the British guns were taken into account. The French and British fought hard and well and artillery took its toll on both sides. It was a campaign of movement and German tanks seemed to be everywhere.

As the campaign progressed supplies of food, fuel and ammunition began to run low for the French and British. There were occasions when British troops shared a tin of meat between several of them if they were lucky. Fuel was at a premium especially high-octane fuel for aeroplanes. There were times when discoveries were made, such as a store of one thousand cans containing 4,400 gallons of fuel found by pilots at the Norrent-Fontes airfield. At Calais, a supply of 7,000 gallons of fuel was unloaded at the docks over two days. But, while useful, such stocks were just a tiny drop compared to what was needed. For the Germans, there was no such problem, with their intact supply lines, even if they were over-stretched. The advancing troops fell on captured stocks of supplies.

Despite pre-war propaganda newsreel films which showed the German army well equipped with motorised vehicles, it still relied heavily on horses for all manner of tasks, including regular cavalry mounts. Just after the campaign in France was concluded it is believed the German army had 750,000 in service, of which some 18,000 were cavalry mounts.

On 23 May Brigadier R.H.R. Parminter, the Deputy Quartermaster General, arrived in Dunkirk from England and immediately headed his convoy for Hazebrouck. The distance was only 27 miles but it took him 24 hours to reach it. He set about distributing 530 tons of stores he had brought over, but again it was too little too late. Drinking water was becoming a problem and with so many troops arriving in the area demand soon outstripped supply. Entering houses and other empty premises did not produce much water either because the fighting had damaged pipes. Realising the emergency, Parminter arranged for 80,000 gallons of water to be stockpiled at points along the beaches at Dunkirk in readiness for the troops as they arrived in the evacuation area. Parminter's hard work was not in vain. An army needs supplies to support itself in whichever direction it is moving, including in retreat. This is something the Germans would also discover later in the war.

At the time of Belgium's surrender on 27 May, the BEF and French troops were fighting a rearguard action to cover the withdrawal of the main armies to Dunkirk from where they were being evacuated to England. The situation had been assessed and the decision made to withdraw the remains of the Anglo-French armies from Dunkirk in an operation codenamed Dynamo; the evacuation lasted from 26 May to 4 June. In that time, more than 338,000 troops were evacuated, a figure which included 113,000 French troops and some troops of other nations. The cost was massive in manpower and materiel which had to be abandoned because there was simply no room on the ships and time was running out.

One of the units to be evacuated was the 1st Armoured Division, whose later record serves as an example of how the British army reformed, trained new troops and

As war approached, women across Britain formed volunteer groups to organise comfort gifts for the troops.

re-equipped. On its return to the UK until August 1941 it was engaged in anti-invasion duties while it built up its strength. It was then deployed overseas to Egypt where it took part in the second Battle of El Alamein in October 1942. Later in the campaign, it was one of the units which took part in the liberation of Tunis. The division had a strength of just under 15,000 men and 343 tanks along with other AFVs for reconnaissance duties, and included artillery and attached units such as signals and engineers. It was just one of many similar success stories.

When the troops returned to England they were taken to depots across the country for processing and those separated from their units in France were returned to their correct regiments. Between 27 May and 4 June, 2,000 locomotives and carriages moved over 319,000 troops running 620 special trains. One transit point was the station of Headcorn in Kent through which 145,000 troops stopped briefly. Around fifty local women volunteered and rallied the local population to provide refreshments for the troops and took it in turn to cover shifts. In that period of eight days they sliced sandwiches using 2,500 loaves each day while 19 stoves boiled water continuously to make tea. The ladies were assisted by forty soldiers who handed out 5,000 meat pies, 5,000 rolls, 5,000 sausages and 5,000 hard-boiled eggs. The BEF had lost 68,111 men

Stately homes, with their huge spaces, were perfectly suited to use as offices for the raising of funds to support the troops.

The donations to troops were sorted, stored and distributed by volunteer groups such as the WVS.

killed, wounded, missing and taken prisoner. They had lost 2,472 pieces of artillery along with 63,879 motor vehicles, and out of some 700 armoured vehicles sent to France only 25 were brought back. The RAF had lost 474 aircraft covering the withdrawal and at sea 243 vessels of all sizes, including six Royal Navy destroyers, had been lost.

Female volunteers helped organise distribution of ration books, evacuation of children and canteens.

Staff at national newspapers helped to raise funds to support the children evacuated from the cities before the Blitz.

As the war progressed, so the ladies in the volunteer groups became better organised.

Belgium, like its Dutch neighbour, had taken a neutral stance when hostilities broke out in 1939, but all that changed when Germany attacked on 10 May. The Belgian army had a peacetime strength of 100,000 men which increased to 550,000 on mobilisation. It had machine guns and was supported with mortars, anti-tank guns and some armoured cars. The troops fought to the best of their ability but after eighteen days they were beaten with 23,350 men killed and wounded. The few armoured vehicles they had were destroyed or captured along with artillery. As a neutral state the country had not seen the need for a large standing army nor the necessity to stockpile large amounts of ammunition and other supplies. Hitler, sensing the Belgians were on the verge of collapse, three days before the country actually surrendered, had written his assessment, expressing how he believed the Belgian soldier '… has generally fought very bravely. His experience of war was considerably greater than the Dutch. At the beginning his tenacity was astonishing.' He went on, remembering that at this point Belgium had not yet surrendered: 'This is now decreasing visibly as the Belgian soldier realises that his basic function is to cover the British retreat.' About this Hitler is incorrect because the Allies were all fighting the same retreat and the average Belgian soldier would have been unaware of any strategy at higher level. The Germans had dropped propaganda leaflets and posters showing the British preventing French troops from evacuating at Dunkirk, but those who got away knew this to be untrue.

The French army had lost 90,000 killed and 200,000 wounded with the remainder of the army, around 1.9 million men, capitulating when the French government signed an armistice on 21 June, seventeen days after Operation Dynamo had ended. During that period, despite being outnumbered in troops and tanks, the French army had fought on, more stubbornly in some cases than at any point in the campaign before Dunkirk. The surrendering French troops were disarmed and taken into captivity and all its remaining trucks and armoured vehicles were eventually taken into German service and given specific titles. In addition to what had been captured from the British army on the beaches at Dunkirk the campaign provided the German army over 5,000 pieces of artillery, 4,260 locomotives and 140,000 railcars, all of which would be used to move war materiel and troops over vast distances. Later, some of these locomotives would be put to a more insidious purpose as they were used to transport Jews to the death camps when the mass deportations began.

With the surrender of France, German forces began to assess their newly-won conquest. In Cherbourg they could look out across towards the British territories of the Channel Islands. There were no British troops on the islands and a broadcast had been made declaring them demilitarised and undefended. On 28 June German aircraft attacked the two largest of the islands, Jersey and Guernsey, dropping bombs in the vicinity of the harbours. Damage was done and civilians killed in these raids. Two days later the first troops landed to begin what would be five years of occupation. During that time the islands, which had no direct military value, were fortified beyond their importance. It was a question of propaganda value for Hitler by seizing British territories and they would come to absorb around ten per cent of the resources put into creating the 'Atlantic Wall'. On Jersey alone, some 11,500 troops would be based and the defences would require 37,000 tons of reinforcing steels rods and 250,000 tons of concrete. The garrison would expand across the islands to a strength of 28,000 troops, one of the greatest concentrations of occupying forces given the size of the islands.

The conclusion of the French campaign yielded some rich pickings for the Germans who seized upon the vast amount of weaponry surrendered by the French army, including artillery, mortars, 315,000 rifles, huge stocks of ammunition, and vehicles. Around 2,170 tanks of all types which had survived the fighting were captured; many would prove unsuitable for front line use but were pressed into a range of other services, as self-propelled guns, flamethrowers or even as internal security vehicles. Over 5,000 pieces of artillery were captured along with four million shells. Raw materials for war production were also captured, including 81,000 tons of copper. The older tanks, like the Renault FT-17 Light Tank, which the Germans termed the PzKw 18R 730 (f), dated back to the First World War and had limited usefulness in a combat role. Most had their turrets removed and were then incorporated into defensive positions as armoured machine gun posts along the French coast. Some were later taken to the Channel Islands, where their turrets were removed and used in the fortifications across the islands. The chassis were then used as towing vehicles or ammunition carriers for artillery units.

Two other examples of captured French armoured vehicles included the Renault AMC 35 Light Tank and the Panhard AMD 178 Armoured Car which became the PzKw AMC 738 (f) and the P204(f) respectively. The suffix letter 'f' was used to denote weapons and vehicles of French origin. At the time of Germany's attack there were around 360 AMD 178 Armoured Cars in service with the French army and most of these were used in the fighting. When France capitulated the Germans readily seized them. A number would be sent to the eastern front in preparation for Operation Barbarossa, the attack against Russia in June 1941. Indeed, it is understood that more than 100 of the vehicles were lost during the fighting. The road wheels were removed from some vehicles and replaced with railway wheels to convert them to run on the rail network and some 43 vehicles may have been configured to this role. The Germans also converted a number to specialised radio vehicles with some being fitted with the so-called 'bed-frame-type' aerial, a distinctively-shaped feature which curved forward over the turret. In 1943, AMD 178s were converted to carry a heavier armament by having their turrets removed and a 5cm calibre KwK L/42 gun fitted in an open-topped turret.

The Germans used even the smallest vehicles they captured, such as the UE Supply Tractor which had been developed by Renault in 1931. At the time of the invasion there were more than 6,000 of these vehicles in service with the French army, known as either the 'Chenillette' (small tracked vehicle) or the 'Tracteur Blindé' (armoured tractor). Weighing just 2.5 tons, these small but powerful vehicles could carry almost 800 pounds of supplies such as ammunition in a cargo bay at the rear and towing additional cargo

Germany used many types of vehicles captured from defeated armies, such as this French AMD178 engaged in Operation Barbarossa in 1941.

Another example of extemporisation by the German army. A captured French Renault UE supply vehicle has been fitted with a PaK36 3.7cm anti-tank gun.

in a trailer. It could reach speeds up to 25mph with an operational range of around 100 miles on roads. The Germans recognised the value of the UEs, which they referred to as 'Infanterie Schlepper' (infantry tractor) and designated them as UE 630 (f). Rather than dismissing the small vehicles they developed them into support roles such as Schneeschleuder (snow ploughs), infantry carriers, radio and observation vehicles and Fernmeldekabel-Kraftwagen (cable laying vehicles) for field telephones. Some were kept in their original role of ammunition supply and others were converted to carry a single MG34 machine gun, called Gepanzerte-MG Träger and used for patrolling airfields from around 1941.

As with the Dutch and Belgian armies, Hitler wrote his assessment of the French army which he identified as containing some 'marked differences'. He noted how in the French army some 'very bad units rub elbows with excellent units. In the overview, the difference in quality between the active and reserve divisions is extraordinary. Many active units have fought desperately; most of the reserve divisions, however, are far less able to endure the shock which battle inflicts on the morale of troops. For the French, as with the Dutch and Belgians, there is also the fact that they know that they are fighting in vain for objectives which are not in line with their own interests. Their morale is very affected, as they say that throughout or wherever possible the British have looked after their own units and prefer to leave the critical sectors to their allies.' The French lost 90,000 troops killed and 200,000 wounded in the campaign, with the remainder of the French army being taken prisoner. Gradually all stocks of captured war materiel would be absorbed into service by the German army.

As the last of the Allies evacuated Europe Hitler wrote his assessment of the British soldier. He believed he understood the mood and characteristics of the British soldier which was based on his experience from the time of the First World War, more than twenty years previously. However, he had only been a corporal in that war and his direct contact with British soldiers then would have been so little as to be of no relevance. Despite this limited knowledge he wrote how, in his opinion, the British soldier was 'very brave and tenacious in defence, unskilful in attack, wretchedly commanded. Weapons and equipment are of the highest order, but overall organisation is bad.'

In his dispatches, Lord Gort, who had commanded the BEF, wrote of his experiences facing the Blitzkrieg commenting, 'The speed with which the enemy exploited his penetration of the French Front, his willingness to accept risks to further his aim, and his exploitation of every success to the uttermost limits emphasised even more fully than in the campaigns of the past the advantage which accrues to the commander who knows how best to use time and make time his servant and not his master.' His words were the first testimony of a British officer as to the nature of this new warfare. He had seen at first-hand what lay in store for future campaigns and Allied commanders would learn from he had witnessed.

To help bring the British army back from Dunkirk small boats such as these were used to ferry the troops from the beaches out to the larger ships waiting in deep water.

The operation at Dunkirk had cost the British army dearly with more than 11,000 killed, 14,000 wounded and 41,338 taken prisoner or reported missing. In terms of vehicles, out of the 68,618 sent to France with the BEF some 63,879 were destroyed or abandoned, including 20,548 motorcycles. Some sources put the figure at 75,000 vehicles and also cite that the BEF lost around 11,000 machine guns of all types and

90,000 rifles. The artillery regiments had taken 2,794 guns of all calibres to France for anti-tank and anti-aircraft roles of which 2,472 were either destroyed in the fighting or had to be abandoned because there was no room for these weapons on the evacuating ships. In addition, 76,000 tons of ammunition was left behind along with a further 400,000 tons of other stores, including food, medical supplies and ancillary equipment. All of this would be put to use by the Germans.

When Operation Dynamo was declared at an end the country was relieved that the British army had been saved. Churchill was the new Prime Minister, but he had witnessed enough crises to realise that worse lay ahead and bluntly reminded people that '… wars are not won by evacuations…' The US radio journalist Ed Murrow, based in London working for the Columbia Broadcasting System transmitting to neutral America, said about calling Dunkirk a victory: '…there will be disagreement on that point.' Churchill knew that saving the manpower was essential and to the population of Britain the news of their rescue did indeed appear a victory.

On 10 June Italy declared war on Britain, no doubt hoping to gain something from the campaign even in its closing stages. Eleven days later Mussolini ordered an attack and on 21 June, thirty-two Italian divisions advanced, but foundered when they encountered French mountain troops who inflicted heavy losses. It was one thing for

Thousands of trucks, such as this refurbished original Morris Commercial 15cwt, were abandoned by the British army as it withdrew from Dunkirk.

On arriving back in England, the evacuated troops of the British Expeditionary Force were given food and hot drinks by civilians. The evacuation was seen by many as a 'miracle' but Winston Churchill had other opinions.

Italian troops to face up to poorly equipped Ethiopian forces but against adequately equipped and better trained forces the Italian soldier was insufficiently prepared. The setback was embarrassing for Mussolini, but, undeterred, he switched his attention and focused on North Africa. It was here that he believed the Italian army would be able to redeem itself. Following defeat in France it did seem that the British army could also be beaten in the new battleground of North Africa.

The thousands of abandoned vehicles littering the roads to Dunkirk became one of the most enduring images of the campaign to be published in newspapers. German propaganda made good capital of the imagery also. Newsreel film taken by German cameramen was distributed to the neutral countries from where copies found their way to England. The films showed the abandoned beaches littered with the debris of war, such as rifles, helmets and uniforms. There were rows of lorries which had been positioned to lead into the water where they served as makeshift staging for the troops to clamber onto the small rescue vessels which ferried the troops out to the larger ships waiting in deeper water. The Germans recovered around 500,000 tons of stores left behind.

One type of vehicle they recovered to be put into service was the Universal or Bren Gun Carrier. As with other captured equipment they gave it a German designation, the Gepanzert Maschinengewehr Träger Br 731 (e), which they adapted into a range of

duties. Some found their way onto the Eastern Front after Germany attacked Russia in June 1941, being fitted with PaK36/37 3.7cm anti-tank gun, machine guns and some to carry 8.8cm Raketenpanzerbuchse anti-tank rocket launchers.

Amidst all the chaos during the evacuation, despite space being at a premium on board the evacuating ships, room was found to get 5,000 vehicles away from France and back to Britain. But as the last remnants of the BEF returned to England the army could only count 200 serviceable tanks.

The country appeared to be standing alone. But it was not, because the dominion and commonwealth countries of the British Empire, including Australia, New Zealand, India and Canada, were dependable cornerstones on which Britain could rely, just as it had during the First World War.

Before the war, the British army had bases and troops in Commonwealth countries around the world. These all had to be supplied with food, ammunition and other vital logistics, especially fuel.

The British army had a long-standing presence in the Middle East. In the 1930s many of the vehicles used were rather dated, but still provided service during the early stages of the campaign in North Africa.

A German soldier at a very early stage in the war.

Chapter 3

The War at Sea

At the outbreak of war, the Royal Navy was more powerful than the combined fleets of France, Germany and Italy, having 2.25 million tons compared to the 750,000 tons, 500,000 tons and 650,000 tons of these fleets respectively. The force included 15 battleships, 7 aircraft carriers, 15 heavy cruisers, along with hundreds of escort vessels, destroyers, minesweepers and submarines. In addition, there were dozens more warships waiting on the slipways at the builders' yards ready to enter service. The war being fought on land could be covered by the journalists of the world. They could observe the action and report on events in newspapers and cameramen could film newsreel for the cinemas. The war at sea was a different matter, being virtually inaccessible, so that events were reported through official channels. Although the German navy, the Kriegsmarine, was only a fraction of the size of the British Royal Navy, through skilful handling and great daring German naval commanders were able to inflict severe losses on the Allies. Germany had fifty-seven U-Boats at sea when war was declared. Indeed, the war was only hours old when one of these boats, the U-30 commanded by Oberleutnant Fritz Lemp, fired torpedoes at a ship he had been tracking in the days leading up to the outbreak of hostilities. His target was the liner SS *Athenia*, taking passengers and evacuees to America. Out of more than 1,100 passengers and crew on board 112 died. They were the first casualties of the war.

Another U-Boat on patrol at the same time was U-47, commanded by Kapitänleutnant Gunther Prien. Between 5 and 7 September, he sank three merchant ships totalling 8,270 tons. A highly successful commander, his most audacious attack was made on 14 October when he penetrated the Royal Navy's anchorage at Scapa Flow and sank the 29,000 ton HMS *Royal Oak*. She had fought at the Battle of Jutland in 1916, but her main armament of eight 15-inch guns still made her a formidable adversary. Over the next eighteen months Prien and his crew sank around thirty ships, totalling some 200,000 tons, and damaged a further ten vessels, before they were sunk in March 1941. It was the actions of commanders such as Prien that led to Winston Churchill later admitting that he was frightened by the U-Boat peril. From the outbreak of war these shipping routes had been patrolled by U-Boats and between September and December 1939 a total of 114 ships, either neutral vessels or registered to Britain or France, representing over 421,000 tons, were sunk.

Holland had been neutral until May 1940 when it was attacked, but its shipping had been vulnerable before then. After capitulation, Dutch shipping was still at sea heading for friendly ports. On 20 June, the 7,500 ton tanker *Moordrecht*, carrying 10,000 tons of oil, was spotted by U–48. At a range of over three miles the U-Boat fired a single torpedo and scored a direct hit. Out of the crew of 29 only 4 survived. Fortunately for Britain and the Allies, things did not always develop in the U-Boats' favour, but for the time being this story was to be repeated many times.

At the beginning of the war the combined tonnage of merchant shipping operated by France and Britain exceeded 24 million tons. The British fleet in 1939 allowed the annual import of around 46 million tons of food and supplies to support and supplement what could be produced by the island nation. Much of this was transported across the Atlantic from various exporting nations, such as beef from Argentina. This flow of maritime traffic represented a wealth of targets for the U-Boats. France had overseas trade routes but being a much larger country and with borders connecting it to friendly countries with which it could trade directly, it was not so dependent on the merchant trade to bring in supplies to the same degree as Britain.

The first major naval engagement of the war was between the 16,000 ton *Graf Spee* and three British warships: HMSs *Ajax, Cumberland* and *Exeter*. The *Graf Spee* sailed from its port at Wilhelmshaven on 21 August and took up station in the mid-South Atlantic on 9 September, ready and waiting for her victims. In the course of eleven weeks she sank nine merchant ships carrying food supplies, totalling over 50,000 tons, before she was engaged by the Royal Navy in a running battle. She took temporary shelter in the harbour of Montevideo in neutral Paraguay. She sailed out on the evening of 17 December and rather than face another battle she was scuttled. Her loss for such a small return was a great price to pay. More successful was the smaller cruiser the *Admiral Scheer*, which sank in excess of 250,000 tons of shipping in the Indian Ocean, Atlantic and home waters.

In the war against merchant shipping the Germans deployed four main weapons: surface raiders, sea mines, aircraft and U-Boats. Sea mines became increasingly sophisticated, especially the magnetic mines, yet they only accounted for the sinking of around 203,500 tons of shipping, or some 6.5% of the total amount sunk. The surface raiders, included the so-called 'pocket battleships' such as the *Scharnhorst, Bismarck* and *Tirpitz*, despite their impressive size and powerful armaments accounted for only 6.1%. More successful surface raiders were the 'Hilfskreuzer' or armed merchantman fleet, many of which actually sank more tonnage than the *Graf Spee*. The Kriegsmarine operated a fleet of eleven such vessels which raided into all the oceans and between them sank over 800,000 tons of shipping, including warships. They had tonnages from less than 4,000 tons and none exceeded 10,000. They were heavily armed in guns, torpedoes and carried floatplanes used to spot targets.

The *Pinguin* captured or sank 32 ships totalling 157,710 tons, of which 52,000 tons were sent back to Germany. The *Kormoran* sank over 68,000 tons, 36,258 tons in the first four months of 1941. Other ships in the fleet had equally impressive tallies, such as the *Thor* and the *Michael* which sank 155,191 tons and 99,386 tons respectively. Ton for ton, they were better than the great pocket battleships.

Long range aircraft such as FW 200 accounted for around 13.4% of all losses, but the greatest threat by far was the U-Boat fleet which sank the remaining 70%. Between each of these methods, their targets included warships and cargo ships carrying supplies and weapons, but mainly it was the tankers carrying fuel. From September 1939 until June 1941, British merchant shipping losses exceeded 5.7 million tons, of which British shipyards could only replace 800,000 tons. In the autumn of 1940 Britain lost 33 ships out of a total of 79 in two convoys. One such was the *San Emiliano*, which sailed from Trinidad on 6 August 1942. She was sunk three days later with her precious cargo of 12,000 tons of high-octane aviation fuel.

In 1940 Britain's merchant marine fleet had a manpower level of 120,000 ratings with 4,500 masters. They were supported by 13,000 deck officers, 20,000 engineers, 36,000 deck ratings, 30,000 engine room ratings and 17,000 stewards. These men were civilians but they faced the same dangers as seamen on board warships. Of the 145,000 British merchant seamen who served during the war, more than 32,000 would be killed, representing a loss of over twenty per cent.

Something had to be done to reduce these losses. Part of the answer lay in the convoy system, which had been used in the First World War, and was reintroduced in 1939. The effect was noticeable. At the end of 1940 around 692 convoys had sailed with a combined total of 17,882 vessels. Of this figure only 127 vessels, amounting to 0.7%, were sunk, meaning that 99.3% got through. The remaining 865 ships sunk that year were mainly sailing alone. Imports of non-essential, luxury items were suspended to make room for material vital to the country's war effort. In reply to these losses the Allies managed to capture or sink some German merchant shipping, but it was nothing compared to the losses they were sustaining. Grand Admiral Karl Dönitz, who had served in U-Boats during the First World War, knew the value of the submarine and calculated that if the German navy could sink 600,000 tons of merchant shipping a month, Britain might be starved out of the war. It was imperative, therefore, that these sea lanes and supply routes be kept open at all costs if Germany was to be defeated. As convoy methods improved so losses dropped. For example, in April 1941, of the 307 merchant ships sailing in convoy only 16 were lost. In 1942 losses were once again high, with 609 ships sunk amounting to 6 million tons. It looked as though Dönitz might achieve his aim. However in 1942, with America in the war and the enormous capacity of its shipyards, combined with that of Britain's output, the two countries built over 7 million tons of shipping, increasing the Allies' fleet capacity to 30 million tons.

Among the new ships being built were special cargo freighters called 'Liberty Ships', designed to transport war materiel to Britain. These ships were constructed using the prefabricated method which greatly speeded up building and in 1942 some 646 such vessels were built. Eventually eighteen shipyards were building Liberty Ships and by the end of the war they had built 2,710 vessels out of a proposed programme of 2,751. At first these ships took on average 230 days to build, but later, with production being supervised by industrialists such as Henry J. Kaiser, this was reduced to 42 days. In an effort to raise public morale a special 'rush' build was reported in the news which covered the construction of the SS *Robert E. Peary*, built in four days and fifteen and a half hours. By the end of the war American shipyards had built 78,000 other vessels, a figure which included 1,200 warships, 3,300 merchant ships and tankers, and some 8,800 other types of naval vessels. In the same period American shipyards built 104 aircraft carriers. By comparison, Japan built only fourteen. Neither Italy nor Germany built aircraft carriers, although they did consider the idea. The Liberty Ship fleet meant that vehicles, tanks, guns and ammunition, along with medical supplies and foodstuffs, could be sent to Britain to maintain its role in the war. Later, these vessels would be joined by the great pre-war passenger liners such as the RMS *Queen Mary* and RMS *Queen Elizabeth* in transporting American troops and all their supplies in preparation for the build-up to invade Europe.

In 1942 there was a drop of five million tons in the amount of supplies reaching Britain, amounting to around 15% of the total. This was partly due to supplies being diverted to Russia being carried by 200 ships. The Russian convoy route was one of the most hazardous of all supply lines of the war. After Hitler attacked Russia in June 1941, Britain saw it as its national duty to support Stalin's communist Soviet state, which was its first new ally in the war against Germany in over a year. Churchill ordered that convoys be sent with supplies to help in the war against the common enemy. These convoys sent to Russia were given the prefix 'PQ' to denote outward bound while those making the return voyage were coded 'QP'. The most infamous incident involving a Russian convoy was that of PQ17 which sailed in late June 1942 with thirty-five merchantmen escorted by destroyers, corvettes and other vessels including tankers. The convoy came under such intense attack from U-Boats and aircraft that it was given the unusual order to 'scatter'. This meant that each surviving ship had to make its own way to its destination. Only eleven eventually reached port. Apart from the loss of 24 ships, 153 sailors had been killed, 430 tanks lost, 210 aircraft, 3,350 other vehicles and 100,000 tons of various cargo. Winston Churchill said, 'The operation is justified if half gets through.' It was a high price to pay but Russia had to be kept in the war on the side of the Allies. Other PQ convoys suffered badly, such as PQ13 which lost 30,000 tons of its capacity of 21 vessels, and PQ18 which sailed in September 1942 losing 13 ships out of 40.

The convoys to Russia sailed mainly from northern ports such as Loch Ewe in Scotland and Rekjavik in Iceland, bound for destinations such as Murmansk or

Arkhangelsk (known to the Allies as Archangel). By the end of the war Britain had sent 78 convoys to Russia of which 87 merchant vessels were sunk and a further 18 Royal Navy escorts ships sunk, costing the lives of 2,773 naval ratings and merchant seamen. They delivered 7,000 aircraft, 5,000 tanks and millions of tons of fuel, medical equipment and other material. Impressive as it was, these figures would represent only a small part of the total number of vehicles sent to Russia by America under the Lend-Lease Act. Initially America did very little, but gradually things changed and in 1943 America sent 210,000 vehicles, 3,734 tanks and two million tyres. By the end of the war America had sent 51,500 Jeeps, 375,000 trucks, 22,000 aircraft, 343,000 tons of explosives, small arms, millions of pairs of boots, millions of miles of cable for telephones, 25,000 telephones, 4 million tyres, 8,700 tractors and 1,900 locomotives (the width of the train track being different between the American standard and the Russian meant these had to be specially produced or modified). Helping to organise all this logistical support was Anastas Mikoyan, who, in June 1941, had been appointed Special Representative of the Soviet State Defence Committee. It was a monumental task, but he set to it with a vigour, knowing the survival of the country depended on it.

When supplies began arriving in quantity he wrote, 'Our army suddenly found itself on wheels – and what wheels!' In 1945, the Red Army had 665,000 trucks in service, not counting those which had been destroyed in the fighting, of which 427,000 were American-built. Mikoyan continued: 'When we started to receive American canned beef, fat, powdered eggs and other foodstuffs, this was worth a lot of extra calories.' In summing up the whole worth of American Lend-Lease, he believed the aid had shortened the war by eighteen months.

Britain's merchant fleet was so large that at any one time there were some 2,000 vessels at sea. There were just too many targets for the U-Boats. Better weapons and better escort ships meant the U-Boat would be conquered but not until after they had wreaked havoc. Mussolini sent his submarines to operate in the Atlantic alongside the U-Boats but they never achieved anywhere near the same level of results. For example, between October and November 1941 Italian submarines accounted for one ship of 4,000 tons. In the same period, German U-Boats sank 435,000 tons.

The Atlantic is a vast ocean, covering 41,000,000 square miles, and no amount of long-range aircraft and escort ships could cover it all. The Germans recognised this and exploited it. The Allies responded by increasing the number of escort ships, introducing better weaponry, and with better training and tactics the U-Boat menace was defeated. The Royal Navy and the Royal Canadian Navy between them provided around 96% of all escort ships for trans-Atlantic convoys. The US Navy provided the rest. It could not provide more because it was committed to fighting the Japanese in the Pacific. The threat of the U-Boat never entirely went away, but its capacity to win the war was in the end beaten.

During the war the Kriegsmarine produced 1,170 U-Boats of all types of which 926 were lost due to enemy action and 42 due to accidents. Only 202 were surrendered at the end of hostilities making losses among the U-Boat crews the highest casualty rate for any branch of a country's armed forces. A search through the records of the twenty highest scoring U-Boat 'aces' of the war shows they sank between them some 3,172,115 tons of shipping. This gives on average 158,600 tons per 'ace' which is comparable to the results achieved by some of the Hilfskreuzer fleet. These vessels did much harm to Allied supply lines and it is not hard for one to imagine what the effect would have been had there been more of them.

Chapter 4

Oil and the Jerrycan

T he term logistics is today defined as 'the branch of military science relating to procuring, maintaining and transporting materiel, personnel and facilities'. Thus logistics covers everything an army needs to remain at a state of readiness at all times but especially during time of war when weapons, ammunition, supplies and vast amounts of petrol, oil and lubricants (POL) are needed. When the German army was being restructured in the mid-1930s it recognised that a future war would be a 'Materialschlacht' (a war of materiel).

As it would discover, especially in the vast desert wastes of North Africa, and in Russia with its extremes in weather conditions, an army without fuel and oil was doomed to failure. In 1935, before Hitler and Mussolini became allied, Italy invaded Abyssinia with a fleet of trucks and tanks which easily rolled over the ill-prepared forces that were poorly equipped and armed. While the attack led to moral indignation at such an unprovoked act of aggression, European countries barely raised any complaint and beyond a few mildly punitive sanctions, Italy was left to its own devices. Had a more stringent line been taken, such as putting in place an embargo on oil, the result would have meant Italy would have been unable to maintain its conquest of the country.

To carry petrol the British army used light tin cans with either 'crimped' or soldered seams which were fragile and easily split during the rigors of transportation. They held four gallons of petrol and General Sir Claude Auchinleck, who had seen service in the First World War, action during the Norwegian campaign in 1940, and commanded British forces in North Africa between 1941 and 1942, criticised them. He believed that the design fault in these tins led to the loss of as much as thirty per cent during the journey from base to the vehicles they were intended to provision. They were so easily damaged in transit that the troops called them 'flimsies'. The author A.A. Nicol, who wrote *My Moving Tent*, an account of his experiences while serving in the 8th Army in North Africa and later Italy, recalled how they were 'no stouter than biscuit tins'. He wrote how he had seen 'a truck loaded with these tins moving up in a supply column and the petrol dripping from the rear, to be sucked up by the greedy desert sand.' One can only sympathize with the troops who, when they '… received such a load, several tins would be empty'. The same design was used to transport water and other liquids, leading to great losses of these essential supplies also.

During the campaign in North Africa the British army captured stocks of German fuel cans which, being made from pressed steel and sealed with welded seams, were far more robust than the flimsies. The design also featured a red enamel coating on the inside to prevent rust, a pouring spout to minimise spillages and an integral sealing cap, making it overall a far superior item than anything produced by the Allies. The same design was used to transport water and other liquids and markings on the body denoted the use. In fact, so impressed were they, the Allies copied it and produced more than 50 million by the end of the war, hence the name 'jerrycans'. Imitation is the sincerest form of flattery. If ever there was an example of that saying, then this was surely one.

The German army fuel can was a superb design and copied by the Allies.

Detail showing the pouring spout designed to minimise spillage.

The so-called 'Jerry-can' was strong and designed to be stacked to make use of space.

Millions of the German-designed fuel cans were produced by both sides and the style is still in use today but using plastics.

Chapter 5

Reforming the Armies and the Rearmament Programme

When Hitler came to power in January 1933 the German military was still abiding by the constraints imposed by the Treaty of Versailles. Because of this, the risk of Germany starting another war was considered low and many European armies, Britain and France among them, reduced their national defence expenditure. Meanwhile, Holland and Belgium reaffirmed their neutral status. Hitler saw all this as weakness but, even so, he knew he would have to bide his time before he could make any overt military move. For just over two years he waited, until in March 1935 he announced his intention to unilaterally dismiss the terms of the Treaty of Versailles, reintroduce conscription, begin increasing the strength of Germany's armed forces, and rearm.

The senior military commanders within the new order realised that it would take time to rebuild the German military, equip it with modern weaponry and train the forces. There were some senior officers from the 'old order' who did not agree with this new aggressive policy. These were the more conservative types and they were bypassed in favour of those who sided with Hitler. In this transition period from Reichswehr to Wehrmacht all the branches of the armed forces expanded greatly. There were already many trained personnel who had served with the Landespolizei who had received military training from their time in the Reichswehr. These men were absorbed into the army proper where they formed a core of trained men who could in turn train the new recruits. More uniforms, boots, helmets and equipment were needed. Manufacturing increased to meet this demand along with the output of new weapons.

The Kriegsmarine expanded and new, heavier, more powerful warships were introduced into the fleet. By May 1941 it had a manpower level of over 400,000. The Luftwaffe received new aircraft and its strength was greatly increased. In 1939 it had around 1.5 million men serving in a variety of roles, including 900,000 in anti-aircraft units equipped with the latest 8.8cm FlaK guns and the lighter 2cm Flak guns. There were 50,000 aircrew and 80,000 in the maintenance and supply chain. In a remarkably short time Germany had gone from having a self-defence armed force to a level which allowed it to deploy over 3,900 aircraft to support 'Fall Gelb', the attack against France and Belgium in May 1940.

Along with the appearance of new warships and aircraft, there were to be further new tank designs for the army. Some of the first of these new designs resembled fairly conventional touring cars, if somewhat large, due to the fact they were fitted with armour plating and carried machine guns. One of the new vehicles was developed as the Maschinengewehrkraftwagen and designated as the Kfz 13, serving in the role of armoured reconnaissance car. In all, a total of 147 such vehicles were built by Daimler-Benz between 1932 and 1934 along with 40 vehicles designated Kfz 14 Funkkraftwagen (radio car). The Kfz 13 and 14 were intended for use with the motorised forces being created and were issued to motorised Aufklärungs (reconnaissance) units. From 1935 the Kfz 13 was augmented by the introduction of the new SdKfz 221 and SdKfz 223, both 4x4 light armoured car designs. This arrangement lasted until 1938, when the Kfz 13 role was completely replaced by later designs such as the SdKfz 221 and 223 armoured cars, withdrawn and issued to reconnaissance units of non–motorised units.

Even so, there still remained a role for the Kfz 13 and 14 and both were used in limited numbers during the invasion of Poland in September 1939. Eight months later those vehicles still remaining in service would be used during the attack against France and Belgium in May 1940. The designs were finally withdrawn completely from frontline service in 1941 and used for basic driver training duties with recruits. They appeared in public for the first time in 1934, along with the first new tank design the Panzerkampfwagen I, which was beginning to equip the German army. Armed with nothing more serious than two machine guns this tank design and the armoured cars gave little if any cause for concern in either France or Britain.

Two years later the PzKw I was joined by the heavier and more powerfully armed PzKw II, equipped with a 2cm cannon in a turret with machine guns. Even with the appearance of these relatively modern designs, the British and French did not seem unduly alarmed. The Germans called their growing fleet of tanks Panzers. To these and armoured cars, along with other specialist vehicles, they gave the prefix lettering SdKfz, standing for Sonderkraftfahrzeug (special motorised vehicle) followed by a unique designation number to denote the type of vehicle. This identification also extended to include the half-track range of vehicles even down to the small motorcycle-style Kettenkrad which was designated SdKfz 2. Even trucks, light cars such as the Kübelwagen and motorcycles all had designation numbers and lettering to identify them. Variations or models would be referred to as Ausfuhrung, abbreviated to Ausf. meaning model or mark. Thus, for example, the Panzerkampfwagen I referred to as SdKfz 101 Ausf. B, meant model B of the tank type 101.

The PzKw I and PzKw II had the nomenclatures of SdKfz 101 and SdKfz 121 respectively, which denoted their special status as armoured vehicles and both would continue to serve in the German army until 1943. In this time more than 1,400 PzKw I tanks were built, along with other variants including supply vehicles and self-propelled guns, and some 3,600 PzKw II had been built in six different models and all variants. While the PzKw II was not the most powerful tank fielded by the German army it was far more advanced than a number of designs in service with other armies at the time, such as the A11 Matilda I Infantry Tank of the British army. The Panzer II was a natural continuation from the design of the Panzer I, but it was better armed and had a faster road speed. The Panzer II may not have been the most powerful tank to see service during the Second World War but the basic design was sufficiently versatile to lead on to the development of several variants including self-propelled guns, recovery vehicles and bridge-laying vehicles.

Using secret facilities in Sweden, the German Ordnance Department had laid out specifications for a tank which would have a battle ready weight of around ten tons because it was thought that anything heavier would wreck the bridges as the vehicles traversed them. From 1934 sufficient numbers of crews had been trained and enough numbers of the PzKw I tanks were in service, so that when the Spanish Civil War erupted in 1936, Hitler could send them to support General Franco. The crews gained valuable experience during the fighting which they could pass on to other tank crews in training. The PzKw II was also used in this war, which enabled crews to identify weaknesses in design which allowed improvements in future models. By 1939 German armaments factories, such as MAN, had already built over 1,200 PzKw II tanks, many of which made up the armoured force deployed for campaign on the eve of the Polish invasion.

The first variant to appear was the Ausf. A, or Model A, of which 100 vehicles were built and it was this series which were the first to enter service with the German army proper in 1936. It was armed with a 2cm KwK30 L/55 cannon in a fully traversing turret with an MG34 machine gun of 7.92mm calibre mounted co-axially. Six main Models of the Panzer II followed, but some features remained unaltered such as the main armament and the radio was always the FuG5. The Ausf. B version was produced from December 1937 with the Ausf. C appearing six months later. A total of only 43 Models D and E of the PzKw II were built between May 1938 and August 1939 and these were deployed with a single Panzer battalion which saw service during the invasion of Poland. The entire series of Models D and E were withdrawn in March 1940 and converted to flamethrower tanks, given the designation of SdKfz 122 Panzerkampfwagen II Flamm Ausf. A and B, and later used on the Eastern Front. The final version of the PzKw II proper was the Ausf. F, which virtually reverted back to the original design. In total some 524 were built between March 1941 and December 1942 and used mainly in the reconnaissance role.

The production programme of the PzKw II continued but the tank versions were phased out in favour of other types based on the chassis. Only twelve vehicles of the Ausf. G were built between April 1941 and February 1942, none of which are understood to have been deployed in a combat role. Four vehicles in the Ausf. H and Ausf. M versions were produced and none of these are believed to have seen actual combat service. Other versions, such as the Ausf. J, were adapted for specific roles such as bridge-laying. Some of the Panzer II fleet were developed into SPGs – self-propelled guns – armed with a range of artillery such as captured Russian weapons of 76.2mm calibre. Another self–propelled gun version, Leichte Feldhaubitze 18/2 auf Fahrgestell Panzerkampfwagen II, designated as the SdKfz 124 or 'Wespe', was armed with a 10.5cm leFH18M gun, and this remained in service until the end of the war. Some 676 versions of the SPG were built and 139 ammunition carrier versions, and the type was considered one the best designs of its kind in the entire war.

In the same year the Germans unveiled the Panzer II, they also revealed the Neubaufahrzeug (NbFz) Panzerkampfwagen V (new construction vehicle or experimental medium tank). It was armed with a turret-mounted 7.5 cm calibre KwK L/24 gun with a 3.7cm co-axial gun and four machine guns in two further turrets, making it the most powerful tank at the time. Yet, the alarms still failed to signal with the British and French. As it transpired, the vehicle, for all its grandiose appearance, never entered service but its revelation was a marvellous propaganda coup for the Germans. The only time it ever saw service was when three of them, along with about 100 other types of tank, were deployed during the invasion on Norway in April 1940. It is believed the three so-called Panzerkampfwagen V tanks photographed in Oslo were almost certainly the three experimental models which were built. They had proved their worth in terms of propaganda purposes and showed the world what German tank designers could do.

The British and French believed their respective anti-tank gun capabilities could deal with the German tank designs, besides which, French tank designs such as the Renault AMC 35 Light Tank with its 47mm main gun were, in theory at least, more than a match for any heavier surprise vehicles. At the time the British army had 136 infantry battalions, 18 horsed cavalry regiments, 4 battalions of tanks and 2 regiments of armoured cars. Some of the tanks were almost vintage in design, having been in service with the British army since 1926, such as the Mk II Medium armed with a three-pounder gun in a turret. Another tank in service of similar vintage was the Vickers Mk VI Light Tank armed with a .303 inch calibre machine gun. Later variants were armed with a .50 inch calibre machine gun, which was comparable to the Panzer I. This design dated back to the 1920s when several types of light tank and carrier were being developed by Carden-Loyd and under consideration for the British army. They were useful vehicles for the time and designed to operate primarily reconnaissance duties.

However, the shape of the British army was changing and so was the type of warfare in which they were to engage. Indeed in 1928, when Carden-Loyd was acquired by engineering giant Vickers, the new design team wasted no time in scrapping designs which were considered to be of no value. One Carden-Loyd design which did survive was the Mk I Light Tank. It entered service with the British army in 1929 and was to be the first in a series of its type to enter service with the army. The vehicle was modern, with a fully traversing turret and several other modifications to the original design.

Like the German Panzer II, the Mk I Light Tank proved to be so successful that it served as the foundation for several other light tanks which Vickers turned out at a rapid rate. The series culminated in 1936 with the Mk VI Light Tank which, in turn, was to run to improved marks ending with the Mk VIC. In fact, this last design was to be the heaviest, fastest and, considered by some to be the best armed tank in the range, being fitted with a BESA 15mm heavy machine gun and a co-axial 7.92mm BESA machine gun. Some versions of the Mk VI Light Tank were equipped to carry .303 inch Bren guns mounted on special turret brackets for low-level air defence. It remained in service with the British army until 1941 and was also used by the Australian, Canadian and South African Armies. The Mk VI was used in service in France during 1940, Egypt in 1941 and even deployed to Malta to be used in the defence of the island. In Egypt the British army used these tanks in the role of mobile artillery observation posts. Those vehicles in the range which had been intended for the Indian army were diverted and ended up in Persia, modern day Iran, when that country was occupied and taken over by the British in a preventative move to protect the oil fields from attack by German and Italian forces.

Following the retreat from Dunkirk in 1940 it became all too apparent that British tank design was inadequate, both in weaponry hitting power and armoured defence. Those older vehicles left in Britain were consigned to training roles. The turrets of the light tank designs were not large enough to accept heavier guns and the armour was not sufficient to protect against battle damage. As the vehicles used in training roles wore out due to mechanical failure they were scrapped to be replaced by more modern designs better suited to the more fluid battlefields of modern warfare, such as the Matilda Mk II. The British army needed new tanks as the situation became ever more urgent. Replacement types such as the Crusader entered service in 1939 and over 3,500 were built. In 1940 the Valentine entered service and by the end of the war around 8,275 had been produced in England. Canada built a further 1,420 and of these some 1,300 were sent to Russia as part of Britain's Lend-Lease support to its Soviet ally. Unfortunately these tanks were still armed with the 2-pounder main gun of 40mm calibre which could not defeat the newer German tanks. Even the Churchill tank which came into service in 1941 was still armed with a 2-pounder, but later versions were more heavily armed. It was not until the Cromwell with its 6-pounder of 57mm calibre and the Comet with its 77mm gun, introduced into service in 1941 and 1944 respectively, did the hitting power of the guns begin to improve.

In the overall assessment on the eve of the outbreak of war there did not appear to be any European country dominating the armour race. Germany had promising tank designs, Britain's were sorely lacking; if there was one country which had the edge in the armour race, it was surely France. With its numerical superiority in designs such as the Char B1 Heavy Tank, Renault R-35 Light Tank and Char Somua S-35 Medium Tank, France, on paper at least, appeared to have the edge.

The increasing demand in the German army for troop transport and prime-mover tractors for towing artillery was served by the half-track. These versatile vehicles were designed from the smallest to the heaviest and proved useful platforms for a wide range of purposes. For example, the SdKfz10, of which 14,000 were built, entered service in 1938 was used in all theatres and remained in use throughout the war. The prototype was built in 1934 and, following further research and development, the SdKfz10 went into production in 1937, with the company of Demag as the leading manufacturer. Two variants of the vehicle, designated SdKfz10/1 and 10/2, were configured to the role of chemical decontamination roles. The SdKfz10/3 was equipped with nozzles to spray poison chemicals, but in the event few vehicles were built for this purpose and no country ever used poison gas during the war which rendered the design superfluous. The SdKfz10/4 and SdKfz10/5 versions were equipped with pedestal mounts to carry 2cm light FlaK anti-aircraft guns as mobile platforms, a role which suited both the army and the air force. The barrel of the gun could be depressed to allow ground targets to be engaged. The army also used the SfKfz10 to tow anti-tank guns and later versions were strengthened to allow them to tow larger, heavier field guns including the leFH18 howitzer of 105mm calibre. Such versatility would become a standard feature of most vehicles used by the German armed forces.

It was the Blitzkrieg which set the Germans apart from all other European armies and the tactic which produced so many victories. Without the tank it could not have been put into practice. Air support and artillery support were essential to allow the army to move forward and to neutralise enemy resistance, but it was the tanks which took the ground to enable the infantry to hold captured positions.

The tanks which would form the 'backbone' of the German armoured division were actually Czechoslovakian designs. Two designs of tank of Czechoslovakian origin in particular were seen as vitally important to the Germans from the moment they annexed the country along with its modern armaments industry. The first of these was to become known as the Panzerkampfwagen 35(t), armed with a 3.7cm gun and two 7.92mm machine guns. The German army actually used few themselves, instead supplying them to their allies. Between 1935 and 1938, 424 were produced. About half were used during the Polish campaign and a few saw action later in France in 1940. The lack of heavy armament and poor armour protection meant it was not entirely useful in the heavy tank battles later in the war.

The second tank, which would become known as the Pazerkampfwagen 38 (t), was the most important. The design began in 1937 when the company of CKD (Praga) built a prototype design known as the Vz38 in a series known as TNHPS, which came out as the overall winner against rival designs during field trials held in 1938. The value of the design was recognised and an order for 150 was placed. However, the political situation at the time led to a cutback in filling orders and it was not until March 1939 that the first vehicle was ready. By then Germany had annexed the country and when the first tanks rolled off the production line they went to the Heer as the Ausfuhrung A version. By now the original production company of CKD (Praga) was under German control and known as Bohmisch-Mahrische Maschinenfabrik (BMM). The first 150 were available to participate in the attack on Poland. Production continued and they were available in sufficient numbers to take part in later campaigns, including the attacks against Norway and France where they were used by units such as the 7th Armoured Division under Rommel.

The next three versions of the Panzerkampfwagen 38 (t) were designated as Ausf. B, C and D and a total of 325 of these were built between January and November 1940, making the first models available to participate in the Blitzkrieg against France and Belgium in 1940. The following year the survivors and newer versions served in the initial attack against Russia in June 1941 onwards, and later in the campaign they would be joined by all other versions of the tank. Variants of the Panzerkampfwagen 38 (t) went on to be deployed to other theatres, including Greece, but none are understood to have served in the fighting in North Africa. The most numerous versions of the tank to be built were the Ausf. E and F, with production running from November 1940 until October 1941 during which time some 525 were built. There were two more models, the Ausf. G and the Ausf. S, with a production run of 321 and 90 respectively, and the output of all versions finally ending in June 1942 after which time other variants such as self-propelled guns were produced.

At the outbreak of war, the British army found itself desperately short of vehicles. The same thing was also experienced by the RAF, but the crisis was not so urgent as with the army. In an effort to make good the shortfall some 26,000 civilian vehicles were impressed into service, a figure which included 5,000 private cars, 7,000 motorcycles and 14,000 trucks. Some vehicles were bought outright from their owners by the government, but, even so, the move only took the total number of soft-skinned vehicles up to 55,000. The fleet of vehicles increased and by the end of the war there were 1.25 million soft-skinned vehicles in service. The same shortfall of vehicles was also experienced in Germany and thousands of cars and trucks were requisitioned. Private owners whose cars had been taken could use public transport to go to work, but there was a limit to the number of vehicles which could be taken from this resource before it created an adverse effect on the country's economy. Trucks and other vehicles had to be left in sufficient numbers to allow food and other goods to be moved for the civilian population.

The army requisitioned thousands of cars to make up the shortfall of vehicles, such as this refurbished original Austin 10.

In Britain one car manufacturing company producing vehicles for the civilian market was the Rootes Group, with factories in Birmingham and Coventry where they were building a series of vehicles under the Hillman marque. Over the years the company had produced several versions of the Hillman Minx, a popular car for civilian use in the pre-war period. It was perfectly suited to liaison duties for the RAF around air bases or to travel between them. By 1939 Hillman moved into building more vehicles for the military and one of the designs was the Tilly (short for 'utility'). Tilly cars were also built by other companies such as Austin and Morris. The Humber Snipe was sometimes converted into 'Beaverette' armoured cars for use by Home Guard units.

The growing German army of the 1930s needed armoured cars. The earlier vehicles, such as the Ehrhardt E-V/4, which had served in the 1920s were now obsolete and others, like the Kfz13, were limited in capability, although their speed and operational range was acceptable. In 1934 the German Army High Command issued a contract to the Leipzig-based company of Bussing-NAG to develop a new armoured car with four axles and full 8x8 all-wheel drive. From time of request through to the first vehicles

As the Home Guard became better organised so it acquired vehicles such as the Beaverette armoured car.

entering service took only three years. This was the Schwerer Panzerspähwagen (heavy armoured reconnaissance vehicle) or SdKfz 232. Entering service in 1937, it was available in numbers to take part in the first phases of the German army's offensive operations.

The vehicle had an impressive cross-country capability which surpassed anything else then in service anywhere. A rear-mounted Bussing-NAG L8V-GS eight-cylinder water-cooled petrol engine produced speeds of more than 50mph on roads and sufficient fuel was carried to give it an operational range of around 170 miles. Armed with a 2cm cannon the SdKfz 232 was perfect for the fast moving Blitzkrieg tactics. It went on to serve throughout the entire war with around 1,235, including other specialised variants, being built. It was later augmented by the SdKfz 234 Puma and the two vehicles served together.

Following the campaigns against Poland and the west, the German army received improved designs as well as completely new designs. For example, between July 1941 and January 1942, a series of replacement and new vehicle designs were built by Daimler-Benz, including the Ausf. B version of the SdKfz 247 armoured personnel carrier. This was another design which remained in service until the last days of the war. It differed from the Ausf. A version by having better armour protection and was slightly larger and heavier as a result, being a 4x4 vehicle based on the chassis of a heavy passenger car.

The SdKfz 222 was one of the first of a new series of vehicles with a building programme lasting between 1936 and 1943 during which time some 989 were produced. It was developed to replace the Kfz 13 and 14, being a more specialised vehicle with

The German army moved fast during the Polish campaign in 1939 using, for example, these SdKfz223 armoured cars.

better armour and heavier armament. The first models of this new armoured car entered service with the German army proper in 1938 and, although the production run was not great, it did serve in all the major campaigns. The design was produced in several versions with the entire production range being built by four main manufacturers, including Bussing-NAG. Production stopped in 1943, but surviving SdKfz 222s continued to be used for the remainder of the war.

A variant of the SdKfz 222 was the SdKfz 223, but perhaps as few as 500 or so were built between 1935 and 1944, which amounted to an average of 50 vehicles per year. This would have been more an inconvenience to produce such small numbers of a specialist vehicle when the workforce could have concentrated on other more important designs.

It was not just armoured scout cars that headed the advance of the German armoured units, motorcycles were also used to reconnoitre to check the roads were clear and to report on the conditions of bridges over rivers. Being small and nimble, they could use their speed to get themselves out of trouble. Even before the introduction of the first tanks, the Munich-based firm of Bayerische Motoren Werke (BMW) was producing a range of motorcycles for the German army, such as the R-12 which was in service from 1935 and the R-61 which was also produced as a combination vehicle with sidecar. But it was the Schweres Kraftrad 750cc mit Seitenwagen, better known as the R-75, with its

Another fast-moving armoured car used in Poland was the SdKfz222 armed with a 2cm cannon.

The Afrika Korps brought a wide range of vehicles into North Africa, including the SdKfz223 which was used for reconnaissance duties.

The BMW R75 was one of the most widely used motorcycles on the Eastern Front. Seen here are some of the mixed vehicles which made up the transport fleet of trucks.

Boxer OHV 2-cylinder 26hp petrol-driven engine and equipped with a sidecar, which emerged as the most popular machine and proved its versatility in many campaigns. By the end of the war more than 16,000 R-75s had been built by BMW. Motorcycle combinations such as the R-75 could be armed by mounting an MG34, with extra ammunition being carried inside the sidecar unit. Additional equipment such as tools, tents and food could be strapped to the rear of the sidecar combination unit to allow the riders to operate with a certain degree of autonomy for days at a time when operating in the reconnaissance role. Typically, the rifle brigade of a Panzer division would include a motorcycle battalion comprising two motorcycle companies, a machine gun company and a mixed company. The armoured reconnaissance battalion of a Panzer division would also include a motorcycle company. These machines could be used as despatch riders to deliver messages and in an emergency evacuate wounded troops. But riders of motorcycles remained vulnerable to rifle fire and during the campaigns of 1939 and 1940 they suffered heavy casualties.

Motorcycles were used by every belligerent nation in all theatres of fighting from the frozen steppes of Russia to the humid jungles in Malaya. The US army used machines built by Harley-Davidson which produced around 90,000 machines and a further 30,000 were supplied to Russia under the terms of Lend–Lease. In 1942 Harley Davidson attempted to copy the German BMW R-71 motorcycle to produce a model known as the XA, but it did not prove successful and only 1,000 were built. It was during the rearmament period of the 1930s that the German army came to realise the usefulness of the motorcycle and how it could fit in with Blitzkrieg tactics, which is why so many machines were produced. Their production for the military had only been achieved by factories re-tooling for the task. Another manufacturer which produced motorcycles for the German army was the company of Zundapp, which built some 18,000 machines during the war.

A range of light cars such as the Kübelwagen, and the amphibious version called the Schwimmwagen, were used for liaison roles, communications and reconnaissance duties. While these vehicles were versatile they lacked the advantage of the motorcycle which could cross bridges which had been rendered unusable by heavier vehicles or enemy action. For example, it was motorcycle riders who located a small, narrow bridge across the River Meuse just north of Sedan which allowed the first German

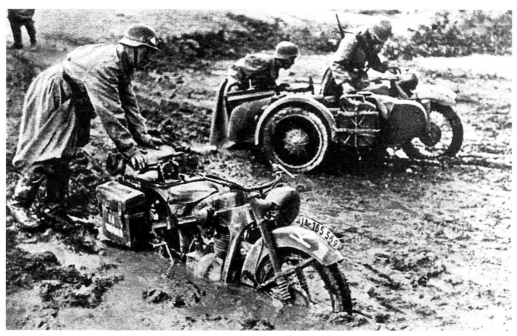

The BMW R35 was a fast, manoeuvrable machine, but it still suffered from the lack of proper roads in Russia.

Motorcycles such as this BMW R12 could transport medics to treat the wounded. This unit is equipped to transport a stretcher on the brackets fitted to the side car unit.

troops to cross the waterway after all the bridges had been destroyed by the French army on 12 May. With both sides of the river secured the engineers could construct a replacement bridge across the river to allow heavier vehicles to cross. But the motorcycle riders did not wait and roared on ahead to scout the route for the tanks long before the bridge was finished.

Even before the rearmament programme, Guderian, commanding a transport battalion in 1931, had conducted military exercises using companies of motorcycles, known as Krad–Schutzen, to represent tanks supplemented with obsolete armoured cars in order to formulate and prove his theory in armoured warfare tactics which would later allow the Panzer divisions to charge across Europe. His dictum would become 'klotzern, nicht kleckern' – smash, don't tap – (this phrase has also been credited to a Major Wenck who served with Guderian in the initial phase of the attack).

After the Anschluss with Austria and the occupation of Czechoslovakia in 1938, Germany had a massive industrial power base at its disposal for the production of motor vehicles. But it was poorly organised, with much duplication and waste of resources. To help resolve the problem Oberst Adolf von Schell was appointed to the task. A career soldier, he was made general plenipotentiary for motor vehicles under General Georg Thomas, himself the head of the War Economics and Armament office. In the

Engineer units of the German army could quickly construct pontoon bridges as temporary crossings to replace bridges destroyed in the fighting.

mid-1930s Schell had visited America on a fact-finding tour to study their methods of production. On his return he formulated a radical restructuring of the German motor industry. He found, for example there were 113 types of truck being produced with no standardisation in designs. In addition, there were hundreds of different types of trailer. In 1938 Schell's proposed new streamlining plan for the motor industry, known as the Schell Plan, began to implement the many recommended changes. One of his proposals was to reduce the number of motorcycle designs from 150 different models to

Engineer units of the German army were well trained and well equipped to keep the army moving by spanning rivers where the bridges had been destroyed.

only 30. The number of truck designs was reduced to 19 and the number of light liaison vehicles such as cars was reduced from 55 different types to 30. His plans extended to ancillary items too. The different number of brakes, starter motors and dynamos were all reduced to standardised types. It saved time, raw materials and money.

The German army had always known how important it was for units to maintain communications at all levels. It was communications which made the Blitzkrieg tactics

HOW ARMY LORRIES ARE TRANSPORTED ACROSS RIVERS

Fig. 3. *Units of the Royal Engineers are attached to every branch of the British Army to carry out all work requiring specialized engineering. This picture illustrates the method by which Royal Engineers, dressed in thigh-boots and life-jackets, and working often under fire, transport comparatively heavy vehicles across streams and rivers on pontoons.*

The British army also had specialist equipment to ferry vehicles and troops across rivers as seen in this illustration from a pre-war publication.

work so effectively. For that reason, they developed a range of vehicles specifically for the role of communication. The vehicles were the SdKfz 260 and SdKfz 261, both termed Kleine Panzerfunkwagen (Small Armoured Radio Cars), entering service in early 1941 and remaining in use for the rest of the war. Externally there was little to tell them apart, except that the former was fitted with a rod aerial for the medium-

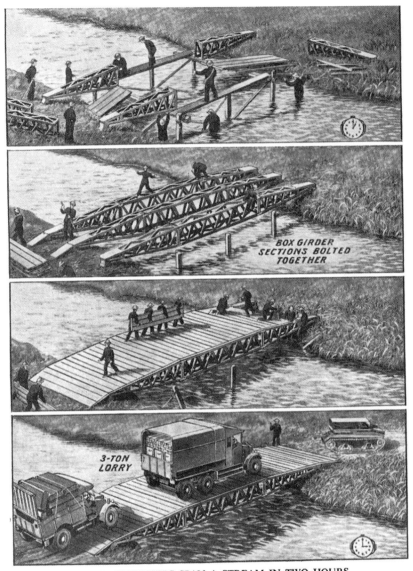

ROYAL ENGINEERS SPAN A STREAM IN TWO HOURS

Fig. 4. *These pictures show how the skill and ingenuity of a unit of the Royal Engineers, such as is attached to each Army branch, make it possible to build in two hours a strong bridge spanning an awkward stream, and drive mechanized vehicles over that bridge. The R.E.s are "building contractors" to the Army, and no job is too difficult for them.*

The Royal Engineers could span rivers with bridging equipment to keep the vehicles moving as seen in this illustration from a pre-war publication.

range radio equipment while the latter featured a collapsible frame aerial for the long-range radio equipment. It was the communications equipment carried on board which made them essential to the headquarters of regiments, brigades and divisions of armoured units to which they were attached, as well as armoured radio companies of the Nachrichten (communications) battalions. Being unarmed and only lightly armoured, the operational life of these vehicles was often short, but the service they rendered was vital.

With the surrender of all the European armies attacked by Germany in 1940, it fell to Britain to resist any further expansion by Hitler. After sustaining such great losses of men, equipment, vehicles and weapons at Dunkirk, the British army had to be rebuilt, and troops trained. Italy declared war against Britain on 10 June and the following day began air raids against Malta, where Britain had bases for aircraft and the Royal Navy port facilities. Three weeks later Italian forces invaded British Somaliland and followed this up by attacking towards Egypt on 13 September. The fighting in Europe was over and now a new theatre of operations was opening in North Africa. The British army had a presence in the region but nowhere as powerful as the Italian army, but they did have tanks and artillery to provide support.

The Matilda Mk II proved effective in the early part of the campaign in Libya in 1940-41. Protected by armour 14-80mm thick it was virtually impervious to the Italian anti-tank guns which were mainly of light calibre, such as the Austrian-built Bohler 47mm and the models 35 and 39 of the Canone da 47/32 of the same calibre. Italian tanks such as the Carro Armato L6/40 and Carro Armato M13/40, which the Italian crews called 'tin coffins', armed with 20mm and 47mm main guns, offered little danger to the Matilda II. The armour protection on the Matilda II was actually greater than

It was only in North Africa where the British army could engage the Italian and German armies in direct action. They were kept supplied by men such as these troops serving with the Royal Army Service Corps.

Troops of the Royal Army Service Corps showing how the climate and conditions took a toll on men, equipment and vehicles.

The Italian army had been in North Africa since the mid-1930s and here a FIAT Spa TL37 truck is seen towing a 77mm Model 28 field gun.

that on the German army's PzKw IV Ausf. E, which was fitted with armour up to 60mm maximum. But when the Afrika Korps deployed to North Africa, the British superiority in tank design began to decline. The newly-raised Afrika Korps also brought with them the powerful 88mm anti-tank gun. With this weapon they could engage the Matilda IIs at ranges in excess of 1,000 yards which was far beyond the capability of the Italian guns. From this point on the crews of the Matilda began to lose faith in their survivability on the battlefield.

The small calibre of the Matilda's main gun was a cause for concern because it could not match the heavier, more powerful 50mm and 75mm guns on German tanks. In the early days of the war the 2-pounder, with a calibre of 40mm, could penetrate the lighter armoured vehicles, but as the war progressed and heavier tanks appeared it was left behind in the gun/armour race. The British tried to correct this and conducted a series of trials into the possibility of increasing the size of the Matilda's main armament up to a 6-pounder of 57mm calibre. A total of 67 rounds was carried for the 2-pounder gun and 4,000 rounds for the machine guns, which reduced the internal space available and made it a tight squeeze. If a larger calibre gun had been fitted, then the amount of ammunition carried would have been less. In the end, the trials proved a failure because the turret of the Matilda II was already far too cramped to accommodate the larger breech mechanism and the gun crew. This was one of the deciding factors that eventually led to the production of the Matilda II being suspended. The last time the Matilda was committed to battle as a frontline tank to engage enemy tanks in direct action was during the first Battle of El Alamein in July 1942, by which time it had gained something of a reputation in desert conditions and the nickname 'Queen of the Battlefield'. At this stage in the war, though, the British army in North Africa was beginning to receive American-built tanks such as the Grant and M3 'Honey' and later the M4 Sherman with the 76mm gun.

As more American-built tanks came into service the question arose of what to do with the surplus Matildas, most of which were still serviceable. The army was loath to write off so many otherwise sound tanks, especially when every tank was needed, but for the time being at least, no-one could see how else they could be usefully employed on the desert battlefield.

The Matilda II was supplied to the Australian army which used them against the Japanese in the Pacific theatre. It was the Australians who showed how more service life could be got out of the ageing Matilda IIs. One idea they came up with was to equip them with flame-throwers to produce a version known as the 'Matilda Frog', used to burn out enemy emplacements. They also produced an earth-moving version to improve tracks through jungle terrain so that wheeled vehicles could be used to move supplies. A number of Matilda IIs were supplied to the Russian army which, despite liking the heavy armour, did not consider the 2-pounder gun to be of any use against the German tanks.

Another vehicle the British army was already using when it went to war was a range of carriers which included the Oxford Carrier and the Windsor Carrier built in Canada. Some were basic and changed very little during the course of the war, while others were built in a variety of designs to suit different roles. The best known of these was the Universal or 'Bren Gun Carrier' which continued to be used throughout the war and became a veritable workhorse, not only for the British army but for several Allied armies as well. The Bren Gun Carrier was a troop and cargo carrier, and became the test bed for a self-propelled gun platform, a flamethrower carrier called the Wasp, and many other experiments. The Australians tried mounting a 2-pounder anti-tank gun on the Carrier, but it did not prove successful and never entered service. They also experimented with heavier guns, including mounting a 25-pounder field gun, which gave varying results. The wartime production run of this utility vehicle exceeded more than 84,000, built in Canada, Britain, Australia, New Zealand and also America where 14,000 were produced for the US army as the T16 with certain modifications.

The Mk I carrier had entered service in 1938 and appeared in a number of the pre-war propaganda newsreel films screened at cinemas across the country to show the British public how well-equipped and modern the country's army was. Such imagery certainly looked impressive as whole battalions of infantry charged around exercise areas being carried into battle on the fleet of carriers. When the BEF was deployed to France in 1939 the carriers went with the infantry divisions so that when the Germans attacked, the Bren Gun Carriers were there for immediate use. During the retreat to Dunkirk it was these same Universal Carriers which were abandoned.

Development of the carrier began in the early 1930s when the design team from Carden-Loyd produced a series of ideas to develop a tracked carrier vehicle for the infantry. The idea of a specialised carrier was not new and had actually been proposed in the early 1920s when a range of carriers was suggested for the purpose of transporting ammunition for the artillery batteries. From this concept it was only natural that it also be used to transport infantry across the battlefield, along with their support weapons such as Vickers and Bren guns, mortars and Boys anti-tank rifles. The term Bren Gun Carrier was actually applied to only one model in a range more correctly termed Universal Carriers, but the name was popular with the troops and it stuck whatever role it served in.

The carrier was little more than an open-topped steel box mounted on tracks. It was protected by armour along the sides of the hull but was vulnerable to even the lightest anti-tank weapons. While that could be seen as a design flaw it did mean that cargo and troops could be loaded and unloaded more quickly than with an enclosed vehicle. It was capable of tackling a wide range of obstacles likely to be encountered on the battlefield and had a very low silhouette. It was versatile enough to serve as a platform on which to mount a range of weapons apart from machine guns. A 2-inch mortar was sometimes mounted to allow the crew to fire smoke grenades to screen their movement across open spaces when natural cover was absent. It served in all theatres of operations from the Far East to north-west Europe, including Italy, and even the Middle East where the dry desert conditions tested it to its limit. It had an average combat range of over 250km which was noteworthy and better than tanks. When towing anti-tank guns, other carriers operating with the group transported ammunition and the crew. Carriers served throughout the entire war and after D-Day in 1944.

Chapter 6

Germany Takes Stock: 1940

W hen the Germans took stock of the huge numbers of vehicles and the amount of supplies and ammunition abandoned by the British at Dunkirk they must have wondered how an army which had left so much equipment behind could continue to function. To many German soldiers it must have seemed as though they had won the war.

The campaign in the west had cost the Germans 27,074 killed, 111,034 wounded, and a further 18,384 missing. But losses of manpower, vehicles and other equipment had not been anywhere near as heavy as anticipated. After so many victories since 1939, recruits would soon be trained and join the ranks to replace the casualties. War materiel would also soon be replaced and even given a temporary boost with the capture of enemy stocks. New troops would go on to join their regiments and divisions deployed to areas where they would become forces of occupation. The German army had captured enough resources to more than compensate for the losses in materiel. The factories in those occupied countries would soon be producing vehicles and equipment for the German army and steel foundries, such as the French companies of Le Creusot and Collembelles, would produce weapons, especially artillery.

The company of Peugeot built over 48,800 trucks and Citroën produced more than 15,000 for the German army while the company of Latil built 4x4 heavy tractors which were used during the Russian Campaign. Citroën also built half-track vehicles such as the Unic Type P107 which could serve as artillery tractors but pre-war strikes meant that only 3,276 were in service when war broke out. When the factory was captured some of the vehicles being produced were designed to permit them to carry light anti-aircraft guns but closer inspection revealed the mountings were suited to weapons used by the German army rather than the Swiss-designed Oerlikon guns. Louis Renault employed his workforce in this role and earned for himself a reputation as being a collaborator. When the country was liberated in 1944 he was arrested by his countrymen, charged with collaboration and held in Fresne prison where he died under suspicious circumstances.

The occupation forces stretched out from Norway, to Denmark, to Poland and across western Europe. Garrisons were established, with divisions being assigned to specific areas. For example, the 319 Infantry Division, raised in November 1940, was posted to the Channel Islands. Along with other attached units, such as medical staff, cooks and clerks, the division would remain on the islands until they were liberated in May 1945. Being islands, everything that was required for their consolidation had to be transported to them by ship. Equipment, vehicles and even captured tanks were sent to the Channel Islands and the workforce of the Organisation Todt was employed in the building of thousands of defensive positions. Miles of tunnels were dug into the hillsides and harbour facilities expanded to cope with the increase in shipping.

Fortifying the Channel Islands would absorb vast quantities of steel and concrete. Hundreds of pieces of artillery of all calibres, including weapons captured from the French, were moved to the islands along with thousands of tons of ammunition. Aircraft were used to transport essential items and high ranking officers to the islands while ships brought in the heavy equipment, troops and vehicles. As the occupation progressed so the Germans consolidated their position by bringing further equipment to the islands, including more military vehicles such as light cars and even some captured French tanks. Sent to Jersey were twelve Char B1 tanks along with five flamethrower variants, around eleven SPG variants of the R35 tank armed with captured 4.7cm Czechoslovakian guns, and at least eight FT17 tanks which dated back to the First World War. Most of the civilian vehicles were commandeered and captured stocks of French and British military vehicles were also brought to the islands. The Channel Islands were unsuitable for heavy vehicles, especially tanks. Nevertheless, the Germans brought them to the islands as a show of force. They also brought standard army trucks such as the Krupp-built 'Protze' L2H 143 which could carry a payload in excess of one ton and also tow light anti-aircraft guns or carry troops or ammunition. It was perfect for the islands, as were other light vehicles such as the Stoewer R200s used in liaison roles during the occupation. This was configured to four main roles, with each being given its own 'KfZ'or Kraftfahrzeug title to designate their role as a military motor vehicle. The KfZ1 was a four-seat personnel carrier for liaison duties, the KfZ2 was equipped with radios for signals, the KfZ3 served in the light survey role, and the KfZ4 was armed with a light anti-aircraft gun which could also engage ground targets.

Artillery was the obvious choice of weaponry in the defence of the Channel Islands including long-range coastal guns, anti-aircraft and anti-tank guns to cover the wide sandy beaches which were natural landing places in the event of an invasion to recapture the islands. Apart from a few half-tracks to serve as artillery tractors no heavy vehicles were required long-term. Light liaison vehicles and motorcycles were very useful on the small islands which could be traversed in only a few hours along the narrow, winding country lanes.

One thing the Germans had to come to terms with was the fact that the local civilian population drove on the left hand side, including horse-drawn carts, the same as on the British mainland, which led inevitably to casualties. Finally, after one year of occupation and a number of fatal crashes involving civilian and military, the Feldkommandantur issued an order that all vehicles would be driven on the right hand side of the road.

As the occupation progressed, the food and fuel situation worsened, particularly after the islands were cut off after the Normandy landings. Rationing was severely imposed and near-starvation conditions developed, which were only relieved when the Swedish Red Cross vessel the *Vega* began delivering food parcels for the civilian population in late 1944 and early 1945.

After the success of its European campaigns, the German army wanted to project the idea that it was more motorised than it actually was. In fact, in September 1939, of the German army's 103 divisions only 16 were motorised, and even this level had only been reached by limiting the numbers of vehicles in service with other units. Typically, an infantry division had fewer than 1,000 vehicles but almost 5,400 horses to draw the fleet of wagons to transport the logistics. This was not much different to the First World War. Even so, a vehicle fleet of this size in each division required twenty tons of fuel each day, while the horses needed fifty tons of fodder, even when not working.

In 1938 the German army had more than 100 different types of truck in service, but rather than making matters easier this disparity of type caused complications and even shortages. In 1939 there was still such a shortage of transportation that 16,000 civilian vehicles were commandeered. After the victories in 1940 the thousands of captured vehicles were distributed throughout eighty-eight infantry divisions.

Before the war, France had a well-developed motor manufacturing industry and several companies, including Latil, Laffly and Panhard, supplied vehicles to the Dutch and Belgian armies. Although a rearmament programme had been initiated in 1936, France lacked modern transport for its own army. In fact, production for the military halved from the annual figure of 40,000 vehicles in 1930 to drop to 20,000 by 1938, and much of the vehicle fleet in service dated back twenty years and was of aged design.

The Germans fell on the resources of the motor industry with the same relish as they had with steel works and armaments factories. Production plants were placed under the control of German companies; the Latil factory at Suresnes, for example, was controlled by Daimler-Benz AG. Other factories either produced French-designed vehicles which were adapted to use by the German army or they built German-designed vehicles. Citroën produced 15,000 trucks during the period of occupation and Peugeot built almost 49,000. The workforce remained largely French nationals, but later forced labour from other occupied territories was brought in.

Factories across France would contribute some ten per cent of the war materiel used by the German armed forces between 1940 and 1944. Factories in occupied Holland and Belgium would add a further ten per cent between them. Poor quality of finished items, along with sabotage, reduced this figure, but never to such levels as to threaten overall supply.

The French tank force was one of the largest in Europe, but poor tactics meant the tanks were not used as effectively as they could have been.

The Citroën Kegresse half-track was used by the French army but later used by the German army to supplement its vehicle fleet as seen here with this refurbished original vehicle.

Another mode of transportation used by the military was the humble bicycle. Indeed all armies in the war used bicycles. The Japanese issued 6,000 to each division during the Malay campaign. During the course of the war the German army used perhaps as many as three million bicycles, including civilians' cycles commandeered for units of the Volkssturm, which were home defence volunteer units in the later stages of the war. Such troops were called Radfahrbeweglichemarschgruppe (mobile bicycle march groups). In March 1944, two of the six battalions of infantry forming part of the 17th SS Panzergrenadier Division were still using bicycles. Bicycles did not require fuel to operate and were even more economical than horses, requiring no food either.

Chapter 7

After Dunkirk and Britain on Its Own

With most of western Europe now under German occupation, the rest of the world, especially America, looked on as Britain appeared to be standing alone. The British army had only 72 infantry and cruiser tanks in the country in June 1940. The figure for artillery at the same time was just as startling: there were only 420 field guns, 163 heavy guns and 54 2-pounder anti-tank guns. Ammunition was woefully short with only an estimated 200 shells for each of the field guns and 150 for each of the heavier guns. Slowly, things began to get better, but only just. At the end of August, the number of tanks had increased to 200 and by September to 438. The country braced itself for imminent invasion which many, including Winston Churchill, thought would be Hitler's next move.

Defences were built around the coast and pillboxes constructed across the country in a series of fortifications called 'stop lines'. These divided the country into regions and were intended to hopefully slow down an enemy attack sufficiently to allow the army to react to the situation. The man behind this scheme was General Sir Edmund Ironside. A highly experienced soldier, having seen service in the Boer War and the First World War, he took to his new appointment with zeal. Among the troops at his disposal were fifteen Territorial Army (Reservist) divisions, home defence battalions and, of course, the newly formed Local Defence Volunteers, later to become the Home Guard. They were not fully trained and lacked weapons, but their enthusiasm was indomitable.

Ironside also had the 8th Royal Tank Regiment, with a small number of tanks and six regiments of armoured cars, but this was still not enough. Ironside saw the only viable option was to construct defences, and on 25 June he submitted his proposals to Churchill's War Cabinet. His plans covered five points:

1. A defensive 'crust' along the coast, able to fight off small raids, give immediate warning of attack, and delay any landing.
2. Home Guard road blocks at crossroads, valleys, and other check points, to stop German armoured columns penetrating inland.
3. Static fortified 'stop lines' sealing the Midlands and London off from the country and to divide the coastal areas into defensible sectors.
4. A central corps-sized reserve to deal with a major breakthrough.
5. Local mobile columns to deal with local attacks and parachute landings.

Fearing invasion was imminent, defences were built across Britain, such as this 'stop line' in Carmarthenshire in Wales. It incorporated brick-built pillboxes and concrete anti-tank obstacles.

These massive concrete blocks in Wales formed an anti-tank obstacle in the event of an invasion.

Men from across Britain rallied to join their local Home Guard units.

Another photograph showing officers and NCOs of Llanybyther Home Guard, No. 8 Platoon.

Given the time available and the resources to hand, it was the best plan he could formulate. The building of such defences called for the construction of at least 40,000 pillboxes. Not surprisingly, it was criticised, with one divisional commander commenting, 'We have become pill-box mad.' But it was all that could be done at the time, and at least the measures gave the public confidence that something was being done.

Another criticism of the plan focused on Ironside's use of manpower to build the defences which took them away from their training. One of these critics was Bernard Montgomery, recently returned from Dunkirk, who wrote that he was 'in complete disagreement with the general approach to the defence of Britain'. He made it abundantly clear that he would refuse to apply it. Montgomery was a realist and did not hesitate to go against the military grain if necessary. For example, in July when he was commanding 3rd Division, which was particularly short of transport, Montgomery informed Churchill that he was prepared to use public transport by commandeering buses to move his men. The idea was reminiscent of the London buses used to transport troops to the front line in the First World War.

Standing on its own after Dunkirk, the British army had to rearm and continue to train the troops with live-firing exercises.

Concrete pillboxes were built at various locations around the country to defend the establishment, such as this example near the RNAS at Yeovilton in Somerset, in the event of invasion.

On 14 May, the Secretary of State for War, Anthony Eden, made an official announcement on behalf of the British government in a radio broadcast calling for volunteers aged between 17 and 65 years to serve in a newly-created unit called the Local Defence Volunteers. Their role would be to guard vital points such as bridges and power stations in case of enemy sabotage. Former soldiers and retirees stepped forward and within a week 250,000 men had joined the ranks. It became the butt of many jokes told by comedians of the day, who referred to the initials as standing for 'Look, Duck and Vanish'. After the withdrawal from Dunkirk the LDV was renamed the Home Guard. People now realised the urgency of the situation as the country now stood alone, with its army in tatters, and without any allies. The predicament stimulated recruiting to the Home Guard and by August the numbers had increased to around 1.5 million.

Defences were built around the coast to mount machine guns, and artillery, some of which was of dubious vintage. The coastal battery built at Brixham in Devon had naval guns mounted which dated back to the First World War and had been intended for use by Japan. Just as General Ironside had proposed, the country was divided in areas with defensive positions forming 'stop lines'. Using a labour force made up of Royal Engineers and local builders, pillboxes appeared across the country at bridges, over rivers and in fields where enemy gliders might land. Speed was of the essence. It was feared the Germans would launch their invasion at any time. Weapons were at a premium.

Some of the defensive positions were manned by the Home Guard, often after they had been at work all day. The men were eventually armed with a range of weapons, especially American-built P17 rifles which fired .30-inch rounds and were identified as such by a red band being painted around the fore-stock or butt-stock to indicate they fired 'non-standard' ammunition; over one million were supplied. The Home Guard also received 25,000 American-made Browning automatic rifles and 22,000 Browning heavy machine guns, also firing the .30 calibre ammunition. A range of other weapons, unique to the Home Guard, were also designed, including the Smith Gun, the Blacker Bombard and the Northover Projector.

As the Home Guard increased in size, its organisation also improved and some enterprising units even created river patrols with small boats for waterways, including the Thames. In rural areas, such as Dartmoor and Exmoor, sections were mounted on horseback. In Kent and Sussex there were some 60,000 men. Around Hythe there were 300 Home Guard. Even some of the most unlikely places, such as the Bank of England and the House of Commons, formed their own Home Guard units. Although never put to the test in engaging German forces, the Home Guard lost 768 men killed and 5,750 injured, mainly due to accidents in handling weapons and mistaken identity when challenged.

The men in these units took their duties very seriously and sometimes converted their own vehicles to produce a range of vehicles unique to Home Guard units, called 'Beaverettes' after Lord Beaverbrook the Minister of Aircraft Production who later became the Minister of Supply. It is estimated that perhaps 2,800 Beaverettes were

Some men in the Home Guard were veterans of the First World War and even the Boer War.

Home Guard units organised large-scale exercises as logistics improved.

eventually built, mostly based on the Standard 14hp chassis, with boiler plate welded on. Another design was the Mk III Standard Beaverette; weighing just over two tons, it was based on a Flying Fourteen saloon car chassis and armed with a Lewis gun in a rudimentary turret. The low number reflected the fuel shortage and the lack of materials to produce an armoured car. Their usefulness in actual battle would have been questionable, but for the purposes of mobile patrols the improvised designs showed what could be produced in an emergency.

Further defensive measures were hurriedly completed and minefields were laid at likely landing places all along the coast, especially in Norfolk and Kent which was closest to enemy-occupied Europe. In some places, defences from the First World War were reactivated and even obsolete tanks were placed in positions where they could be used as barricades on the roads. The Home Guard may have been willing, but in the early days they were far from being ready and able, lacking as they did any real armament. Members often paraded with shotguns and sometimes items of historic vintage. By the time the force was 'stood down' in December 1944, which is to say they were paraded and then dismissed for the last time, there were over 1.7 million men serving in over 1,000 battalions. Of this figure, some 141,676 were engaged on anti-aircraft duties, 7,000 with coastal artillery such as the site at Brixham in Devon, and another 7,000 on bomb disposal duties. The force had allowed more men to be freed up for other war duties and service overseas.

Hitler's plan for the invasion of England was very real and given the codename Sea Lion. It called for a combined airborne and amphibious assault, involving an initial attacking force of 260,000 men, supported by 34,000 vehicles and almost twice as many horses. The British believed that the main weight of any attack would concentrate on Kent, because it was the closest point to France. Invasion forces of the 9th Army, part of Army Group A under General von Rundstedt which had attacked France, would leave the harbour at Le Havre and land at points including Brighton and Ventnor on the Isle of Wight. Further west, elements of the 6th Army, part of Army Group C, commanded by General Ritter von Leeb, would sail from Cherbourg to land on the Dorset coast at Lyme Regis. The Kriegsmarine would require two million tons of shipping just to transport such an invasion force and further ships to supply the almost 2,000 tons of supplies required daily to support the landings. This was a weight of shipping which the German High Command did not have. Even with ships captured in France and Holland, they could not make up the amount required. Of course, all this was unknown to the British, but had the attack come in such force the British army would have been stretched to its limit and probably beyond. The RAF and the Royal Navy would have to stop an attack before it landed, if the country were to stand any chance of survival.

Free countries around the world, especially the USA, were watching Britain's fate with concern, believing it was only a question of time before Germany attacked and defeated a battered Britain. But they had not reckoned with the unconditional support of the Dominion and Commonwealth forces of the British Empire. These nations had stood by Britain in earlier conflicts and now, once again, their involvement would help with the problem of manpower. They would also help produce vehicles and weapons. Canada, with a population of around eleven million, declared war against Germany on 10 September 1939; some 1.1 million men and women would go on to serve in its armed forces and factories. The war would eventually cost the country 21 billion Canadian dollars and they would suffer 45,000 killed and 54,000 wounded. The merchant fleet would expand and embark on 25,000 sailings to transport thousands of tons of food

Around 1,771 Covenanter tanks were built and although they were in service between 1940 and 1943 they were never used in North Africa. Instead, they were used as training and a stop-gap in the event Hitler had invaded.

such as dried milk and eggs, tinned goods, wheat, and tens of thousands of vehicles and heavy weapons.

Canada's industries supported the Allied war effort by producing more than 50,000 armoured vehicles and some 815,000 other vehicles, which was a greater output than the combined efforts of Germany, Italy and Japan. In fact by the end of the war around 38% of Canada's production had been for Britain and included 1.7 million small arms, 43,000 heavy guns, 16,000 aircraft and two million tons of explosives.

Canada also built locally-designed armoured vehicles such as the Mk I Fox Armoured Car which was based on the British army's Humber Armoured Car. It was not one of the best vehicles of the war, suffering from problems with the steering, which made it unpopular with the troops. Nevertheless, Canadian General Motors produced some 1,500. More successful Canadian-designed armoured vehicles included the Ram cruiser tank, of which 1,900 were built by the Montreal Locomotive Works and some 2,150 Sexton self-propelled guns fitted with 25-pounder guns which were built at the plant in Sorel. On top of these came the production of thousands of other specialist vehicles, including Kangaroo personnel carriers and the Badger flamethrower vehicle.

Another vehicle produced by Canadian factories was the Ford F30 truck which served as the tractor for the Bofors 40mm light anti-aircraft gun, as an ambulance,

Some Vickers Light Tanks were used in France in 1940 but later served as training vehicles.

and saw service with the Long Range Desert Group in North Africa. Canada also produced some 13,000 Chevrolet C8A Heavy Utility trucks which served in the role of ambulance, signal vehicle and troop transport. She also produced some 4,000 GM C15TA Armoured Trucks for carrying troops, and 1,400 Valentine tanks, most of which were sent to the Soviet Union after 1941.

One of the lesser-known, but still important vehicles produced by the impressive Canadian armaments manufacturers was a design known as the 'Car, Light Reconnaissance, Canadian GM Mark I Otter'. This was built to the same general specification as the British Humber Mk III Light Reconnaissance Car, but using components manufactured in Canada to produce a vehicle markedly different from the

Humber. For example, the engine bonnet was shorter but higher, which gave the vehicle a pronounced hump-like appearance. Originally it had been intended that the Otter should carry the same armament as the Humber, but a decision was taken that the vehicle be armed with an entirely different complement of weapons. Into the turret was mounted a Bren .303inch MG, which with its 500 rounds per minute cyclic rate of fire, gave all-round defence. Mounted in the hull front, next to the driver, was a Mark 1 Boys anti-tank rifle which fired ammunition of .55inch calibre that could, under ideal conditions, penetrate 20mm of armour at a range of 550 yards. The weapon had been withdrawn from frontline units in 1941 because of its inadequacies against tanks with thick armour, but in the case of the Otter, which would be operating in a mainly reconnaissance role, it was believed the Boys anti-tank rifle would be sufficient for its purpose. Around 1,761 vehicles were produced and used by units of the British and Canadian armies. The Royal Air Force Regiment also came to realise its usefulness and used some for assisting in airfield defence by patrolling the perimeter. The RAF fitted them with a 20mm cannon in the front of the hull and twin Browning machine guns in the turret.

Canada never shirked its responsibilities. By the end of 1942 she had some 177,000 men serving overseas in the army. They would go on to participate in some of the hardest-fought actions of the war including the ill-fated raid on Dieppe in 1942 and have Juno Beach assigned to them during the D-Day landings at Normandy in 1944. Canada's war effort is often overlooked, but there is no denying that she helped the Allied cause tremendously.

As isolated as it was, Australia proved that it too could help the Allied war effort. In 1939 the country had a small regular force of only 3,000 men and a volunteer force, albeit fully trained, of 80,000 men, but these were home service only. Australia declared war against Germany on 3 September 1939, but was obliged to keep a close watch on developments relating to Japan. There was no shortage of volunteers coming forward and when fighting in North Africa began in earnest, it deployed three divisions to the region in spring 1941, by which time it had over 108,000 men in uniform. Australia's heavy industry was not as advanced as Canada, but what it had was mobilised and it went on to produce around 5,600 Bren Gun Carriers and much other equipment besides. It surprised many by producing a locally-developed tank called the 'Sentinel', used mainly for home defence, and some 700 tracked armoured fighting vehicles, based on British designs, were produced.

The troops Australia sent to North Africa had a long journey ahead of them. At the critical point in the campaign, access to the Suez Canal became threatened and convoys sailing to and from Indian and Australia were forced to sail via the Cape of Good Hope, which increased sailing distances from 6,000 miles to 11,000 miles. This had a 'knock-on' effect by reducing cargo carrying capacity by 25% to allow extra fuel to be carried to make the voyage which had once taken 90 days but now took 122 days.

Australia's position changed after 7 December 1941 when the Japanese bombed Pearl Harbor. The enemy was now at the country's back door and when the port of Darwin was bombed on 19 February 1942 there was a very serious fear of further attacks and a possible Japanese invasion. The Prime Minister John Curtain declared 'Australia is facing the gravest hour in her history,' and home-based troops were placed on alert. Australian troops who had been fighting overseas since the early part of 1941 realised that their comrades at home were now facing a serious threat.

During the Second World War, Australia, like other countries of the British Empire, undertook to support the Allied cause by producing as many vehicles and weapons as they could manage. Anything and everything they could produce helped ease the burden on Britain which was trying to keep pace with demand and replace losses incurred in battle.

New Zealand declared war on Germany on 3 September 1939, thereby expressing its solidarity with Britain and the other countries in the British Empire. What it lacked in ability to produce heavy equipment (it did build some 520 Bren Gun Carriers), it more than made up for with manpower. At the beginning of the war the country had a very small regular army of only 578 men, but a territorial force of over 10,300. It introduced conscription in 1940 and by May that year the army consisted of 19,500 men. Before that, in early February 1940, over 6,500 men of the 4th New Zealand Infantry Brigade arrived at the Suez Canal.

More troops followed later in the year and into 1941. Some 7,700 New Zealand troops were sent to defend the island of Crete where the force suffered 671 killed, 967 wounded and 2,180 taken prisoner when the Germans invaded in 1941. The country had a population of only 1.7 million, but its armed forces eventually numbered 157,000, sustaining 12,000 killed and 16,000 wounded, representing an enormous commitment. Fighting in the Middle East accounted for the greatest number of these casualties with 5,363 killed, 15,000 wounded and almost 8,400 taken prisoner.

Another Commonwealth country to make its contribution to the war effort was South Africa which mobilised 140,000 out of a population of 10.7 million. The condition of the country's heavy industry was sufficient to allow it to produce around 2,694 Daimler Armoured Cars and 3,630 Marmon-Herrington Armoured Cars. South African troops fought in North Africa and Italy where they proved themselves to be tough, formidable troops many times over.

The vast country of India produced not only a remarkable number of troops, but also proved capable of turning out vehicles. The first troops were mobilised on 3 September 1939 and two years later Indian troops were deployed to North Africa and the Middle East serving in Syria, Iraq, Persia, and protecting the Suez Canal. In 1940 the population of the country was 388 million from which 2.4 million were mobilised to serve in the army, navy and air force. They fought against the Japanese in the Far East from 1942 and by the end of the war had sustained 48,000 killed and 65,000 wounded.

Despite not being used to producing specialised military equipment, heavy industry in India produced a series of locally-designed vehicles known as Armoured Carriers, such as the wheeled I.P Mk II, and the AOV, building around 4,655. They would be used in various theatres of war, but were especially useful in the Far East. From across India, some eight million civilians were recruited were recruited and engaged in war work, such as building airstrips and roads. One project which absorbed a labour force of 50,000 was the Burma Road running into Imphal and Kohima. Indian labourers were employed in the maintenance of this route which was vital for the movement of supplies and troops. Indian factories began producing a wide range of essential supplies to support the Allied war effort, from fresh food to ammunition. Wool from the millions of sheep was processed to produce over one million blankets and over 41 million other items of equipment ranging from uniforms to webbing equipment. Two million parachutes were produced and 16 million pairs of boots. Indeed, by 1943 Indian factories were producing more for the war effort than the combined output of Australia, New Zealand and Canada. There was a price to pay, and Britain had to pay for all this materiel as well as protect the country from invasion by the Japanese. It was a contentious point and one which rankled politicians such as Leo Amery, the India Secretary, and Winston Churchill.

While Britain had its Commonwealth to add to its output this materiel had to be transported in convoys. With so many factories now under German control in the occupied countries, they could move supplies around by rail with relative impunity.

These five countries were the main nations supplying troops, vehicles and equipment along with manpower, but they were not the only countries supporting the British Empire. Smaller states, such as the Caribbean islands making up the British West Indies, Malta in the Mediterranean and other forces including Rhodesia, Palestine and Transjordan, all sent what troops they could. These may not have been great in number, but they were significant in showing they were allied in cause against a common enemy. Men who had left the Channel Islands to join their regiments in 1939 would not know anything about the welfare of their families until 1945. In truth, with such support behind it, Britain was far from being alone. Yet, despite their best efforts, more was needed to face an enemy which daily grew stronger.

One of the Britain's leading motor vehicle factories was the Luton-based company of Vauxhall, which produced some 66,000 Bedford MW 15 cwt trucks between 1939 and 1945. These were fitted with 3.5 litre six-cylinder petrol engines to give a top road speed of 45mph with a fuel consumption of around 12 miles per gallon. They were used by all branches of Britain's armed forces, but mainly the army, whose drivers called them 'Pneumonia Wagons' because they lacked protection against weather.

All over Britain, companies such as Scammell, which had several factories across the country, were engaged in producing heavy-duty trucks for the British army, including

The British company of Bedford also supplied trucks to the army and these served in various roles, such as this refurbished OYC original vehicle configured as a petrol tanker.

The refurbished OYC Bedford petrol tanker carried fuel to the forward bases for tanks and other vehicles.

This refurbished example of a Bedford MW truck illustrates the kind of vehicles used by the British army throughout the war.

a design known as the 'Pioneer', which was first produced in 1935 and used in the roles of prime-mover for artillery, tractor units for tank transporters, as well as recovery. By the end of the war around 3,572 of these heavyweight vehicles had been built. Between 1939 and 1944 factories across Britain would produce more than 919,000 trucks of all types, but an army never admits to ever having enough of anything. It always wants more and if that means getting extra equipment from somewhere else, then explore that avenue and exploit it to the fullest. With supplies coming in from Canada and troops from the other Dominions and Commonwealth countries deploying to other theatres of war, Britain was safe for the moment but her future was far from being secure. The opposing sides were engaged in an arms war and Britain's survival depended on outlasting Germany. Britain would get assistance but only after protracted talks, agreements made, and the financial cost would be enormous.

There was moral support for Britain in some quarters, but what the country needed most was guaranteed support. With little or no possibility of assistance the country busied itself in replacing losses after Norway and France. Replacing so much war materiel was a slow process. For example, weekly tank production in September 1940 was only fifteen vehicles per week for infantry tanks and nine vehicles per week for cruiser tanks. Total British tank production in 1940 was 1,399 (Germany, by contrast, built 1,460 in that year, a number only greater than Britain's effort by a very narrow margin). Workers increased their output, but later they slowed down as fatigue set in. Designs for new anti-tank weapons, including the 6-pounder gun to replace the ageing 2-pounder, were on the drawing board. But factories went back to producing the old type weapons, citing the reason that re-tooling would slow down production. Besides which, the army claimed the troops were already trained in the use of the old weapons. In other words, something was better than nothing. It may not have been the right way, but, at the time, perhaps it was the only way.

The production of unarmoured vehicles was not a problem. For example, the Humber Heavy Utility Car, based on the civilian design Humber Super Snipe chassis which had entered production in 1939, was modified in design to make it suitable for military use. Fitted with an 85hp six-cylinder petrol engine it could reach speeds up to 48mph on roads and had a good operational range for the duties in which it was engaged. It had a large, spacious interior which was well suited to the liaison role and it was this which made it popular and useful as a communications, staff and command vehicle. Because of its shape and size the troops nicknamed it either the 'Box' or the 'Battleaxe'. It could be equipped for various duties and there was accommodation for six passengers. Map boards were fitted to the rear of the front seats which could be folded down so that personnel in the rear could use them as tables for writing surfaces. The Box was used by the army, Royal Navy and RAF and even some AFS units during the Blitz. It entered service in its new role in 1941 and some 6,500 were produced for the British armed forces throughout the war, including around 1,100 ambulance versions.

During the war the Royal Navy increased in size to reach almost one million personnel, including 78,000 Royal Marines and 74,000 Women's Royal Navy.

The American car manufacturer Ford established its first British production plant at Trafford Park in Manchester in 1909 and over the following years built other manufacturing plants across the country. The company had been exporting cars to Britain since 1903 and by 1914 the plant at Trafford Park was building cars at the rate of twenty-one vehicles an hour. In 1918 Ford opened a plant at Dagenham in Essex and the company's future in Britain was affirmed. Throughout the inter-war period and the 'Depression' the company continued to produce vehicles. Even though American-owned, the Ford factories in Britain played a vital role in the country's war effort. The Dagenham plant alone built 360,000 vehicles and the factory at Trafford Park produced 34,000 Rolls-Royce Merlin engines

The Royal Air Force had a manpower level of over one million service men and women, including personnel from the Dominions and Commonwealth countries.

which were used to power Spitfires, Hurricanes, Lancaster bombers, the Mosquito, and the P-51B/C versions of the USAAF Mustang. Ford also produced around 60,000 15cwt WOT2 trucks. Like its British motor industry counterparts, Ford suspended manufacture of all civilian cars to free up space for the war effort.

Ford became one of the most important companies to supply the British army and its modern assembly line process meant it could produce vehicles at a very fast rate. Before hostilities, one of the company's most popular vehicles for the civilian market had been the Model 62, and, like the Humber Super Snipe, it was discovered that a militarised version could be produced from the chassis powered by a 30hp V8 engine. Two versions were produced, the WOA2 and the WOA2A and both were classified as 'Heavy Utility' vehicles, because of the weight which was around 1.5 tons. The WOA2 acronym stood for: W=War Office; O=1940; A=Passenger vehicle and 2 identified the period of the Second World War. Between 1941 and 1945 Ford produced around 11,754. A post-war document published in 1950 by HMSO entitled 'Report on the Motor Industry' contradicts the accepted production numbers and states that Ford built just over 9,000 of these vehicles. Why there should be such a discrepancy is a mystery. It could be that Ford did produce the numbers stated, but only 9,000, or so, entered service.

Across the Channel the Germans were poised to launch their invasion. The troops were tired, but they were jubilant at having won a great victory. They had weapons, supplies and good support. In fact, there was no reason why an attack should not be launched. But first, in order to make it happen, Hitler needed mastery of the air and control of the sea lanes if his plan, known as Directive 16, was to work. The British army waited and the RAF stood by to engage the Luftwaffe, which everybody knew must come. On 10 July, the waiting was over when the first attacks were detected by Britain's secret radar which gave details about the enemy's approach.

Over the coming weeks the air battles intensified and losses on both sides mounted. All the while,

The British army would reach a strength of almost three million men by 1945.

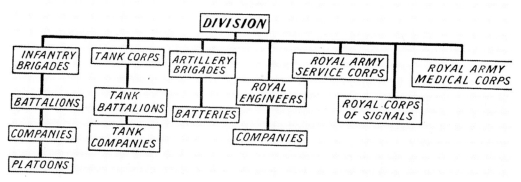

Breakdown of a division in the British army, showing the support branches including the Royal Army Service Corps and Royal Engineers.

The Royal Navy Air Service, Fleet Air Arm, flew aircraft from carriers for escort duties to protect the convoys and as reconnaissance against surface raiders such as the Scharnhorst and Bismarck. In 1945 there were 72,000 personnel with 3,700 aircraft in the Fleet Air Arm.

preparations were being made and an invasion fleet was being assembled with barges being converted into extemporised landing craft. German bombers, operating from forward airfields in France, attacked coastal freighters moving supplies as well as attacking the airfields from which the RAF operated. This was the first phase of the preparatory attacks, designed to win control of the Channel. Known to the Germans as Kanalkampf, Channel Battle, it was designed to force the Royal Navy out of the sea lanes in order that the Kriegsmarine could conduct operations. The date for the operation was set for 15 August.

This was the Battle of Britain that Churchill had spoken about in his radio broadcast. Pilots of the RAF had little respite as they fought to protect shipping in the Channel and their own airfields from attack by bombers and fighters. There were two factors going in their favour. The first was, that fighting over their own country, a pilot shot down would be cared for and if not too badly wounded could return to the fight. For every German shot down over England, it represented one less to return to fight again. On 12 August, the Luftwaffe changed its tactics and specifically targeted the RAF airfields. Despite Goering's reassurances that the Luftwaffe was gaining the upper hand, Hitler remained unconvinced. The day of the planned invasion of 15 August came and went as the Luftwaffe continued to battle on.

Try as hard as they might the pilots of the Luftwaffe could just not get mastery of the air. The Kriegsmarine had never been a match for the Royal Navy and without air supremacy the invasion would never sail. The air battles continued into the beginning of September, when on the 7th of the month, the bombers targeted London. They concentrated on the area around Woolwich Arsenal and the docks and warehouses, all the essential points for supplies. After 15 September the Luftwaffe began to target London more and to bomb factories. This was the beginning of the Blitz which would thrust the civilian population directly into the front line. Air raids would continue for the rest of 1940 and into May 1941, when Hitler changed his plans.

The Royal Navy remained intact and controlled the waters around Britain and with winter gales the threat of invasion was reduced. The RAF was bloodied but not bowed and could still fight on. The threat had passed and Britain had won through. What Churchill and the other war commanders did not know was that Hitler had plans to attack Russia. It has since been opined

In September 1940, the war took another direction with cities being bombed, including London, as seen here, along with Liverpool and Bristol.

that Hitler was never serious about Operation Sea Lion. Indeed, it is now known that it did not have the full support of his general staff. There were those who criticised the plan, such as General Kesselring. Instead he wanted to invade Gibraltar to seal off the entrance to the Mediterranean to the Royal Navy. This would have impacted severely on Britain's conduct of the campaign in North Africa; but in the end, this operation was never implemented. Britain's cities in the meantime were still being bombed, but the factories continued to produce tanks and lorries for the army and their weapons and uniforms.

The British government called on women to go into the factories. A drive to collect scrap metal was launched and answered with considerable relish, especially by young boys who salvaged pots and pans to recycle the aluminium to make aircraft. Church bells were sacrificed for the war effort and iron railings were removed from around buildings, including many village churches. While such imagery made for good propaganda in

Despite being 'bombed out', businesses continued to operate, and morale amongst the civilian population, although affected, was never broken.

the newsreels seen in cinemas, showing how everyone was doing their bit, the truth was that the metal did not necessarily make good raw material for producing weapons. Nevertheless, along with salvaging newspaper, textiles and old tyres, it was all morale-boosting to the civilian population. With the resources of occupied Europe now at his disposal, Hitler did not have to resort to such measures.

Chapter 8

The War Widens and Towards Lend-Lease

W hen Mussolini declared war on Britain the strength of the Italian army stood at around 2,000,000 men organised into 73 divisions, including three armoured divisions and two motorised divisions. Mussolini had sent 300,000 troops to Libya supported with 1,811 pieces of artillery, 339 tanks, along with 8,039 trucks for transportation of troops and supplies. To provide air support there were 151 fighters and bombers. On paper, this force looked impressive enough and their position seemed secure. In Ethiopia, which Italy had seized in 1935, the Duke of Aosta as the commander-in-chief of the Africa Orientale Italiana (the Italian Army in East Africa) had a force of 88,000 Italian troops with 200,000 colonial troops. Again, the force seemed impressive on paper, but Aosta believed he would only be able to fight for six to seven months in the event of war. He was to be proved correct in his estimation when he surrendered four months after the British invaded Ethiopia in January 1941 and succeeded in destroying several major supply dumps of fuel and ammunition.

Italy's armoured force in 1940 comprised 1,000 light tanks, meaning that at least one third was in Libya alone. The size of the force was not substantial but as an ally to Hitler, these vehicles could prove valuable during operations. Unfortunately for the Italian army they were mainly based on out of date designs and locked in with the infantry. Italian output of tanks was never given high priority and production only allowed for a slow build up. The country did not have an advanced heavy industrial capacity; its steel production, for example, was only a fraction of that of Britain. Nevertheless, Italians did manage to produce some good designs, such as the M14/41 Light Tank and the Semovente tank destroyer, but fewer than 800 were built.

Mussolini had ordered a rearmament programme in 1932, long before other European countries. Italy was advanced in the production of light vehicles, such as motor cars and trucks, built by companies such as Alfa Romeo, Fiat and Lancia. Heavy trucks were also produced, by companies such as Breda and La Moto-Aratrice. In addition to producing their own designs these companies also built vehicles based on German designs such as the Fiat 727SC half-track. While some of these designs, including the Alfa-Romeo 800 8-ton trucks and Fiat 665/666 range, were modern, many of the other vehicles were based on old designs. These were all very well for campaigns in Ethiopia and Somalia, but in a fast, mobile war in Europe they would not be effective.

Italian vehicles were used in North Africa, but the country could never hope to reach anywhere near the scale of output as Germany, nor match the quality of its designs. In 1939 the Italian army already had four years more fighting experience than its ally Germany, and both sent troops and equipment to the Spanish Civil War. Even so, the country was still poorly prepared for a European war.

Britain had been forced out of mainland Europe but it was in North Africa where the army had the opportunity to keep in contact with the enemy. General Wavell was commander-in-chief in the Middle East with a mere 30,000 troops, compared to ten times that number of Italian troops. The British had troops in Egypt and more spread out across the region to protect the area which was vital to Britain for the oil and the Suez Canal through which convoys could pass to transport supplies. The odds did not look favourable for the British forces, equipped as they were with obsolete Vickers Light Tanks to provide armoured support. There had been several clashes between the British and Italians, such as the attack against the Italian garrison at Fort Capuzzo on 13 June. During the engagement, in which 200 Italians were taken prisoner, it was demonstrated that machine gun fire from British armoured cars and light tanks could penetrate the light armour of the Italian vehicles. The Italian commander Marshal Rodolfo Graziani, who had taken over after Italo Balbo the commander-in-chief of Africa Settentrionale Italian (Italian North Africa) was killed when his plane was shot down in June 1940, was ordered by Mussolini not to delay any further and to attack.

On 13 September, Graziani ordered a general attack by 167,000 men in two armies, including six divisions of infantry, supported by artillery, 300 tanks and a fleet of 8,500 vehicles. This force greatly outnumbered the British and it looked set to be a one-sided affair. Using a combination of motorcycles, lorries and horses to accompany the armoured units, everything was in favour of the Italian Tenth Army gaining a great victory. The Italians continued to advance virtually unopposed for four days, covering sixty miles into Egypt. Then, on 17 September, quite inexplicably, they stopped to 'dig in', and began preparing a series of defensive positions extending fifty miles south from Sidi Barrani on the coast. Graziani explained away his unexpected halt to Mussolini by claiming he was building up his reserves of supplies and waiting for the cooler weather before resuming his advance.

The British wasted no time and used the opportunity to rush much-needed reserves and supplies to bolster Wavell's forces. With the safe arrival of reinforcements British forces now stood at 80,000 men, 48 anti-tank guns, 48 25-pounder field guns, 20 light anti-aircraft guns and armoured support of 154 tanks. The question was now, who would make the next move? Time was something of which there was precious little if the British were to avoid a disaster. The outcome of the battle still looked to be stacked in favour of the stronger Italian forces.

In charge of the forthcoming battle was Major General Richard O'Connor, commanding the Western Desert Force. He had used the intervening period wisely and sent out a series of patrols which located gaps in the Italian defences. More importantly, these patrols had located the positions of minefields and where the heaviest defences were sited. The British plan of battle was codenamed Operation Compass and O'Connor was leaving nothing to chance. Taking advantage of one of the gaps located in the Italian defences he intended to thrust fifty tanks ahead to support the 4th Indian Division, while more tanks from the 7th Armoured Division would move to a blocking position around Buq Buq, to the rear of the Italian positions.

In the early hours of 9 December, O'Connor ordered his force of 25,000 men to attack along a forty-mile front of the Italian defences. A short but intense artillery barrage opened fire on the Italian garrison at Nibeiwa, catching them completely unaware. Before they could react, the Matilda tanks of the 7th Armoured Division had moved in to destroy twenty-five Italian tanks before turning their attention to the artillery. Motorised infantry, transported in trucks, came in to join the battle. The attack punched a gap fifteen miles wide in the defences from Nibeiwa to Rabia. In London Winston Churchill was being kept appraised of the situation as it unfolded. One message which caught his attention was the signal from an officer of 7th Armoured Division who radioed to headquarters to communicate that he had 'arrived at the second B in Buq Buq'. Another signal from the battle informed General O'Connor that they had captured 'about five acres of officers and two hundred acres of other ranks'.

Before the battle a young British soldier had been watching the build-up and later wrote that the trucks in the supply column were 'loaded with the everyday paraphernalia for making war in the wilderness – rations, ammunition, petrol and that most precious of all requirements, 4-gallon flimsy aluminium containers of water, all carried in three-ton canvas-covered Bedfords…5-cwt [quarter-ton] Morris Scout trucks with the section officer or battery captain standing up in the passenger seat, divisional pennants fluttering in the wind-stream; a couple of RHA 25-pounder guns, cylindrical water bowsers skittering on two wheels behind a 15-cwt. Sometimes a troop of Hussars' light tanks, their tracks screeching and rattling and bouncing over the boulders, their long, slender wireless aerials bobbing and waving. The rolling convoy moved in unison, fanned out in open order, fifty yards separating each vehicle, sand streaming from the wheels like spray in heavy rain.' It would have been an unforgettable sight.

The British captured 38,300 Italians prisoners in four days, during which time the tanks had been in continuous action and the older Vickers Light Tanks almost worn out. Capturing enemy-held territory was one thing and seizing his equipment and weapons was another, but the problem now arose over what to do with so many prisoners. Small numbers of the enemy had been captured before, but nothing on this scale. They had to be removed from the area, put in prison camps, fed, accommodated and guarded. This posed a serious logistical problem.

Known as 'flimsies' the British army used the one type of can to transport all types of liquids. They were marked appropriately: W for water; P for petrol; O for oil.

The cans were carried on the vehicles and were prone to damage resulting in much wastage.

At the start of the war, the method of supplying troops had hardly changed from the previous war of 1914-18.

The first prisoners taken captive by the British had been German sailors from U-Boats. The crew rescued from the U-39, sunk on 14 September 1939, were taken first to Scotland from where they were transferred to PoW camps in Canada. The following week, the U27 was sunk. Thirty-eight men were rescued and interned in PoW camps. The war was barely three weeks old and these few dozen prisoners did not place any great undue burden on the system. At the time, there were only two PoW camps in the whole of Great Britain. Six years later the number of camps had risen to over 600 and were holding tens of thousands of men.

While the haul of prisoners 'put in the bag' following O'Connor's operation was impressive, such large numbers had never been anticipated and placed a huge strain on British resources and logistics. The Italian prisoners were placid and compliant, but they still had to be guarded, which meant pulling men away from other duties. Under the terms of the Geneva Convention, PoWs had to be removed from the battle zone to camps away from the fighting. They had to be escorted away from the battle area, transport had to be found, and the wounded had to be given medical treatment.

Even dental treatment was provided for their welfare. They were sent to England on ships where they were transported to newly-established camps across the country. In Somerset for example there were PoW camps located at Yeovil, Norton Fitzwarren,

The Italian army surrendered in its hundreds of thousands. They were brought to England and kept in PoW camps around the country. Some, such as this man, were employed as labourers on farms.

Bridgwater and Wookey Hole, along with other sites. These at first were used for the internment of Italians, but later they were used for German prisoners.

Except for officers, prisoners were put to work, to keep them occupied as much as anything else. Those put to work on farms helped with food production. Indeed, at one point it was estimated that PoWs provided perhaps as much as fifty per cent of the work force on British farms.

Operation Compass had yielded an unexpected bonus in the capture of great stocks of Italian supplies. Around 700 vehicles of all types were seized at Bardia and these helped the British army with its problem of transportation. Sensing a great victory still lay ahead, O'Connor maintained the pressure on the Italians. Using stocks of captured enemy food and fuel to augment his own supplies, he continued moving forward. In the space of two months the British army advanced 500 miles, capturing or destroying almost 400 tanks, 1,290 pieces of artillery and taking a further 130,000 prisoners. The Foreign Secretary Anthony Eden paraphrased Winston Churchill's famous speech concerning the Battle of Britain the previous month saying, 'Never has so much been surrendered by so many to so few.'

Among the supplies captured were stocks of Italian tinned meat which was labelled 'AM' to identify it as Administrazione Militare. The Italian troops did not relish this product and referred to it as 'Arabo Morte' (dead Arab). Later in the North African campaign, when the Germans arrived, they called them 'Alter Mann' (old man), 'Anisus Mussolini' (Mussolini's anus) or 'Alter Maulesel' (old mule). It was not high quality, but at least it was nutritional food and to hungry troops it was something to eat. German tinned food was known as Marschverpflegung (march rations) and included cheese, meat, sardines, and various spreads for biscuits or bread. Much later in the war, the artist Bill Mauldin, whose work appeared in *Stars and Stripes* forces newspaper, served as a sergeant with the US 45th Infantry Division in 1943 during the campaign in Sicily and Italy. He remembered the quality of the German food as being very good, remarking how the Germans '… [perhaps] didn't know much about vitamins, but their stuff was filling. It was always a great day when our patrols found caches of Jerry food…their sausage is good, and they have marmalade that comes packed in a big wooden box and isn't bad at all…The Germans have a pretty good chow system…all their best stuff [goes] to the front. One prisoner told me that he had transferred from a cushy job in the rear echelon to the infantry so he could get something to eat.'

Throughout history troops have used whatever they have captured from the enemy. In North Africa nothing was wasted. The Germans, whose foodstuffs were so appreciated by the Allies when it was captured, in turn appreciated the stocks of food they seized, especially the British rations. One German veteran recalled how 'our vehicles, petrol, rations and clothing were all English…' He also remembered how he once 'breakfasted off two tins of milk, a tin of pineapple, biscuits and Ceylon tea'.

The vehicles to which this soldier was referring would almost certainly have been the Austin 4X2 K3 General Service truck. This was a standard supply vehicle weighing three tons, capable of towing light anti-aircraft guns or being fitted with hard bodies to be used as field workshops. At the beginning of the war only 10,000 were in service, but

The British company of Austin supplied thousands of trucks for the British army as shown here with this example of a refurbished original vehicle.

The Austin K3 truck was a standard vehicle for the British army and used in all theatres of war to transport troops and supplies. This is a refurbished original vehicle.

by 1945 around 390,000 Austin trucks had been built in all versions and variants and used in all theatres of the war.

Using the enemy's equipment and vehicles also had its disadvantages. With each side using so much captured equipment, especially vehicles, it was inevitable that confusion would arise. For example, a group of British troops were surprised to discover that what they observed to be friendly vehicles approaching their positions, turned out to be captured British trucks being used by German troops. On another occasion a division of Italian troops readied itself for battle on seeing British vehicles driving towards their positions. Just before they opened fire they realised that German troops were using the trucks.

Meanwhile, on the other side of Mediterranean Sea, events were unfolding that would affect the situation in Libya. On 28 October Mussolini ordered an attack against Greece using 160,000 men as the Italians opened another theatre of operations. The Greek army numbered 209,000 men, with only a few vehicles at its disposal, relying instead on a force of 125,000 mules and horses for transport due to the mountainous conditions in the region. The Italians had believed it would be a short campaign, but they had reckoned without the sub-zero temperatures and the tenacity of the Greek soldiers. Faced with these difficulties the Italians were not only halted but were forced back by the Greek army.

Despite the protestations of naval and army commanders, who were still engaged against the Italians in North Africa, Churchill sent a force of 57,000 men with 100 tanks to support the Greeks. 'W' Force, under the command of Lieutenant General Wilson, was formed by taking men from Lieutenant General Cunningham's command. As it was shipped to Greece, the convoy was constantly attacked by Italian aircraft. Arriving at the end of November the Australians, New Zealanders and British troops took up their defences in northern Greece along positions called the Aliakmon Line. It was hoped they would be able to deliver another victory against the Italians, but the British had reckoned without the intervention of Hitler.

Relief for the Italians came on 6 April 1941 when the Germans attacked with a force of 680,000 men supported by 700 aircraft and 1,200 tanks. Meanwhile the Italian allies had built up their forces to 565,000 men with the support of 163 tanks and 463 aircraft. The Greek army was now also fully mobilised with 430,000 men but only 20 tanks and very few anti-tank guns. The Germans rapidly bypassed defences such as the Metaxas Line and quickly advanced.

Hitler ordered this operation on the same day the German Second Army attacked Yugoslavia with 1,000 tanks, along with support from its Italian, Hungarian and Romanian allies. With this latest development, Germany was heading for a war on three fronts. The forces in Western Europe were garrisoning defences along the French coast and, although they knew Britain could not mount an invasion of any size, they still had to be vigilant. The situation in North Africa was not certain and now Yugoslavia had absorbed troops and tanks; but Hitler believed the situation was still within the capabilities of his armies.

He appeared to be vindicated when, two weeks later, Yugoslavia was added to his list of Blitzkrieg victims. On 23 April, after seventeen days of fighting, Greece surrendered, with one of the largest forces, the Greek East Macedonian army of 60,000 men, becoming prisoners of war. The day before, on 22 April, the British began to evacuate Greece. Force W had been in the country just over three weeks. The Royal Navy evacuated 51,000 men, but lost four transport ships and two destroyers sunk in the process. The troops had been saved but they had been forced to leave behind all their heavy equipment and supplies.

During the operation, the Luftwaffe had flown air support missions to attack targets, and bombed shipping moored in the harbour of Athens. One air raid in particular produced results which were catastrophic in terms of losses. A single Ju88 bomber made an approach and dropped its bomb load hitting a 12,000 ton freighter, the *Clan Fraser*, which was delivering supplies along with several other vessels in its convoy. The bomb set off a chain reaction by detonating 350 tons of ammunition on board which, in turn, destroyed ten other ships in the harbour, around 41,000 tons in total, with the loss of the crews and the stores of ammunition, food, fuel and weapons. In less than three weeks the British army had lost 2,200 killed and wounded and left behind many to be taken prisoner. It had been another demonstration of the strength of the German army to the world and another retreat for the British.

The campaign in Greece had been a disaster waiting to happen. General O'Connor believed that had he been allowed to finish the campaign in Libya he would have been in a better position to deal with the situation in Greece. He told Churchill that British forces could not deal with both situations at the same time. Stripped of manpower the British army in North Africa was more vulnerable than ever before.

One country which still held faith was America, where President Roosevelt declared that the country must become the 'great arsenal of Democracy'. In May 1940 Roosevelt presented Congress with his plan to increase the country's defence budget to $1.2 billion saying, 'These are ominous days... Americans must recast their thinking about national protection.' This was a reference to their opinion poll in September 1939 which showed that only 2.5% thought America should enter the war. Around 37.5% said that the country should not take sides, with 29.9% saying America should do absolutely nothing. This left 30.1% undecided. Supporting Roosevelt's increase in the defence budget was Admiral Ernest Joseph King, who served as Commander in Chief US Fleet and Chief of Naval Operations during the war. He remarked that 'The war has been variously termed a war of production and a war of machines. Whatever else it is, so far as the United States is concerned, it is a war of logistics.' How right he was.

Churchill increased his calls asking America to reconsider selling weapons and vehicles, but American newspapers carried features which called for Roosevelt to keep the country out of the war. The president responded by vowing to keep the country out of any war in Europe and this satisfied the voting public who did not wish to enter the war either. After Hitler invaded France and the Low Countries in May 1940 there was a shift, with some 60% realising the importance of defeating Germany. America, for the time being at least, would remain neutral. But being neutral was no guarantee that a country would remain unaffected by events unfolding in the war. For example, the Republic of Ireland had a pre-war merchant fleet of 56 vessels, but its position of neutrality did not prevent 16 of these being be sunk, resulting in the loss of 136 lives.

Such unprovoked attacks were as a direct result of Hitler's policy of unrestricted submarine warfare which included neutrals. In 1939, Holland had also been a neutral state with a merchant fleet of 1,532 vessels totalling 2,972,871 tons. After the country surrendered in 1940 those surviving vessels were made available to undertake convoy duties to transport troops and supplies. One outstanding civilian Dutch vessel was the massive 36,000-ton luxurious liner the *Nieuw Amsterdam*. She was in America in 1939 when war broke out and it was decided she would remain there for the duration.

In 1940 she was requisitioned by Britain as a troop ship, a role in which she became distinguished. Capable of speeds up to 20 knots, she could carry 6,800 troops in a trip. By 1945 she had transported 350,000 troops to various destinations and sailed over 530,000 miles in her role.

Republican Wendell Wilkie crusaded to keep America out of the war and was joined among others by the pioneer aviator Charles Lindbergh, who had become an influential public figure after his successful solo flight across the Atlantic in May 1927. As a prominent figure, he had an audience and they listened when he spoke. Another Republican to oppose Roosevelt's Lend-Lease Bill was Robert Taft, senator for Ohio. Nevertheless, Roosevelt continued to press to supply Britain with more goods, arguing the virtues of leasing or lending equipment to any nation 'whose defense the President deems vital to the defense of the United States'. Despite resistance the Lend-Lease Act was put before Congress and the Senate in the House of Representatives in March 1941. There was overwhelming support for it, with 60 to 31 and 317 to 71 respectively. This meant that America could now openly provide material to support Britain's war effort. Winston Churchill said of the deal that it was 'the most unsordid act in the history of any nation'. Two months after the Lend-Lease Bill had been passed, President Roosevelt ordered that two million tons of shipping be built as part of the deal. It would mean the survival of Britain. Later, the likes of Willkie, Taft and Lindbergh would all come to change their minds about America becoming involved in the war.

Lend-Lease was a lifeline for Britain, but its enactment left American ships open to attack by German U-Boats and there were several major incidents during the second half of 1941. In September the USS *Greer* was attacked, a destroyer which had been tracking the position of a U-Boat and passing on the information to a Royal Navy aircraft carrier on patrol in the area. The German commander attacked the *Greer* because he interpreted its actions as hostile. When the incident was reported in the newspapers no mention was made of the *Greer*'s communication with the aircraft carrier. This was followed on 17 October by a U-Boat attack on the destroyer USS *Kearny* which resulted in the deaths of 11 crew, and the destroyer USS *Reuben James* was attacked and sunk by a U-Boat on 31 October with the loss 115 crew.

Initially, Britain would receive $7 billion of aid, but this was later increased to $30 billion. In September 1940, Churchill approached the Americans asking for naval assistance in helping to secure the trans-Atlantic shipping routes bringing supplies to Britain, taking the opportunity of accepting Roosevelt's declaration that America would 'extend to the opponents of force the material resources of this nation'.

Churchill and Roosevelt reached an agreement known as 'Destroyers for Bases' whereby in exchange for fifty ageing destroyers Britain would allow America a 99-year lease on British island territories in the Caribbean, including Bermuda, Jamaica and Antigua. Churchill did not like the terms and said, 'Empires just don't bargain.' US

Attorney General Robert Jackson replied, 'Republics do.' Between July and October 1940, 144 unescorted merchant vessels had been sunk by U-boats and a further 73 in convoy. The destroyers supplied by America were virtually obsolete but the Royal Navy could make use of them all the same. Some were sunk by U-boats and others were later transferred to Russia.

Britain was not the only country in the Allied camp to receive Lend-Lease aid. America would go on to provide the equivalent of $50 billion in Lend-Lease aid to forty-four countries. China, which had been at war with Japan since 1937, received $1.6 billion in aid. The level of Lend-Lease France would eventually receive would amount to $3.23 billion, mainly after June 1944. Russia received $11 billion with oil, tanks, aircraft and vehicles. America would supply tanks, artillery and aircraft in vast numbers to Britain under the Lend-Lease Act, especially during the build-up phase for the invasion in Europe. At the time the strength of the US army stood at around 1.4 million men with an armoured force of 300 light tanks. By 1945 the US army would have eight million men under arms and the factories would have built many thousands of trucks and tanks for these troops and overseas allied armies.

Despite having advanced heavy industry, during the period of 1939-40 America produced only 325 light tanks and six medium tanks. It would not produce its first heavy tank until 1942. But by the end of the war American factories had built more than 88,000 tanks, 41,000 other tracked vehicles, and 3,200,436 trucks and other wheeled vehicles. In the same period Germany would produce less than 28,000 tanks of all types. Against such capacity Germany could never hope to compete, not even with the help of the occupied countries. The strength of the combined US Army Air Forces would reach a peak of 2,411,294 service men and women between July 1940 and August 1945 and accept into service more than 229,000 aircraft of all types, such was the capability of the nation. By comparison, between 1939 and 1945 German output for aircraft of all types was less than 100,000 machines.

Behind the scenes, even as the last engagements of Operation Dynamo were being fought, British agents were discussing arrangements to buy numbers of the new M3 Lee-Grant medium tank. This was equipped with a 37mm gun in a fully traversing turret and a 75mm gun was mounted in a side sponson. It was an unusual layout because at the time armaments manufacturers in America could not build a turret to take the powerful 75mm gun. The M3, protected by armour up to 80mm thick, was heavier and more powerfully armed than anything then in service with the British army. The negotiations succeeded in securing a quantity of M3s but the first batches would not arrive in North Africa until early 1942. The first deliveries would arrive in North Africa in November 1941. A deal was also struck to purchase 500,000 obsolete rifles, mainly P17s of First World War vintage which would be used to equip Britain's Home Guard, and 900 pieces of artillery of 75mm calibre with 1,000 shells for each gun. Such weaponry was hardly war-winning, but it was something.

Another tank design which caught the attention of the British team was the M3 Light Tank. Known as the 'Honey' by the armoured regiments in the North African campaign which used it, it was one of the most widely used light tanks to serve with the British army during the Second World War. Development began in 1935, when it was known as the M2A1, and went on to be built in three variants. The basic design featured a 37mm gun as the main armament mounted in a turret capable of traversing full 360 degrees. After some modifications were made to the design it was accepted as the M3 standard light tank for the US army in July 1940. It was agreed that the M3 tanks to be supplied to Britain under the Lend-Lease Act would be sent directly to North Africa. About eighty-four M3 Light Tanks arrived in July 1941, just in time for the crews to be trained before being committed to battle for the first time in November 1941 at Babr Saleh, as part of the Operation Crusader offensive.

The M3 Light Tank was built by the American Car and Foundry Company, which by August 1942 had produced more than 5,800 vehicles. The design was declared obsolete in July 1943 and by the October, when production was finally completed, the company had built over 13,800 M3s. Although no longer produced, it remained in front line service. It was used in all theatres of war, including the Pacific 'island hopping' campaign against the Japanese.

Chapter 9

1941: A Turning Point

The year of 1940 had ended with good prospects for the British army in North Africa. Things were still looking good at the beginning of 1941 as General O'Connor's Operation Compass seized Bardia and Derna, and most importantly the port of Tobruk, which had been the forward point for receiving Italian supplies. On 7 Februrary 1941 the Australians entered Benghazi and advancing towards El Agheila. What had begun as a limited operation had turned into a full-blown rout of the Italian army. The cost to O'Connor was a casualty figure of less than 2,000. It had been made largely possible by using additional captured Italian supplies.

In 1940, Hitler had tried to persuade Franco to get Spain to join Germany and Italy as a third member of the Fascist alliance. Franco was tempted, but he asked a high price if he was to commit the Spanish army. Among his list of demands was 400,000 tons of fuel, 500,000 tons of coal, 200,000 tons of wheat, 100,000 tons of cotton and other commodities. Now, with the British successes against Italy, Franco declined to side with Hitler, but as a staunch Fascist he remained sympathetic to the cause.

The same day Churchill withdrew 57,000 troops from the North African theatre to defend Greece, the first German forces began to arrive in Libya. This was the newly-created Deutsches Afrika Korps under Rommel, who had acquitted himself during the campaign in France. Here was an officer who got things done and the British knew he would not waste time. Their arrival would change the course of the war in the region. Bolstered by the arrival of their German ally, morale among the Italians was raised to return to the offensive.

From a commander's point of view, the North African desert, with its sparsely populated vastness, was a perfect battleground where there would be no repeat of the high numbers of civilian casualties and lines of refugees clogging the roads as there had been in Europe. Here, armies could manoeuvre great distances without hindrance. In this harsh terrain one mistake could cost a man his life or many lives. General Johann von Ravenstein, who would command the 21st Panzer Division and serve as Rommel's second-in-command, said of the desert that it was 'a tactician's paradise and a quartermaster's hell,' and the military historian Martin van Creveld has opined that 'For all Rommel's tactical brilliance, the problem of supplying an Axis force for an advance into the Middle East was insoluble.'

The arrival of the Afrika Korps turned the war in North Africa in favour of the Italo-German forces. It was armed with artillery such as this 150mm Feldhaubitze 18.

Once committed to the campaign in North Africa, the Afrika Korps poured into the theatre of operations, along with fuel, ammunition and all other logistics to support it.

For the British there was still the question of the Italians in Ethiopia and Italian Somaliland, where there were 250,000 troops. Admittedly more than 180,000 were Askari natives with questionable fighting capabilities. The Italian presence here threatened the southern end of the Red Sea and convoys exiting into the Indian Ocean after they had left the Suez Canal. The British were now faced with the possibility of having to fight two separate campaigns in the region.

On 19 January, Major General William Platt launched an attack from the north and was soon making better headway than Brigadier William Slim's attack the previous November had achieved. Fighting was fierce and conditions were dreadful with men reduced to two pints of water per day, later reduced to one pint. Drinking water remained a problem for both sides and clean, fresh supplies had to be brought to the troops as well as food. At one point during the operation drinking water became so critical that the British used the Royal Navy to land 1.5 million gallons from a convoy at Sollum in Egypt. Platt's attack in the north was supported by Cunningham, recently appointed to command the East Africa Force, who launched an attack in the south of Italian Somaliland on 11 February and headed towards Kismayu.

The two commanders were made aware of the German arrival in Libya but there was never any possibility of their intervening in Ethiopia. Realising the Germans did not pose any threat, Platt and Cunningham maintained the pressure from the north and south. Fighting continued into March with conditions all the while deteriorating, but the British remained determined. On 27 March the Royal Tank Regiment attacked with Matilda tanks, supported by infantry in Bren Gun Carriers, cutting the Dongolaas Road and forcing the last of the Italian resistance to crumble. By 6 April the British were in Addis Ababa, and after eight weeks, during which time Cunningham's men had covered 1,700 miles, the fighting had cost the British only 500 killed and wounded.

However, Italian resistance was far from over and fighting continued. Platt and Cunningham's forces now began to converge on the mountainous range dominated by Amba Alagi (11,300 feet) where the Italians had prepared defences and built up supplies of food, ammunition and fresh water from natural streams. This was infantry fighting as the British edged up the steep rock faces. For almost three weeks British and Indian troops fought to clamber up the sides of the mountain. British artillery managed to hit and destroy several Italian supply dumps. The loss of these, which included ammunition, broke the Italians' ability to resist. On 19 May, the commanding officer, the Duke of Aosta, surrendered. After the campaign, Churchill commented on the low Allied casualty figure, to which Wavell responded by saying, 'A big butcher's bill is not necessarily evidence of good tactics.' In addition to the battlefield casualties the British suffered over 74,500 men stricken by sickness and injured in accidents. 300,000

Italians were captured. With the south-east now secure and the threat to the Suez Canal removed from the southern end of the Red Sea the British could turn all their attention to the greater threat posed by the Germans and Italians further to the west in Libya.

Meanwhile, in Britain as 1941 dawned, the country had become the temporary home for tens of thousands of troops who had fled from countries which were now under German occupation, including Poland, France, Holland, Norway, Czechoslovakia and Belgium. Some were fully trained and experienced troops who had escaped to make their way to Britain. Some volunteered for new units which were being raised such as the Commandos and the Parachute Regiment. Some were trained pilots and joined the RAF to fly in national squadrons. For example, by 1945 there were 2,099 Norwegians with 483 officers serving with the RAF flying eighty aircraft in five squadrons.

In the early days, these forces in exile were equipped and armed by the British army, wearing battledress uniform, but with national badges. One of the largest single groups from France was the Light Mountain Division, some 15,000 men, evacuated from Norway in 1940. In July 1940, French troops were assembled and formed into the Legion de Gaulle referred to as the 'Fighting French' by the British. At the end of 1940 there were almost 11,000 Polish troops with 3,500 officers in the country. Like their French counterparts they were issued with British uniforms, equipment and weapons. In 1940 a group of around 1,500 Dutch soldiers was formed into the Royal Dutch Brigade which was renamed the Princess Irene Brigade in late August 1941. When General Sergey Ingr of the Czechoslovakian army escaped to France he managed to take with him over 11,000 troops. They took part in some of the fighting in 1940, and the survivors later escaped to Britain where they were trained and equipped by the British army.

Denmark was occupied and, incredibly, almost 800 Danes escaped to reach Britain where they joined British forces. In the beginning, the numbers from Norway were tragically low – 110 officers and 1,100 other ranks. Following the Commando raid on the Lofoten Islands in March 1941 and an evacuation of Spitsbergen in July, numbers increased and by the end of 1942 around 250 officers and 2,300 other ranks had been trained and equipped by the British army. Some of these joined the Special Operations Executive to be returned to Norway to destroy military installations and recruit resistance fighters.

At this stage, mainland Europe was a no-go area regarding any type of campaign, besides which the British army was in no condition to undertake an assault of any size. The only way of engaging the Germans was through nuisance raids. The first Commando raid was undertaken on the night of 24/25 June 1940 by No 11 Independent Company which sent a party to gather information from the Boulogne and Le Touquet part of the French coast. Between July and September the same year, several further raids were mounted, which included operations in Guernsey for the purposes of intelligence gathering.

In 1941, as U-Boats continued to sink shipping, it was calculated that Britain could survive on 26 million tons of imports, which was less than half that of pre-war totals. This could not be done without imposing rationing of commodities in all quarters. Such a move was considered an emergency and would last for a short period. It was believed to be unsustainable, but if the situation did not improve, then the whole country and armed forces would suffer. The situation was critical and unless something was done reserve stocks would soon be depleted. The air force would be grounded due to lack of fuel and warships would have been stranded in port. Civilians were rationed and cards were issued to regulate foodstuffs. A typical weekly allowance for an adult included three pints of milk, 2oz of tea, 4oz of margarine, 2oz of butter and 8oz of jam. Sugar was rationed to 8oz per week, if available, 2oz of cheese, 4oz of bacon, and meat was a luxury. Dried foodstuffs came in from Canada and America, including milk and eggs.

As well as the Home Guard, men served as Special Police Constables and Air Raid Wardens.

Britain by now had been standing against Germany for two years during which time the country had faced off the threat of invasion and the Battle of Britain had been won by the fighter pilots of the RAF. Now, the country's cities were reeling under attack as German aircraft dropped hundreds of tons of bombs in the nightly air raids known as the Blitz. London had first been bombed on 24 August 1940, but it was soon joined by other cities as they became targets, including Liverpool, Bristol, Birmingham and Plymouth. Birmingham, where factories produced small arms such as rifles and machine guns, had 365 air raid alerts and was bombed on 77 occasions during which 2,241 people were killed and a further 6,700 injured. More than 12,900 buildings were destroyed or damaged, including 302 factories, making it the third most heavily bombed city after London and Liverpool. Birmingham was an important centre of production for aircraft and aircraft engines, along with a whole raft of other items for the military. As well as the fire services the city had around 22,000 volunteer air raid wardens. The work they did in rescuing people after the raids was vital in saving lives, but, being volunteers, they did not get paid.

The midlands city of Coventry was an industrial centre with factories, such as Humber and Daimler, producing vehicles, tanks, aircraft and munitions. The city was attacked seventeen times during August and October 1940, but it was the air raid during the night of 14 November that proved particularly devastating. Over 500 aircraft dropped 500 tons of bombs and thousands of incendiary devices. The attack left 568 people killed, and 4,300 houses and 111 factories producing war materiel destroyed; 60,000 other buildings were damaged and 100 acres of the city levelled. German propaganda under Goebbels was quick to capitalise on the success of the attack and coined a new word for the press to describe the effects of the raid: 'Coventriert', literally meaning 'Coventried' (reported in the British press as 'Coventrate'). Goebbels declared that the word meant 'completely destroyed'. While the air raids did disrupt life and industrial output, they did not destroy the city nor the people's resolve to carry on.

Vehicles could double up in their duties, such as this refurbished original Bedford van, used by the police but also serving as an ARP vehicle.

The ruins of Coventry Cathedral after the Luftwaffe raid on the night of 14 November 1940.

To maintain morale, King George VI visited factories across Britain, such as this plant producing 25-pounder field guns.

The railways in Britain were vital for moving the heavy volume of supplies needed by the British army. Special Gunpowder Vans such as this preserved example served the factories producing ammunition.

Another example of a preserved Gunpowder Van which transported materials to the ammunition factories.

This shows how the wooden crates were stored in the railway wagons for transportation by rail.

The vast amount of movement meant there would inevitably be some damage to supplies, but it was at an acceptable level.

London suffered the heaviest raids and between September 1940 and May 1941 more than 20,000 people were killed. One of the worst raids occurred on 10 May 1941 when 1,436 people were killed, 155,000 families were without water, gas or electricity and a third of the city's streets were rendered impassable. Civilians took to sheltering in the underground railway system and each night at the height of the Blitz some 177,000 sought refuge in the tunnels. By the end of the war in all the raids four million homes had been damaged, 200,000 destroyed and 70,000 civilians killed, including in the V-weapon attacks from June 1944.

Following the evacuation of the British forces from Greece, the country was delivered with yet more bad news when the Germans attacked Crete. Between 20 and 28 May, the garrison of the British army, along with Greek, New Zealand, and Australian troops, numbering around 40,000 men, commanded by General Bernard Freyberg, put up a sterling fight. The Germans poured 29,000 troops on to the island, including 15,000 elite Fallschirmjäger (parachute) troops. By the end, the Allies had lost 4,000 killed and 17,500 taken prisoner. The remainder were evacuated in an operation reminiscent of Dunkirk and Greece the previous month. The operation

Damage was only to be expected among the thousands of tons of supplies being transported daily.

Charitable gifts for the troops organised by the WVS were distributed by the railways, in this case, as seen here by the Great Western railway.

cost the Royal Navy twenty warships lost. It had been a costly affair for the Germans too who lost 1,900 killed, 1,700 missing and 2,000 wounded. The Luftwaffe lost 284 aircraft and a further 700 damaged. In fact, after the attack Hitler ordered that no more such operations involving airborne troops be mounted.

It was only in North Africa that the British army and the Dominion forces remained in direct contact with the enemy on the ground. Rommel and his Afrika Korps had gone on the offensive almost as soon as they had unloaded the transport ships.

The British and Italian armies were acclimatized to local conditions which put them at an advantage over the newly-arrived Afrika Korps. However, they were also tired after so many months of fighting. Much of the equipment, particularly tanks, were virtually worn out from constant battle. And the British tank in use at the time, the Matilda Mk II, had been useful against the Italian tanks but would prove useless against the heavier German tanks. The gun/armour balance was only tipped marginally back in favour of the British when the Valentine arrived, with its 6-pounder gun.

Rommel's forces were fresh, well trained, experienced and better supplied with new equipment. His tanks included Mk II and Mk III Panzers armed with 2cm and 5cm guns respectively, along with machine guns. Other armoured vehicles included

It was vital that the Suez Canal remain in allied hands to allow supplies and reinforcements to reach North Africa.

armoured cars, liaison vehicles and prime movers for towing artillery, especially for the 88mm anti-tank guns which would prove so deadly at long range. The tanks that were left with the Italian armoured units were barely adequate, being lightly armed and armoured. These were the survivors of the earlier battles, such as the M13/40 which was armed with a 47mm gun and protected by 40mm of armour, with a speed of only 20mph and operational range of 125 miles which further compounded its already limited capabilities. By comparison the British Cruiser tanks may have been armed with only a 40mm gun and protected by 40mm of armour but they could reach speeds of up to 27mph and had an operational range of 200 miles, which out-performed the Italian tanks. Also, with 110 rounds of ammunition carried for the main gun and 4,500 rounds of ammunition for the two machine guns the Cruiser could continue to fight on for a lot longer than most Italian tanks. The Panzer IIIs had a range of only 100 miles but would prove to be a different matter altogether. The Panzer II suffered from lack of hitting power but when the Panzer IV came into the theatre of operations, with a 75mm gun, it could have tipped the balance of power. Unfortunately for Rommel, this tank suffered by having only an operational range of only 120 miles.

The nominal commander of the Axis forces was General Italo Gariboldi, the Italian commander-in-chief in North Africa, but Rommel had complete operational command and was answerable only to the German High Command in Berlin. By the time of Rommel's arrival in Libya, the Italians had had a presence in Africa for almost eight years. The British army had maintained garrisons in the Middle East since the end of the First World War. Although this made the Germans the newcomers to desert warfare, Rommel and his troops showed they were fast learners and they quickly gained the necessary skills. The Afrika Korps had been raised especially for the campaign and together with the Italians they would be termed the Deutsch-Italienische Panzerarmee. It has been opined that the campaign in North Africa was nothing more than a 'sideshow' for Hitler, who at the time of their deployment already had his mind set on attacking Soviet Russia. Later in the campaign, the Afrika Korps would find itself short of supplies and competing for replacement vehicles, weapons, troops and supplies as the Russian campaign absorbed everything.

Six months earlier, in October 1940, Major General Wilhelm Ritter von Thoma reported directly to Hitler, stating that in any future war involving German troops in the North African theatre the 'overriding consideration' in his opinion would be one of logistics. Thoma had visited Libya personally to assess the future battleground and drafted his report which emphasised the importance of logistics and supply lines. He wrote: 'The decisive factor will be the problem of supply. This not only because of the climate and terrain difficulties in the desert, but because of the British navy's command of the Mediterranean. It will be extremely difficult, if not impossible to supply and maintain a large army. If Germany does send a force to support the Italians, it should be an armoured force and at least four divisions to ensure success…' He summarised by saying, 'This is also the maximum force that could be effectively maintained with supplies.' He could not have been more correct in his predictions.

Rommel's orders were simply that he was to conduct an 'aggressive defence'. He would retake the region of Cyrenaica in eastern Libya and capture the main town of Benghazi, thereby pushing the British back from their territorial gains of late 1940. This limited him and went against his tactical and strategic battlefield policies which embodied the much-quoted principle that 'the best form of defence is attack', a doctrine which is sometimes attributed to Napoleon. This was the man, after all, who had written the book *Infantry Attack* and he wanted to come to grips with the enemy. Rommel later wrote of his decision to launch an attack: 'There'll be consternation amongst our masters in Tripoli and Rome and perhaps in Berlin too.' He went on to outline the fact that he alone was responsible for the decision and would take the blame in case things went wrong, writing, 'I took the risk against all orders because the opportunity seemed favourable…' He was used to taking risks and driving hard and fast.

Wavell did not believe the Germans were in any state of readiness to mount an attack, given the time they had been in the country. He thought they would need to spend more time organising themselves and building up their reserves. He was proved wrong when, on 24 March, Rommel made his first move. Dividing his force into three columns he set out, using the 5th Light Division combined with the Italian motorised division. British forces were still in a weakened state having sent troops to support the campaign in Greece and they fell back. Rommel advanced rapidly, covering the ninety miles from his start point to reach El Agheila the same day. Tanks had never been subjected to such punishing use and the toll on men and machines was exhausting. His advance had been covered using motorcycles, with trucks transporting supplies and troops to escort the tanks.

With ample supplies, both from his own lines of support and using captured British stocks, he maintained the pressure. A week later he was approaching Agedabia. On 2 April, he completed his initial planning brief when he captured Benghazi. He had not had it all his own way, as proved when he encountered tanks of the 5th Royal Tank Regiment. Sergeant Jake Wardrop wrote of the situation: 'We sat behind a ridge and waited until they came, then popped up and let loose. There seemed to be nothing in front but tanks coming on, but we kept firing and they slowed down and finally halted and shot it out stationary.' However, Rommel was undeterred and he pressed on. To his south one of his tank columns had captured fuel stocks at Msus and Mechili, which allowed them to continue to Gazala and the coast road. His third column, commanded by Lieutenant Colonel Count von Schwerin, completed a wide encircling manoeuvre around Ben Gania, past Mechili and Derna. It resulted in the capture of 3,000 prisoners from the 2nd Armoured Division, including General O'Connor who had pushed the Italians back six months earlier, along with Brigadier John Coombe and General Philip Neame.

The 2nd Armoured Division had only been in Egypt since the beginning of the year, having been sent as a reinforcement unit. Raised in December 1939 it did not begin to receive any vehicles, tanks or troops until March 1940 when the 1st Armoured Brigade took into service around 150 Vickers Mk VI Light Tanks. This was an aged design and the vehicles were armed with either a .50inch machine gun or a 15mm heavy machine gun mounted in a turret with a single .303inch machine gun mounted co-axially. One of the reasons for the slow build-up was because priority in tanks and equipment was allocated to the 1st Armoured Division serving with the BEF in France. When the 2nd Armoured Division was finally completed its strength in October 1940 stood at 344 tanks, all of which were inadequately armed for the task which lay ahead, and 10,750 men. The tanks now included Cruisers such as the A9, A10 and A13 Mk III, all of which were armed with 2-pounder guns in their turrets with short range and limited penetrating capability.

When the 2nd Armoured Division landed in North Africa in early 1941 it was viewed as a great boost to General O'Connor in his Operation Compass which was pushing the Italians back. Now, four months later, it was caught in a pincer movement between the Italian 10th Bersaglieri Regiment and the German 5th Light Division and 15 Panzer Division at Mechili. Some men were lucky to escape and make their way north to the port of Tobruk. The remainder were either killed or taken prisoner. On 10 May 1941, less than eighteen months after being formed, the 2nd Armoured Division was officially declared disbanded and did not reform again during the war.

The Cruiser tank design, as used by the ill-fated 2nd Armoured Division, was the result of the tank rearmament programme in response to tank developments being unveiled in Germany in the 1930s. Britain may had been instrumental in introducing the tank to the battlefield during the First World War, but in post-war years had lost any advantage it enjoyed and failed to maintain the impetus of armoured warfare. The tank designs which did enter service were often slow, with limited combat range and armed with a main gun which was less than up to the task of engaging enemy tanks. The Cruiser Mk IV, officially termed the A13 Mk II, was among those designs to suffer from inadequate armament and combat range.

The Germans were learning how to cope with the difficulties of fighting in the desert. They had always understood the importance of maintaining their vehicles properly and keeping them operational. After any engagement, German engineers would go onto the battlefield and recover damaged tanks which they would take back to their bases and repair. The British developed a grudging respect them. Some envied the standard of German organisation. John Butler, an Australian serving in the garrison at Tobruk, wrote, 'We can learn from the Germans. Their battalions are complete units, with anti-tank guns, tanks, air force and field workshops, ack-ack [anti-aircraft artillery] and artillery.' He was not the only one to comment on the way things were being run.

The British army used transporters like this to move tanks, as seen here with this Matilda Mk II.

The Crusader Mk II Cruiser tank was used by the British army in the desert, but its light armour left it vulnerable to anti-tank fire.

Lieutenant Michael Kerr wrote, 'The standard of infantry training was really quite terrible. Soldiers were unable to understand what they were meant to be doing and what everything was about.'

Veterans have since often remarked how, when the fighting had stopped after a battle, the Germans remained on the battlefield to salvage what they could. For example, after Operation Battleaxe, the failed British attempt to relieve Tobruk in June 1941, the Germans showed what they had learnt in fighting in such hostile conditions by recovering 88 of the 100 tanks knocked out in the fighting. These would be cannibalised to repair other tanks or repaired and returned to the battle. The Germans had transporter vehicles, such as the SdKfz 9 half-track which could tow a 60-ton-rated trailer. This combination, known as the BsAh 642, could also be used to recover abandoned tanks from the battlefield, and allowed tanks to be brought forward thereby saving wear and tear on the tracks. By contrast the British had few transporters, which meant their tanks had to move forward under their own power to the battle area and then fight.

Recovery units equipped with specialist vehicles such as the Panzer-Bergegerat SdKfz 179, were developed to help recover damaged tanks from the battlefield. These engineers became masters of this operation and established workshops on the battlefield. Each tank regiment had its own workshop company which comprised two

The Matilda Mk II was not the best tank in North Africa but its heavy armour earned it the nickname 'Queen of the Desert'.

The Crusader Mk I tank had a small 40mm calibre gun. Around 5,300 of all variants were built and served between 1940 and 1943.

repair platoons, one recovery platoon and several sections that specialised in different aspects of repair. There were repair sections right down to tank company levels. If repairs could not be undertaken in the field the damaged vehicle would be towed back

The Valentine proved to be a versatile tank and served in the desert from 1940. It was also supplied to Russia as part of Britain's Lend-Lease from 1941. It was also built in Canada.

to the workshop company which may be located up to twenty miles to the rear. If the vehicle was not damaged beyond repair, then it could be expected to return to the front in twelve hours.

By 11 April Rommel had captured Bardia and seized Sollum, but bypassed Tobruk. He left a garrison of 23,000 in his rear area, but with few resources to launch a counterattack and insufficient manpower, they did not amount to a threat to the British.

Commanding the defence at Tobruk was Major General Leslie Morshead, a tough, no-nonsense Australian, who said about the beleaguered position, 'There'll be no Dunkirk here.' He continued his rousing address to his troops, which included 15,000 Australians, 500 Indians and 7,000 British, 'If we should have to get out, we shall fight our way out. There is no surrender and no retreat.'

The defensive perimeter around Tobruk extended for thirty miles and was based on the fortifications built by the Italians who had occupied the port until being driven out two months earlier. The Allies constructed two lines of defence, the outer 'Red Line' and the inner 'Blue Line' with a minefield in between. Seventy strongpoints were built and an anti-tank ditch some thirty feet wide was dug. The 1st Royal Tank Regiment with Cruiser tanks provided armoured support and, with a deep-water harbour behind them through which they could be supplied, the garrison looked secure.

The position resembled a medieval siege, with Rommel having sealed off all lines into and from Tobruk. He tried a direct assault using thirty-eight tanks to smash through the defences. They managed to advance two miles into the perimeter before being stopped. The Australians used 25-pounders and captured Italian coastal guns, turned to face inland, to break up the attack. The attack cost Rommel almost half his tank force. The German artillery maintained a bombardment which continued around the clock, day after day. Finally, on 4 May, Rommel called a halt to the attacks and left the garrison to its own devices. However, he could not ignore Tobruk entirely. He had advanced 250 miles, a route along which all his supplies must travel from the ports at El Agheila and Benghazi. If Tobruk, which lay only 75 miles from the Egyptian border, could be taken he would have a forward supply base to support his push into Egypt and the Suez Canal. If the British could hold the port, then Rommel would be denied the luxury of a forward supply base and any further advance would only stretch his supply lines, which were already over-extended, even further.

In the early hours of 13 April, under the cover of darkness, the Germans began to probe the defences and in the late afternoon had managed to penetrate the Red Line outer defences. The Australians resisted and during a counter-attack Corporal Jack Edmondson won a posthumous Victoria Cross. The Germans managed to advance and by 5am the next day their tanks were about half a mile beyond the Red Line but the Australians were ready for them with anti-tank guns. As the tanks advanced they were fired on from the flanks to hit them in the side where their armour protection was

The Panzer III was the mainstay of the German armoured units in North Africa although other types were also used.

weaker. British tanks joined in the battle. At one point Cruiser tanks of the 1st RTR and Panzer III tanks fired at one another across the anti-tank ditches surrounding the position like some land-based naval battle, giving a foretaste of the type of fighting which lay ahead. At such close range the light 2-pounder guns could inflict damage, and both sides could hardly miss. After two hours fighting the Germans withdrew leaving behind seventeen destroyed tanks and many dead and wounded. The next day air raids started as the Luftwaffe, supported by Italian aircraft, bombed targets in the harbour and the defences forming the perimeter around the port.

Over a period of four days, 13 to 17 April, Rommel ordered a series of attacks to be launched, sending in the German 5th Division, while the Italians sent in the Brescia Division and the Trento Division. The Australians repulsed them conclusively and inflicted particularly heavy losses on the Ariete Division which lost ninety tanks. The Australians took enormous risks to maintain and improve their defences and continuously mounted aggressive patrols. German propaganda referred to the 9th Australian Division as 'rats in a trap', a term which the Australians turned into a nickname and called themselves the 'Rats of Tobruk'. Rommel recognised their fighting spirit and paid them the compliment of calling them 'an elite formation of the British Empire'. All the while, Major General Morshead had the welfare of the men in mind and made sure that they were well supplied and received the best medical care possible.

For two weeks, the opposing forces faced off one another across the defences, with the Australians bracing themselves for the next round. The Germans brought forward more 88mm guns to provide support as anti-tank guns. A limited attack late in the evening of 30 April alerted the Australians that a bigger attack was imminent. They positioned anti-tank guns and brought forward several Matilda tanks to meet the expected line of attack. Bad weather delayed the attack which was finally launched at 8am. The Panzers pressed past the anti-tank guns and drove into a minefield. Fighting continued throughout the day, during which the Germans lost a further seventeen tanks and were driven back. The Matildas moved forward to complete the victory only to be met by the 88mm anti-tank guns. The Germans were always numerically weaker in tanks than the British and to counter this Rommel lured unsuspecting tank crews into areas commanded by his anti-tank guns. This was a tactic he had learned in the Spanish Civil War. His anti-tank guns inflicted a severe toll on the Allies and preserved his vehicles for the main attack. It was easier to resupply anti-tank shells than it was to bring up more tanks.

Both sides had to be supplied by convoys sailing across the Mediterranean Sea. For the Germans and Italians, it appeared a simple matter of sailing from ports in Italy and southern France. For the British, their convoys had to sail the length of the Mediterranean. The Royal Navy had mastery of the Mediterranean and with aircraft operating out of Malta they could attack the German and Italian supply convoys. Such was the intensity and success of these attacks that on average, the Afrika Korps would only receive about half of the supplies and equipment sent during the campaign. The worst month was November 1941 when Rommel only received 30,000 tons of an expected delivery of 70,000 tons of fuel and ammunition. Such losses not only limited the operational capability of Rommel's tanks but also restricted the amount of food issued to his troops, thereby limiting their ability to fight. The Italians told Hitler that convoys sailing across the Mediterranean had to be suspended because 'the British [RAF and Royal Navy] on Malta are slaughtering us!'

The British, with naval escorts and aircraft carriers, could send their convoys through, if not with total impunity, then certainly with a better chance of getting through. Malta had to be supplied with fuel if air and naval operations were to continue. Italian and German air forces bombed the island relentlessly trying to prevent supplies getting through. In August 1942, the most famous convoy of the war arrived in Malta. The Operation Pedestal convoy set sail on 2 August, comprising fourteen merchant ships escorted by destroyers and aircraft carriers. Eight days later it ran the gauntlet of the Straits of Gibraltar. Over the next three days it was under incessant air attack by German and Italian aircraft which took a high toll. Finally, on 13 August, just three battered merchantmen arrived at the island, but there was no fuel tanker with them. Two days later, the tanker *Ohio*, barely able to steer,

Despite suffering severe losses to the ships bringing in supplies, enough still managed to arrive to allow the Germans to continue fighting.

entered the Grand Harbour at Valletta, lashed between two destroyers. In total, five merchantmen arrived, including the *Ohio* which delivered 11,500 tons of fuel and oil. This allowed Malta to continue to operate as a base from where Rommel's convoys could be attacked.

The British army too was learning lessons and began a programme to modify tanks to better cope with the extreme conditions of desert warfare. Initially the British army

British convoy under attack as it delivers supplies to North Africa. Despite the intensity of the attack the British still managed to get through.

HMS *Indomitable*, which took part in Operation Pedestal.

British convoy under heavy air attack. The bravery of the Royal Navy meant that supplies continued to reach the British army in North Africa.

lacked the means to recover tanks in the desert, but the engineers in the specialist support regiments such as the Royal Electrical & Mechanical Engineers (REME) and Royal Army Ordnance Corps (RAOC) fitted winches and cranes to trucks for this purpose. The RAOC was also concerned with the handling of supplies including replacement vehicles. During the North Africa campaign the RAOC distributed 11,000 vehicles of all types and 73,000 tons of shells.

Tobruk was a thorn in Rommel's side which he could just not dig out. The defending garrison were stubbornly denying him what he so desperately needed to support his advance into Egypt. Conditions inside the defences were grim, with water being one of the most pressing problems. At one point men were reduced to six pints of water per day for all purposes. Realising he could not break into the position, Rommel departed from Tobruk on 4 May, leaving sufficient forces to hold down the garrison. Fuel was critical for Rommel to continue his attack and he noted in his diary, 'Unfortunately our petrol stocks are badly depleted, and it was with some anxiety that we contemplated the coming British attack, for we knew that our moves would be decided more by the petrol gauge than by tactical requirements.' One German motorised division needed 360 tons of fuel per day to keep moving, a feat which required the logistical support of almost 1,200 trucks driving 600 miles from Tripoli to Tobruk. The Italian army had around 7,000 trucks and was suffering a fuel crisis too.

Lieutenant General Sir Noel Beresford-Peirse took over command of the Western Desert Force as the replacement for General O'Connor who had been taken prisoner. More importantly, the British received a delivery of equipment and supplies when Convoy Tiger docked at Alexandria on 12 May. Deliveries included 50 Hurricane fighters and 200 tanks. There would have been more, but the 9,200-ton *Empire Song* hit a mine and sank, taking with it members of the crew, 57 tanks, several trucks and 10 aircraft.

On 15 May Wavell, encouraged by Rommel's failure to capture Tobruk, launched Operation Brevity. In command was Lieutenant General William 'Strafer' Gott, who with twenty-nine Cruiser tanks attacked the Italian's positions at Fort Capuzzo. Meanwhile, a slightly smaller force of twenty-four Matildas attacked German positions in the Halfaya Pass on the Libyan-Egyptian border. The aim of Brevity was to consolidate ground which would allow the British to launch a stronger attack to relieve Tobruk. The British scored a victory over the Germans and Italians at Halfaya Pass, driving them back, destroying 300 tanks and killing, wounding or taking prisoner 38,000. The outcome of the battle was favourable, but Gott became concerned about fighting in open terrain and the operation was terminated two days later.

The Germans spent the intervening time consolidating their forces and bringing up more supplies. Rommel made his next move on 26 May when he ordered a force of 160 tanks with infantry support to advance towards the Egyptian border. As it turned out, this was a ploy, but the British believed it and fearing they would be caught in a flanking attack, began to withdraw from the pass. Wasting no time, Rommel, the 'Desert Fox', rushed his forces into the pass and fortified it with artillery, including 88mm anti-tank guns which British tank crews were learning to fear. The Allies would soon come to call the position 'Hellfire Pass' and with good reason.

The next planned operation by the British was Battleaxe and had the same intention as Brevity in that it was meant to relieve Tobruk. It began on 15 June, but the Germans had advance knowledge through radio interceptions which referred to the operation by the codeword 'Peter'. The Germans knew of the British intentions because the Italians were intercepting the coded messages from the American military attaché in Cairo, Colonel Bonner Frank Fellers, which were then deciphered. Colonel Fellers was a most conscientious and capable officer, but unknown to him, or indeed anyone else at the embassy, was that a member of the Servizio Informazione Militare was working at the US Embassy in Rome and had stolen the so-called 'Black Code' in September 1941, copied it and returned the original to the embassy. Fellers was privy to British military plans and was passing on details to the Military Intelligence Division in Washington, which the Italians were intercepting, decoding and sending to Rommel. Such information was probably more vital than a convoy of supplies, because of the time and effort it saved. At the time America was not in the war and still had diplomatic relations with Italy. It is impossible to calculate how much damage had been done by the time the leak was finally discovered in June 1942 and the stream of information plugged.

Both sides were experiencing mechanical troubles with their vehicles, especially their tanks, with sand entering the air filters and clogging the air intakes. General Wavell assessed the shortcomings in British tank designs stating, 'Our infantry tanks are really too slow for a battle in the desert, and have been suffering considerable casualties from the powerful enemy anti-tank guns. Our Cruisers have little advantage in power and speed over the German medium tanks. Technical breakdowns are still too numerous.' The British attacked Halfaya Pass two days after the operation had opened, losing tanks in the fighting, but succeeded in pushing the Germans out of the Pass. Although other objectives were taken, Wavell decided to halt the attack which had cost him 969 casualties, killed, wounded and missing, and 91 tanks. The German and Italians had suffered a combined casualty rate of 1,270 killed, wounded and missing and lost 50 tanks. They remained on the battlefield to demonstrate to recover what they could, which included some British tanks. In the end, they managed to salvage all but twelve vehicles which could be returned to the battlefield. The British tanks were painted in German colours and used against their former owners in future engagements.

There now followed a pause in the war in North Africa. The Afrika Korps had regained all the territory the British had captured from the Italians. Churchill had hoped for a better outcome and on 1 July he replaced Wavell with Auchinleck as commander-in-chief in the Middle East. Meanwhile, against all odds, the garrison at Tobruk was holding out against the besieging Germans surrounding them. They had taken severe casualties and despite hardships, morale was still high. They were receiving supplies brought in under cover of darkness and these deliveries became known as the 'spud run'. The crews making these deliveries from Mersa Matruh and Alexandria, distances of 240 miles and 350 miles, became proficient at unloading their vessels quickly and embarking any casualties for the return trip. The garrison came to view a single cargo ship with just 5,000 tons of supplies worth the equivalent of twelve convoys. Then, the British managed to pull off the seemingly impossible and evacuated the men of the 9th Division with its Australian, Indian and British troops. Between August and October, three operations took out the exhausted garrison and replaced it with fresh troops and supplies. The first was Operation Treacle, conducted between 19 and 29 August. This was followed by Operation Supercharge, 19 to 27 September. The last was Operation Cultivate, between 12 and 25 October. In September, the Western Desert Force, which had achieved so much under General O'Connor, was now renamed the 8th Army and General Cunningham was appointed to command it.

Suddenly, in the early hours of the morning of 22 June, the main emphasis of the war was shifted away from North Africa as Hitler embarked on his next phase of the war. The war was twenty-one months old and still going in Germany's favour when Hitler ordered Directive 21 or 'Case Barbarossa', the code to launch the attack against the Soviet Union or Russia, as many still termed the country. Now the world would witness the full power of the Blitzkrieg as it was unleashed against a vast but largely unprepared enemy. Planning for this had been in place for several months with General Franz Halder being one of the senior officers involved. However, in May 1941 he found his attention being diverted away from the matter in hand due to events in North Africa. Rommel had been in command of the Afrika Korps for three months, but reports were being received which gave some cause for concern over his ability. General Halder commented: 'Rommel hasn't given us a clear report for days. I have a feeling something's gone wrong. All the comments I read in the officers' reports or in personal letters indicate that Rommel is in no way up to his leadership task. He storms around all day long with formations strewn all over the place, launches reconnaissance missions, fritters away his troops…'

Halder despatched his quartermaster, General Friedrich von Paulus, to assess the situation and complete a report. It was a critical moment in the planning stage of the forthcoming Russian campaign and a diversion Halder could have done without. Nevertheless, Hitler had to be appraised of what was happening in North Africa. On arriving, von Paulus wasted no time and set about preparing his report. The main trouble was pinpointed to Rommel's supply line which was in a terrible state of organisation. More weapons, tanks and aircraft would be needed but most importantly the advancing forces would need a minimum of 50,000 tons of supplies each month and the coastal shipping bringing the supplies forward could only cope with half that amount. Once delivered, the supplies had to be transported overland by trucks. If something was not done, the German army would suffer its first defeat of the war.

When he learned of the situation Halder stated, 'By overstepping his orders, Rommel has brought about a situation for which our present supply capabilities are not sufficient.' But by the time the situation report reached Halder, Rommel was on the Egyptian border which more than satisfied Hitler. In view of his success, more resources were sent to support Rommel. The attack against Russia would, over time, have a serious effect on the campaign in North Africa, which faltered as both campaigns vied with one another for resources.

Now all that mattered was the attack against Russia. All other aspects of the war, including the campaign in North Africa, seemed secondary. Hitler had never attended a military academy and his grasp of military strategy was, at best, fundamental, bordering on impulsive. He had no idea of the enormity of problems which lay before the German army in Russia. The historian Martin van Creveld commented, 'For the Russian campaign, the Wehrmacht never had sufficient means available, and this was even more true of raw materials, reserve stocks and means of transportation than it was of combat

Despite the propaganda, the German army relied on hundreds of thousands of horses to move supply wagons and artillery.

In Russia, the motorcycle proved invaluable. They could operate in either the liaison or reconnaissance roles.

forces.' The huge distances covered with apparent ease during the early phase of the campaign led Hitler to believe that another great victory lay ahead.

The Red Army was believed to have some 24,000 tanks. German intelligence believed most of these were obsolete and would not pose any problem to the modern tank forces of the German army. Likewise, the Soviet Red Air Force, with its outdated aircraft, would be shot out of the skies by the Luftwaffe's modern Messerschmitt Bf 109s flown by battle-experienced pilots. Within days of the start of the campaign German troops advanced deep into Russia with seemingly nothing to stop them. Anything which did stand in the way was either swept aside or simply bypassed and left to be dealt with by follow-on troops.

The scale of the attack was unprecedented and included three million troops in 146 divisions supported by three air fleets with over 1,800 aircraft. Seven armies and four Panzer groups with 3,580 armoured fighting vehicles, 7,184 pieces of artillery, 600,000 other vehicles for transport and liaison roles, and 750,000 horses were committed to the attack. The tank force included 1,440 PzKw IIIs, around 500 PzKw IVs, 410 older PzKw Is and 746 PzKw IIs, and a number of PzKw 35 (t) and 38 (t) tanks. This was Blitzkrieg on a grand scale and it had to be so because it was taking on a massive enemy.

Those senior commanders who privately believed that Hitler had taken on an enemy that was too strong for his armed forces soon forgot their worries when no serious opposition was encountered. Some commanders thought the Soviets were too weakened by the army 'purges' of 1937/8 when Stalin had ordered the liquidation of around 35,000 officers, which left the army with only ten per cent of its generals. One of the victims of the purges was Marshal Mikhail Tukhachevsky, an exponent of tank warfare who predicted that Germany would attack Russia. He believed that the country would survive because 'In the final result, all would depend on who had the greater moral fibre and who at the close of operations disposed of operational reserves in depth.' Almost two hundred years earlier Frederick the Great recognised this and placed emphasis on the provision of supplies for his troops while at the same time disrupting the enemy's lines of communication which would lead to the collapse of their supply lines.

The attack against Russia split Germany's forces which were now faced with war on three fronts: North Africa, the Eastern Front and occupying forces across western Europe. This latest move took some of the pressure off the Home Front in England by diverting aircraft away from bombing cities and factories. Winston Churchill in a conversation with his secretary John Colville said, 'If Hitler invaded hell I would at least make a favourable reference to the Devil in the House of Commons.' In a speech he said, 'No one has been a more consistent opponent of Communism than I have, but all this fades away before the spectacle that is now unfolding…Any man or state who fights on against Nazidom will have our aid.' Finally Britain now had an ally which could fight in Europe.

Despite Russia's great strength of arms on paper, Churchill sensed how unprepared the Russian army was in the face of the Blitzkrieg and he ordered that supplies be despatched with the first convoys sailing in August. In October Matilda Mk II tanks were sent to Russia even though the British army needed them for the fighting in North Africa. Stalin called for Britain to open a 'Second Front' (ignoring the fact that the British army was already at grips with the Germans in North Africa) and insisted that an attack be made against mainland Europe. Such a move was, in any case, impossible because the British army simply wasn't strong enough or sufficiently equipped.

Hitler said, 'We have only to kick in the front door and the whole rotten edifice will come tumbling down.' But his generals urged caution and tried to warn him against fighting on two fronts. He dismissed their opinions in characteristic manner.

Stalin at first refused to believe that Germany had attacked; after all the two countries had signed a non-aggression pact in 1939. It seemed even more extraordinary in view of the fact that only days previously Russia had sent Germany 1.5 million tons of wheat and 2 million tons of oil transported by train.

The attack against Russia was made along a front 500 miles wide and the Panzers made good headway as they seized bridges intact across the River Bug. Each day as they drove deeper into Russia their lines of supply became ever more stretched.

The German army pushed onwards under the umbrella of full air support. Within hours, tanks, trucks, motorcycles and other AFVs had advanced more than twenty miles. The Panzer IIIs and IVs rolled on, with trucks carrying infantry to keep pace, and bringing up fuel and ammunition to keep them supplied for battle. One unit of the LVI Corps, commanded by General Eric von Manstein, operating in the north, had advanced fifty miles before darkness fell on the first day. Army Group North, under Field Marshal Ritter von Leeb, smashed a gap 100 miles wide in the Russian defences and pressed toward Leningrad. By September this major city, lying on an isthmus, being bordered to the east by Lake Ladoga and to the west by the Gulf of Finland, was cut off and isolated, with German troops to the south and their Finnish allies to the north. It was now under siege, a situation which would last 872 days and not be lifted until 27 January 1944.

By the end of the first day's fighting almost 1,500 Russian aircraft had been destroyed, mostly on the ground, and those machines which did take off were shot down. The Russians conducted a brave fighting retreat, hoping to gain some time to allow them to consolidate, but the Germans were relentless and pressed onwards. Army Group Centre under Field Marshal Fedor von Bock pushed on towards Minsk as their primary objective, beyond which lay the greater prize, the city of Smolensk. Army Group South under von Rundstedt was temporarily slowed in its advance but was soon on its way again to lay siege to the port facilities at Odessa on the Black Sea and then on to the Crimea.

Just over a week after the commencement of the attack, German tanks were 200 miles into Russia and Army Group Centre was on the outskirts of Minsk. Once that had been captured the way would be open to Moscow. Resistance in Minsk, however, was much greater than the Germans had anticipated and the city was not captured until 9 July. By now the Russians had lost 324,000 troops captured along with 3,300 tanks and 1,800 pieces of artillery. Each delay in seizing their targets cost the Germans valuable time because they wanted to conclude the campaign before the onset of winter. They failed to recognise that the Russians were trying to buy time and as they fell back they left nothing for the Germans who would have to fight hard for anything they wished to capture.

Some of the German commanders, like Major General Hans von Greiffenberg, who served as Chief of Staff in Army Group B, later Army Group Centre, commanded by von Bock, realised that they were following in the footsteps of Napoleon's ill-fated campaign of 1812, but later stated, 'We did not think that the lessons of the 1812 campaign applied to us. We were fighting with modern means of transport and communication… We thought that the vastness of Russia could be overcome by rail and motor engine, telegraph wire and radio. We had absolute faith in the infallibility of Blitzkrieg.'

If the Germans understood the comparison, so too did their Russian counterparts. By falling back, they were using the tactic that had defeated the French in 1812. Everything of use to the French had been destroyed in the wake of their advance. 'Scorched earth' denied food and fuel to the invader meaning they could not live off supplies obtained locally. Stalin went on the radio to broadcast to the Russian people on 3 July and declared a 'national patriotic war', calling for everyone, soldier and citizen alike, to do their duty. He declared that not 'a single railway engine, a single wagon, a single pound of grain' should nor would be left for the enemy. If the broadcast was not heard, the words were published in newspapers and spread by word of mouth. The side effect was the starvation of the civilian population.

Such drastic measures meant the Germans would have to bring everything forward or face the prospect of the campaign collapsing. It looked as though history was going to repeat itself. Every mile the Germans advanced meant another mile further to bring food, ammunition and fuel. It has been opined that the most inhibiting factor in the conduct of land operations, except the combatants' morale and fighting ability, was logistics. If a nation is possessed of enough space and can maintain its will to fight, then an invading enemy army will eventually reach a point when it must stop short of complete conquest due to logistic failure. Russia had the space to fall back and in doing so it was giving the Germans the impression that they were winning. The Russian officers ensured that morale held and meted out harsh punishments, including executions, for those who failed. Officers who failed in their duty were expected to commit suicide such as the commander of the air force Lieutenant General Kopets who shot himself. Lulled into a false sense of security the Germans continued with their advance and captured huge numbers of prisoners and materiel and destroyed tanks, trucks and artillery. The Russian will to fight would remain unbroken.

Meanwhile, the fighting in North Africa continued and as winter approached both sides were making their preparations for attack. This time, however, it was the British who knew Rommel's intentions because the German code had been broken. Armed with this advantage the British launched Operation Crusader on 18 November. The two sides clashed at Sidi Rezegh, where a small but useful airstrip was located. The British 7th Armoured Division with 453 tanks, including some American M3 Honeys, was facing the 15th and 21st Panzer Divisions with 272 tanks, many of which were in desperate need of maintenance. The intention of the attack was to drive the Germans back and so relieve the garrison at Tobruk. In addition, there was the British 1st Army Tank Brigade attached to XIII Corps with another 135 tanks including Matilda Mk IIs and the newer Valentines which were fast but still lacking heavy guns.

The weather was appalling with heavy rain but the British advanced and made good gains. The following day the 22nd Armoured Brigade, equipped with Crusader tanks, engaged the Italian Ariete Division at Bir el Gubi and destroyed 34 tanks, but lost 25 in the process. The brigade lost a further thirty due to mechanical failure and were forced to retire. At Sidi Rezegh the Crusader tanks of 7th Armoured Brigade took the Italians by surprise and managed to destroy a number of their aircraft on the ground. The Italians quickly rallied and prevented the British from linking up with the garrison at Tobruk.

At Gabr Saleh, some fifty miles south of Tobruk, the German unit known as Kampfgruppe Stephan, with eighty-five tanks, engaged the 4th Armoured Brigade equipped with the light M3 tanks in the first large-scale tank battle of the desert war so far. The Germans had artillery support and anti-tank guns and although each side claimed a victory it was the British who withdrew, having lost twenty-three tanks.

Rommel turned his attention against Tobruk, having issued orders on 22 November directing the 15th and 21st Panzer Divisions to concentrate on Gabr Saleh and move on to Sidi Rezegh. This was what the British wanted, but it did not go as well as they hoped because Rommel had made better preparations and virtually destroyed the 7th Armoured Brigade which was left with only ten serviceable tanks after the engagement.

General Ludwig Crüwell headed to Bir el Gubi where he joined forces with the Italian Ariete Division. Together they exploited a gap in the line between XXX Corps and XIII Corps, but Crüwell was prevented from breaking through by the 5th South African Infantry Brigade. During the fighting the South Africans lost 3,400 killed or taken prisoner. The remnants of the 22nd Armoured Brigade with only 34 tanks and some artillery were also in the gap and they made a stand. Crüwell had 160 tanks and a further 100 Italian tanks and with such superior numbers he charged recklessly at the British positions. It cost him dearly with the loss of 70 tanks, but the action had also caused the British to spend their last reserves and they were forced to withdraw. Night was falling. Rommel was watching events at Sidi Rezegh and wrote, 'Visibility was poor and many British tanks and guns were able to break away to the south without being caught. But a great part of the enemy force still remained inside.' He went on, 'hundreds of burning vehicles, tanks and guns lit up the field.' He called the scene 'Totensonntag' (Sunday of the Dead).

Serving as a tank commander with the 4th Armoured Brigade was Lieutenant Cyril Joly who later wrote about his experience of Sidi Rezegh: 'It was a frightening and awful spectacle – the dead and dying strewn over the battlefield, in trucks and Bren-carriers, in trenches and toppled over in death, others vocal with pain and stained by red gashes of flowing blood or the dark marks of old congealed wounds. Trucks, guns, ammunition, odd bits of clothing were smouldering or burning with bright tongues of fire. Here and there ammunition had caught fire and was exploding with spurts of flame and black smoke. Tanks of all kinds – Italian, German and British – littered the whole area.'

Operation Crusader was continuing with mounting losses on both sides. On 24 November Rommel travelled towards Tobruk where he met General Crüwell who believed that most of the British forces were destroyed. The fighting was proving an anxious time as men's nerves were tested to the limit. One of those who gave in under the strain was General Cunningham who believed that the Germans were about to score a great victory over British forces. General Auchinleck, now nicknamed 'the Auk' by the troops, came forward to relieve him of his command. The Auk had 750,000 men in North Africa, with a fleet of 10,000 vehicles, mostly assigned to garrison and support roles to maintain the supply lines, and drivers and mechanics to service the trucks. The force gave the British numerical superiority over the Germans and Italians, but such numbers placed a strain on the supply chain because each man had to be fed and the vehicles supplied with fuel.

Auchinleck put paid to any notion of a retreat from Sidi Rezegh. Crüwell discussed his options with Rommel and suggested they counter-attack towards Sidi Rezegh with a view to holding the airfield. Rommel agreed, knowing full well that his manpower was weakened and his supplies running short. The attack was launched regardless. The British held their positions but adopted a new tactic of allowing the tanks through then closing the gaps to separate them from their supporting infantry and supply columns. These units were then systematically destroyed. Auchinleck now brought in Major General Neil Ritchie to take over the duties of Cunningham as commander of the 8th Army. He had taken part in the Dunkirk campaign and was known for his calmness and decision-making abilities. Auchinleck also ordered General Freyberg VC, with his tough 2nd New Zealand Division, to push through towards Tobruk.

Tobruk was still under siege by the Germans but the garrison of Australian and British troops was holding on. While they held this port facility they could still receive supplies which helped their position. But it was not a situation which could last indefinitely. It was becoming increasingly apparent that logistics were the key factor which would decide the outcome. Whichever side had the best supply lines and most abundant stocks would ultimately win.

The Italians had the most experience in fighting in North Africa, yet they failed to recognise the importance of building supply dumps of food, fuel and ammunition along the intended route of advance. They had to bring their supplies along the same route as the Germans and the same distance from Tripoli up to Sollum, almost 1,000 miles. As the campaign continued, the Italians faced a shortage of vehicles of all descriptions, but mainly trucks. It had been a problem almost from the beginning of the North African campaign in 1940 and by 1942 it was reaching crisis point. Shortages of trucks meant shortages of everything else from water to ammunition and fuel. Out of a fleet of 8,600 trucks in mid-1941, around half were not serviceable. This was down from the original fleet of 16,500 trucks in 1940. In August 1942, the Italians had around 40,000 men engaged in logistics. They required a minimum of 11,000 replacement troops each month but this number was not forthcoming. Their refusal to build supply dumps affected their operational capabilities. They failed to understand the importance of such measures and preferred to move supplies as and when needed. If they had static lines they could be supplied but when the forces were mobile they were often let down.

German supplies had to be sent from ports in Italy and landed at Tripoli. From there, everything had to be loaded onto trucks and driven along the single route known as the 'Via Balbia', which stretched almost 500 miles to El Agheila, then on to Tobruk another 500 miles. The cost in fuel was extraordinarily high, but there was no alternative if supplies were to be moved. Italian trucks broke down under the strain and servicing and repairs were a constant feature which slowed down deliveries. The Germans considered air lift as an option, which was one reason why the airfield at Sidi Rezegh was important to Rommel.

This long route was open to attack by aircraft of the RAF and also long-range raiding units such as the Long Range Desert Group (LRDG) and the Special Air Service (SAS) which struck fast and withdrew. The Germans began escorting their supply columns with armoured cars which were fast and carried heavier fire power than the LRDG.

In 1941, at the start of Hitler's involvement in the North African campaign, German troops and supplies were sent to Italy where they embarked on German ships for transportation to Tripoli. But losses to British aircraft and Royal Navy submarines operating from Malta forced the Germans to use Italian ships as replacements. Air lifts were used because they were faster, but transport aircraft such as the Junkers Ju52 could not carry a sufficient payload and its own fuel for the flight to make it worthwhile. Shipping was the only solution, even though losses were high. For example, in September 1941 almost one fifth of all German supplies were sunk.

The quartermaster-general's branch was given the task of organising deliveries of supplies. The Kommandeur Rückwärttiges Armeegebiet (rear commandant) or Koruck was responsible for delivering supplies to the Panzergruppe and stockpiling supplies for future operations. Supplies were sent along the coast road to the front, and then despatched to those units operating in the interior to the south such as Msus and Bir Hakeim. Shortages and threats to Rommel's supply dumps by the British during Operation Crusader meant that he would be restricted in what he could achieve. For example, on 22 November the 2nd New Zealand Division forced the 21st Panzer Division near Gamut to evacuate its supply dumps. Ammunition stocks of all calibres became critical, including tank shells, but especially 2cm anti-aircraft ammunition. In fact, it would be this shortage of supplies that forced Rommel to break off the attack. It was the only option left open to him. When he withdrew west the British advanced, which meant it was now their turn to extend their supply lines. Now, with shorter distances to cover, Rommel's fuel and ammunition could be brought up and stockpiled in readiness for the next offensive.

On 24 November 1941 Rommel advanced with a mixed force of 106 Italian and German tanks making a grasp at the Egyptian border. It failed and would prove to be his swansong in this round of the fighting. Some of the garrison at Tobruk fought their way out and headed towards Sidi Rezegh where they attacked the Italians and forced them away from their positions. Freyberg's New Zealand troops joined in the fight and turned the Italian defeat into a complete rout. Down to his last remaining forty tanks Rommel finally turned westwards and headed past Tobruk and on towards Derna. On 10 December, British troops entered Tobruk to relieve the garrison. Churchill, on 11 December, addressed the House of Commons to relay the good news, stating, 'The enemy, who has fought with the utmost stubbornness and enterprise, has paid the price for his valour, and it may well be that the second phase of the Battle of Libya will gather more easily the fruits of the first than has been our experience.' He continued, 'I will go so far on this occasion as to say that all the danger of the Army of the Nile not being able to celebrate Christmas and the New Year in Cairo has been decisively removed.'

Rommel realised the campaign was over but was sufficiently experienced to know that although he had lost the battle, the war was far from being over. The fighting had cost the Germans and Italians more than 38,000 killed, wounded and captured along with 340 tanks destroyed or damaged. Gathering his forces together with his last few remaining operational tanks he conducted a well organised retreat, all the while being strafed by aircraft of the RAF. It was not only on land he had been beaten, but also at sea where his supply ships were being sunk. In November alone the Royal Navy and RAF had sunk sixteen supply ships vital to the fighting capability of the Afrika Korps, amounting to a total of 60,000 tons of fuel, ammunition and other equipment. The cost of Operation Crusader to the British and Commonwealth troops was 17,700 killed and wounded and more than 800 tanks destroyed, battle damaged or broken down. Most importantly, they had managed to deny the port facilities at Tobruk to Rommel.

The British had advanced almost 500 miles against the Italians between December 1940 and February 1941 until Rommel arrived and pushed them back almost to their starting point. Now, as the end of the year approached, they were poised to advance once again and cover the same old ground. The experienced troops, the 'old soldiers', called the campaign the 'Benghazi handicap' or 'Benghazi stakes' as if it was a horse race. This time, though, things would be different. They now had the M3 Honey. Later, more American-built tanks would be sent to the theatre, including the M3 Lee-Grant Medium Tank, under the Lend-Lease agreement. Factories in America were now producing hundreds of tanks and between July and December 1941 some 2,000 Lee-Grant tanks were built. In fact, these designs and other American equipment would be tested in battle by the British many months before America entered the war. Rommel lacked such supplies of replacement equipment and his forces frequently pressed into service captured British vehicles such as Matilda Mk IIs and Marmon-Herrington armoured cars.

The Mk I Marmon-Herrington entered service in 1940 followed by the Mk II in the same year. By the time of the North African campaign around 900 had been produced, some of which were deployed against the Italians in East Africa in March 1941. The Mk II Marmon-Herrington had armoured protection between 6mm and 12mm and could reach speeds up to 50mph. Armed with a Boys .55inch anti-tank rifle and two .303inch machine guns it had an operational range of 200 miles. Modifications produced the Mk III and Mk IIIa versions and some of these had their weaponry changed on the battlefield to mount heavier calibre weapons including captured enemy weapons with 20mm and 47mm calibres taken from Italian and German vehicles.

Other vehicles to be used in North Africa included the Mk IV Cruiser tank, already mentioned above. The British tank used in North Africa had entered service in late 1938 and by the time production ended in 1939, only 335 vehicles had been built. The Mk IV had been used in France in 1940 and although its armour protection between 6mm and 38mm gave protection against machine gun it was not sufficient against anti-tank guns such as the PaK 36 3.7cm or PaK 38 5cm and certainly not against the heavier guns. It was armed with a 2-pounder gun, a co-axial mounted .303inch calibre Vickers machine gun, and smoke grenade dischargers on the turret. The turret had sharply sloped faces to deflect projectiles, but the lower half of the turret sloped sharply inwards towards the hull which could allow anti-tank shells to become trapped or deflected to the base of the turret. The Cruiser went into service with some units of the 7th Armoured Division and the Christie-type suspension performed well in the desert conditions. Overall the

The Marmon-Herrington Mk III was an armoured car designed and built in South Africa and used by British and Commonwealth forces in North Africa for reconnaissance roles.

tank was useful, but it was finally withdrawn from that theatre of operations in 1942. While the Germans often pressed into service any useful vehicle or weapon the Cruiser tanks do not appear to have been worth their while. Instead, they stripped captured vehicles of anything useful and what was left consigned to the scrap heap.

The war in North Africa was defined by regular forces organised into battalions, brigades, divisions and corps, and newspapers reported on the battles between these units. Cameramen for cinematic newsreel also filmed these engagements to be shown to the public in their respective countries. The side of the war they did not, indeed could not show, were the operations conducted by the so-called irregular forces. One of the first of these units to come into being was the Long Range Desert Group, the LRDG. The LRDG was formed on 3 July 1940 and initially comprised 11 officers and 76 NCOs and privates. They used vehicles such as the Chevrolet WB 30cwt (1.5 ton) trucks and mounted their first operations in August and September that year. The aim of their mission was to disrupt the supply lines of the Italians, who at the time were fighting on their own, and destroy their fuel dumps. They also gathered information regarding enemy movements, dispositions and the size of their formations.

Over the next two years the LRDG continued to increase in size and firepower and by March 1942 there were some 350 men with 110 vehicles of various types such as Bedford and Chevrolet trucks, along with American-built Jeeps. The vehicles carried

The Vickers Mk II Light Tank was a product of the 1930s and obsolete before the outbreak of war. It served as a training vehicle for tank crews.

all the equipment and supplies needed for extended patrols and with supply dumps they could remain on patrol for weeks and cover thousands of miles. By creating supply dumps along their lines of operations the LRDG could extend their operational range to more than 1,000 miles, which allowed them to penetrate deep behind enemy lines. The method of creating supply dumps to allow the period of operations to be extended was nothing new. The tactic had been used by the Duke of Marlborough during his campaigns in the eighteenth century. Now, over 200 years later the same principle was being used in modern warfare.

The supply of water was a major problem facing all armies in North Africa and any way of conserving supplies was important. Water was also essential to vehicles which used it in their radiators to cool the engines and required filling up periodically. One method devised by the LRDG to conserve water was to use a system to condense the water by fitting a hose to the radiator which led into a container secured to the front grille of the vehicle. As the steam vented from the radiator it would turn back into water as it cooled, to be saved in the container to be poured back into the radiator. It was simplicity itself and many vehicles in the desert were fitted with the method. Major R.A. Bagnold of the Royal Signals, attached to the LRDG, remembered this method and how it worked. He recalled how 'one lost water when the radiator began to boil, and blew water off through the overflow. So instead of having a free overflow pipe, we led the water into a can half full of water on the side of the car, so it would condense in the can. When that began to boil too it would spurt boiling water over the driver, who would have to stop. All we had to do was turn into wind, wait for perhaps a minute [while a vacuum built up], there'd be a gurgling noise, and all the water would be sucked into the radiator, which was full to the brim.'

The year after the LRDG was formed a new unit was created, called the Special Air Service. For its size the SAS inflicted huge losses to the Italians and Germans out of all proportion to the size of the unit. Raised in July 1941 in North Africa as the idea of Captain David Stirling of the Scots Guards, who had earlier served in No 8 Commando, the unit worked closely with the LRDG and learned much from it. Operating over great distances, being independent and self-contained, they hit at pre-planned targets and targets of opportunity. These 'hit and run' tactics frustrated the enemy and tied down troops who would otherwise be engaged in frontline battles. Five months after being formed the SAS helped the British campaign in North Africa enormously when, during two weeks in December, patrols destroyed some ninety aircraft on the ground. Such attacks denied Rommel air cover during his operations. Eighteen months later, on 10 July 1943, an SAS patrol attacked a battery of artillery at Capo Murrodi Porco, destroying six guns and killing many.

An offshoot of the SAS was the Special Boat Service (SBS) and, like their counterparts, they too tied down large numbers of enemy troops. While the SAS operated primarily on land the SBS used kayaks to paddle to their objectives and sometimes used captured vehicles to help complete their mission. For example, on Crete during the night of 13 June an SBS group destroyed aircraft and supply dumps at Kastelli. Nine days later they struck again, this time attacking four air bases including the airfield at Peza, where they destroyed 4,400 gallons of fuel along with more aircraft.

As the campaign in North Africa was being fought, the German advance into Russia was continuing and penetrating deep into the country. The front was broad and at times commanders found themselves engaging in inter-unit rivalry as they competed with one another to see who could capture the next target. One such officer was Heinz Guderian, who had charged into France in 1940, and was now invariably to be found way out in front. From the very beginning of the attack his 2nd Panzer Group was out in the lead. In only 25 days, between 22 June and 16 July, the unit had covered 413 miles from Brest-Litovsk to Smolensk, covering an average distance of more than sixteen miles per day. Breakdown rates for tanks was still around 30% and to prevent this from becoming worse, armoured advances were often slowed or halted after 300 miles to carry out maintenance, and resupply with ammunition and fuel. Any long delays, it was thought, would give the Russians an opportunity to withdraw, regroup and prepare defences. The more the Russians withdrew, the more German commanders saw it as a chance to pursue an enemy they believed was broken. The problem was, they sometimes forewent the vital maintenance needed to keep the vehicles operational and paid the price at a later date.

Field Marshal Gunther von Kluge, commanding the Fourth Panzer Army, recognised Guderian's eagerness to press on with the aim of capturing the city of Smolensk which at the time lay 200 miles further east. Telling Guderian 'Your operations always hang by a thread,' he nevertheless allowed his subordinate to charge ahead. It was a calculated risk which paid dividends when the city was captured on 16 July.

Some German tank crews had combat experience from previous campaigns, but most of the Russians had never been in a battle before. The only Russian general with recent battle experience was Georgi Zhukov, fighting in the defence of Leningrad in the north. One of his engagements had been the Battle of Khalkhin Gol on 20 August 1939, where he had enjoyed armoured and air superiority with 500 tanks against some 180 Japanese tanks. His 500 aircraft gave him air cover to support his tank force which comprised of Bistrokhodny BT-5 and BT-7 designs which dated from 1935 and were armed with 47mm guns. Protected by armour plate 22m thick and capable of speeds up 45mph, at the time they had been equal to the Japanese tanks, but now against heavier, more powerfully armed German tanks they were no match.

From the time of Germany's attack in June to December 1941, the Russians lost at least 17,000 tanks in battle while the Germans lost only 2,700. The reason for such high losses was not just down to poor designs of Russian tanks, but also poor tactics on the battlefield. Russian commanders at the time did not have the skill to compete with

German commanders. One tank design which did hold its own against German tanks was the KV-1 (Klim Voroshilov) which was heavier and armed with a 76.2mm calibre gun which could knock out Panzer III and Panzer IVs. Unfortunately, the Russians only had some 500 such tanks in service, but they did have greater numbers of T34 entering service, also armed with a 76.2mm main gun. The Germans had yet to meet this formidable design in combat and if they guessed at its existence they were still taken by surprise when it made its first appearance.

Following the opening stages of the attack the Russians lost tens of thousands of tanks, trucks and pieces of artillery, but later their capacity to replace these losses would astound the Germans. Between 1941 and 1945 Russian factories produced 100,000 tanks, the same number of aircraft and 175,000 pieces of artillery. The supplies the Western Allies sent were useful and at first were the only way of ensuring the country's chance of survival, but later were dwarfed by what the country could produce for itself.

Russia may have been caught unprepared but it soon stirred itself into action and stunned the world with what it could achieve. The most pressing task they faced was to prevent the armaments factories and other vital industry from falling into German hands. To this end the Russians moved over 1,500 factories hundreds and even thousands of miles east of the Ural Mountains, which put them beyond the reach of the Germans. In terms of percentages, 15% was sent to the Volga district, 44% to the Urals, 21% to Siberia and 20% to Soviet Central Asia. The move required the support of 1.5 million railway wagons. The entire factory staff of 16.5 million went with their machines, tools and equipment. Within a year of this upheaval the factories managed to produce 24,500 tanks in the second half of 1942. The following year this figure peaked at 30,000 vehicles. The men and women worked up to twelve hours a day often six days a week in half-completed factory buildings in sub-zero temperatures. Russia had forty-two factories dedicated solely to the production of tanks and between them they built 18,000 KV tanks and 40,000 T-34 tanks.

As the weeks passed the weather began to change with the first rains of autumn to be followed by the winter freeze. This was the period the Russians called 'Rasputitsa', the time without roads, when vehicles could not move. Apart from the main routes, the country's road network consisted largely of unprepared dirt roads which would be rendered impassable by the weather. In fact, across this vast country there were only 40,000 miles of roads which had been properly engineered with metalled surfaces and the railway had only 50,000 miles. Snow, rain and ice would turn the roads into muddy routes which sucked in everything and slowed vehicles to a crawl. Colonel General Erich Hoepner, commanding 4th Panzer Group, wrote that 'The roads have become quagmires – everything has come to a halt. Our tanks cannot move. No fuel can get through to us, the heavy rain and fog make airdrops impossible.' On a more optimistic note he continued, 'give us fourteen days of frost. Then we will surround Moscow.' The frosts came, but with such severity that everything froze, including oil, and frostbite was endemic without adequate winter clothing. The same conditions affected the Russians, but they knew the terrain and conditions and being more experienced in dealing with such hardship they could cope.

The initial phase of Barbarossa had been launched using 3.6 million men and 3,600 tanks, supported by 2,700 aircraft. It represented the largest attacking force in history. Standing against this tidal wave of military power the Russians had 2.7 million men, organised into 140 divisions and forty brigades supported by 10,000 tanks and 8,000 aircraft. From the beginning, the attack had gone in Germany's favour but several weeks into the campaign, with continuous combat, troops were becoming exhausted and vehicles, especially tanks, were beginning to require maintenance.

German High Command had estimated that the main bulk of the fighting would be over after six to eight weeks and the way would be clear to advance on the strategic centres of Moscow, Leningrad and Kiev. On 3 July, General Halder wrote, 'It is no exaggeration to say that the campaign in Russia has been won in 14 days.' He was, of course, being frightfully over–optimistic. The following month he had cause to revise his assessment, when on 11 August he stated that 'It is increasingly clear that we underestimated the Russian colossus…We believed that the enemy had about 200 divisions. Now we are counting 360. These forces are not always well-armed and equipped and they are often poorly led. But they are there.'

On 8 July, von Bock made his own report on the successes of the campaign so far, which had only just entered its third week. In it he listed that Army Group Centre had destroyed four Soviet armies comprising 32 infantry divisions, 8 armoured divisions and many other elements including 3 cavalry divisions which resulted in hundreds of thousands of Russians killed and more than another 287,000 taken prisoner. The Russians had lost over 1,500 pieces of artillery and 2,500 tanks. Two weeks after the first situation reports had been filed the Germans calculated they had captured or killed three million Russian troops and destroyed 12,000 tanks and 8,000 aircraft.

As in North Africa, German recovery units were usually able to send repaired tanks back to the line in twelve hours. In theory and when spares were available that level could be achieved, but as the advance moved further into Russia and with the onset of winter things became more complicated. The campaign had begun with a fleet of 200,000 trucks to support the supply routes but this figure consisted of more than 200 different types of vehicle, including vehicles captured from France, Belgium and Poland. When these broke down it was almost impossible to locate spares for even the most basic of repairs. In such cases the vehicles had to be written off which compounded the problem of shortages.

On 11 July while the generals were delivering their verdicts their armies were still ten miles short of Kiev and a halt had to be called for vehicle maintenance and resupplies to be brought forward if the attack was to continue. By now, the tanks had covered hundreds of miles on their tracks. In one instance, the tanks of one unit advanced an incredible 72 miles in 24 hours. The lighter trucks and motorcycles were covering thousands of miles as they traversed backwards and forwards along the supply routes carrying orders and moving supplies. Engines had to be overhauled and repairs made but all the time they were expected to keep up the pressure and attack. Army Group North, commanded by General von Leeb, headed north to invest Leningrad to the east of the Finnish border. It was planned to besiege, reduce and capture the city.

By now, stocks of ammunition and fuel were beginning to run low and lacking sufficient numbers of suitable supply vehicles with good cross-country abilities to reach units in the remote areas, things were slowing down to allow supplies to be brought forward. Even so, the Germans managed to capture the important centres of Bialystok, Minsk and Smolensk on the route towards Moscow. The southern flank of Army Group Centre moved towards the city of Kiev which the Russians had designated as the Kiev Special Military District with a defence force of 56 divisions supported by 5,600 tanks including 1,000 of the new KV-1 and T-34 types.

Frontline troops had their own opinions of the campaign, especially among the tank crews, who discovered their guns, not even the 75mm calibre, were powerful enough to penetrate the armour of the heavier Russian KV-2 and T-34 tanks. They devised a method to deal with them. The tactic was radical and called for them to move in very close and very fast with the intention of shooting off the tracks, thereby crippling them to be dealt with by anti-tank guns. This realisation their guns were not sufficiently powerful to destroy the latest Russian tanks led to the Germans entering a gun/armour race. In the factories, German designers developed ways to fit ever more powerful guns to the tanks, such as the 88mm, and improving on the performance of ammunition. All these improvements would benefit the soldiers on the front line, but these developments took time to implement and filter down the supply lines to the soldiers themselves.

On 12 September, Kiev was finally surrounded but the fighting continued to rage for nearly another week. Cut off from reinforcements and with ammunition and supplies running out the Russian defenders were left with no choice but to surrender. This left the Germans having to deal with 600,000 prisoners of war. The Russian soldiers had lost heart to resist, and, being largely of peasant stock, were quite passive after their commanding officers had been removed.

The campaign against Russia was now 100 days old, 3.5 million men had been taken prisoner and by all estimates the bulk of the tank force, artillery and air force had been smashed. The campaign had cost the Germans 400,000 casualties but in view of the odds, it was still looking favourable for them. The number of prisoners were a strain on logistics, having to feed them, and guard them. If they worked they would be fed, otherwise they starved. On 13 November, Eduard Wagner, quartermaster-general, issued orders to his heads of department instructing them that 'prisoners of war who are not working will have to starve.' By early February 1942 it is estimated that as many as sixty per cent of the Russians taken prisoner in 1941 had died. By 1945 the Germans had taken 5.7 million Russians prisoner, of which over 3.3 million died, mainly as a result of Wagner's order.

On 1 October 1941, Hitler ordered his next move in the campaign, Operation Typhoon, which called for the all-out advance against Moscow. This was something which Field Marshal Walther von Brauchitsch had proposed to Hitler in December 1940 during the early planning stages of Barbarossa. In drawing up his plans to attack Russia, Hitler had not originally identified the importance of Moscow as a target, seeing it merely as a 'geographical expression' rather than the centre of operations and the headquarters from where Stalin ruled. Now, almost a year later, he had changed his mind and committed 1.9 million men with 14,000 pieces of artillery, nearly 1,400 aircraft and 1,000 tanks, to the task of capturing the city.

As impressive as it all sounded, by now his armies were weakened with tank losses of up to fifty-six per cent on average and ammunition supplies depleted to a level which was only sufficient for four days fighting. At the start of the campaign there had been an ammunition stock for sixty days continuous fighting. Fuel was in short supply and lack of food was affecting the troops. Nevertheless, the operation went ahead and two weeks later the German spearhead tanks were approaching the outskirts of Moscow. At this stage in the campaign the Germans had captured 47% of Russia's agricultural lands, seized 41% of its rail network and were in possession of 62% of the country's coal output along with 68% of its steel and 60% of its aluminium production.

The bad weather which the Russians had hoped for began to set in, bringing with it the first autumn rains that washed out the roads and reduced the German advance to a slow crawl. On 10 October Stalin appointed Zhukov to the task of defending Moscow. The Russians took advantage of the delay the bad weather caused to the Germans and used the time to build up reserves. In a space of only three weeks 84 divisions had been moved to the west away from Siberia, giving Zhukov 1.25 million men to defend the city. They were supported by 10,600 pieces of artillery, 930 aircraft and 850 tanks including more units equipped with the new T-34 and KV tanks. It had been a prodigious feat of logistics and, best of all, the Germans were not aware of the move. Over the following two weeks more reinforcements were sent into the city. Over 100,000 men arrived along with another 1,000 pieces of artillery and 300 tanks. The railway system serving Moscow was intact, despite being attacked by the Luftwaffe's bombers. Damaged tracks were repaired to keep the flow of supplies and reinforcements entering the city. On their return journey locomotives took out machinery and evacuated 500 factories from around Moscow, along with other manufacturing equipment to prevent it from falling into German hands should they capture the city.

On 7 November Stalin addressed the defenders of the city who were assembled in the Red Square outside the Kremlin. He declared that if 'the German invaders want a war of extermination against the peoples of the Soviet Union. Very well then! If they want a war of extermination, they shall have it.' The country had a manpower reserve of 16 million men of military age it could call on to commit to the fight, and 50 divisions and 3,000 aircraft in the east to guard against an attack by Japan. Moreover, when the Japanese bombed Pearl Harbor on 7 December 1941, turning their attention against Singapore and Malaya, the Russians realised they were no longer at risk of attack from the east. The majority were moved to reinforce the western front. As these troops arrived in Moscow they were ushered onto all available civilian transport including taxis and buses, which had been commandeered to move them to their positions on the western front in a scene reminiscent of London and Paris in the First World War.

The workers and civilians of Moscow were also mobilised into work details numbering 450,000 and between them they dug 60 miles of anti-tank ditches and 5,000 miles of trenches.

Finally the ground had frozen sufficiently to allow the German tanks to move once more, but there were other complications. Temperatures frequently plummetted to below minus 30 degrees. The Russians refer to this as 'General Winter', one of their greatest defending officers. Radiators burst, water-pumps froze and fuel and oil solidified in the tanks and sumps of the fleet of 27,000 vehicles supporting the advance. The Germans had never experienced anything like it and had made few if any preparations for these extreme conditions. Men froze to death and frostbite weakened units. The weather was causing more casualties and destroying more vehicles than the fighting and General Winter was living up to his reputation. Fodder could not be brought forward for the horses and they died in their thousands.

Yet, even under these conditions the Germans somehow still managed to advance so that on 27 November they were less than twenty miles from the centre of Moscow. On the same day General Wagner, quartermaster-general, stated, 'We are at the end of our resources in both personnel and materiel. We are about to be confronted with the changes of deep winter.'

The German army had been living off the land in Russia, to the cost of the civilians and farmers whose food they stole. They took 7 million tons of wheat, 17 million head of cattle, 20 million pigs, 27 million sheep and goats, along with a hundred million chickens and other domestic fowl. The army could feed itself this way but it was not a long-term proposition. With farms destroyed and the farming communities killed, this stock could not be replaced.

Day by day the rate of the German advance became perceptibly slower, a fact which did not go unnoticed by the Russians. On 4 December, the last operational tank in service with the 1st Panzer Division, which the troops nicknamed 'Antony the Last', finally broke down. On 5 December, the Russians launched their counter-attack across a front 600 miles wide. German weapons were frozen solid and could not fire. The Russians, supported by T-34 tanks, some straight from the factories and not even painted, attacked in overwhelming numbers and forced the Germans back, leaving behind in their wake the abandoned vehicles which were useless in any case due to the weather and lack of fuel. The attack would continue until March 1942, all the while pushing back the Germans, in some place ninety miles and more than twice that distance in other places. One Russian soldier wrote, 'We sped forward, slowed only by the terrain.' Thousands of villages and towns which had been captured by the Germans only months earlier were now being liberated. The German army had never encountered such an attack and by early spring 1942 they had lost 500,000 men, 1,300 tanks, 2,500 pieces of artillery and 15,000 other vehicles including transportation trucks. Field Marshal Fedor von Bock voiced his concerns as early as 16 December reporting, 'Because of the shortage of fuel and because of icy roads I am not getting my motorised units back; I am not even getting my horse-drawn artillery back because the horses cannot manage the weather.' Russian tanks with their wider tracks and the trucks with higher ground clearance than the German vehicles meant they could cope with the snow and mud better than the German designs.

The only failure was at Demyansk, where the Russians hoped to encircle the 96,000 troops of the II Corps which was part of the 16th Army. They had managed to manoeuvre to take up positions on three sides, but they could just not manage to close the gap at the rear to cut off the unit. It was decided to use the Luftwaffe to supply the encircled position, a task which required an air fleet of 500 Ju 52 transport aircraft. Over a period of ten weeks they flew up to 150 flights per day to transport 65,000 tons of supplies, at an average delivery rate of over 900 tons each day, and evacuated 34,500 wounded on return flights. The operation had been costly and the Luftwaffe lost 265 aircraft in the process. Going in their favour was the fact the Soviets had few aircraft to intercept the supply aircraft. The men at Demyansk would not be relieved until the end of April 1942.

In the north, the Luftwaffe mounted a similar support action, but on a much reduced scale, at Kholm, south of Leningrad. Here the operation managed to support a garrison of 5,500 troops by air supply between 23 January and 5 May 1942 after it was cut off for 105 days. At this stage in the campaign the Germans were still capable of mounting such rescue missions because they had the resources.

Being a Communist state there was no private enterprise in Soviet Russia. The state owned everything, including all manufacturing. There was a motor industry to produce vehicles for a range of purposes including the military, but like the collective farming policy which controlled agricultural output, there was a 'Five Year Plan' which governed how industry should operate. Stalin had come to power in 1922 and four years later the first Five Year Plan was implemented, running from 1928 to 1933, during which time the AMO factory near Moscow began producing Italian-designed 1.5 ton trucks. The GAZ factory was built at Gorky, covering an area of 256 acres and employed a workforce of 12,000, making it the largest plant of its type in Europe. GAZ also produced 1.5-ton American-designed trucks called the Model AA and together these two factories increased production from 50,000 vehicles in the first Five Year Plan to more than 200,000 by the second Five Year Plan. Other factories were also built, including the ZIS (Zavod Imieni Stalin) and YAG (Yaroslav Automobilini Zavod), which added to the output of trucks.

The Russian army used the 2.5ton AAA built by GAZ as the standard truck. Apart from transporting troops and supplies it could also be fitted with mountings for weapons, such as quadruple machine guns for the anti-aircraft roles. Other trucks, including the 6X4 ZIS-6, were adapted to carry the rocket artillery systems nicknamed 'Stalin Organs', which terrified the Germans with their shrieking noise. Russia produced 2.5-ton half-tracks for use as artillery tractors and between 1933 and 1940 well over one million trucks were built by the factories of GAZ and KIM. The Americans supplied vast numbers of vehicles including the utilitarian Jeep, which did not fail to impress the Russians. In fact, the vehicle designers at the GAZ factory produced a variant known as the GAZ-67. This was a heavier vehicle than the Jeep and the factory built thousands. As impressive as this output of trucks and light vehicles was, it was country's production of AFVs, especially tanks, which bolstered the army and gave it the fighting force necessary to take on the Germans.

As the end of 1941 approached, Hitler's forces were now engaged on three fronts. The campaign in Russia was absorbing more resources in manpower and weaponry than could be afforded, but Hitler refused to deny it the resources to support it, even to the cost of his other theatres of operations. In France, the Germans realised they must begin constructing defences to guard against an Allied landing. The Organisation Todt, with its massive labour force, began building Festung Europa (Fortress Europe) which would become known as the 'Atlantic Wall'. As these defences grew in number and size, stretching from Sweden to the borders with Spain, the building absorbed millions of tons of concrete, steel and vast arrays of weapons. The weapons captured from France and Belgium, along with others seized from several other engagements, including some British weaponry, were ideal to use in these static defences. Anti-tank guns of Czechoslovakian origin were used in bunkers and even obsolete weapons, provided there was sufficient ammunition, were put in the pillboxes and bunkers springing up across occupied territories.

In North Africa, things could have been better. Rommel had been repulsed but the setback was only temporary. The British knew that he would return because the oil fields in the Middle East were a tempting prize. And even if he could only threaten one end of the Suez Canal it would close the waterway to Allied shipping. Capturing the oil fields in Iraq and Iran would have denied the British almost 15 million tons of oil, the combined annual capacity the two countries were producing. Denying this to the British and claiming it for his armies would have suited Hitler, but it was the 35 million tons capability which Russia produced annually that was the greatest prize. Hitler still viewed North Africa as a sideshow and he realised that capturing the oil fields in the Ukraine, with their refineries, was more important. Furthermore, these were within his grasp, and with Army Group South he had means of threatening this region. Since October 1940 Hitler had gained access to the vast oilfields in Romania when the country became a German ally. The country would provide almost 1.25 million troops but it was oil which was most important. The largest oil refinery produced around two million tons per year.

As the war progressed the Germans began modifying increasing numbers of captured enemy tanks to replace losses in the Russian campaign. These were mainly French designs, such as the Char Somua S-35 Medium Tank which the Germans designated as Panzerkampfwagen 35C 739 (f), but these and the other armoured vehicles did not always prove suitable for purpose. For instance, captured examples of the French AMC-35 Light Tank, designated by the Germans as PzKfpw AMC 738 (f) were pressed into a variety of miscellaneous roles, but ultimately they proved to be of limited service value to the Germans, especially on the Russian Front where they were next to useless.

When the French army surrendered the Germans seized on a tank force of some 2,170 vehicles which had survived the battles in May and June 1940. The French army was numerically stronger in tanks than the German army at the time. Some designs of French tank were better than their German opposite number, being armed with guns of heavier calibre and having better armoured protection. The Renault-built AMC-35 light tank, which entered service in 1935 and went to make up the French army's tank force of some 3,000 tanks of all types on the outbreak of war in September 1939, was armed with a 47mm calibre gun. The level of armour protection was only 25mm but that was better than some of the early German designs.

Another Renault vehicle captured by the Germans was the AMR 33 VM Light Tank which had been used throughout the French campaign in 1940. AMR stood for Auto Mitrailleuse de Reconnaissance (machine gun reconnaissance vehicle). The AMR 33 VM weighed only 4.9 tons and was compact in design. The armament comprised of only a single 7.5mm machine gun in a fully traversing turret of riveted design rather than a heavier calibre main gun.

A variant of the AMR 33 VM was fitted with an 85hp Renault engine which gave it a road speed of 34mph and combined with other modifications produced a vehicle weighing 6.3 tons. In all, a total of 200 of these tanks were built and entered service with the designation AMR 35 ZT. Two men operated this vehicle which could be armed with either a standard 7.5mm calibre machine gun, a 13.2mm Hotchkiss machine gun or a

25mm cannon. The Germans pressed into service those examples of the AMR33VM and AMR35ZT which had not been destroyed in the fighting, giving them the designation PzSpWg VM701 (f) and PzSpWg ZTI 702 (f), until they became worn out and had to be replaced by other vehicles. When the vehicles were declared obsolete the turrets were removed along with their armament and used as extemporised armoured machine gun posts set onto a concrete base as static defences. Some examples of the light tanks after removal of their turrets were converted into mortar carrying vehicles to provide mobile fire support to infantry units.

By late 1941 it was becoming increasingly clear to many people that it was only a question of time before Japan entered the war as a belligerent nation. After all, it was a signatory of the Tripartite Pact which made it an ally of Italy and Germany. Japan had been engaged in hostilities since it invaded China in the invasion of 1937. It had also fought brief but bloody border engagements with the Russians in 1939, making it the second most combat experienced country after Italy. For all its militarism, Japan had few natural resources of its own to support its armed forces. Demand for industry outstripped supply and the country had no choice but to import raw materials for manufacturing and oil to power its industry. Much of what it imported came from

The Phaenomen Granit 1500A was a versatile truck, being used for transporting troops and supplies as well as serving as a platform on which to mount weapons, such as this refurbished original vehicle which is fitted with twin MG42 machine guns for anti-aircraft or ground support roles.

The range of trucks, such as this refurbished original example of an Opel Blitz, were the foundation of the logistics supply line for the German army. Fuel shortages in the later stages of the war forced more horses to be used.

The SdKfz 250 half-track was a versatile vehicle, being capable of transporting troops, evacuating wounded and towing artillery and supplies.

French-built Citroën trucks, both civilian and military, were taken into service by the German army. This example of a refurbished original vehicle has been equipped as a field workshop.

The German army also used French-built Renault trucks which supplemented German-built vehicles to transport troops and supplies.

A captured French AMR35 tank has been modified by the German army to serve in the role of self-propelled mortar carrier.

America but the country's increasingly aggressive actions in China, such as the massacre of the populace in the city of Nanking in 1937, led to America threatening to place an embargo on certain commodities to get Japan to stop military actions against China.

Relations between America and Japan, which had been deteriorating for some time, finally reached crisis point and on 7 December 1941 Japan used aircraft, flying from aircraft carriers, to bomb the US Navy base at Pearl Harbor. The attack was unprovoked and came without warning. President Roosevelt, addressing Congress, called it 'a date which will live in infamy' and declared war against Japan. Japanese aircraft bombed the British colonies of Singapore and Hong Kong in the early hours of the morning of 8 December. Britain responded to the attacks by declaring war on Japan later the same day. Two days later, Japanese aircraft sank HMS *Repulse* and HMS *Prince of Wales* off Malaya and Japanese troops captured Guam and landed in the Philippines. On 11 December Hitler and Mussolini declared war against America in an act of support for their Japanese ally. In the months that followed, Japanese forces rapidly expanded across the Pacific to invade other territories such as Borneo, Timor and Malaya.

The Japanese Admiral Isiroku Yamamoto said after the Pearl Harbor attack, 'I fear all we have done is to awaken a sleeping giant and fill him with a terrible resolve.' Hitler and Mussolini would have done well to heed such prophetic words, but they wanted to show their full commitment to the Pact of Steel. America would indeed become the 'arsenal of democracy' as Roosevelt had declared and as the armoury of the Allies it would change the entire course of the war. Its factories would produce 297,000 aircraft, 14 million small arms, and 193,000 pieces of artillery. In 1939 the amount of the American gross national product given over to defence was around two per cent; by 1945 this had increased to a staggering forty-two per cent. In 1939 America had a small army of only 174,000 men. In 1941, at the time of its entry into the war, the strength of the country's army had increased almost ten-fold to nearly 1.5 million. Even so, this figure represented a relatively small military force by comparison to either Germany or Russia. By the end of the war the total number of personnel serving in America's armed forces peaked at fifteen million, eight million of which were in the army, and represented twenty-five per cent of total Allied strength.

When Winston Churchill first heard the news of the attack on Pearl Harbor he could scarcely contain himself because he realised that with America as an ally the defeat of Germany was almost certain. In February 1941, an impassioned Churchill had broadcast a speech calling for America to 'Give us the tools and we will finish the job.' Only a few weeks later the Lend-Lease Bill was passed. After the war, he wrote about his reaction to the bombing of Pearl Harbor in his multi-volume work *The Second World War*: 'So we had won after all!' and 'No American will think it wrong of me if I proclaim that to have the United States on our side was to be the greatest joy...'

Churchill travelled to Washington where between 24 December and 14 January 1942 he conducted a series of talks with Roosevelt in what is referred to as the Arcadia Conference. During their discussions, they agreed to combine all the resources at their disposal and that the defeat of Germany was to be the main priority. The meeting was not just a question of nodding together in agreement; it had to be much more than that. Churchill knew that America and Britain were the only two countries in the world which were in any position to resist the Axis forces. Britain as a nation was experienced in this war, but at the same time was tired, having stood up to Hitler and Mussolini for eighteen months since June 1940. It had endured the Blitz, the treat of invasion and was being worn down by losses of supplies due to the U-Boats. America was fresh, but it was also keen and had the industrial capacity and manpower which could defeat the Axis forces. America would provide the bulk of the equipment, but Britain would act as the springboard from which the invasion of Europe could be launched. As 1942 started, the great industrial might of the country began the gradual process of shifting into the production of tanks, guns and planes for the battles which lay ahead.

Chapter 10

The War Widens: The Campaigns of 1942

In North Africa, the beginning of 1942 boded well for the British army with Bardia being captured on 2 January. The fighting had cost the Australians 456 killed and wounded but it had yielded up 400 guns and 130 tanks captured and 40,000 Italians killed or captured. Further actions achieved more successes with another 208 guns and 87 tanks seized, along with another 25,000 PoWs. With such losses, the burden of continuing the campaign in North Africa was falling more heavily on Germany. The British moved westwards to establish the so-called 'Gazala Line' which was a series of self-contained defences, each approximately two miles square, intended to support one another in the event of an attack. With the port of Tobruk, now garrisoned by 2nd South African Division of General William Gott's XIII Corps, securely behind their own lines, the British were receiving supplies. Meanwhile, the convoys transporting supplies to Rommel were under constant attack from aircraft and submarines operating from Malta. Count Ciano was not exaggerating when he told Hitler they were being 'slaughtered'.

In France, the occupying forces were largely self-supporting except in manpower, but the war in Russia was draining in respect of everything, especially petrol and ammunition. Hitler's operations in the Balkans against Yugoslavia had diverted resources and now the German war machine was expected to supply military support to its allies in eastern Europe, including Hungary, Bulgaria and Romania. Even Finland, holding the northern end of the Karelian Isthmus to besiege the city of Leningrad, was receiving military support. Volunteers from Spain fought in Russia, but the country remained neutral. That did not prevent it from becoming a hotbed of intrigue for both Axis and Allied spies who used it as a centre for espionage and counter-espionage throughout the war. It was a role which Spain was happy to serve.

Hitler's attempt to 'bribe' Franco to side with him as an ally was a tactic he had used before. In a meeting with Mussolini on 25 August 1939, Hitler had hinted to the Italian leader that Germany was going to attack Poland. He enquired if Italy would be understanding in the event of such an action. Count Ciano, the Italian Foreign Minister and Mussolini's son-in-law, directed Mussolini to reply that Italy was not in a position to go to war. The country was already committed to a campaign in Ethiopia, as well as supporting Franco's forces in Spain, and had just invaded Albania four months earlier in April that year. Germany, by contrast, apart from Spain, had not committed any troops overseas.

This was a reply that Hitler did not expect and would not accept. In response, he pressed to ask what it would take for Italy to ally itself with Germany and go to war. The following day he received a list asking for 18,000 tons of coal, along with other vital raw materials such as tungsten, steel, oil and other essential metals which Italy had to import. Ciano stated that it would require 17,000 carriages to transport such a load, and was beyond the capacity of the Italian rail system. Rather than offer to transport it for the Italians, Hitler reduced the amount offered. Not unsurprisingly, the negotiations collapsed and Italy would not, for the time being at least, be bound to enter the war.

Incredible as it might seem, at the time of these discussions Britain actually controlled around eighty per cent of Italian imports arriving by sea due to her domination of the world's mercantile fleet. Most of Italy's coal already came from Germany, but being shipped from Bremen to ports in Italy the German ships had to pass through the Straits of Gibraltar which were controlled by the British. At the other end of the Mediterranean, Britain had air and naval bases on Malta, which meant that all supplies of raw materials could be attacked in the event of war. When Germany went to war it needed all the coal it produced for its own use. This reduced Italy to importing coal from neutral Holland. Italy was viewed with suspicion in some quarters, but not as a belligerent. Mussolini proved them all wrong when he declared war in June 1940.

Crete had been lost and the campaign in Greece had been a disaster, but with good positions in North Africa and the Mediterranean (Malta and Gibraltar) the country was standing off against Festung Europa in a stalemate. The situation in the Far East, where the British territories including Hong Kong and Singapore were being targeted by Japan, things were looking dire. The strength of Japan's army at the time of the attack on Pearl Harbor stood at 1.7 million men in 51 divisions. By 1945 this figure had increased to five million men in 140 divisions. At the peak of its expansion Japan controlled an area measuring 3,000 miles by 3,500 miles, much of it spread out across the Pacific Ocean with garrisons established on islands. Japan probably had the worst trouble of any belligerent country when it came to trying to produce armaments. The country, itself comprising of a range of islands, had a population approaching 73 million, but with insufficient natural resources of its own and no raw materials to support heavy industry, everything from oil to iron ore had to be imported. Convoys also had to transport everything out to the island garrisons across the Pacific. Later, as the war progressed, Allied submarines would take a huge toll on the convoys.

By 1944 the Japanese had a working population of around 33 million, working shifts of eleven hours a day to support the war effort. The country produced some remarkable gigantic warships, such as the almost 73,000 ton *Yamato* and *Musashi*, and built 70,000 aircraft between 1941 and 1945. The workforce of Britain and the Commonwealth numbered 20 million, worked a 60-hour week, and produced 135,000 aircraft and more than 160,000 tanks and other AFVs mainly due to better production methods and access to raw materials. From 1931 until 1938 the Japanese only built 1,700 tanks and during the entire war they only built around 6,000 AFVs of all types. In the second half of 1942 Japan only built 500 tanks, ten per cent of Germany's output for the same period, illustrating the Japanese military preference for warships and aircraft.

The decision between Britain and America to first defeat Germany would lead to the European theatre of operations dominating the conduct of the war, but that is not to say the fighting in the Far East was any less important. Japan's military expanded to occupy vast tracts of land in China along with Burma, Thailand and Malaya. Capturing the larger islands of Sumatra, Borneo and Mindanao gave them more land and occupying the greater northern end of New Guinea and Timor allowed them to operate aircraft from where multiple-engine bombers such as the 'Betty' G4M with a range of 3,000 miles could threaten Australia. Naturally, the Pacific war was mainly conducted at sea with land engagements on the islands, involving a series of amphibious landings as the Americans leapt from one island to another, all the while advancing towards the main Japanese islands. Tanks used in these operations were the same as those used by the Allies in North Africa and later Europe. The Japanese tended to use small, light tanks with low armour protection, armed with small calibre guns and used mainly to support the infantry. Although allied to one another in the so-called Pact of Steel, Japan was separated by thousands of miles from Italy and Germany and consequently they were unable to directly support one another's campaigns. In fact, on several notable occasions each acted without informing the other of its intentions. For example, when Hitler attacked Russia he did so without informing Italy or Japan. The Japanese attack at Pearl Harbor may have been guessed at by Germany, but because of the secrecy involved, Hitler was never told.

At the time of the attack against Pearl Harbor the Japanese were reduced to six months of aviation fuel reserves and overall some 50 million tons of oil. The Japanese Navy was using 9,300 tons per day and with such levels of consumption it would soon reach critically low levels.

The aircraft which attacked Pearl Harbor were launched from aircraft carriers 275 miles away. Successive waves sank or damaged 19 capital warships and destroyed or damaged nearly 350 aircraft, killing 2,403 men and wounding a further 1,178. The sixteen huge fuel tanks with a holding capacity of 4.5 million barrels were not hit during the attack. Whether this was intentional or an oversight is not entirely clear. If the oil storage facilities were deliberately avoided it could have been that the Japanese intended to use the supply for themselves. If they were not attacked due to confusion, then the mistake cost the Japanese dearly. The tanks had only just been refilled to capacity and had they been destroyed the ships at sea at the time of the attack could not have been refuelled and put back to sea. Admiral Chester W. Nimitz said of the attack, 'Had the Japanese destroyed the oil, it would have prolonged the war another two years.'

Pearl Harbor was not the only target attacked that day. Japanese aircraft struck at territories of the Dutch East Indies and other areas controlled by Britain and France. On 8 December, the Japanese attacked the British colony of Hong Kong where a garrison of 14,000, including Canadian troops, were defending the harbour and other installations. The British resisted but surrendered on 25 December when the fresh water supplies were captured and cut off. Before doing so, they had destroyed much of the supply stocks, including oil tankers in the harbour, to deny them to the Japanese. The fighting had cost the British 2,223 killed, 2,300 wounded and the rest taken into captivity. The operation cost the Japanese fewer than 2,700 killed and wounded. Within weeks of the attack on Pearl Harbor the Japanese appeared to be everywhere at once and newspapers were full of details recounting the success of their advance.

Landings were made by the Japanese 25th Army in Thailand, which spread out to move southwards down the coastal routes either side of the Malayan peninsula. They were working to a timetable set by Lieutenant General Tomoyuki Yamashita, giving the force of 50,000 men 100 days to seize the peninsula. At the southern tip was the prize, 620 miles away from the landing points, the British island colony of Singapore, vital to the Japanese because from here it controlled all regional lines of communication. The Japanese 5th Division advanced with a few tanks and other vehicles in support, but it was 6,000 bicycles which gave them the most mobility. As the rubber tyres wore out they continued to ride them on the metal rims of the wheels, making such a noise the British and Commonwealth troops believed they were being attacked by tanks.

The speed of the advance was greater than Yamashita expected and on 8/9 February, forty days early, the first troops were crossing the Jahore Strait separating mainland Malaya from the island. Over the following week the British garrison with Australian and New Zealand troops fought to hold back the Japanese, who captured great quantities of stores. The Australians destroyed oil stocks. Unknown to the defending garrison was the fact that the Japanese were running dangerously low on ammunition. Food and water were not a problem to the Japanese infantrymen who knew how to live off the countryside and were prepared to do so. Yamashita called a bluff and demanded the surrender of the garrison commanded by General Arthur Ernest Percival. On 15 February, the island was in Japanese hands. It had cost the British 5,000 killed and wounded with the remaining 80,000 being taken prisoner. The Japanese had lost 5,000 killed and wounded but gained the supply of stocks not destroyed before the surrender, including the remnants of 1,800 trucks, artillery and other vehicles. The surrendered Allied troops were taken into captivity and kept in horrific conditions. They were put to work as forced labour to construct a railway network along the Malaya peninsula.

By the time Hong Kong and Singapore were captured, the Japanese had also landed in the Philippines and were engaging the combined force of 151,000 American and

Filipino defenders in fierce fighting which would last 105 days. The last American and Filipino troops surrendered on 9 June 1942. The fighting had cost them 25,000 killed and 21,000 wounded with 100,000 taken prisoner. The Japanese force of 130,000 had lost 9,000 killed and 13,200 wounded. With the Philippines in their hands the way was open for the Japanese to expand their military sphere and occupy the Dutch East Indies of Java and Sumatra with its resources of oil. Other islands and mainland territories yielded up other resources including ore deposits and rubber. The loss of rubber, used mainly for tyres, would hit the Allies hard.

In the 1920s and 1930s most vehicle production in Japan used American technology. In 1929 Japanese companies produced 437 cars but American companies built 30,000. In 1936 the introduction of the Motor Car Manufacturing Enterprise Law meant that half of all holdings in vehicle production plants must be Japanese. By 1939 the Foreign Exchange Control Law banned the production of foreign vehicles, which meant American vehicles. At the time Japan was almost entirely dependent on America for scrap metal which was melted down and processed for use in the production of vehicles, but as relations between the two countries worsened so this trade dried up.

Japan had invaded Manchuria in 1931 and further expansion into China in 1937 gave some access to raw materials but Japan would always struggle to get supplies and this would have a telling effect.

If Japanese tank production was not up to supplying vehicles in quantity, then the motor industry was not much better at providing trucks. Between 1941 and 1942 Japan produced 45,433 trucks, half designated for civilian use. Compared to other countries where vehicle production increased, Japan's output declined year on year. Between 1942 and 1943 production of trucks dropped to 36,483 vehicles. From 1943 to 1944 output was down to 25,672 vehicles and a year later this had dropped to 21,743. In the last five months of the war from April to August 1945 Japan's truck production was 6,726 vehicles. To make up for this shortage the troops were compelled to use huge numbers of captured civilian vehicles and military trucks which caused them the same problems in maintenance and spare parts as the Germans experienced. Examples of Japanese-made vehicles included the 6x4 Isuzu 'Type 94' with a 1.5-ton load capacity, various staff cars, and the 5-ton half-track Ikegai 'Ko-Hi' used as artillery tractors.

As the Japanese continued to expand southwards they made landing on Papua New Guinea. On 14 February 1942 they parachuted 360 troops into southern Sumatra and naval activity pointed to the likelihood of an invasion of Australia. Australia was becoming ever more isolated, supply routes were becoming increasingly vulnerable, and essential war materials both to and from the country could not be guaranteed. On 19 February 1942 aircraft flying from bases on the Celebes islands bombed the harbour installations at Darwin. It was to be the first of 62 air raids launched against the port and its environs over the next 21 months.

Prior to the outbreak of Japanese hostilities, Australian military authorities, probably sensing the growing hostile attitude of Japan, had decided to produce a tank of local design, which would be built in Australia and meant only for use by Australian troops. An engineer was sent to America in early 1940 to study tank building methods and by November that year the first specifications for the Australian tank had been drawn up. The new tank, known as the Australian Cruiser 1, was to be armed with a 2-pounder gun. The project was approached with urgency and by January 1942, with little or no previous experience in these matters, the first designs for a wholly Australian-built tank had been drafted. The turret was a single one-piece casting, which was a remarkable feat of engineering, given the fact that Australia lacked the experienced workforce to undertake the production. The hull was to be produced in the same manner, which further stretched an already strained manufacturing industry. In fact, at the time this work was being undertaken the country did not even manufacture motor cars.

The tank was driven by three Perrier Cadillac '75' V-8 cylinder petrol engines linked together to provide a single unit. It had a top speed of 30 mph and an operational range of 200 miles, which was more than adequate for Australia's needs for home defence. The tracks were supplied by American manufacturers and identical to the type used on the US army's M3 Lee-Grant Medium Tanks. The project came to be known by the informal name of Sentinel. Despite being quite literally cobbled together from resources available, the Mark I Sentinel had armour protection of between 25mm and 65mm and a combat-ready weight of 28 tons. The Sentinels were built by the New South Wales Railway Company at Chullora.

By 1943 the war in the Pacific had turned in favour of the Allies and American-built tanks were being shipped to Australia. As American forces gathered strength and began to force the Japanese back, so the pressure on Australia and the likelihood of invasion subsided. American-supplied tanks were sent to Australian forces serving in the Pacific theatre and the need for the Sentinel tank passed. As a stop-gap measure it had worked and shown what a country could achieve if the situation demanded it.

On the other side of the world the war in Russia was raging. In April 1942, both sides had just come through the first winter on the Eastern Front. The Germans had suffered badly. The Russians had fared slightly better and were in good spirits with hopes of regaining the city of Kharkov. Marshal Semyon Timoshenko, commander of the Red Army's south-west front, made plans for its recapture. Stalin ordered that it be taken, for which task Timoshenko committed the Soviet 6th Army to attack north towards the city while the 28th and 38th Armies attacked from the north-east and south-east respectively. Unknown to them, the Germans, under the command of von Bock, were also planning an offensive, called Operation Fridericus, using their own 6th Army in the north supported by forces to the south. The Russians got in first by attacking on 12 May. The Russians had deployed 640,000 men and 1,200 tanks, including the new

T-34 with its 76.2mm main gun. The attack had pre-empted the Germans attack by six days and they managed to break through the German lines. The Germans responded by putting in a full-scale attack and even though Russian officers on the spot realised the danger, Stalin ordered things to be left as they were. On 17 May, von Bock launched Fridericus in strength and within a week had moved to cut off the Russian 6th and 57th Armies. By 28 May it was all over with another resounding victory for the German army which had killed or captured more than 277,000 Russians and destroyed more than 2,000 pieces of artillery and 1,250 tanks. Hitler now began looking at the oil fields in the Caucasus and the great industrial city of Stalingrad.

By March 1942, the fighting in Russia had cost the Germans one million men killed, wounded or taken prisoner, 3,100 armoured vehicles had been destroyed along with 115,000 other vehicles and 10,500 pieces of artillery. They had also lost 260,000 horses which were used for transporting supplies. In July, Mussolini saw the opportunity to support Hitler and sent the newly and specially raised Armata Italiana in Russia (Italian army in Russia) to the Eastern Front. Known also as the Italian 8th Army, it comprised some 235,000 troops commanded by General Giovanni Messe. The force also had 16,700 trucks, tanks and over 1,000 pieces of artillery, including anti-tank guns. The Italians took part in various operations, but it was at Stalingrad that it suffered most. In January 1943 Mussolini ordered them to withdraw and the survivors fought their way back through Soviet lines. They returned to Italy, having lost around half their number and most of their equipment.

At the northern end of Russia, at the same time as Operation Fridericus, the campaign against the city of Leningrad was bogged down in stalemate with 300,000 Germans holding the southern end of the isthmus and the Finns holding the northern end. The Finns and Germans had not managed to link up their front lines which would have cut off the southern edge of Lake Ladoga. This left the Russians in possession of Lednevo with its railway links and Novaya Ladoga with road links from where supplies could be transported into the besieged city. The Finns may have been allies of Germany but as far as they were concerned they had reconquered the territory they had lost in 1940 during the war against Russia and they were satisfied. They were not prepared to go any further and this left open the water route into Leningrad. The Russians had built defences on the outskirts of the city but with a population of three million the problem was feeding the people. In October 1941, the city was being supplied with 1,000 tons of food daily brought in by boats from Novaya Ladoga but after November, when the waters froze, that rate dropped to half. The problem was compounded when a German attack captured a stretch of the rail link at Tikhvin and severed the route into Lednevo.

The Communist party secretary in Leningrad, Andrei Zhdanov, ordered that a route be cut through dense forest so that trucks could carry supplies from the railhead at Zaborye to Novaya Ladoga from where convoys could continue to Lednevo and across the waters of the lake. The route, to be hacked through the forest to connect Zaborye to Novaya Ladoga, was fifty miles long; in just over four weeks, between 9 November and 6 December, it was completed. It was a prodigious feat of work by labourers, many of whom were on the point of collapse from hunger. The terrain was so steep in places that the trucks had to be physically pushed up the inclines. When a Russian counter-attack seized back the railhead at Tikhvin, drivers took their trucks across the frozen surface of Lake Ladoga. By January 1942 there were daily up to 400 trucks driving the treacherous twenty miles across the frozen lake from Lednevo to Osinovets, from where they could continue overland to Leningrad or the railhead could take supplies direct to the city. The civilians called it the 'Road of Life' but to the drivers who risked crashing through the ice it was the 'Road of Death'.

Seven months earlier some 54 trains had removed 1.2 million works of art and national treasures from Leningrad in a month-long operation to prevent them from being captured by the Germans. By the time of the first thaw in April 1942 some 53,000 tons of supplies such as fuel and ammunition and a further 42,500 tons of food had been driven across the Lake Ladoga ice road. The siege of Leningrad would last for 890 days, until 13 January 1944, with 1.5 million being killed or dying of starvation. The struggle to save the city and keep it supplied was one of the greatest examples of logistics in action during the war. Andrei Shdanov declared, 'We must dig Fascism a

This refurbished original Bedford MW truck in desert colours shows the type of vehicle the 8th Army used for transporting supplies.

grave in front of Leningrad.' The cost to the German army and its Italian and Finnish allies saw 680,000 killed, wounded or taken prisoner. The operation tied down hundreds of thousands of German troops, tanks, trucks and other equipment, denying them to be deployed elsewhere.

Since his defeat following Operation Crusader in December 1941, Rommel was pushed back almost 300 miles, first past Derna and then Darce, before arriving at Benghazi. The British maintained the pressure and pushed him even further back, to El Agheila on 6 January 1942. It had taken Rommel almost six months to reach his furthest point of advance in 1941, now he was back to his start line in only weeks. In typical fashion, Rommel acted swiftly. On 21 January, even though he had only 560 tanks (of which 332 were German, the rest being Italian or captured vehicles), he mounted his offensive. The following day he had advanced and captured Agedabia. The British 8th Army commanded by Lieutenant General Neil Ritchie was equipped with 850 tanks including Matilda Mk IIs, Valentines and M3 Stuarts, but now, and most importantly, he had 167 M3 Lee-Grants armed with 75mm guns which would prove invaluable. By May, Rommel had captured Tmimi on the coast, which put him twenty miles away from the Gazala Line. But it was another one of his ploys as the true line of attack revealed itself on 26 May when he struck in the south towards the defensive position of Bir Hakeim held by a garrison of 3,600 Free French, which included troops of the French Foreign Legion commanded by General Pierre Koenig.

For more than a week Ger-man sappers worked to clear a way through the minefields while the Luftwaffe pounded the position with a series of air raids. On 3 June, Rommel attacked using the German

An unusual view of a Leyland truck from the 1930s as used by the British army in North Africa. It shows the large size of the vehicle.

15th, 90th and 21st Divisions along with the Italian Ariete and Trieste Divisions. The position of Bir Hakeim was being held by the French. He left the 90th and Trieste Divisions to attack Bir Hakeim, while his remaining four divisions swung south around the French position to attack two of the defensive boxes held by Indian troops and destroyed them. Initially the Trieste Division failed to capture the position, but later in the day they combined to attack once more. For more than a week the Germans allowed the French no respite, attacking and probing the defences day and night. The position was virtually surrounded except for a narrow corridor. Earlier, on 29 May, Rommel's forces had penetrated the Gazala Line to the north of Bir Hakeim, but they were soon struggling due to lack of supplies, especially ammunition and fuel. He ordered them to hold and form a defensive crescent. This created a salient known as the 'The Cauldron', bulging eastwards into the British lines. The British did not have long to wait. On 5 June Rommel ordered his troops to attack east out of the position, inflicting 6,000 casualties on the British and destroying 150 tanks in the process. The attack forced the British to retreat and over the following week Rommel's Afrika Korps and the Italians captured more ground so that by 17 June he was, once again, threatening Tobruk itself.

The British, meanwhile, had been providing as much support as they could to the French defenders. The Germans made repeated calls for their surrender, but, despite shortages of supplies, they stubbornly held on. Then, on the evening of 10 June, under cover of darkness, General Koenig, realising he could do no more, led the 2,700 survivors of his command out of the position and made their way through the desert to a pre-arranged rendezvous point. Here they met a fleet of British trucks which had been sent out to transport them back to safety. When Rommel's troops entered Bir Hakeim on 11 June all he found were 300 men who were too seriously wounded to be evacuated and the graves of 600 other defenders.

Tobruk, which was so essential for supplying the Allies, and had eluded Rommel the year before, was now at his mercy. The garrison at Tobruk comprised 35,000 men including Indian, South African and British troops with sufficient supplies of food and ammunition to last for at least ninety days. In February, Auchinleck made his opinions known about the position of Tobruk, stating, 'It is not my intention to continue to hold it once the enemy is in a position to invest it effectively. Should this appear inevitable, the place will be evacuated and the maximum amount of destruction carried out in it.'

On 18 June aircraft of the Luftwaffe began to bomb the positions, sappers cleared the mines, and tanks of the 21st Panzer Division attacked defences held by the 2nd/5th Mahrattas. Lacking anti-tank guns and heavy support the Indians were overwhelmed but the survivors fought on with the Cameron Highlanders until finally they were forced to surrender. Realising that they could not hold, Major General Henry Klopper, commanding the Tobruk garrison, following Auchinleck's instructions, ordered supplies to be destroyed. Fuel, oil and ammunition were blown up, but even so, when the garrison finally surrendered on 21 June, Rommel reaped a rich harvest, including 5,000 tons of supplies, 2,000 vehicles and, most importantly, 500,000 gallons of fuel. It was shattering news to the Allies and Churchill in particular, who confided to Roosevelt that its loss was 'one of the heaviest blows I can recall during the war'. Hitler was delighted with the news and promoted Rommel to the rank of Field Marshal. The way to Cairo and the Middle East with its oil supplies appeared to be wide open. Roosevelt responded by immediately sending 300 of the new Sherman tanks to help the British and Commonwealth troops.

Rommel and his Afrika Korps in North Africa were adding to the German army's victories by capturing the defensive positions of El Duda and Belhamed outside the town port of Tobruk. He also captured British supply depots near Bardia and the airfield at El Adem. Sensing the victory which had eluded him several months earlier he wrote, 'Evidence of the British defeat could be seen all along the roads and verges… Vast quantities of material lay on all sides, burnt-out vehicles stood black and empty in the sand. Whole convoys of undamaged British lorries had fallen into our hands, some of which had been pressed into service immediately by the fighting troops, while others were now awaiting collection by the salvage squads.'

Trucks which fell into German hands included the Morris CS8 built by Morris Commercial Cars based in Birmingham. Production had started in 1937, and the British army would eventually have about 26,000 of these useful little vehicles in service. They were nicknamed 'Gin Palaces' by the troops because they were so comfortable. Built in three versions, one of which was for communications, being manned by the Royal Corps of Signals, they were also used to transport supplies and troops, for which purpose they were fitted with wooden slatted seats, and evacuate the wounded. The rear body was built up from wooden slats with a tailgate which dropped down to make loading and unloading easier.

Other abandoned vehicles captured by the Germans were 4x2 Morris PU 8cwt trucks. Some had already fallen into their hands after Dunkirk in 1940. These vehicles should have been wrecked to prevent them being used by the enemy, but demolition actions were not always totally destructive; beyond draining the sump and running the engine till it seized up not much else could be done to render them useless. To good mechanics it would not have been too much of a problem to get the vehicle back on the road. PU 8cwts were used by British and Australian troops as radio trucks and supply trucks and those captured intact by the Germans were put to the same use. Built between 1936 and 1941 with Canada producing many they were also used in India. Like other military vehicles it was versatile and could carry troops, supplies and tow light anti-aircraft guns. With so many of their own vehicles being used on convoy routes the Germans eagerly seized on the opportunity to supplement their fleet of vehicles, which were in much need of replacement or extensive servicing.

The British forces in North Africa did not collapse as might have been expected. Instead, Auchinleck ordered his forces to consolidate and take up positions called 'boxes'. There were several of these strongly defended positions, so-called because of their all-round defence. The largest of these enclosed El Alamein in a wide sweeping arc which ran from the coast east of the town, continued south and then ran west before moving northwards back to the coast. Cairo was Rommel's goal and prize, but it lay 150 miles further east. To get to it, he first had to smash these 'boxes'. On 1 July, he sent in 15th and 21st Panzer Divisions to attack the positions at Deir el Shein, completely avoiding the positions around El Alamein. The Deir el Shein box was held by the 18th Indian Brigade and, despite the bravery of the defenders, the combined weight of the German attackers supported with tanks succeeded in capturing the positions the same day. The 90th Light Division followed a feature known as the Miteirya Ridge to the south of El Alamein, skirting the defences, to advance towards the box held by the 4th Armoured Brigade, outside the perimeter defences to the south-east. The Germans became tangled in a minefield, and artillery fire from the El Alamein defensive perimeter added to their losses. Auchinleck had guessed that such a movement would take place and sent 155 tanks of the 7th Armoured Division to positions south of the Deir el Munassib box held by the New Zealand Division. In the centre the 1st Armoured Division was positioned to counter any attacks there and the 6th New Zealand Brigade held the Bab el Qattara box.

The Italian Ariete Division advanced to attack the New Zealanders' positions on 3 July. Learning of their approach the New Zealanders headed out to engage them, rather than wait for them to come close. It was an unexpected move and after a brief engagement the Italians were forced back. Rommel's men were becoming slightly over-confident with their successes, when, on 4 July, they were given a sharp reminder that they still faced an undefeated enemy. Elements of the German 15th and 21st Panzer Divisions moving eastwards to the south of the newly-captured Deir el Shein positions encountered units of the British 1st Armoured Division. The fighting ended equally with both sides falling back.

For the next week Rommel and Auchinleck ordered thrusts to be made, such as the attack on 10 July by Australians against positions held by the Italian Sabratha Division which fell back. The next day was no better for the Trieste Division which abandoned its position at Tel el Eisa when the Australians attacked. By 14 July Auchinleck still had 400 tanks he could commit to battle while Rommel was down to only 30 serviceable tanks. Even when facing such odds, the German tank crews fought on determinedly. By now, though, Rommel's artillery had run out of ammunition and his Italian allies were crumbling fast and could not be relied on for support. On 21 July Auchinleck mounted a night attack, but at Deir el Shein, formerly held by the 18th Indian Brigade, his tanks ran into an ambush and anti-tank guns and mines claimed eighty-seven Valentine tanks either destroyed or damaged and which had to be abandoned.

The fighting continued until the end of July, during which time Rommel was receiving supplies and reinforcements either by road convoy along the coast road or through the harbour at Tobruk. But movement along these routes was not without its dangers as bombers of the RAF continued to attack the supply lines. The Luftwaffe was over-stretched and could not provide complete air cover to protect the routes. Rommel wrote, 'They were shooting up our transport columns and sinking one barge and coastal vessel after another. No ship lying in the harbour is safe.' Fighter aircraft of the RAF were shooting up anything that moved, their presence being given away by clouds of dust which pilots spotted and engaged. Rommel noted this also, remarking that 'All movement was instantly stopped by the low-flying attacks... Soon many of our vehicles were alight and burning furiously.' He was always alert to the dangers aircraft posed to his supply lines, but with little or no support from the Luftwaffe there was nothing he could do except hope that sufficient supplies got through. In another entry, he wrote, 'The enemy is in hot pursuit… There is [a] serious danger they will break through and destroy our supplies.'

Auchinleck was reluctant to engage in another battle so soon. He wanted time to build up his reserves of manpower, supplies of fuel, ammunition and food, along with more tanks and artillery. Churchill saw this as a sign of weakness and decided that he would replace the Auk with someone who was more aggressive and willing to take risks. The Germans had respect for Auchinleck, but their opinions counted for nought. In his place, Churchill appointed General Harold Alexander, who had overseen the evacuation of the some of the last British units to leave Dunkirk in 1940. He had also coordinated the defence of Britain when the German invasion was still possible. For the time being, at least, the war in the desert was at a stalemate once more. General Montgomery was appointed commander of the Eight Army, and he would make a difference to the war in the desert.

The British army was using increasing numbers of American-built tanks such as the M3 Lee-Grant and the earlier M3 Honey Light Tank. In fact, these designs were being battle-proven before America entered the war proper. The demonstrations under such conditions showed to the American army how their tanks coped in combat and highlighted any defects. In 1939 America was not involved in the war in Europe, but that did not prevent military observers from taking an interest in developments and sending reports to various departments. One such observation from 1939 reported that tank guns at the time were proving inadequate, especially those in the 37mm calibre bracket. Events of 1940 with the over-running of Western Europe spearheaded by Panzer Divisions confirmed this and tank designers in America began to examine ways of fitting guns of 75mm calibre gun into vehicles. The problem was that turret designs of the time were not capable of supporting such a large calibre gun and so an alternative method was devised. This was known as 'sponson' mounting, a design more commonly used on warships. But while this solved the problem of getting a large gun into a tank it raised the problem of how to obtain all-round traverse of the weapon. Sponson mountings permit only a limited traverse across the side of the vehicle on which it is mounted, whereas a turret can traverse through 360 degrees for all-round protection.

In July 1940, the US Ordnance Committee which advised on such matters designated that a new tank design using the sponson method for mounting a 75mm gun should be developed and termed it the M3 Medium Tank. Previous contracts for other tank designs were cancelled and the Chrysler Corporation of Michigan was awarded the contract to produce the M3 tank. The company already had experience building vehicles for the military and for this project it acquired a site on which to build a purpose-built tank factory at Warren in Michigan. By the end of the war the company had produced around 25,000 armoured vehicles, of which 3,352 were M3 tanks.

A British tank commission sent to America in June 1940 found itself facing obstacles regarding the purchase of tanks because American producers believed that Britain was about to surrender following the country's defeat at Dunkirk. They were also reluctant to build a tank to British specifications. In their opinion, if Britain was defeated, who would pay for the vehicles? Undeterred, the British delegation decided that the M3 Medium Tank would suit the needs of the British army and eventually convinced the company to accept an order. Chrysler used sub-contract companies to produce them: the Pullman Company and the Pressed Steel Company would eventually build 500 and 501 M3 tanks respectively, Baldwin would produce 1,220 and Alco built 685. Not all were destined for Britain and Canada, Russia was also supplied with the tank from 1941. American heavy industry made a significant difference by introducing the same mass-production methods to build tanks as was applied to build civilian cars. It greatly eased assembly and speeded up production rate.

The M3 was built in several versions including the standard M3A1 design through successive models to reach the M3A5 and then afterwards used on other variants to produce the M7 'Priest' self-propelled gun. Other versions included a vehicle recovery model, workshop vehicles and mine clearance. In service with the British army the M3 was known by two names, these being the 'Lee' after General Robert E. Lee and the 'Grant' after General Ulysses S. Grant. The M3 was the Lee I; the M3A1 the Lee II; the M3A3 the Lee IV; the M3A3 (fitted with a diesel engine) the Lee V and the M3A4 the Lee VI. These versions kept the original small cupola-type turret mounting a .30inch calibre machine gun on top of the turret of the 37mm gun. This was the design also used by the American army but the British did not much care for a tank with such a high profile of over ten feet in height. The M3A5 version had the machine gun cupola removed and this design was called the Grant II. The Grant I was produced by Pullman and the Pressed Steel companies using a turret of British design and it was this version which was used at the Battle of Gazala in May and June 1942 where, for the first time, tanks of the 8th Army stood anything like a chance against the German's PzKw IV.

Later in the desert war, when the M4 Sherman tank became available in greater numbers they replaced the M3 which the British removed from North Africa. They were deployed to India and the Far East where they, in turn, replaced the Matilda Mk II, Valentine and lighter M3 Honey. The M3 Medium Tank was finally declared obsolete in early March 1944, but it was still useful in other roles such as training purposes.

Jake Wardrop was serving with the 5th Royal Tank Regiment and he remembered how the 'new tanks were arriving now and they were super, the finest things we had ever seen. They had a nine-cylinder radial engine, were quite fast and had a crew of six…. The gun was a 37mm and the bottom one a 75mm.' In action the tanks acquitted themselves well, being able to dish out punishment to the German tanks and withstand the fire from anti-tank guns.

The crews were concerned about being resupplied with fuel and ammunition to keep up the fight. One tank commander recalled how relieved he was when 'The ammunition and petrol lorries duly reached us, after a fairly adventurous journey. All the Grants were refilled with ammunition, and the light squadron was brought in a troop at a time to fill up with petrol.' The troops called the battle the 'Gazala Gallop', fought between 26 May and 21 June 1942, during which 167 Grants were committed. German 88mm anti-tank guns destroyed almost half the number. By October 1942 another 350 M3 tanks were in theatre of which 210 were present at the Battle of El Alamein along with 270 M4 Shermans.

The one great universal fear which was common among tank crews of all armies was the dread of catching fire during a battle. If the vehicle exploded completely on being hit the chances were no-one knew anything. When the vehicle caught fire it was terrifying. A tank crewman remembers how 'There was one particularly nasty form of ending one's days if one is trapped in a tank and the tank blows up and is on fire. Nobody who's been involved in this will ever lose the awfulness or the horror of screams of men trying to get out of their vehicles. If a tank is shot up and burning it didn't matter whose side it was on, the crew had to escape. Once they'd escaped from this tank I know of no occasion when they were ruthlessly shot down by machine guns. They had the elements to face, they had sand and thirst and hunger to face and the fact that they were out of their tank and couldn't make it back to their base was sufficient. If you could take them prisoner you would, but you wouldn't do anything out of hand.' Tank crews did not have the facilities to take prisoners. They were handed over to the infantry to sort out, escort back, and put into 'the bag'. This applied to both sides.

The Afrika Korps entered the war in North Africa bringing a range of vehicles with them, including various types of tanks. At first these included Panzer II and III designs but later included the more powerful Panzer IV. The prototype for the

Panzerkampfwagen IV had appeared in 1937 and proved so successful that it went on to be built in various models and would remain in production throughout the war. Indeed, it has the distinction of being the only German tank to continue to be built and serve in action from 1939 to 1945. In all, some 8,540 gun tanks were built of which around 3,774 were Ausf. H, making it the most numerous model produced. In addition, there were hundreds more chassis produced for other roles such as the 'Sturmpanzer' assault gun armed with a 150mm gun and the 'Panzerbeobachtungswagen' (observation post tank). The Panzer IV had the specialist designation of SdKfz 161 and was produced by various companies, including Krupp-Gruson, Vomag and Nibelungenwerke, between 1938 and 1945. The company of Nibelungenwerke built around 1,758 Ausf. J versions of the tank between June 1944 and March 1945, making them among some of the last tanks to be produced in a collapsing Germany.

The M4 Sherman was the third American-built tank to be used by the British army in North Africa, where it was given its baptism of combat experience before America had committed troops to any theatre of war proper. It incorporated a 75mm gun fitted into a new cast turret which would allow a full all-round traverse capability of 360 degrees. This new design enjoyed several benefits and after consideration it was standardised in September 1941 as the M4 medium tank, but commonly known as the 'Sherman'. It entered service in 1942 and by the time of the Battle of El Alamein, which began on 23 October 1942, there were some 270 in service with the British 8th Army along with 210 M3 Lee-Grants. They represented the first of almost 17,000 tanks and other armoured vehicles the British army would take into service. Other Allied armies such as the Canadians, Free French and Polish would all be equipped with the Sherman. The Russians took delivery of over 4,000 Shermans, some of which they fitted with the 76.2mm gun, this being the weapon which was also fitted to the T-34. The Sherman tank was built by three main manufacturing plants, Ford, Chrysler and General Motors, and by the end of the war they, along with subsidiary factories, had produced some 49,234 tanks between them. Using the same technique to build tanks as commercial motor cars on the assembly line using prefabricated parts, it has been calculated that a Sherman tank could be assembled in thirty minutes. The Sherman was not the best tank used during the war, but it was the most numerous.

It was adaptable and saw service in all theatres of the war from Europe to the 'Island Hopping' campaigns in the Pacific against the Japanese where the temperatures and humidity were greater than even the desert of North Africa. The Sherman was developed into a range of specialist roles, one of which saw it being fitted with large cylinders or rotating drums with heavy chains mounted on the front of the tank. As the vehicle advanced the drum would rotate to beat the ground with the chains to pound a path through minefields. This was used during the Normandy campaign in 1944 where it also successfully destroyed barbed wire obstacles. Rocket-launching frames were fitted above the turret and these were known as 'Calliope' but probably the most unusual concept was the idea by the 1st Coldstream Guards in 1945, when they fitted their Shermans to fire 60-pound aircraft rockets from either side of the turret. This was called 'Tulip' and was used during the Rhine crossing.

At first, tank production in America was slow, but it gained momentum as factories got underway in mid-1940. This was a result of Roosevelt's 'Selective Service Acts' being passed by Congress, which included military conscription and a $15 billion budget for domestic rearmament. This came on top of the $1.5 billion Naval Expansion Bill of two years earlier. The size of the army increased from 140,000 in September 1939 to 1.25 million in 1941. The Armored Force, commanded by Brigadier General Adna R. Chaffee, was created, with the First Armored Corps activated in early July, comprising the 1st and 2nd Armoured Divisions based at Fort Knox and Fort Benning. More units followed so that by 1943, sixteen Armored Divisions had been formed, each with their own tank battalions, infantry battalions and artillery support.

The Sherman tank was an evolving and changing design which affected its weight and dimensions as it evolved to meet the variants being developed from the original basic model. The first production M4 weighed 29.8 tons, the later M4A6 weighed 31.25 tons, and the design known as the M4A3E2 'Assault Tank', armed with a 7-inch gun in a turret, weighed 37.5 tons. Some 254 of these heavyweight versions, nicknamed 'Jumbo', were built and ready in June 1944.

The M4 chassis went on to be used by the Canadians to produce the RAM and Kangaroo carrier. A flamethrower version, known as the 'Adder', was also developed. The Sherman influenced some other tank designs, including the Australian 'Sentinel' and the Argentinian 'Nahuel'. The British army used the M7 for a time, but later adapted the Canadian-developed SPG which used the 25-pounder field gun and was known as the 'Sexton'. This was built initially at the Montreal Locomotive Works in Canada and was another design based on the M4 chassis. One of the most powerful versions of the Sherman was a British development called the 'Firefly', fitted with a 17-pounder anti-tank gun in replacement of the 75mm gun. The original gun could defeat most German tanks but against the heavier types such as the Tiger and Panther it was ineffective. It was for this reason the British developed the Firefly.

As the war progressed, the Americans had proposed fitting a 90mm gun onto the Sherman in order to deal with the heavier German tanks, but that would have meant a completely new turret being designed. The British approached the problem by investigating a 76mm calibre gun firing a 17-pound shell fitted into a modified turret. In October 1943 engineers at Woolwich succeeded and once other technical details had been sorted it was decided to fit 600 M4A4 Sherman tanks with the Mk IV L/55 76mm gun for which 78 rounds of ammunition would be carried inside the tank. The Americans had initially resisted the idea of using the Firefly but some 160 vehicles were made available to them and the design was in service with crews trained in readiness for the Normandy Landings on D-Day 6 June 1944.

Another diversified variant to be based on the chassis of the M4 Sherman was a vehicle which became the M7 self-propelled gun (SPG) which was used across Europe and other theatres too. The pilot models for the proposed M7 SPG were produced by the American Locomotive Company in June 1941 with the project number T-32 appended and sent to the army for trials at the Aberdeen Proving Ground in Maryland. These trials were successful and proved the system to be workable with remarkably few design faults so that the army placed an order for 600. The only real criticism levelled at the T-32 design was that the configuration lacked an anti-tank capability. This was rather unfair because the design was intended to be what the artillery classified as a howitzer, which meant it was to be used to provide fire support with the weapon firing ammunition at high angles of trajectory. As a weapon the self-propelled gun was nothing new in service, but it was the flexibility which the design gave to the artillery which made it important during the Second World War. In fact, all fighting nations would deploy their own form of self-propelled guns which were usually based on the chassis of existing and proven tank designs.

The advantage of the newly-developed American design, however, was the speed it was produced which made it quite extraordinary. In fact, within only eight months of the pilot models of the T-32 appearing the new weapon was standardised as the M7 Howitzer Motor Gun Carriage and accepted by the US army in February 1942. Five months later a batch of 100 of these new vehicles was dispatched to the British 8th Army in North Africa but unfortunately the ship carrying them was sunk by a U-Boat, and it looked as though the British army would be denied the opportunity of giving another American AFV its baptism of fire.

The American Locomotive Company had already tooled up its factory to begin building the M7 and using the assembly line technique had produced sufficient vehicles to allow another ninety to be sent out as replacements for the British army. These guns were sent by convoy and in September 1942 handed over to units in the front line, including the 11th Regiment Royal Horse Artillery which was serving with the 1st Armoured Division. Two months later the 5th Regiment Royal Horse Artillery, also serving with the 1st Armoured Division, deployed their M7 self-propelled guns and used them to engage and destroy German anti-tank guns which had been well dug in to fire at British tanks during the later stages of El Alamein. The gunners of the Royal Artillery were impressed with the new American guns and typical of the British army they nicknamed the gun 'Priest' because of the pulpit-like mounting for the 12.7mm heavy machine gun. In view of its success in battle the British Tank Commission in America requested that a further 5,500 M7 Priest SPGs be delivered by the end of 1943. Even with all its industrial might this was an optimistic request for America's armaments industry and it became obvious there was no way this number of guns could be supplied to the British army, while still supplying numbers to the US army, especially after events in December 1941. In the end the numbers entering service with the British army would fall short of the requested amount.

The Pressed Steel Company was engaged to maintain output of the M7, eventually building some 826 types. The American Locomotive Company remained the main producer and built 3,314 vehicles. The Federal Machine and Welder Company built 127 M7 SPGs, giving a total wartime production of 4,267 M7s of all types. The unarmed versions were used for transport to carry ammunition and observation roles for other artillery batteries.

Of all the different types of tanks used by the British army and Commonwealth forces in North Africa, it could be said that the Valentine was perfect for the war in the desert. It was not much to look at and certainly not a heavyweight either in armour or weaponry, but it was capable of remarkable feats of endurance. For example, after the Battle of El Alamein in November 1942 some Valentine tanks in service with the 23rd Armoured Brigade were driven 3,000 miles on their own tracks as they pursued the Afrika Korps westwards. The story goes that the design was submitted for approval on 14 February 1938, St Valentine's Day, from which came the name Valentine. The War Office did nothing for over a year but then in July 1939, sensing the impending outbreak of war, ordered Vickers to build 275 of the new tanks without delay. The first tanks, officially designated Infantry Tank Mk.3, entered service in May 1940 and were among the first vehicles to make good the losses of tanks either destroyed or abandoned during the fighting in France.

Production continued until early 1944 by which time 8,275 had been built. The Canadian Pacific Railway workshops built 1,420, most of which, along with 1,300 British-made tanks, were sent to Russia after June 1941. In British service the Valentine saw action in North Africa, Madagascar and the campaign in the Far East. Even after it was replaced as a battle tank the chassis were serviceable and these were converted for use as the basis for a number of specialist vehicles such as bridge-layers, flame-throwers, and swimming tanks. It was also used for the Bishop self-propelled 25-pdr gun and the Archer self-propelled 17-pdr gun. The turret design changed throughout its service from the early model which was operated by a two-man crew and then later a three-man crew. The main armament was originally a 2-pounder gun, but the tank was up-gunned with later versions being armed with a 6-pounder (57mm calibre) and then to a 75mm gun. The Russians considered the 2-pounder guns of the Valentines sent to them to be better suited to shooting sparrows and removed them to be replaced by a 76.2mm gun, the same as they did with some Sherman tanks.

American industry not only introduced new innovations in production methods, it also developed new ideas to extend the service life of components. For example, the introduction of rubber blocks and rubber-jointed tracks for tanks increased service to 3,000 miles compared to 600 miles for those tanks fitted with all-metal jointed tracks. The Americans also learned from the combat experience provided by the British in North Africa and soon moved away from the early riveted designs on the M3 Stuart Light Tank and M3 Lee-Grant Medium Tank to develop the M4 Sherman with a welded and cast construction which would become the mainstay of the Allied tank force. The M5 Light Tank was an improved version of the M3 having a welded design with improved layout and would go on to serve to the end of the war after its introduction in 1942. The Americans also introduced a whole range of trucks and utility vehicles in a series called 'WC' which were designed and built by Dodge of Detroit, Michigan. Some thirty-eight different types were developed each with an identification code and intended for various roles, such as the WC 9 Ambulance and the WC 7 Command Car.

Detroit was the historical centre of the American motor industry, which led to it being termed 'Motor City'. In the early weeks of 1942 Major General Brehon B. Somervell described its importance when he said, 'The road ahead is dim with the dust of battles still unfought. How long that road is, no one can know. But it is shorter than it would have been had not our enemies misjudged us and themselves. For, when Hitler put his war on wheels he ran it straight down our alley. When he hitched his chariot to an internal combustion engine, he opened up a whole new battle front – a front we know well. It's called Detroit.' Over the coming twelve months, the US army would receive 180,417 Jeeps and over 2,166,000 trucks. Well might the Axis forces have grave concerns about resupply and vehicle output in the face of such production figures.

Another of Dodge's vehicles in the WC series was a design designated as the pick-up open cab or WC4. It had a payload capacity of 1,000 pounds and could tow either trailers or anti-tank guns such as the 37mm M3 which weighed 900 pounds. These would become some of the first vehicles to be used by specialist units operating in the role of tank destroyer, capable of towing the gun while also carrying the gun crew and ammunition. The WC4 remained in service until replaced by the WC51 three-quarter-ton truck which was better known as the Weapon Carrier. Around 5,570 WC4s were built and they served well until heavier and more versatile vehicles came into service. Although many men entering the American armed forces could already drive, the Chrysler Corporation established a special school to teach the handling characteristics of military vehicles to troops and the WC4 was used for this purpose.

The motor manufacturing company of Dodge had been established in 1914 by two brothers, John Francis and Horace Elgin Dodge, and almost immediately began production of light trucks which were work vehicles. The design interested the military and by 1916 the company was supplying vehicles to the US army for use in the Pancho Villa Expedition of the same year. It was only natural therefore that the company should once more produce vehicles for the military during the Second World War. It was in

1939 that Dodge produced its first prototype of a purpose-built military vehicle in the form of a 4x4 half-ton in what was then the 'VC' series. Some designs were built in very small numbers while others were produced in their thousands. Between 1940 and 1942 the company produced 79,771 half-ton ton trucks.

One of the truly outstanding features of Dodge designs was the high degree of interchangeability in parts. Spares could fit many vehicles which made maintenance easier.

The most widely used of the WC series was the design referred to as Weapon Carrier, of which some 182,655 were built between 1942 and 1945. This was produced in two types known as the WC51 and WC52, both of which were 4x4 with a ¾ ton load rating classification and only differed in design by the latter version being fitted with an integral winch over the front bumper. The WC51, weighing 2.5 tons, was the most numerous with 123,541 being built. It could carry six to eight men, including driver and co-driver, with weapons and personal kit. The WC52, of which 59,114 were built, was slightly heavier at 2.6 tons. Even when the larger 6x6 trucks entered service the WC51 continued to be used, mainly to carry supplies leaving the larger vehicles to carry troops and heavier cargo loads as part of the specialist convoy systems which were developed to supply troops in Europe after the Normandy Landings in June 1944. The WC51 and 52 were versatile and could be armed with machine guns and other devices. They were used by other armies during the war with Russia alone receiving 25,000 Weapons Carriers where the vehicles were assigned to such duties as towing the ZIS-3 76mm calibre anti-tank gun.

Another of the most numerous WC designs was the purpose-built ambulance designated as the WC54 with around 26,000 being built between 1942 and 1944. This was just one of the standard military ambulances used during the war and served with the US Army Medical Corps in all theatres of operations. Its capacity to transport either four wounded as stretcher cases or seven seated casualties plus a medic made it an indispensable vehicle for the movement of casualties from the battlefield to rear areas and better hospital treatment. Wartime photographs show it on the beaches at Normandy and later during the campaign to push inland after the landings. The WC54 replaced the WC27 ambulance and some other older designs. During its production run the vehicle underwent some minor design modifications, but all featured a heater for the comfort of the casualties.

Before entering the war, America had been considering the purchase of 20,000 horses to augment its vehicle fleet. Yet only a couple of years later the country's motor industry was producing more vehicles than any other army at war. Trucks and other vehicles would replace the horse.

The various automotive producers would supply hundreds of thousands of trucks and tanks as the war progressed but in January 1942 the USA was still coming to terms with the fact it was now involved in a global war. With the decision to defeat Germany having been made between Churchill and Roosevelt at the Arcadia Conference it was vital that troops, equipment and aircraft be sent to Britain. The first troops arrived in April to be joined later by aircraft which would join the bombing campaign against Germany. The USAAF built airbases across Britain, with the main concentration in the Suffolk and Norfolk areas. Personnel were billeted in specially constructed camps. Large country estates were also commandeered and troops were billeted in the grounds which were vast enough to serve as vehicle parks for the trucks and tanks. The 28th Infantry Division, the 'Keystone' Division, was sent to Wales where they took over various locations including Margam Park near Port Talbot and used the more than 800 acres surrounding the manor house to practise training. In Northern Ireland an air depot was established at Langford Lodge near Belfast where thousands of American aircraft stopped over on their way to war. The grounds of Dunster Castle in Devon were taken over for training purposes as was the land around Bowood House in Wiltshire. Littlecote House in Berkshire would be used by the 101st Airborne Division, Braunston Park in Leicestershire was used by the 82nd Airborne Division and at Saltram near Plymouth in Devon the estate, owned by the Parker family, was used by a number of specialist units along with the 4th Infantry Division and other infantry units. The grounds of Saltram were also used as a vast vehicle park and maintenance facilities were built to service the tanks and trucks. This was called the 'Friendly Invasion' by the British and they welcomed their American allies. Over the coming months millions of American service personnel, hundreds of thousands of trucks, tanks and artillery, and millions of tons of supplies arrived in Britain.

In Russia, the German army was still recovering from the powerful counter-attacks which had pushed it back from the outskirts of Moscow. Stalin was calling for the Western Allies to open a 'Second Front' by invading Europe. The Russians believed they were bearing the brunt of the fighting and would not accept that such a campaign could not be mounted until sufficient equipment and troops had been assembled to be certain of success. The Western Allies, Britain in particular, wondered how much longer Russia could last after losing so much in the way of men and equipment. Although it had been forced to withdraw from its primary objective, the German army was far from being defeated and proved as much by tightening its grip around Leningrad in the north.

Nearly 1,300 miles away to the south from Leningrad, units of Army Group South had made the first moves in November 1941 to invest the city of Sevastopol in readiness for another siege. In December von Manstein's 11th Army had attacked and forced the defenders back from their first line of defences which comprised two miles of trenches, anti-tank ditches and minefields. The city lay on the coast in the Crimea which itself was virtually an island, being attached to the Ukrainian mainland by only a narrow isthmus to the north. In such a position the city and its population, which included a defending garrison of 100,000 troops, had their backs to the sea.

German operations against Kerch to the east led to the capture of 170,000 Russian troops, 250 tanks and 1,100 pieces of artillery which could have been used to support Sevastopol. Manstein continued to build up his forces which included bringing forward the massive 800mm calibre railway-mounted gun called 'Dora' to add to the weight of the artillery which would shell the city. The defenders had 600 pieces of artillery, 38 tanks and only 55 aircraft. The Germans had 600 aircraft, as well as long-range guns and rocket artillery called 'Nebelwerfers' which could add to the bombardment. They also had the support of their Italian allies along with Bulgarian and Romanian troops. Three rings of defences surrounded the city with minefields, pillboxes and concrete bunkers all of which had to be broken through before Manstein's forces could enter the city proper.

The fighting continued with the defenders being squeezed in tighter with each day of fighting. Finally, on 3 July 1942, the last of the city's defenders surrendered, presenting the Germans with another 100,000 prisoners. The engagement had lasted 247 days and the Germans had fired 46,000 tons of artillery shells in addition to the aerial bombs dropped on the city. The fighting had cost them over 71,000 killed and wounded in what was a sideshow. Had they cut off the isthmus route into the Crimea they could have isolated and starved out the garrison for a minimum of losses. One small benefit which came with the capture of Sevastopol was a stock of 50,000 tons of artillery shells which could be fired against the Soviets using captured pieces of artillery,

The Dora, along with the 'Gustav', was the largest calibre railway artillery piece ever built and had originally been developed by the company of Krupp with the specific intention of bombarding the French Maginot Line. In his book *Lost Victories*, Manstein described Gustav as 'A miracle of technical achievement. The barrel must have been 90 feet long and the carriage as high as a two-story house. Sixty trains had been required to bring it into position along a railway specially laid for the purpose. Two anti-aircraft regiments had to be in constant attendance.' He went on to say of the Gustav railway gun, 'The effectiveness of the cannon bore no real relation to all the material, manpower and expense that had gone into producing it.' In other words, the whole thing was a ghastly drain on resources.

The Gustav gun was dispatched to Sevastopol in 1942 to participate in the siege of the city. It required a crew of more than 1,400 men for its operation and defence, in addition to the anti-aircraft units. The Gustav was formally known as '80cm K (E)' and was built in sections to allow it to pass the railway loading gauge. The fully assembled weapon was over 140 feet in length, 33 feet in width, 38 feet in height and weighed 1,328 tons. It took three weeks to assemble and prepare it ready for firing. The Gustav was assembled using a four-rail double track, with two outer tracks for the assembly crane. The two halves of the bogie units were placed into position and the gun carriage built up on top. The barrel, which came in two sections, was assembled by inserting the rear half into the jacket, connecting the front half by means of an enormous junction nut and mounting the whole assembly on the cradle. The gun was dismantled into breech ring and block, the two barrel sections, jacket, cradle, trunnions and trunnion bearings. All of these sections were transported on special flatcars. The mounting was split longitudinally for movement and dismantled from the top downwards. The sections were transported on additional flatcars hauled by trains. The logistics invested in moving this massive weapon could have been better used transporting conventional and more useful supplies.

Hitler was planning a change of strategy in Russia, where his armies spread out across the vastness in a state of organised chaotic confusion. There had been some reverses but generally the war was not going too badly for Germany. Now Hitler revealed his plans for Army Group South, setting for it a huge target which, if it succeeded, could weaken Russia's ability to fight. On 5 April, he announced Führer Directive 42 or Operation Blau which involved mounting a two-pronged attack, with one advancing in the direction of Stalingrad and the other heading south into the Caucasus and the oil fields. He claimed the move would divide the Soviet forces and ordered preparations be made.

From the rear echelon area, he ordered huge troop movements to the south along with fifty-one divisions supplied by his Bulgarian, Italian and Romanian allies. Italian support for the operation included an Alpine Corps complete with 20,000 mules and 1,100 pieces of artillery. When the movements had been completed there were nine of the nineteen panzer divisions in Russia under Field Marshal Fedor von Bock's command along with four of the ten motorised divisions and half of all infantry divisions. In other words, Army Group South had fifty per cent of all the German army's resources at its disposal. The Italians also made great use of horses in Russia and deployed regular mounted cavalry which on occasion could produce startling results. For example, on 23 August 1942 the Italian 3rd Dragoons of the Savoia Cavalry Regiment of the Prince Amedeo Duke of Aosta (Celere) Division, armed with Model 1891/38 Carcano carbines, but as mounted cavalry also armed with sabres, were ordered by Colonel Betton to charge Russian positions held by the Siberian 812th Infantry Regiment. The charge cost them 40 killed and 70 wounded but they killed 150 troops, captured 900, and seized 60 mortars and other pieces of artillery along with machine guns.

With so much weaponry, equipment, troops and support available for the campaign ahead senior officers believed it would be successful. Any doubts they may have harboured about turning south instead of pushing on eastwards appeared to be without foundation and failure was never considered an option. The opening moves saw a wide-sweeping pincer movement against the city of Voronezh, some 300 miles to the south of Moscow. Other sizeable towns such as Staryy, Oskol, Millrovo and Morovsk were captured as the 6th Army continued its advance towards the target of Stalingrad in Operation Heron. From here Hitler could launch Operation Edelweiss, the strike towards the oilfields of the Caucasus. He had every faith in the 6th Army under General von Paulus, after all they had been successful in every campaign in which they had participated so far.

If the 6th Army could capture the vital oil resources the Russian army would be crippled by lack of fuel while the Germans would be self-sufficient. From early July to early August the Germans moved forward to try and encircle the city of Stalingrad. During that time they had captured the city of Rostov with its massive industrial centre. The advance was opposed by the Russians who put up enough resistance to cover a planned, orderly withdrawal. Hitler was jubilant, proclaiming, 'The Russians are in full flight! They are finished!' But it was to prove the undoing of the Germans in Russia and change the course of the war.

The city of Stalingrad proper stretched for about fifteen miles along the western bank of the River Volga, but its environs extended much further. At its widest point, the city is over four miles wide and so its shape was linear which would force any attacker to stretch his forces long and thin. That is exactly what von Paulus did and although his troops would eventually capture some ninety per cent of the city they never made any incursions across the Volga, which left the east bank of the river securely in Russian hands. The city had factories producing weapons and tanks, three of which were very important: the Barrikady, the Red October and the Tractor Factory.

The distances expected to be covered were enormous and placed great strain on supply lines, men and machines. The 4th Panzer Army commanded by General Hermann Hoth had to cover more than twenty miles to help support General Ewald von Kleist's 1st Panzer Army which had encountered fierce Russian resistance in the Don Basin. The two forces met but the Russians had withdrawn, leaving nothing of any consequence to be captured. Reflecting later, Kleist said of the operation that in his opinion 'Fourth Panzer Army could have taken Stalingrad without a fight at the end of July, but it was diverted to help me crossing the Don. I did not need its aid, and it simply got in the way.' In fact, the amount of traffic on the roads caused congestion and delays. Hitler then ordered Hoth to return to the thrust on Stalingrad, adding to the mileage to be covered, while Kleist continued southwards towards the oilfields.

The Russians had come into possession of a full set of detailed plans outlining Operation Blau in advance, so were not entirely unaware that a major offensive was about to be launched. They had gained the papers when the aircraft in which Major Reichel, chief of operations for the 23rd Panzer Division, made a forced landing close to Russian lines. The capture of such sensitive documents seemed too convenient to Stalin who held the belief that the Germans still planned to attack Moscow. Despite their

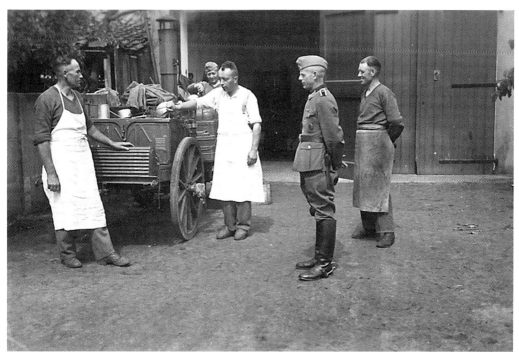

Feeding the troops was essential and food had to be cooked, making it it a vital part of the logistics supply lines. Here, cooks with a field kitchen, known to German troops as the 'Goulashkanone', are preparing a meal.

Millions of horses were used by the German army on the Eastern Front as seen here pulling a wagon through the mud.

A whole supply column with horses to pull the wagons. Petrol was needed for the vehicles, but the animals had to be fed.

In the early stages, German troops were well equipped with everything for a campaign. Later everything became more scarce, including proper uniforms.

The Germans made extensive use of the rail network in all occupied countries. Here, the troops are queuing to be fed, presumably somewhere in Russia, with their mess tins at the ready.

appearance to the contrary Stalin dismissed the captured plans as a plant to deceive the Russians by subterfuge. Nevertheless, when the German attack came and the Russians realised what the object of the attack was they immediately mobilised the one resource they had in ample supply and that was manpower. A labour force made up initially of 90,000 civilians was put to work between August and September and set with the task of building defences. The work continued day and night without pause such was the urgency to halt the Germans. More workers joined and eventually they constructed 100,000 defensive positions including 70,000 pillboxes using concrete and bricks. They dug 500 miles of anti-tank ditches, 200 miles of anti-infantry obstacles and 1,000 miles of trenches for their infantry. Roads were sealed off and mountain passes were blocked. The tanks and infantry of von Kleist were effectively stopped by this human endeavour and the Caucasian oilfields were safe.

Paulus and his 6th Army with 25 divisions, 2,000 pieces of artillery and 500 tanks supported by the VIII Fliegerkorps capable of flying 1,000 sorties per day were at the gates of Stalingrad. Facing them the garrison commander Lieutenant General Vasili Chuikov had a force of 54,000 men in the 64th Army supported with 900 pieces of artillery and mortars and 110 tanks. On taking up his command he reported to his superior, General Andrei Yeremenko, 'We shall hold the city, or die there.' The city had been invested ready to be besieged and from 24 August heavy fighting patrols were

being sent out to probe the Russians' defences, but the first serious attack was not
made until 14 September. The combined weight of the attack with Hoth's troops
brought the total strength to 200,000 men.

German tanks entered the city in support of the attack and the Russians defended every
building, street and cellar. The Germans were not used to fighting in such conditions
and tanks are unsuited to fighting in built-up areas with buildings all round. Once they
had entered the city the Germans did not withdraw and poured more men and reserves
into its capture. The Russians did not evacuate the civilians from the city and brought
reinforcements and supplies into the city by ferry across the River Volga. These boats
were constantly attacked by German aircraft and bombarded by artillery but the supply
lines into the city kept operating. By the end of the battle these boats, known as the
Volga Flotilla, had made 35,000 crossings to bring in supplies and 122,000 men and
evacuated only those most seriously wounded. The fighting continued throughout the
rest of the month by which time the Russians had lost 80,000 men killed and wounded.
In September alone, the German 6th Army fired around 25 million rounds of small
arms ammunition, 750,000 mortar bombs, 685,000 shells for artillery and tanks, and
thrown 178,000 hand grenades. All this had to be replaced and reserve stocks delivered.

At the same time as the Germans were approaching the outskirts of Stalingrad, the
Western Allies were putting into action a plan to launch a limited attack on the French
coast. On 19 August an Anglo-Canadian force including fifty-one US Rangers and
some French commandos landed at Dieppe in an action called Operation Jubilee. The
object of the operation was to make an assault to gain experience in trying to capture a
port installation which would be needed to support an amphibious landing. As Winston
Churchill saw it the operation was 'a reconnaissance in force' in order to 'test the enemy
defences… [to] discover what resistance would have to be met in the endeavour to seize
a port'. The Western Allies had been harangued by Stalin to launch a Second Front by
attacking in the west but they just did not have the supplies or specialist vehicles and
equipment in 1942 to undertake such an assault. Furthermore, they had no experience
in large-scale amphibious landings. The British had plenty of experience in withdrawing
troops using amphibious forces, following Dunkirk, Norway, Greece and Crete, but not
landing troops and vehicles.

The attack against Dieppe was designed to give the Allies practical experience at all
levels, with the emphasis placed on how important it was to get armour ashore from
the landing craft. The bulk of the force was infantry, made up of 4,963 troops from the
Canadian 2nd Infantry Division supported by a squadron of twenty-eight Churchill
tanks. The Germans later remarked that they considered the attack to be serious
because it was too large to be an ordinary commando raid. They recognised it was an
attempt to land a force in strength on a beach, but they understood it was too small to
be the anticipated invasion. The infantry managed to move inland away from the beach

and fighting was fierce, but against defensive positions held by superior numbers and even with air cover they could only do their best. The operation began to collapse as the casualty rate among the British and Canadian infantry mounted and the Royal Navy lost more vessels.

The first landings had been made before 5am, but by 9am it was becoming clear the operation was foundering. Major General Roberts commanding the Canadians organised for the RAF to provide air cover to allow the infantry to withdraw. At 11am the landing craft approached the shore to embark the men and by midday the operation was all but finished. It was an unmitigated disaster with the Canadians losing 900 men killed and a further 3,367 wounded and taken prisoner. The British lost 275 killed, wounded and taken prisoner. Two of the tanks had sunk in deep water as they were landed, a number became bogged down in the shingle and fifteen made it to the sea wall and began to move off the beach before being halted by obstacles. The Germans lost 519 killed and wounded.

In the grand scheme of things, compared to events on the Russian front the Dieppe raid was a pinprick. The Allies did learn many important lessons from the mistakes made at Dieppe and they would correct many by the time of their next attempt at amphibious assault. The Germans had learned not to underestimate the Allies' resolve to invade Europe. Indeed, the Allies came to realise the limitations of ordinary armour and recognised the importance of developing special armoured vehicles to break through defences and that a port installation was vital for supplies to be ferried in to support the assault. It also demonstrated to Stalin that his Western Allies were trying. Three days later, Brazil declared war on Germany. While sounding insignificant, it meant that the waters around South America were being patrolled and that the meat produced by the country and shipped out would help support the Allies.

At Stalingrad, the populace was mobilised to build barricades, women soldiers served on anti-aircraft guns and to a man they were resolved to defend the city come what may. The German situation looked strong but in reality they were at the end of a very long and consequently very fragile supply line. Furthermore, they had no reserves of anything to speak of. In their advance to invest the city, the tanks and other AFVs had spearheaded the attack followed by the supply convoys with the infantry bringing up the rear. Even so, the advance had been so fast they had outpaced some of the supply columns. The Russians continued to fall back, avoiding battle and this further added to the Germans' false sense of victory and they pressed on ever deeper into Russia.

On 23 November Hitler asked the army chief of staff, General Kurt Zeitzler, a specialist in logistics, for his assessment of the situation. Zeitzler began his analysis, based on statistics compiled by his staff, and presented his findings: 'Allowing for all the stocks at present with the 6th Army, allowing for absolute minimum needs and the taking of all possible emergency measures, the 6th Army will require delivery of

300 tons per day. But since not every day is suitable for flying, as I myself learned at the front last winter, this means that about 500 tons will have to be carried to the 6th Army on each and every flying day if the irreducible minimum average is to be maintained.' Goering replied, 'I can do that!' without basing his declaration on any hard facts. Zeitzler replied by saying it was a lie that such an operation could succeed. Hitler sided with Goering and dismissed any further opposition to the task which lay ahead by declaring, 'The Reichsmarschall has made his report to me, which I have no choice but to believe.' Zeitzler concluded his assessment by giving a cautionary notice to take care of the positions to the north of Stalingrad where the Italian, Hungarians and Romanians held the line. He also pointed out that the southern sector and the 6th Army's right flank were also exposed. The Germans had never before had to fight in such conditions where men hid among the ruins of buildings and the battle was costing them 20,000 killed and wounded per week. The streets were strewn with rubble which reduced the tanks to a crawl and exposed them to anti-tank weapons.

Stalin proclaimed a policy of 'Not one step backward,' and that there was 'no land beyond the Volga'. In other words the Russian army had to stand and fight where it was. Snipers took their toll and battles ebbed backwards and forwards with buildings changing hands many times. Using the ferries the Russians moved 122,000 men into the city to carry on the fight but this represented only a small proportion as the greater numbers of men, vehicles, supplies and weapons, amounting to 27 infantry divisions and 19 armoured divisions, were sent to assembly areas to wait in readiness for the attack.

When the Volga froze, the conditions allowed trucks to be driven over the ice like Lake Ladoga at Leningrad. Over the course of seven weeks the Russians managed to move over 18,000 trucks and 17,000 other vehicles, including tanks and self-propelled guns, into the defence of the city this way. The build-up continued until, by mid-November, the Russians had husbanded together a force of one million men, 900 tanks, thousands of trucks, 13,500 pieces of artillery, and Katyusha rocket-firing trucks, supported by 1,100 aircraft. Some of the tanks were supplied by America under the Lend-Lease Act but the Russians believed them to be 'no good' because the 'valves go to pieces, the engine overheats and the transmission is no use'. The Germans were running out of fuel to the degree that between September and November the tanks of the 22nd Panzer Division could not operate. Finally, the preparations were complete and the Russians launched Operation Uranus on 19 November, attacking the Romanian positions to the north of the city, just as Zeitzler had predicted and tried to warn against. The powerful T-34 tanks, which the Germans had already encountered, were used in large numbers. The Romanians had no defence against them and fled their positions. The collapse left a gap fifty miles wide in the German lines and the Russians poured through.

The attack to the south of Stalingrad was equally effective and the Russians streamed through the German lines. Their advance was so fast that German army military police directing the flow of traffic became confused and could not tell the difference between friend and foe. Russian troops on trucks seized bridges and secured them. On 23 November the two arms of the Russian pincer movement met up thirty miles west of Stalingrad and the Germans inside the city were surrounded and cut off. The Russians believed they had trapped 75,000 men but the figure was actually 250,000. There was no chance of moving reinforcements into the city to support them; the Russians could move with almost total impunity and were getting stronger every day.

Three days after the attack von Paulus assessed his situation. He estimated that he had food for only six days and fuel and ammunitions stocks were running critically low. He signalled Hitler asking that he be allowed to fight his way out of the city. Hitler forbade such a move and told him that supplies would be flown to him. The trapped 6th Army needed at least 120 tons of fuel and 250 tons of ammunition each day to continue. Other supplies such as medical aid and food would push this figure up to 600 tons. Despite all promises, Goering's Luftwaffe could only deliver half the required amount.

General Martin Fiebig, commanding VIII Air Corps, knew the enormity of the task and as the two great pincer arms of the Russian forces were closing in around Stalingrad he voiced his doubts to senior officers: 'It is impossible to resupply a whole army by air. The Luftwaffe hasn't got enough transport aircraft.' He was later proved correct, but at the time no-one would take his side to try to convince Hitler, who had already made up his mind.

The Luftwaffe would have to fly from bases at Tatsinskaya and Morozovsky, three-hour round trips which meant aircraft could only fly one mission per day. There were 225 Ju 52 transport aircraft available, but they were slow and lumbering which made them vulnerable to attack by Soviet fighters. To support the operation He III bombers were pressed into service and although they were faster, each aircraft could only carry 1.5 tons of supplies. The claim that the trapped 6th Army could be supplied by air depended on all aircraft being serviceable and airfields inside the city being held by German forces. In the event, the best they could achieve was eighty serviceable aircraft per day and when the Russians captured the airfields the amount of supplies which could be flown in fell to less than sixty tons per day.

On 4 January 1943, 250 tons of supplies were flown in and the following day this figure was down to 150 tons. Two days later only 45 tons of essentials were flown to the beleaguered fighters and after 21 January no supplies were delivered. The attempt to airlift supplies cost the Germans 488 aircraft shot down or crashed. Manstein, now commanding the newly-formed Army Group Don, formulated Operation Winter Storm, which was intended to break into the city to relieve the 6th Army.

By now the Russians had pushed eighty miles west past Stalingrad, but General Hoth with his 4th Panzer Division began his mission on 12 December. In his column he had a convoy of trucks carrying 3,000 tons of supplies. They battled on against Russian attacks, worsening weather conditions and rugged terrain. His progress slowed and finally on 23 December he was ordered to withdraw. He was thirty miles away from his destination, but given the conditions it may as well have been thousands of miles. As Hoth retreated, the 6th Army was effectively abandoned to its fate. The distance between the German front line and Stalingrad grew longer each day as the Russians continued to advance. The 6th Army somehow continued to fight on but groups were surrendering. The Germans finally surrendered on 31 January 1943. The fighting had cost them 150,000 killed and the Russians took a further 100,000 prisoners. The Germans had lost so much equipment it was calculated that it could have supplied twenty-five per cent of the German army in the field. The Luftwaffe had lost almost 500 Ju 52 transport aircraft alone in the five-month period. It had been a costly demonstration of how important good logistical support was to a modern army.

The lesson of Stalingrad and how difficult it was to supply ammunition and fuel in sufficient quantity to an army was not lost on the Allies, but the Germans did not appear to have learnt anything from the experiences at either Demyansk or Kholm earlier in the year. No army could continue to lose weapons, vehicles and troops at the rate Germany was and still expect the army to function. Yet, here was Hitler, still urging his forces to go on with depleted resources and minimal supplies.

Eleven days before the Russians launched Operation Uranus at Stalingrad, the Western Allies launched Operation Torch, an amphibious landing on the North African coast of French Morocco and Algeria. It demonstrated to Stalin what they were capable of. It should have also served as a warning to Hitler what to expect in Europe.

French Morocco and Algeria were being held by troops of the Vichy government of Marshal Phillipe Pétain, who supported Hitler. It was decided to land at three points along a 700-mile stretch of the coast, extending from Casablanca to Algiers. The Western Task Force would land on the western coast of Morocco. The Centre Task Force would land around the port of Oran, while the Eastern Task Force would land at Algiers.

It was an ambitious plan. It would be the first time in the war American troops had engaged an enemy on land. Next, the distances to be covered in transporting everything to the landing points were great. Also, it was the first Anglo-American operation of the war. Much depended on its success, not least the future of the war in North Africa.

The areas in which the Allies were to land were believed to be defended by 125,000 troops with artillery and armoured support. If necessary, they could be ordered to move east to support Rommel. There was also a sizeable naval presence in Casablanca which could harass Allied naval forces entering the Mediterranean Sea. If a successful landing could be effected, it would achieve two aims. Firstly, it would secure the southern coastline entering the Mediterranean. Secondly, it would threaten Rommel's rear in the west and the shipping lanes of his supply ships. Rommel was already suffering badly from losses and the rates were increasing. In July he lost 15,386 tons, in September 33,791 tons, and in October he lost over 56,000 tons.

The assault forces comprised 107,000 troops, mostly American, none of which had ever been in combat before. They were transported to their landing points in 500 transport ships with an escort of 350 warships. The American force sailed direct to North Africa and maintained the supply line. The landings were made on 8 November 1942 and the Americans hoped for a quick campaign. They met some resistance but not on the scale they imagined. The firepower of the naval guns supported the landings and kept the French fleet at bay. The Vichy French had 210 ageing tanks, but they were to prove no match against the 630 modern American Sherman tanks and anti-tank guns. After a week of fighting the Vichy French surrendered. They had lost 3,200 killed and wounded and all their weapons and equipment. The Allies had got off lightly with around 500 killed and some 720 wounded. Importantly, they had secured harbour facilities and airfields in Morocco and Algeria which would allow supplies to be brought in.

With the success of these new landings in North Africa Rommel was now faced with an improbable situation of fighting on two fronts, each having to be supplied. When he was informed about the Allied landings he wrote in his diary, 'This spells the end of the army in Africa.' The Germans responded to the Torch landings by sending 17,000 reinforcements with General Jürgen von Arnim.

Commanding the landing operations was an officer by the name of Dwight David Eisenhower who had never before held a combat command. At the time of Operation Torch, he was a relatively unknown factor, but soon the whole world would recognise him and know him by his more familiar nickname of 'Ike'.

Eisenhower had graduated from West Point in 1915 and during the First World War he held various training posts, proving himself to be a capable and skilled organiser. He was refused the opportunity to serve overseas in the First World War and instead was appointed to train tank crews. Promoted to the rank of brigadier general in October 1941, his capabilities as an administrator were becoming widely recognised. His first post when America entered the war in December 1941 was Deputy Chief in charge of Pacific Defences. He was assigned to the General Staff in Washington where among his many duties he was responsible in drawing up plans for the defeat of Germany and in May 1942 he arrived in England with Lieutenant General Henry Arnold. In June 1942 he was appointed Commanding General European Theatre of Operations, followed by Supreme Commander Allied (Expeditionary) Force of the North African Theatre of Operations for the Torch landings, during which period he strengthened his command skills. Further promotions and changes in his appointment came during 1943 and by the end of that year President Roosevelt appointed him Supreme Allied Commander in Europe.

Several other prominent American commanders would emerge during Operation Torch, including George Patton, Mark Clark and Omar Bradley. The Americans were still relative newcomers, but they were learning the rules fast. One of these was the importance of supplies. One American General was heard to remark: 'My men can eat their belts, but my tanks gotta have gas.'

Four months before Operation Torch, the month of July had been an uncertain time for the British 8th Army which was on its back foot and waiting for Rommel to make his next move, believing it was only a question of time before he returned to the attack to deliver the knockout blow. With only minimal resources he had achieved the seemingly impossible with the capture of Tobruk. It was all very different from his position in May when he was within a day of surrendering due to lack of water. He had been saved by the huge stocks of supplies he had captured at Tobruk. Like their counterparts in Russia, the Afrika Korps was at the end of a very long and fragile supply line, which was being attacked by the LRDG and SAS which had penetrated deep behind their lines. Rommel was being promised much but receiving very little. In preparation for his forthcoming attack, planned for August, Field Marshal Kesselring, Commander in Chief South and therefore Rommel's commanding officer in North Africa, promised a delivery of 6,000 tons of supplies. As a matter of urgency, Kesselring declared that 1,000 tons would be flown in. Rommel stressed the importance that such a delivery be made. His main problem was supply convoys not getting through. On one occasion a convoy of six tankers was intercepted and four sunk. Despite having only 203 battle-worthy tanks, Rommel still made his preparations.

In August Churchill flew to Cairo to announce changes in command, which included replacing General Auchinleck with General Alexander. He had intended to appoint General Gott commander of the 8th Army, but when Gott was killed on 7 August, General Sir Alan Brooke, Commander Imperial General Staff, suggested Montgomery be appointed to the position. He was a 'no-nonsense' leader who expected much from everyone under his command. His orders, issued directly from Churchill, were straight to the point: Destroy the German-Italian army commanded by Field Marshal Rommel. Montgomery was a man of action and he immediately set about making his preparations for the battle which lay ahead.

The expected attack came on the night of 30/31 August with Rommel using the 15th and 21st Panzer Divisions supported by the Italians including the Littorio and Ariete Divisions. Things did not go well and they sustained heavy losses. Rommel was ill but he was still capable of command. On 1 September, he visited the forward area to see how the battle was proceeding. The weather changed and sandstorms tore across the area. Rommel tried to forge ahead but by the evening of 2 September he had only sufficient fuel to continue for 100 miles. This was not enough and he began to withdraw. He had been promised an emergency airlift of fuel but he needed much more than could be flown in if he was to keep up his offensive. The fuel crisis was his main problem which he pointed out on 27 August when he said, 'The whole battle depends on it.'

Facing him, Montgomery had some 400 tanks in defensive positions supported by screens of 6-pounder anti-tank guns and 300 additional tanks in reserve. The defensive screen had blunted Rommel's attack and the battle had cost him 50 tanks, 400 trucks and 55 anti-tank guns. The British had lost 67 tanks and 17 anti-tank guns. Montgomery had only been in Egypt two weeks and here he was stopping the Germans in his first action against Rommel.

Montgomery was pleased with the way his men had fought at the Battle of Alam el Halfa and seeing his foe was not going to advance further he called off the battle. Rommel's health was deteriorating and believing the British would probably not be ready to attack until December, he took the opportunity to return to Germany on 23 September. He left matters in the hands of General Georg Stumme who had arrived in Egypt on 19 September. Lieutenant Colonel Friedrich von Mellenthin, serving on Rommel's staff, summed up the position by describing the battle as 'the turning point of the desert war…the first in a long series of defeats on every front which foreshadowed the defeat of Germany.'

The British were receiving reinforcements, replacement tanks, supplies and new weapons. Each side began to lay vast numbers of mines which claimed many victims, both human and vehicle. Eventually the Germans laid almost 250,000 anti-tank mines with 14,500 anti-personnel mines. The infantry referred to these minefields as the 'Devil's Gardens'. To clear paths through them the British used Matilda Mk II tanks called 'Scorpions' which were fitted with chain flails. Some M3 Lee-Grant Medium Tanks were also converted to this role. In addition, infantrymen were trained to use their bayonets to probe the ground to locate mines, and the Royal Engineers used mine-detector devices.

Throughout the rest of September and into October 1942, Montgomery continued the build-up for his planned attack. Troops were rigorously trained, and stores, weapons, fuel and ammunition were stockpiled. He was determined to deliver the knockout blow which would put the Germans in full retreat. Churchill tried to pressure him into making an attack, but Montgomery was determined he would not do so until he knew everything was ready.

The RAOC handled 40,000 tons of stores delivered to depots and issued 595,000 separate items which amounted to around 29,000 tons of equipment. Nothing was too insignificant. For example, almost 100,000 boots were repaired. At the other end of the scale, field workshops repaired more than 1,000 tanks and other AFVs belonging to X Corps and returned them to battle during a period of three weeks. The Eighth Army also received specialised ten-ton rated recovery trucks from America which supplemented the lighter three-ton lorries that formed the backbone of the British army's transport flout. The heavier vehicles were produced by companies experienced in the manufacture of heavy-duty lorries for use on massive projects such as the construction of dams in America. These rugged 4x4s were ideal for use in the desert. In earlier wars food for troops and forage for the horses had formed the bulk of supplies being transported. Here in the desert and other theatres, this would fall to ten per cent as petrol, oil and ammunition took priority. The British by now had learned the importance of their vehicles and veterans of the campaign recall how 'Your vehicle was your life, quite literally. We loved our vehicles and we'd do anything to keep them going.' They did too, and marvels were worked in maintenance.

After weeks of preparation, Montgomery was satisfied that everything was ready and he could begin his attack which would be a three-pronged assault in three phases. The main attack would be made in the north with diversionary attacks in the south with dummy tanks, trucks and fuel dumps made from inflatable models, canvas and empty crates. Radio signals added to the illusion and kept the Germans guessing where the main thrust would come. In the north, the British moved XXX Corps forward, supported with artillery, trucks, engineers and all the attendant supplies.

On 23 October at 9.40pm, two months earlier than Rommel had predicted, Montgomery launched his attack with an opening artillery barrage from 1,000 field guns. Fifteen minutes later, all firing stopped. Then, suddenly, after a pause of five minutes, it all began again with shells being fired at the rate of 1,000 per minute. This was the 'rolling barrage', a wall of high explosive designed to keep the enemy under cover while the British army advanced. On average, Montgomery's forces were almost twice as strong as the Germans.

Montgomery had 195,000 troops compared to a combined Italo-German army of 104,000. Among his arsenal he amassed 1,351 tanks, which included 422 American Shermans and Grants, and almost 1,300 anti-tank guns, including 753 of the new 6-pounder. Major General Sir Francis de Guingand, who served as Chief of Staff to the 8th Army between 1942 and 1943, recorded over 900 pieces of field artillery, including 832 25-pounder field guns. The Germans had about 600 tanks, half of which were Italian. Of this force, only 38 were Panzer IV which had the capability of matching the Sherman. German artillery comprised of 800 anti-tank guns, of which only 86 were of the powerful 88mm calibre and a further 500 field guns. The two sides were almost on parity in aircraft with the RAF having 530 to the Luftwaffe's 500. The difference came in the fact that the Germans had only 350 serviceable aircraft and their fuel shortages restricted their operational readiness, which actually meant the RAF had air superiority.

On 24 October, General Stumme while moving between locations in his staff car was attacked by aircraft. Although uninjured, Stumme died of a heart attack a few days later. Rommel returned to the front line but by that time his forces had taken a terrible mauling. By the evening of 25 October the 15th Panzer Division was down to only 31 tanks, having lost 88 in only 48 hours of fighting. Montgomery kept up the pressure and units were entering the battle as his strategy unfolded. At an engagement on 2 November, British artillery contributed to the 117 German tanks destroyed at El Aqaquir.

Rommel assessed the situation and declared it hopeless, ordering his troops to withdraw. They fell back sixty miles to Fuka. He informed Hitler of his decision on 4 November who immediately exploded in a rage and forbade any such action. The Germans conducted a fighting retreat and managed to beat off an attack by 200 tanks. Hitler, in a rare change of mind, conceded Rommel's decision and allowed the Afrika Korps to retreat. The Germans commandeered the Italians' vehicles so they could withdraw, all the while being pursued. The Italians, without transport, short of food, water and ammunition, surrendered in their tens of thousands. Rommel had nothing left with which he could turn and fight and his forces were now in headlong retreat. Over the next few days the rearguard units destroyed their last tanks. The weather broke and torrential rain turned tracks into seas of mud so that the trucks carrying the infantry could only trundle along at little more than walking pace. They were saved by the fact that the weather was so appalling it grounded the RAF.

Montgomery kept in contact but maintained a distance just in case Rommel could muster a counter-attack. Passing through Sidi Barrani another eighty miles back German sappers destroyed bridges and roads in the rear. The Battle of El Alamein was over and had cost the Germans 50,000 killed, wounded or taken prisoner. They had lost hundreds of trucks, 450 tanks, the Italians had had to abandon 75 tanks through lack of fuel, and over 1,000 pieces of artillery had been destroyed or captured. Montgomery had lost 13,500 killed and wounded with100 pieces of artillery destroyed. Figures for the loss of British tanks vary, with some sources claiming that of the 500 tanks lost only 150 were beyond repair. Other sources claim that 600 were knocked out of which 350 could be repaired, while a third source claims 200 tanks were destroyed and 300 were repaired. The true cost was probably an average of the three figures – about 266 tanks destroyed and the same number damaged.

In a speech made in November 1942 Winston Churchill said of the Battle of El Alamein, 'Now this is not the end. It is not even the beginning of the end. But it is, perhaps, the end of the beginning.' He could have been speaking for all the Allies, including Stalin and Roosevelt, as together the campaigns and operations of 1942 were forcing the Germans back on all fronts. Even so, these leaders realised that there was still a long way to go before Germany was beaten. Montgomery knew the Germans had lost the battle but they had not lost the war in North Africa, but he was determined to complete his orders from Churchill. It would take time, but with Allied forces in the west waiting to receive the retreating Afrika Korps he was confident that the outcome was inevitable and Churchill's orders would be fulfilled. The opposing sides had 'see-sawed' back and forth east and west across the desert five times covering thousands of miles. The vehicles were worn out and the troops exhausted.

The British pushed the Germans on to Benghazi. At that point Rommel was given the devastating news that ninety per cent of a convoy bringing his supplies had been sunk. At El Agheila on 12 December, the 7th Armoured Division overran German positions and on 25 December the British army was at Sirte. They had advanced 800 miles in two months, but that now meant their supplies had to come that distance. The difference, though, was the British had the resources to achieve it.

British troops resupplying and refuelling their Churchill tanks.

Chapter 11

1943: More Lessons are Learnt

As 1943 dawned, the war was entering its fourth year as a global conflict. Germany had taken severe blows on the Eastern Front with the loss of the entire Sixth Army following its surrender to the Soviet army at Stalingrad on 31 January. In North Africa, the Afrika Korps and the Italian forces were being hemmed in following the success of the Anglo-American landings to the west in November 1942, which put large numbers of troops to the rear of Rommel's forces, obliging him to face the Allies on two fronts. Despite these setbacks, Hitler's forces in the field remained far from being defeated. In both situations it was oil, or rather the lack of it, which lay behind the problems besetting the Germans. The Western Allies had good supplies to support their operations in North Africa while Rommel's supply lines were being attacked by sea and air as the ships bringing in his oil and ammunition were sunk. In Russia, the Red Army was beginning to benefit from improvements in their supply lines, especially oil. The Germans, surrounded and trapped in Stalingrad, received very little in the way of supplies. Reviewing each of these situations, one is reminded of the words of George Curzon 1st Marquis of Kedleston after the First World War: 'the Allies floated to victory on a tide of oil.' It looked as though the Allies would again be victorious due to their control of oil.

Rommel had realised all along the importance of logistics, especially fuel, to keep his army operational. He also knew how important it was to have air support. These two considerations took up much of his time. In one set of records he outlines both points together and comments, 'Whoever enjoys command of the air is in a position to inflict such heavy damage on the opponent's supply columns that serious shortages must soon make themselves felt. By maintaining a constant watch on the roads leading to the front he can put a stop to daylight supply traffic and force his enemy to drive only by night, thus causing him to lose irreplaceable time. ... an assured flow of supplies is essential; without it an army becomes immobilised and incapable of action.' It was as though he was seeing his own future in North Africa.

At the beginning of 1943, America, despite being the newest belligerent to the war, was showing the world just how quickly it was responding to the war footing on which it now found itself. American troops were now in action in North Africa, it was fighting a war in the Pacific, and the USAAF had joined the RAF flying bombing missions over Germany. However, without doubt, it was the vast industrial might of the factories producing tanks, guns and vehicles in ever-greater quantities which was proving to be the vital lifeline for Britain and the Soviet Union.

Everything America produced was on a massive scale. The story of the Willys Jeep begins in 1940, when the war in Europe was widening across the globe and threatening to drag in other nations. America had adopted an official non-involvement stance, but even so, there were some industrialists who realised that it was only a question of time before an incident occurred which would force the country into action. There were those in the military who harboured similar opinions and began pressing for new vehicles. There were calls for reliable, sturdy vehicles to meet the needs of the military in a future war. In 1940, the US Ordnance Technical Committee produced a specification for a new military vehicle which had to meet a certain level of criteria for what was termed as a 'utility car'. The specifications called for the new vehicle to be four-wheel drive, be light with an upper weight limit of 1,300 pounds and capable of carrying a payload of 600 pounds.

The request for the new vehicle was sent out to 175 specialist engineering and automobile companies. Urgency was the order of the day, and the request set a delivery date with a lead time of eleven weeks in which each company could submit their models for consideration. It was a tight deadline and in the end only two manufacturers responded.

The Jeep became the workhorse of the Allies' armies in a wide range of roles.

Airborne forces found the Jeep fitted their needs.

The American Bantam Car Company produced a prototype known as the Bantam Reconnaissance Command. It was delivered in September 1940 and put through a series of field trials at Fort Holabird. These tests showed the vehicle had potential but it was lacking in power and not nearly rugged enough to withstand the rigours of use and abuse on the battlefield.

At Willys-Overland Motors, the chief engineer, Barney Roos, believed the specifications laid down were not realistic and any design would be too constrained by them, especially when it came to the question of overall weight of the finished vehicle. Roos began working to design a vehicle which he felt was more suited to the needs of the US Army and decided to ignore the weight limits. He worked closely with the engineers from the US Army Quartermaster Corps and between them they produced a vehicle ready for testing in November 1940. Early trials showed it to be successful in every instance and it looked promising.

Meanwhile, the Ordnance Technical Committee had made some concessions regarding the new 'utility car' and the weight limit was now raised to 2,160 pounds. Invitations for a new design with the amended specifications were sent to the companies of Ford, Willys-Overland and Bantam asking for their vehicles. In the end the Ford and Bantam designs were found to be inadequate. The Willys design exceeded the new weight limit by some 120 pounds, but it was more powerful, giving over fifty per cent more engine capability than the other designs. Roos returned to examine the vehicle and stripped out all unnecessary items to bring it to just within the set limits. The hard work paid dividends and the new 'utility car' was accepted into service in 1941, just in time for America's entry into the war after Pearl Harbor. An initial order for some 16,000 vehicles was placed and these were referred to as model MA. As production proceeded, some modifications were made, such as fitting a larger fuel tank and these became the Willys Model MB with production commencing in December 1941. The Ford Motor Company was also contracted to build the vehicle to Willys' design and these were called Truck, Command and Reconnaissance, ¼ ton, 4x4 Ford Model GPW.

The new vehicle soon acquired the name 'Jeep', a nickname which all reference sources agree was a contraction of the initials 'GP' – General Purpose. The name stuck and is still used today. The Jeep proved invaluable as a cargo carrier, capable of towing a trailer load of 1,000 lbs and carrying loads of 800 lbs on the vehicle itself. It was also versatile enough to serve as a weapons platform onto which heavy machine guns could be mounted or recoilless rifles for anti-vehicle roles and destroying bunkers. The Jeep's improvement to battlefield mobility was immediately obvious and proved useful to infantry, artillery, medical services, marines and air force alike. With the artillery, it could tow light anti-tank guns up to 57mm calibre. It was used by the British Long Range Desert Group and Special Air Service who fitted them with a range of machine

The Jeep could cope with most conditions from mud to sand.

Capable of being heavily armed for its size the Jeep suited all purposes.

Light, reliable and easy to handle the Jeep was a 'go anywhere' vehicle.

The Long Range Desert Group and the Special Air Service also found the Jeep met their needs.

Even in a liaison capacity the Jeep could be depended on.

gun configurations including twin Vickers 'K' Guns, Bren Guns, and .30 and .50-inch machine guns. Jeeps were also capable of being driven directly from landing craft during amphibious assaults such as North Africa, Salerno, D-Day and the landings in the Far East, such as New Guinea and Okinawa.

The Jeep was used personally by Montgomery and Patton, and Rommel ordered that captured vehicles be pressed into service. In the ambulance role, the Jeep could carry up to three stretcher cases. At Normandy and Arnhem they were stripped down to reduce weight and carried into battle by gliders.

The Jeep was used for a range of experimental trials including a half-track version and long wheelbase. The American 82nd Airborne Division are known to have modified some of their Jeeps by fitting armour plate for improved protection when in battle. A nasty trick used by some Axis forces was to stretch wire across the road at about neck height in the hope it would catch a despatch rider on a motorcycle. Open-topped Jeeps also encountered this deadly trap and to counter it lengths of angle iron were fitted upright at the front of the vehicle higher than the driver's head.

Under the terms of the Lend-Lease Bill which came into effect on 11 March 1941, America supplied Britain with thousands of vehicles including many Jeeps. Russia too benefitted from a similar plan and in 1943 alone received over 210,000 vehicles, a figure which included thousands of Jeeps. The Jeeps were transported as 'Partly Knocked Down' or 'Completely Knocked Down' and had to be assembled on delivery. In Britain after D-Day the Jeeps were assembled in hastily prepared barns on recently liberated farms. A typical Jeep could carry four men plus the driver along with personal equipment and a heavy machine gun. By the end of the war over 639, 000 Jeeps had been built.

Many more companies were involved in the production of the Jeep and experiments were conducted to produce other variants of the design. One such trial produced the GPA or amphibious design, sometimes known as the 'Seep' (Sea-going Jeep), which could reach 50mph on land and the propeller allowed it 5.5mph in the water. It was useful for moving small loads, such as medical equipment, quickly over short distances and through water obstacles, and around 12,778 were built, but it was never popular, being difficult to handle in the water and prone to being swamped.

The Jeep was also popular with irregular forces created during the war, such as the unit nicknamed 'Popski's Private Army', named after and commanded by Major (later Lieutenant Colonel) Vladimir Peniakoff. Born in Belgium, Peniakoff had an in-depth knowledge of the region and had served in the French army in the First World War. The unit was raised to raid deep into enemy territory in the western desert and later in Italy. Peniakoff was irregular and unconventional and devised some unusual ideas for conducting warfare. He also had a penchant for fitting strange devices to vehicles; he mounted smoke generators on his Jeeps. He was audacious in his undertakings such as the night time raid at Gravina, a German-held town in Italy. Driving their Jeeps into the town late at night on 13 September 1943 they posed as Italians and entered the headquarters building where the 1st Parachute Division was garrisoned. They grabbed papers and documents and an officer who turned out to be Major Schultz who was responsible for supplies to the officers' mess. Although Schultz was of relatively minor importance, the documents Popski and his men grabbed provided detailed information concerning German defences and unit strength in the area which was very important. In an earlier operation, in Tunisia the PPA destroyed thirty-four aircraft on the ground. It also proved effective at hitting Rommel's supply lines by destroying 118 vehicles and 450,000 gallons of fuel supplies as well as taking prisoners for interrogation.

Perhaps one of Popski's more incredible ideas was to develop a flamethrower version of the Jeep. Known as the 'Wasp' there would be, as far as research can tell, only ever the one of its type built. Popski conceived his idea and approached British army engineers and mechanics to ask if it were possible to create a flamethrower system to fit onto a Jeep to destroy pillboxes, machine gun posts and bunkers. The RAOC and the REME both considered the task and reported that in their opinion it could not be done because the vehicle was too small to carry all the equipment and fuel for it to be a useful flamethrower. Vehicle-mounted flamethrowers were already in service, but these were mounted on heavier vehicles such as the type fitted to the Universal or Bren Gun Carrier known as 'Flame Thrower, Transportable No 2' which used Popski's nickname, the Wasp.

Popski, nevertheless, pressed on with his idea undeterred and eventually engineers managed to fit an improvised flamethrower into a Jeep. To cope with the additional weight, the front panels were strengthened using lengths of angle iron and the frame bolted through to the chassis of the vehicle. Fuel for the flamethrower was projected using gas or air from a cylinder. This was piped to an evaporator in front of the driver's position and water heated by the engine expanded the gas which then passed through pipes to the fuel tanks located at the rear of the Jeep. The bonnet (engine hood) of the Jeep had to be cut to allow the pipes to pass through. The fuel passed an ignition circuit and, as with the Wasp, flames shot out 50 to 100 yards. It is known that after the system's successful testing there was an apparent reluctance among vehicle crews to use the device. As a close-quarter weapon it would have been devastating against defensive positions but no doubt the crew were disinclined to sit on so much fuel, exposed and vulnerable. It is not known if it was ever used in combat, but it was a remarkable design and showed just how versatile the Jeep could be. We know the Wasp was built because of the evidence which has been left behind, including all the photographs which show a remarkable illustrated record of a unique vehicle from the war.

Still fresh in the minds of the British and Americans were the humiliating defeats inflicted on them by the Japanese in 1942. The Japanese had forced the surrender of

Singapore with its garrison of over 88,000 men, while the Imperial Japanese Army and Navy were fanning out to capture the islands across the region. In doing so, they captured resources vital to their war effort, including the oilfields on Sarawak and Java and the installations at Balikpapan on Borneo. On the mainland, the Japanese turned north to push the remaining British forces up the length of the Malay Peninsula, obliging them to conduct a fighting retreat as they headed towards the Indian frontier, almost 1,500 miles distance. In their wake, the British lost 13,000 men killed and wounded and abandoned much equipment. Many abandoned vehicles were salvaged by the Japanese.

The oil installations in Burma were destroyed to deprive the Japanese of the resources. Robert Morris, serving with the 7th Hussars, was in Rangoon and witnessed this destruction: 'All we saw were blazing fires and oil dumps set alight. Mounds of equipment such as aircraft marked "Lease-Lend to China from USA" lay in crates ready for assembly. At Pulau Bukum around 200,000 tons of oil were destroyed. The number of lorries lined up ready for shipment to China amazed us. The port had been deserted and ransacked.' Out of all this destruction the Japanese managed to salvage much which they used to supplement their own supplies.

The Japanese had been at war with China since 1937 before the attack on Pearl Harbor.

In China, the American General Stilwell ('Vinegar Joe') commanding the Chinese Fifth Army against the Japanese was also forced to retreat. Although recoiling, the Allies were preparing to build up and regain lost ground. They knew it would take time, but they were optimistic, as Stilwell told journalists: 'I claim we got a hell of a beating. We got run out of Burma and it is as humiliating as hell. I think we ought to find out what caused it, go back and retake it.' That endeavour would take time, but it would happen.

The year began with another series of meetings between Churchill and Roosevelt, this time when they met at Casablanca on 14 January for a series of talks codenamed 'Symbol'.

The Japanese used horses to cover long distances in China, as these signallers are doing to lay telephone lines.

It was easier for Japanese troops to use horses for transport in China because they did not need petrol and forage was plentiful.

Railways and bicycles were also used by Japanese troops.

For ten days, the two men spoke about plans for the next stages of the war. Top of the agenda was the question of conducting the war with the aim of forcing Germany's unconditional surrender. They were in complete agreement that nothing less would be considered. This point naturally included the air war against Germany and the bombing of strategic targets. The bombing offensive, codenamed 'Pointblank', was discussed and it was decided that the aim would be 'the progressive destruction and dislocation of the German military, industrial and economic system and the undermining of the morale of the German people to a point where their capacity for armed resistance is fatally weakened'. It was agreed that the RAF would continue to bomb by night and the USAAF would bomb by day, allowing no respite. The bombing campaign on its own could not halt production but it would have the effect of making

The USAAF used B-25 bombers in the Pacific and the RAF also used them for missions in Europe.

the Germans decentralise which reduced output as parts had to be transported for assembly.

There were other subjects on the agenda, including continued support for Russia. Stalin did not attend the talks, he wanted to remain in Moscow to oversee the final defeat of the Germans at Stalingrad. French Generals Charles de Gaulle and Henri Giraud were present, but they did not figure in the overall planning strategy. Churchill and Roosevelt agreed to provide sufficient resources to support the war against Japan with America pledging thirty per cent of its war effort to the defeat of Japan. Churchill managed to persuade Roosevelt to accept his plan to invade Sicily as a precursor to invading mainland Italy later in the year. The next phase of the war in Europe was covered and it was agreed an invasion should take place. This operation would become known as 'Operation Overlord' D-Day. The meeting was reported in the free press of the world and Hitler and his generals would have been aware of the outcome.

The bombing offensive was the only way the Allies could attack Germany directly and it had always been a contentious matter from the beginning. At the start of the war the RAF had been reluctant to bomb factories in Germany, on the grounds these premises were privately owned even though they were producing tanks and artillery. Now, three years later, attitudes had changed. The Germans had not hesitated at bombing British cities and armaments factories on the outskirts of Birmingham and Coventry.

London had come through the Blitz of 1940 and 1941, bowed but unbeaten. These attacks had the effect of temporarily disrupting production, but the bombing never halted output and the factories remained centralised.

With Hitler's attention focused on Russia, giving Britain some respite from air raids, the RAF began to plan a change in strategy. At the start of the war they flew daylight operations which proved costly in terms of losses. The main bomber in service at the time was the tough and resilient Wellington. It had a range of over 2,000 miles, but it could only carry two tons of bombs. It had entered service in 1938 and remained in operation throughout the war. In May 1940, Wellingtons had been used to attack oil installations at Duisburg and the railway marshalling yards at Monchengladbach. Shortly afterwards, daylight operations were suspended and attacks would instead be made at night, but still losses mounted.

On 22 February 1942 Bomber Command received a new commander with the appointment of Air Marshal Sir Arthur Harris as Air Officer-in-Command. He had different ideas to his predecessor, Air Chief Marshal Sir Richard Peirse, when it came to planning bombing operations. Within days of taking office, Harris ordered an attack

The Manchester bomber was retired from frontline service by the RAF in 1941, but it was retained for training purposes to give crews experience in delivering supplies.

The Wellington bomber remained operational throughout the war and was even used to transport troops.

by 235 aircraft to bomb the Renault factory at Billancourt which was producing vehicles and components for the German army. The attack on 3 March was a resounding success and put the factory out of operation for several months. Harris kept up the pressure and on 8 March aircraft bombed targets around the steel production centre of Essen. His offensive approach earned him the nickname 'Bomber' but to the bomber crews he was 'Butch' short for 'Butcher' because of the high casualty rate.

Bomber Command was now flying regular sorties to attack targets of importance to the German war machine. Harris had no doubt in his mind that his tactic of bombing was correct. The new heavy bomber, the four-engine Avro Lancaster, could carry several tons of bombs and had a range of over 1,500 miles. Bomber Command now planned its most audacious operation of the war to date. A plan to attack targets in Germany was devised but it was unlike anything before planned. Targets had been bombed in Germany but what made this operation different was the scale. Codenamed Operation Millennium, it would involve over one thousand aircraft of all types.

It was not an easy task to assemble so many aircraft to fly on the mission, mainly because nothing like it had ever before been tried. The fuel, bombs, ammunition for the guns and the crews themselves all had to be readied, at fifty-three airfields around the country. On the morning of 30 May, word was received that 1,046 were available. The air fleet took off. It stretched over seventy miles as it crossed the North Sea, preceded by a force of fifty fighters to provide advance cover against German aircraft. The armada flew on towards the target city of Cologne where, at around 12.47am on the morning of 31 May, the first bombs were released. The raid lasted around two and half hours during which time almost 35,000 bombs were dropped, killing 500 people, injuring over 5,000 and destroying some industrial installations but also almost 18,500 homes. The next night, 1 June, a force of 956 bombers attacked Essen, but they missed the steel-producing plants and other factories in the industrial district. The importance of Essen to the German war effort can be measured by the fact that it reacted to 830 threats of air raid during the war. Three weeks later Bremen received an air raid of over 1,000 bombers. These attacks showed the Germans what they could expect in the future. To America, it showed what the RAF could achieve and, no doubt, set their minds to doing the same.

In Germany, the civilian population was beginning to feel the real effects of the war in day-to-day living standards. One aspect was a severe rationing of coal in 1943. In the factories, around 450,000 were employed in processing steel, 160,000 producing tanks, and a further 210,000 producing weapons from rifles to artillery. In 1943 these factories produced over 18,300 tanks and other armoured vehicles. But impressive as it sounded, such output was only a third of the more than 54,000 vehicles produced by the Allies in the same period. German factories in the Ruhr were targeted and caused the Germans to divert anti-tank defences to protect the centres of industry, the rail network, and coal mining areas.

Factories in France, such as the Renault plant at Montbéliard, were being used to produce tank turrets and engines for fighter aircraft. In July 1943, the RAF attacked the plant but missed the main building. More than 260 French workers were killed in the raid. Another air raid was out of the question but the plant had to be destroyed. It was decided that resistance fighters would attack and on 5 November 1943 a group infiltrated the factory. They laid explosive charges, parachuted in by RAF aircraft, and succeeded in destroying plant machinery and a stockpile of some 6,000 tyres. The plant was out of production for several months.

On the night of 16 May 1943, nineteen Lancaster bombers of the specially created 617 Squadron, converted to carry a new type of bomb, took off from their base at RAF Scampton to head for strategic targets deep inside the industrial heartland of Germany. They were going to attack the great hydroelectric dams producing electricity for the factories making steel. The Mohne and the Eder dams were destroyed with the third, the Sorpe, being damaged. Eight aircraft were lost in the attack codenamed Operation Chastise. In the torrent of water which cascaded from the dams 11 factories were destroyed, 114 damaged, and almost one thousand homes destroyed. Thousands of people, many slave labourers forced to work for the German war effort, were killed in the raid. Power was reduced and the output of coal was reduced by 400,000 tons, all

Daytime bombing raid by the USAAF over Berlin to hit military targets and factories.

German factories producing tanks and self-propelled guns were targeted in air raids by the RAF and USAAF.

of which affected war production. Further afield, the flood water destroyed crops and drowned animals, leading to a severe drop in food production. The attack had the side effect of forcing the Germans to divert more anti-aircraft guns and aircraft away from the operational fronts to protect the factories.

This factory building half-track vehicles has been badly damaged but could be put back into production.

In mid-1942, the RAF began to receive their American Allies with great relief as the first arrivals of bombers such as the B-17 and B-24 began to arrive in Britain. As their numbers built up, so the weight of aircraft sent against targets in Germany increased and with it the weight of bombs. For example, in March 1943 a raid by 1,000 bombers could drop around 4,000 tons of bombs. Two years later, this figure had increased three-fold.

The Mohne Dam in 1943 before the raid by 617 Squadron.

The breach in the Mohne Dam following Operation Chastise.

Between January and December 1943, the Allied bombing offensive dropped 135,000 tons of bombs on various targets in Germany alone. In July 1944, the RAF and USAAF had a combined bomber force of 5,250 aircraft which, in theory, could drop over 20,000

A German labour unit used to clear up after bombing raids and repair roads and bridges.

tons of bombs. The net result was an increase in the output of anti-aircraft guns which rose from 20% of all production of artillery to 30%. Personnel to serve these weapons increased from 439,000 in 1942 to around 900,000 in 1944. Special warning posters were put up to remind civilians about the dangers of falling splinters from the exploding shells containing the words: 'Bei Flakfeuer; gegen Splitterwirkung sofort; Deckung Suchen!'

On 17 August 1942, the USAAF made its first daylight raid against a target in France when twelve B-17 Flying Fortresses attacked a railway marshalling yard in Rouen. It was a success and for the remainder of 1942 a further 1,547 sorties were carried out. Targets included submarine pens to prevent U-Boats from sailing to attack convoys. Losses were low compared to those of the RAF. After the Casablanca Conference, the raids were increased and the targets now included locations deep in Germany. On 1 August 1943, 178 B-24 bombers of the USAAF flying from bases in North Africa took off to attack oil installations at Ploesti in Romania in an operation codenamed Tidal Wave. The attack was pressed home but in doing so 54 aircraft were lost and 58 badly damaged, resulting in 310 aircrew killed and 114 taken prisoner. The net result was some damage to the installation and plant facilities but it was all repaired within weeks. In fact, the attack had the opposite effect and rather than force a decrease in fuel production, the Ploesti oil installation increased its output.

On 17 August 1943, the USAAF was tasked with another equally dangerous mission, when 376 were sent to bomb the ball-bearing factory at Schweinfurt. The attack was intercepted and the Americans lost 147 aircraft. A second attack was planned for October and this too suffered extremely high losses with 60 aircraft shot down and 142 damaged. Photographic reconnaissance showed the factories to be badly damaged. Yet despite appearances, full production was resumed with a month.

To accommodate American aircraft operating from bases in Britain an expansion was called for in the construction of airfields. In 1939, there were only nine military airfields in the country which had paved runways, but by 1945 more than 440 had been completed, of which 50 were for exclusive use by the USAAF. It took on average between six and seven months to complete an operational airfield and work on them absorbed almost a third of the UK labour force. One historian has calculated that by 1945 there were almost 1,000 airfields in operational use across Britain, taking up some 360,000 acres of land. It was not just airfields which had to be built, but ancillary storage areas were required for bombs and fuel. At the beginning of the war in 1939 the RAF used 10,000 tons of fuel per week but by 1945 this figure had risen to 112,000 and facilities for storing it had to be built.

In July 1943, military planners decided to use the combined weight of the RAF and USAAF in a series of air raids designed to show to the Germans they were unstoppable. On 24 July, the first raid in a series of attacks known as Operation Gomorrah was flown against the city of Hamburg, which had a population of 1.2 million, but which was also a major industrial and military centre. U-Boat pens, oil refineries and armaments factories made it an important target to attack to cripple the German ability to produce materiel for the war

American pilots fought a long, hard war in Europe and in the Pacific.

The USAAF used vast amounts of fuel on its missions against targets across Europe.

effort. For a total of eight days and seven nights 2,630 aircraft from the combined air forces dropped 4,300 tons of bombs. Around 44,600 civilians and 800 military personnel were killed in the attacks and whole housing districts were destroyed. The bombing also destroyed 183 out of 524 large factories, 4,118 smaller factories out of 9,068 and a further 580 premises producing ammunition, vehicles and weapons. Destruction had been great but within five months the factories were back to at least eighty per cent operational capacity. After the war, German officials stated that had the Allies put in further such raids the country would have been forced out of the war. Fortunately for the Germans the Allies were not able to maintain such a weight of attack but they could still mount air raids which had the effect of forcing the Germans to decentralise their production facilities. One Hamburg housewife wrote of the difficulties the bombing caused: 'For days we have had no water; everything is chipped and broken and frayed; travelling is out of the question; nothing can be bought…' Yet, life still went on and daily routines, going to school and work, continued.

The German war effort proved to be remarkably flexible, as demonstrated when the Faun factory producing trucks for the army was destroyed in 1943. Production was relocated to a new site at Lauf near Baden and vehicles were once again being built.

In early 1943 the Germans were producing 760 tanks a month but by the end of the year they were building 1,229 despite decentralisation. Aircraft production in that year would exceed 25,000 and in 1944 more than 39,200 aircraft were produced.

Such achievements were only possible with the efforts of forced labour from occupied countries and concentration camp inmates. At one aircraft production plant around eighty per cent of the workforce was made up of Russian PoWs. Inspired by the 'Total War' speeches of Goebbels in 1943, German factories turned out ever more military armaments. Some establishments produced goods for the civilian market and even managed to manufacture around 13,000 tons of wallpaper, despite all the bombing.

The toll of the bombing campaign against Germany would cost the RAF 10,123 aircraft between September 1939 and May 1945. Bomber Command lost 55,435 killed, 8,403 wounded and almost 13,000 taken prisoner out of a total force of some 125,000 aircrew. The USAAF lost 26,000 aircrew killed from bomber squadrons out of a strength of 100,000 men; tens of thousands were wounded and 20,000 were taken prisoner. The USAAF lost 5,548 bombers between 1942 and 1945. The combined effort of the two air forces dropped an estimated 1,576,921 tons of bombs on targets in Germany and occupied countries.

Britain started its preparations for bombing as early as the 1920s by excavating subterranean storage facilities to keep stock levels of bombs secret. One such storage site was built in a disused quarry near Corsham in Wiltshire. This site was started in 1928 and extended for six acres to allow up to 12,000 tons of bombs to be kept secure. As the political situation worsened throughout the 1930s this site was extended. When war broke out the tunnels were further extended to cover 125 acres with the capacity to store 300,000 tons of bombs.

Although the exact location was secret, a journalist from the *Daily Express* was granted a rare opportunity to visit the facility and report on his observations. His report, after careful censoring by the War Office, informed the public: 'Many thousands of lights burn continuously in this land of forbidden cities…Warm conditioned air flows through arterial channels of concrete and limestone. Shells painted a gay yellow rock endlessly on a conveyor belt, to be stacked in a twenty-foot honey-combe, or to be shipped to a theatre of war. Here, carved from the living rock, is a great bomb-proof cloister hundreds of feet long, supported by square thirty-foot columns hewn out of stone. Already scurrying blobs of khaki have piled it high with war stores. And here on rock covered with smooth concrete, engineers have built a great powerhouse, with whirring giant dynamos, winking signal lights and shiny black controls. Fluorescent bars throw a daylight effect over the spotless asphalt floors.' This was just one of hundreds of similar locations across the country.

Another site prepared as an ammunition supply dump was at the RAF base at Fauld, Hanbury, Staffordshire. In 1936 the Air Ministry had decided that the war reserve stock of bombs should be kept at 98,000 tons at least. In April 1937 the Luftwaffe supporting General Franco's Nationalists bombed the town of Guernica to destruction. After that stocks were increased from 158,000 tons to 632,000. Other facilities were prepared and the underground site at Fauld was extended. On 27 November 1944, tragedy struck when a massive explosion ripped through the storage facility at RAF Fauld, destroying everything and killing at least seventy people. It is estimated that at least 4,000 tons of bombs detonated, as well as some 500 million rounds of ammunition. The blast created a crater 750 feet in diameter and 100 feet deep. The force of the explosion also ruptured a nearby reservoir, releasing 450,000 tons of water to add to the devastation. This loss of munitions was great but it did not stop or even slow down the bombing campaign against Germany.

As the air war evolved, the Allies developed more powerful aircraft capable of carrying heavier bomb loads over greater distances. Heavier bombs were also developed, such as the 6-ton 'Tallboy' and 12-ton 'Grandslam', designed by the aircraft designer Barnes Wallis, who had also designed the bouncing bombs used to destroy the hydroelectric dams in Operation Chastise. Numerically, the Allies' air forces also grew stronger and in all theatres achieved air superiority and then aerial domination, but the Luftwaffe could never be written off entirely and with new aircraft designs, such as the jet-powered Messerschmitt Me262, continued to pose a threat to the bombers attacking targets in Germany.

The underground bomb store at RAF Fauld at Hanbury in Staffordshire which was destroyed when it blew up.

Following the successes produced by Pointblank, the Allied air planners devised a new strategy in February 1944, codenamed Transportation Plan or Transport Plan, which had the aim of destroying the German rail network and attacking oil supplies. A secondary aim of the operation was to disrupt and destroy the rail system in France and disrupt supplies sent from the factories in occupied territories, including Holland and Belgium. It would also hamper supplies and reinforcements being sent to France after June 1944. Joining the planning group in February 1944, as the new commander of the USAAF 8th Air Force operating out of bases in Britain, came Lieutenant General Carl Spaatz. He was a career officer, having served as a pilot with the 13 Aero Squadron in France in 1918 when he had shot down three aircraft.

As bombers began to attack targets in France, especially the railway network and focusing on the area around Normandy, Spaatz had a plan of his own, called the Oil Plan. He knew that by cutting fuel supplies he would slow down the German army on the ground and reduce the number of combat missions the Luftwaffe could fly. On 12 May 1944, he ordered the first mission, which was carried out by a force of 886 bombers attacking oil installations at Leipzig. The cost was high, 46 aircraft lost, but the mission achieved results. The attack was followed up by two more raids on 28 and 29 May, before the damage could be repaired. It worked, and by autumn 1944 Spaatz had need of only fifteen per cent of his bomber force to keep monthly output to a trickle, down from what had been a monthly output of almost one million tons six months earlier.

The German Armaments Minister, Albert Speer, wrote about Spaatz's new tactics: 'Until then we had managed to produce approximately as many weapons as the armed forces needed, in spite of their considerable losses… a new era in the war began. It meant the end of German armaments production.'

The effectiveness Transport Plan was having on German supply lines was recorded in a report compiled by the German air ministry dated 13 June 1944, one week after D-Day. The bombings had: 'caused the breakdown of all main lines; the coast defences have been cut off from the supply bases in the interior…producing a situation which threatens to have serious consequences … large scale strategic movement of German troops by rail is practically impossible at the present time and must remain so while attacks are maintained at their present intensity.' In September 1939, Germany had gone to war with one of the most powerful and modern air forces in the world. By mid-1944 it had been reduced to a shadow of its former self. Losses continued to mount and fuel shortages produced by the effective Allied bombing campaign crippled it by keeping the aircraft on the ground for much of the time.

In 1944 Germany produced over 34,000 aircraft. It does raise the question: why build so many aircraft if one does not have the fuel to fly them? Germany did have fuel, but not a reliable stock. The aircraft were being built in readiness for the time when oil was in ample supply.

Despite their belief in the effectiveness of their bomber forces, Harris and Spaatz must have realised that the bomber alone would not win the war. They could inflict heavy damage but could not prevent repairs from being made. Only ground forces could do that by capturing the facilities. Meanwhile, the bombers would continue to disrupt supply routes in Germany and occupied territories. The success of the bomber echoed the words of Stanley Baldwin, who in 1932, had stated, 'The bomber will always get through.'

As well as having heavy bomber capability and escort fighters, the Allied air forces also had squadrons assigned to provide support for special operations. Aircraft would drop weapons and equipment, usually by means of parachute, deep into German occupied territory. These special squadrons were formed for the specific purpose of delivering these supplies to resistance organisations across occupied Europe, the British Special Operations Executive (SOE) and the American Office of Strategic Services (OSS). These formations helped organise and train resistance groups in the use of explosives to destroy railway tracks and bridges which would hamper the movement of troops and supplies by the Germans. One of these special units was RAF squadron No 161, formed in February 1942 from the disbanded No 138 Squadron which had already completed successful missions in support of resistance groups. Flying Lysanders, Whitleys, Hudsons, Halifaxes and Stirlings, the squadron operated out of Newmarket in Suffolk. The last operational flight by No 161 Squadron was on the night of 5/6 September 1944. By the end of the war the squadron had flown around 200 missions. Perhaps not the greatest number of operational flights, but during that time it had flown 1,000 people, including SOE agents, and dropped 42,800 tons of supplies and weapons to resistance groups in France and other occupied countries.

Another specialist RAF squadron was No 148 (Special Duties) Squadron which before the war had something of a chequered history, having been disbanded and reformed at various times between 1919 and 1943. Originally formed in February 1918 it operated as a bomber force to attack German airfields and railway systems transporting supplies for the army. The squadron was disbanded in 1919, but was reformed in 1937 during Britain's rearmament period. It was once again disbanded in April 1940 and eight months later was reformed again and sent to Malta where, for the next two years, it operated Halifaxes flying bombing missions in support of the campaign in North Africa, intercepting enemy shipping sailing in convoys, and sinking Rommel's oil supplies. In December 1942, No 148 was again disbanded but in March 1943 phoenix-like it rose again, with its Special Duties designation, still operating Halifax bombers, but now with American-built B-24 Liberators to carry heavier loads over greater distances. The main role of the squadron now was to fly missions to supply air drops of equipment and weapons to partisan groups fighting in the Balkans, Yugoslavia, Greece and Poland. In

April 1944, the aircrews devised a system whereby they could air-drop a jeep from their Halifax aircraft. However, the method had to be curtailed because it was believed that it endangered the aircraft unnecessarily. Typically, a Halifax carried 4.7 tons of weapons and equipment which was dropped from heights between 500 and 800 feet. During May 1944, the squadron delivered 272 tons of supplies flown in 196 sorties. In August 1944, No 148 flew missions to drop supplies to Polish resistance fighters during the Warsaw uprising against the Germans, delivering 100 tons of weapons and three million rounds of ammunition and losing five aircraft in the process. In January 1945, No 148 Squadron increased the number of supply drops made to the Yugoslavian partisans led by Marshal Josip Broz, better known as Tito. Tito had 800,000 men and women in his army of resistance fighters, receiving supplies from the Allies and anything they could recover from operations against the Germans.

Meanwhile, at sea, the losses of ships, even when sailing in the relative safety of a convoy, was having a telling effect on all the armies. In the Mediterranean, the Allies were attacking Rommel's supply lines with submarines and aircraft operating from Malta to sink his fuel tankers. The German U-Boats in turn were operating in the Atlantic, where they continued to be a problem and claimed many victims. Churchill remarked: 'The only thing that ever terrified me during the war was the U-Boat peril.'

Yugoslavian partisans fighting against German troops. They are using captured Italian weapons.

Female Yugoslavian partisans of Tito's forces fighting the Germans.

As the figures showed, he was right to be concerned. Between 1941 and 1942 U-Boats and surface raiders sank 1,459 vessels amounting to 7,619,000 tons of shipping.

In 1942 Britain was on the verge of being starved if such losses were maintained and fuel supplies were also becoming critical. In the month of March 1943, 108 vessels were sunk, but aircraft with extended range provided air cover and helped keep the U-Boats at bay. In May, fifty ships were sunk, but specialist weapons, improved tactics and technology such as ASDIC and radar allowed the Allies to sink forty-one U-Boats. U-boats would continue to be a menace to supply routes but their ability to range at will largely unmolested had been stopped. By the end of the war, U-Boats had sunk 175 Allied warships and 14 million tons of shipping including the weight of the cargo the ships were carrying. But the cost to the U-boats was high: 785 out of 1,162 were sunk.

By the end of 1943, the threat from Hitler's surface raiders had been eliminated. The *Bismarck* had been sunk by the Royal Navy in May 1941 and the RAF had damaged the *Gneisenau* so badly on 26 February 1942 that she never again sailed. The *Scharnhorst* was sunk on 26 December 1943 and the other large ships, the *Admiral Scheer*, *Tirpitz* and *Hipper*, were not to sail again. The pressure was off and the build-up for the invasion of Europe could continue.

After the Torch landings, the Americans realised how the fighting in the North African desert was unlike anything they could have prepared for and they came to understand what a vast unforgiving area the battleground was, covering as it did many thousands of square miles. The British, Italians and Germans had learnt many lessons over the past three years and now it was the turn of the Americans. One of the main considerations they had to understand was just how few roads there were and even fewer maintained to a level which allowed travel. The Allied forces making up the Operation Torch landings comprised the Western Task Force of 25,000 men commanded by General Patton. The Central Task Force of 39,000 men was under the command of Major General Lloyd Fredendall, and Major General Charles M. Ryder commanded the Eastern Task Force comprising 23,000 British and 20,000 American troops.

By using the northern route, following the coast road, the British and Americans, virtually unopposed, advanced on Algiers which promptly capitulated. From here the US II Corps continued eastwards to capture Philippeville and Bone, crossing the border to enter Tunisia from the north. Further south, the British First Army, commanded by Lieutenant General Kenneth Anderson advanced to present a second line of advance against German positions. Anderson had seen service in the First World War and had fought during the Dunkirk campaign. Known as an organiser, his battle experience did not make him a good commander in the field. He covered over 400 miles of hostile terrain in six weeks, and although not held in high regard by his contemporaries, Anderson kept his supplies with him. His timely arrival and handling of reinforcements and logistics certainly played a crucial part in the defence of the Kasserine Pass. On the conclusion of the campaign Anderson returned to England where his skills were used in training troops in readiness for Normandy.

Over in the east, Montgomery kept up the pressure and by late January 1943 had succeeded in pushing the Afrika Korps all the way back across the Libyan border and into Tunisia. The operation also pushed Rommel's forces closer to General Arnim, commanding 5th Panzer Armee. The Allies could afford to take their time if they wished and they manoeuvred to take up positions along the Dorsal Mountains, a vast natural barrier which could only be penetrated through a series of natural passes.

By now, supplies of fuel, stores and reinforcements had been reduced to only a fraction of what the Afrika Korps needed. However, what did arrive were deliveries of the new Tiger tanks. Armed with an 88mm gun and weighing 56 tons, it was the most powerful tank in North Africa. The Tiger was formed into battalions comprising thirty vehicles and the Germans sent two battalions to the North Africa theatre of operations between November 1942 and March 1943. Of all the varied tank types to be produced by Germany during the Second World War, the one design which stands out from all of them is unarguably the Tiger. The very name struck fear into Allied infantry and tank crews alike. The Russians had already encountered the Tiger and now the

Western Allies were about to meet it for the first time in North Africa. However, if Hitler thought that this tank alone could turn the tide he was gravely mistaken. What was despatched was too little too late. The fact that Tiger tanks were sent to North Africa at all is surprising. It may have been more prudent to send them to the Russian Front. Hitler may have rated the campaign in North Africa as a side show but he was not going to abandon it without a fight.

On 14 February, American forces under the command of Fredendall began to move forward but they were unwittingly stumbling into an elaborate trap. Using the effects of a sandstorm to cover their movements, the Germans moved armoured units forward, including Tiger tanks, through the Faid Pass. The 10th Panzer Division and 21st Panzer Division linked up to surround an American force of 2,500 men. The next day the Germans attacked with air support and destroyed 46 tanks and killed almost 350 men. Only 300 Americans managed to escape. The rest of the American force fell back towards the Kasserine Pass through the Dorsal Mountains which had to be held to prevent the large supply base at Tabessa from falling into German hands.

Rommel wanted to pursue the retreating Americans, no doubt with a view to capturing the supplies which he could have used, but von Arnim, who was technically superior to him, and with experience of fighting in Russia, was cautious and did not want to take the risk given their limited resources and shortage of supplies. The difference of opinion was only resolved with the personal intervention of Field Marshal Albert Kesselring, who had flown in from Rome to assess the situation and gave his support to Rommel's plan. German tanks entered the Kasserine Pass on 19 February in pursuit of the Americans. The natural feature is barely one mile wide at its narrowest point and the Americans prepared their defences; using artillery and anti-tank fire they made a stand which halted the German tanks. The next day the Germans renewed their attack using artillery and another weapon new to North Africa, Nebelwerfers (rocket artillery), which forced the Americans to fall back again. The British gave support to their Allies and sent eleven tanks from the 2nd Lothian and Border Horse, but these were destroyed in the fighting.

The way appeared clear for the Germans to move the short distance across the border into Algeria and capture Tebessa, with its prize of stocks of fuel and other supplies, and after that Thala. Rommel experienced a rare moment of caution because he expected the Allies to mount a counter-attack which caused him to hesitate in making his move. Instead he decided to adopt a defensive stance. When the expected attack did not materialise he renewed his advance, but the Allies had not wasted the moment and had used the opportunity to their advantage to strengthen their positions. The Americans held fast and defended Tebessa, denying the supplies there to the Germans. The British however were forced back by the Tiger tanks of the 10th Panzer Division, to Thala where they established defences.

The following day artillery support arrived from the US 9th Division which had covered the distance of 600 miles from Oran in just four days. On 22 February, the German advance was halted but the Allies did not put in a counter-attack but preferred instead to hold their positions. The Germans began to withdraw from the Kasserine Pass and Rommel, recognising the weight of reinforcements and supplies reaching the Americans, knew he did not stand a chance against them with their superior numbers and equipment. No more attacks were ordered, but even so it was another twenty-four hours before the Americans discovered he had pulled off a master stroke and completely melted away. The Americans had been unprepared for such a frightening initiation into war – the fighting had cost them 6,500 killed, wounded and captured. The British had lost 2,500 men and the whole effort had cost the Allies 183 tanks destroyed. The Germans and Italians had lost 2,000 killed, wounded and captured and 34 tanks destroyed.

The Italian army had been in the field far longer than any other European force but the experience did not make them better soldiers. Almost from the very beginning there had been a chronic shortage of everything. The situation had been like it for so long that troops became resigned to the constant lack of equipment. Shortages of food, fuel and medical supplies compounded the problems and the soldiers suffered. It was no secret that Italy was unprepared for war but Mussolini had decided to support his ally Adolf Hitler. Now, after several years of fighting, the Italian Empire in North Africa was crumbling. The travelling range of armoured vehicles used by the Italian army was among the worst of any of the belligerent nations. There are many reasons for this and, apart from the Semovente which is generally regarded as the best Italian armoured vehicle of the war, the remainder of the Italian designs were not well thought out.

Italy had been engaged in military campaigns since 1935 when it invaded Ethiopia and in Spain from 1936 where Mussolini deployed more troops than Germany and fielded light tanks such as the M13/40 which were later sent into action during the disastrous Greek campaign of 1940. The inadequacies of these tanks were highlighted in these campaigns and the Italians realised, somewhat late, that better designs were required if they were to stand a chance on the battlefield. In 1941 the Italian army finally developed and put into production a light tank design which did show some promise of being useful on the battlefield, but even so it was a classic case of too little too late. The new tank was the M14/41 served by a crew of four and armed with a 47mm calibre main armament with 104 rounds of ammunition carried. The M14/41 promised to be better than the earlier Italian tank designs, but in the later phases of campaigns in North Africa it fared no better when it encountered anti-tank guns or British units using America-built tanks such as the Sherman. The Italian Centauro Armoured Division used M14/41 tanks in action at the Kasserine Pass in 1943 and lost many during the heavy fighting against the American forces.

Built by the motor manufacturing company of FIAT the full title of the new tank was Carro Armato M14/41 – M for Medium, 14 tonnes, and 41 the year of introduction into service. It was in fact a 'light' tank and little more than a modified version of the earlier M13/40 light tank. Armour thickness varied from 6mm to 42mm, but even so it was still far short of posing any threat to the newer American tanks entering service in North Africa. The M14/41 was constructed using a riveted design and looked old-fashioned compared to most other tank designs which were either cast or welded. As well as the 47mm main gun, it carried two Modello 38 machine guns of 8mm calibre as secondary armament for which over 3000 rounds were carried.

The M14/41 was produced from 1941 until 1942 during which time some 800 vehicles were built, but even with its upgrading the tank was obsolete even before it entered service. The flaws in its design became apparent when it was deployed to North Africa. For example, it had a tendency to catch fire easily when hit. When the Italian forces withdrew, they abandoned many of their vehicles, often for no other reason than lack of fuel. The Germans, with better supply lines and more fuel, seized on this as an opportunity to add something to their armoury. They recovered the abandoned Italian vehicles, refuelled them and absorbed them into service, giving them the designation M14/41 736 (i). The British army captured a few and pressed them into service for a short time, but the British were not short on tanks and the Italian tanks were eventually abandoned. Some M14/41 tanks were deployed by the Italian army to serve on the Eastern Front and these too ended up being used by the Germans.

In March 1943, at his headquarters near Benghazi, Rommel confided to Colonel Hans von Luck, 'The war is lost.' Luck replied that he did not understand: 'We are very deep in Russia, we are in Scandinavia, in France, in the Balkans, in North Africa. How can the war be lost?' Rommel gave his reply: 'I will tell you. We lost Stalingrad, we will lose Africa, with the body of our best-trained armoured people. We can't fight without them. The only thing we can do is ask for an armistice. We have to give up this business about the Jews, we have to change our minds about the religions.' He was absolutely correct in his assessment in both the tactical and strategic situations.

Although he never served in Russia, Rommel would have been acutely aware of the logistical problems facing the German Army there, just as he revealed that he knew about the persecution of the Jews. He would have been aware of the waste of resources it entailed. The logistics required to move these millions by rail to concentration camps, the fuel needed to move the trains, the troops to guard the Jews under transport along with the other services – if Hitler had redirected these resources the lines of supply and logistics would have been much improved to support the campaigns in Russia and North Africa.

In the meantime, Rommel was not prepared to go down without a fight, and eighty miles to the east had established a defensive line of strongpoints, including bunkers, tank traps and minefields. This was the Mareth Line, originally built by the French but now strengthened and improved by the Germans from where they could gather their resources as they prepared to launch an attack. Rommel intended to launch an attack against the British-held town of Medenine, but what he did not know was that the British had an advantage when it came to intelligence. They were intercepting German radio messages and decoding them. One set of these messages contained Rommel's orders and with this information the British were provided with ample warning of the impending attack and made their preparations. In fact, so accurate was their decoding, that not only did they know the date of the attack, 6 March, they also worked out the direction from which it would be launched and deployed their anti-tank guns to be ready and waiting.

The British had learned a great many lessons when it came to desert fighting, especially how to deal with attacks by German armour. For example, the anti-tank gunners had learned to hold their fire, allowing the German tanks to come within 400 yards. This was a tactic which had been used by the Afrika Korps and here it was being used against them. The gunners opened fire and destroyed fifty-two of Rommel's ever-diminishing tank force. On 9 March, Rommel flew to Berlin to personally request Hitler that he be allowed to evacuate from North Africa what was left of the Afrika Korps. The request was denied and Rommel remained in Germany while von Arnim took over command of Army Group Africa. They were to be left to their fate.

Fredendall was replaced by Patton on 6 March who brought with him more Sherman tanks. A firm advocate of attack using tanks, he was also made of sterner stuff than his predecessor, and for the next three weeks he kept up the pressure by attacking the passes through the southern end of the Dorsal Mountains at El Guettar and Maknassy. He benefitted by having good supply routes and fresh troops but even with such support, in the end, there was little to show for his efforts. However, Patton's tactics did have the effect of forcing the Germans to take tanks out of the defences making up the Mareth Line, a move which helped Montgomery who ordered the New Zealand 2nd Division, some 25,000 men under the command of General Freyberg, to attack south-west in a wide swinging movement which outflanked the Mareth Line. Once past the defensive line, the New Zealanders moved north-east to link up with Montgomery's main thrust.

During their advance of 200 miles, the British had used the routes which had been plotted by the Long Range Desert Group. Indeed, when it came to charting routes across the inhospitable wastelands of the desert, the LRDG achieved nothing short of miracles. During their patrols, units often traversed long distances using minor routes which were considered by normal units as being unreliable, because the track could be blown away during violent sandstorms. The LRDG used dead-reckoning, which eliminated the need to use landmarks to gain a bearing. In that respect it was rather like navigating at sea. Accuracy was all-important and the slightest error could lead to the destination being missed.

The LRDG used, among other vehicles, the Canadian-built CMP F30 truck (Canadian Military Pattern, 30 cwt/1.5 tons), a 4x2 truck with a payload of over one ton. It was fitted with a 239 C1 Ford/Mercury petrol engine, and its twin fuel tanks with a combined capacity of 24.5 gallons allowed it to cover 150 miles without refuelling. It was a rugged design that could carry everything needed by a patrol, from water and ammunition to extra fuel. Canada built around 400,000 CMP trucks out of a wartime production total of 815,729. In fact, Canada on its own built more trucks than Germany for the same period.

Like the LRDG, the SAS penetrated deep behind enemy lines. To extend their range they sometimes established forward supply dumps which they could use to replenish their on-board stocks. Some patrols could go out on operations for days and even weeks at a time using such techniques.

By using information provided to them by the LRDG and the SAS, the main advancing British units linked up with other elements of the British 8th Army, all the time moving over great distances as they headed northwards towards their goal of Tunis. On 7 April the British linked up with the US II Corps. By now the Germans were using up all their reserves and conducting a fighting withdrawal to take up defensive lines sweeping in a wide arc on the tip of Tunisia.

On 21 April 1943, at Medjez-el-Bab, No. 4 Troop, 'A' Squadron of the 48th Royal Tank Regiment, equipped with Churchill tanks, engaged German forces equipped with Tiger tanks, and had a remarkable stroke of good luck. It was a fierce engagement, during which one of the Churchill tanks fired on a Tiger, hitting it and, against the odds, disabled it. The crew, with no other option, were obliged to evacuate the vehicle and leave it abandoned on the battlefield. After the fighting, the British consolidated the area and the knocked-out Tiger was recovered from the battlefield by 104 Army Tank Workshops of the REME and the 25th Tank Brigade Workshops of the REME. Here, for the first time, the Allies had an intact version of the German army's latest and most powerful tank. It was taken to Tunis ready for shipping back to England and full inspection. It was put on display at Horse Guards Parade in London where it was seen by King George VI along with Winston Churchill and Anthony Eden. After it had been displayed the tank was taken apart and examined. The examination showed the battle damage was only superficial. The shot which had disabled the Tiger had first hit the underside of the barrel of the tank's great 88mm gun, ricocheted off and become jammed in the space between the turret and the hull, preventing the turret from traversing. Opportunities like this did not come along very often, but when they did, the Allies, not unnaturally, took full advantage.

On 22 April, the fighting continued with British artillery joining American units to pound German positions prior to an attack. General Bradley, who had taken over from Patton, ordered an attack by seventeen Sherman tanks to support an infantry attack against a feature known as Hill 609 (from its height measured in metres). The Germans, literally with their backs to the sea, had only 175,000 men to oppose an Allied force of 380,000 men with 1,200 tanks, 1,500 pieces of artillery, 3,000 aircraft and unlimited supplies. The Germans had 400 aircraft, 130 tanks and stocks of ammunition sufficient for three days, if the 400 guns they had left were careful. A massive artillery barrage by 600 guns pounded the German positions on 6 May which further weakened them. The next day the Americans were only fifteen miles outside Bizerta and elements of the British 11th Hussars entered Tunis. Units such as the 10th Panzer Division continued to fight until forced to surrender when they ran out of fuel. By 12 May the Germans and Italians had expended everything and General Hans Cramer sent a message to Berlin: 'Munitions expended, weapons and war equipment destroyed.'

The following day, 13 May, General Alexander sent a signal to Churchill to report that the campaign in Tunisia was finished and the enemy surrendered. North Africa was clear and the Allies could now concentrate on enemy forces in Europe from France to Italy. The North African campaign was to prove to be one of the longest of any theatre of land operations. The success of the Allies had been down to better supply lines and greater quantities of logistics. The Germans had understood the value of good supply lines, but their routes were over-extended and vulnerable to attack. Until America's entry into the war, which swung the odds in Britain's favour, the opposing forces in North Africa had been evenly matched. That is evident from the number of times each side had advanced and retreated. The Torch Landings had broken that cycle and the weight of logistical support destroyed any chance of a comeback by the Germans into the North Africa theatre of operations.

The combined losses sustained by the Germans at Stalingrad and the surrender of their forces in North Africa were huge by any standards. They had lost thousands of trucks, tanks, artillery, millions of tons of war materiel and most importantly manpower. However, despite these losses the German army still had some 10.3 million men under arms in the field in mid-1943, including allies and volunteers from occupied territories who came forward to freely serve in the armed forces. There were almost 7.5 million forced labourers and PoWs, mainly Russian, producing vehicles, weapons and uniforms in factories across the territories under occupation. At the BMW plant in Munich there were some 16,600 PoWs working on the production of vehicles. General Keitel claimed these prisoners were 'working for Germany'. Such a statement implies they were working on their own free will when it was anything but the case. This impressed workforce accounted for more than 20% of the total workforce, including Jewish inmates from camps, and allowed the German armaments industry to increase productivity to supply the army by 80%. This figure is remarkable when one considers the disruption caused to factory output by round-the-clock bombing, with the RAF attacking at night and the USAAF by day.

On the other side of the world, in the Pacific theatre, by 1943 the Japanese Empire had expanded to reach the zenith of its power. Garrisons were established on many islands across the region, airbases were built from where aircraft could operate to attack American shipping and provide air support for their own naval forces. The Allies could not bypass these bases, nor could they be ignored. The Americans realised that it would require an entirely different approach to attack each one in turn. One of the main problems was the vast distances involved. Following their massive defeats at Singapore and in the Philippines the Allies knew they could not continue to fall back in the way the Russians had been able to in front of Germany's attack. Around 500,000 civilian refugees joined in the flight towards India to escape the Japanese, clogging the roads heading north. It was a repeat of the scenes witnessed in Poland and France, but the difference this time lay in the fact that far more died, perhaps as many as 80,000. The British Army retreated to the borders of India covering around 1,000 miles in over five months, fighting all the way and losing over 13,000 men killed, wounded and missing. They abandoned whatever they did not need and the Japanese army trailing them made use of stocks captured intact, especially the food and fuel, referring to these as 'Churchill's supplies'.

Things could have been worse for the British army and its losses much higher but for good coordination, organisation and a determination to survive. The army was moving fast to save itself, leaving in its wake much equipment. Before the war, the British army had employed a pre-war local civilian workforce of around 20,000, employed in menial tasks as labourers to load vehicles and dig ditches. Now, following the Japanese invasion, 14,000 of these either ran away or defected to work for the Japanese. For more than six months the Japanese kept up their pursuit until, in July 1942, the British began to slow down and set about reorganising themselves. Out of 150 pieces of artillery they had just 28 guns left and from a fleet of several hundred trucks they were left with just 80 serviceable vehicles.

In March 1942, General Slim, the troops' 'Uncle Bill', was appointed to command the Burma Corps or Burcorps. He later wrote: 'To our men, British and Indian, the jungle was a strange, fearsome place; moving and fighting in it was a nightmare. We were too ready to classify jungle as 'impenetrable', as indeed it was to us with our motor transport, bulky supplies and inexperience. To us it appeared only as an obstacle to movement and to vision; to the Japanese it was the welcome means of concealed manoeuvre and surprise. The Japanese used formations specially trained and equipped for a country of jungles and rivers, while we used troops whose training and equipment, as far as had been completed, were for the open desert. The Japanese reaped the deserved reward for their foresight and thorough preparation; we paid the penalty for our lack of both.' The problem lay not in the troops lack of experience or training and equipment, just that it was the wrong type. They would have to learn different methods of fighting.

In October 1943, Slim was appointed to command the newly-created 14th Army, which would benefit from well organised air support and by the end of the war have around one million men in its structure. One of Slim's first moves was to give his new command what he called 'an injection of ginger'. He made sure there were adequate supplies on the Assam front, including ammunition and medical stores. Four new major routes were built across the region running from Chittagong on the east coast of India to Arakan. Another ran from Dimapur through Kohima south to Imphal. A third connected Imphal with Tiddim; and finally from Ledo in the north of India the fourth route ran down the Hukawng Valley south to Myitkyina to the Chinese border. This would become known as the Ledo Road and, along the with other routes across the region, was vital for the transportation of supplies to British and American troops as well as their Chinese allies.

One of the first officers to organise troops to fight back was Brigadier Orde Wingate, who was an expert in guerrilla warfare, having created special groups in Palestine and later established 'Gideon Force' in 1940 which operated against Italians in Ethiopia. His idea was to form a unit (the Chindits) which would attack the Japanese supply lines using hit-and-run tactics. At Jansi in the summer of 1942, Wingate created his first unit and set about training them for the task of 'long-range penetration', like a jungle-based version of the LRDG. After learning the skills of jungle operations and handling mules which would carry supplies, the first mission, Operation Longcloth, was ready to be launched in February 1943 with 3,000 men. Logistics for the operation were short in supply. Each man carried a load weighing sixty pounds, which included food, water and ammunition. They would have to forage for food in the jungle and trade with local villagers for extra food. It was not an ideal situation, but Wingate did not want to delay and rather than wait and argue for more supplies, he ordered the operation to go ahead.

On 13 February, the Chindits crossed the Chindwin River. Their force was divided into several columns and their mission was to locate and destroy supply dumps, railway tracks and blow up bridges. The columns marched through miles of jungle to reach their targets, encountering Japanese patrols along the way which had to be fought off. After more than five weeks of operating behind Japanese lines, Wingate decided it time to withdraw. On 25 March the columns began their return trek to India. Of the original force of 3,000, over 2,000 returned, but many of them were in terrible health with tropical illnesses and wounds. They had achieved some success by destroying roads and bridges, but had proved that such operations could be successful with better planning and support. Wingate was granted permission by Churchill to expand the Chindit force and ordered to prepare for a more enterprising operation in August. For this operation, the Chindits would have air support to fly in supplies and they could also count on support from the Chinese.

Meanwhile, at sea, the US Navy had fought a major naval battle against the Japanese fleet in the Coral Sea and won another costly victory in the battle at Midway between

The Bren Gun Carrier lived up to its real title, Universal Carrier, by serving in all theatres of war, including the Far East.

American troops fire heavy mortars on Bougainville. The shells being fired would have all been carried into place by the troops.

4 and 7 June 1942. Together, these actions broke the Japanese naval dominance in the Pacific. American planners decided to invade the Solomon Islands, but first they would have to capture the island of Guadalcanal which lay to the east. To defend the islands in the group, made up of Tulagi, Florida Island and Guadalcanal, the Japanese had deployed almost 4,000 men and 100 aircraft. The Americans assembled a fleet of 75 warships and other ships to transport the invasion force, which included 16,000 US Marines for the assault, along with vehicles and supplies. At this stage in the war America had no combat experience of amphibious landings. The force had been assembled very hastily. The attackers were issued with only sufficient ammunition for ten days and their supply levels had been reduced from three months to only two months.

The first wave of Marines landed at Lunga Point on Guadalcanal on 7 August 1942, which, by coincidence was the day before the US troops landed in North Africa during Operation Torch. From the beginning, fighting was fierce and the Japanese showed how they would rather die fighting than surrender. The Americans enjoyed naval and air support. To resupply their forces on Guadalcanal the Japanese resorted to using a fleet of destroyers. The scheme was the idea of Rear Admiral Tanaka and it was intended the operation would deliver supplies, reinforcements and ammunition under cover of darkness. Destroyers were faster than supply convoys but the downside was that each ship could only carry 150 troops and 40 to 50 tons of supplies. Although not equipped to carry heavy equipment such as tanks or heavy artillery, the destroyers on occasion did deliver replacement artillery. In October 1942, several convoys managed to deliver artillery and further reinforcements. The Americans nicknamed these supply operations the 'Tokyo Express' and plans were made to intercept these deliveries to sever the supply routes. On the night of 11/12 October, ships of the US Navy successfully engaged one of the Tokyo Express convoys in an action off Cape Esperance. The fight for the island lasted until 7 February 1943 and despite growing losses the Tokyo Express remained operational throughout the campaign. The Japanese tried so-called 'High speed convoys' which achieved some success although severely hampered by American operations.

It had cost the Americans almost 1,800 killed and 4,359 wounded and the Japanese had lost over 19,000 killed. The logistic support for the operation had been confused but eventually it was resolved and much was learned from the experience. The US Marines had been supported by M3 Stuart light tanks. The Japanese had little to oppose the tanks which literally crushed everything beneath them as they attacked the Japanese positions. General Vandegrift, commanding the 1st US Marines on Guadalcanal recorded: 'rear of the tanks looked like meatgrinders' – from the bodies they had driven over with their steel tracks. It was the first operation in the island hopping campaign and every shell, vehicle, gallon of petrol and soldier would have to be transported in readiness for every amphibious landing, each of which would be unique.

Guadalcanal had been costly in terms of lives and equipment, but it was the only possible strategy given the enormity of the task which lay ahead. The planners of the Joint Chiefs of Staff realised that 'strategically speaking the Central Pacific route is decisive.... success here is most certain to sever the homeland [Japan] from the overseas empire to the south.' Naval sea and air power would be the key to success, even though some aspects were still unproven. For example: 'carriers and carrier aircraft are at a disadvantage when exposed to shore-based air [craft] is subject to revision when large carrier forces become available... There are strong reasons to believe that carrier aircraft, although untested, are equal to the task of supporting amphibious operations against island fortresses.' They were to be proven correct as naval task forces increased in strength and gave air support to operations such as Iwo Jima and Okinawa.

The term 'island hopping' was coined to explain how the Americans would advance by leap-frogging forward from one island to the next with the rear area secure. There was nothing new in the idea – books had been written on the strategy, such as *Seapower in the Pacific* and *The Great Pacific War* by Charles Bywater, published in 1923 and 1925. These volumes, like those on the Blitzkrieg written by Rommel and Guderian, were available but hardly anyone took any notice of them. In 1921, Major Earl Hancock Ellis of the United States Marine Corps had written on the strategy of amphibious warfare too. The essentials were there to be used, but they were being overlooked, probably because of the sheer scale of the operation being undertaken.

With the fighting in North Africa over, the Germans now concentrated on how best to prepare defences to counter an allied invasion of Europe which Hitler and his generals knew must surely come. Europe had been under occupation for three years and although defences had been constructed, it was only now that efforts were redoubled. The building programme also extended to the Channel Islands, which in October 1941 Hitler had ordered to be fortified. Over the next three years these defences would be strengthened and expanded and the islands would become part of the Atlantic Wall which stretched along the European coastline from Norway to the border of Spain. In November 1944, there were almost 1.4 million workers engaged in constructing defences, including Germans, foreign workers, PoWs and other 'criminal' elements, a category into which the Germans placed the Jews. In 1944, records show there were more than 25,000 service personnel deployed across the three main Channel Islands of Jersey, Guernsey and Alderney. Most of these were from the 319 Infantry Division, with the remainder comprising Luftwaffe and Kriegsmarine along with attached specialist troops for signals and engineering. The islands provided what they could in terms of foodstuffs, but the majority had to be imported from France and certainly all fuel.

German wartime propaganda made a great deal of the much-vaunted Atlantic Wall protecting Festung Europa (Fortress Europe). In 1944 Oberleutnant Walter Kohler wrote for a military magazine that 9.3 million cubic metres of concrete had been poured along the wall stretching for 2,100 km into which 6,000 guns were placed. At the Pas de Calais where Batterie Todt was built there were four 38cm guns which could fire shells almost thirty-five miles to bombard Dover with its port facilities for handling merchant ships transporting food and coal.

After North Africa, Rommel had been sent to Greece, where he arrived on 25 July 1943 and almost at once was ordered to Berlin. He was sent to Italy, but his command there turned out to be only temporary. In November, Hitler appointed Kesselring as commander of Italy and sent Rommel to France where he was to organise the defences in preparation for the Allied invasion of Europe. It was a task which would require all his energies and skills as a commander befitting his new rank of Field Marshal.

He took to his new appointment with eagerness, all the while pushing for the defences to be improved and strengthened with more mines, guns and obstacles. He believed the Allies would have to be stopped on the landing beaches. He knew that if the British and Americans were permitted to land in strength and consolidate, nothing the German army could do would dislodge them. He was faced by critics who held the opposite view, one of whom was his Commander, Field Marshal von Rundstedt. On taking over his new command, one of the first things he did was to complete a tour of the defences, which he found inadequate. He undoubtedly reflected on his time in North Africa and drew comparisons. The situation must have reminded him that 'Whoever enjoys command of the air is in a position to inflict such heavy damage on the opponent's supply columns that serious shortages must soon make themselves felt.' When the Allies landed, with air support, it must have seemed to him as though history was repeating itself. Rundstedt had his own opinions about the efficacy of the Atlantic Wall believing it to be 'a myth, nothing in front of it, nothing behind – a mere showpiece. The best that could be hoped for was that it might hold up an attack for twenty-four hours, but any resolute assault was bound to make a breakthrough anywhere along it in a day at the most. And, once through, all the rest could be taken from the rear, for it all faced out to sea and became quite useless.'

In Russia the fighting never ceased. Across the vast expanse of country there was always movement and fighting, ranging from localised to major offensives. To keep the Russian front buoyed, Hitler stripped men and equipment from France to redeploy in the east. In a desperate recruitment drive, a call was also put out for men from those occupied countries to volunteer to serve in German units. This extended to units of the SS with specially created regional units, such as the Charlemagne (French) SS which probably had 11,000 men at its peak strength in 1944. These men were known as 'Freiwillige' (volunteers) and were recruited from the Baltic States, Latvia, Estonia and Lithuania. From Croatia a force of 17,000 were formed into the 'Handschar' Division. A further 114,000 Croatians served in the army and another 38,000 in territorial units. From Belgium, some 2,000 men served in the Walloon SS and an equal number joined from Norway to serve in the Nordland Division. Around 7,000 Dutch served in the Niederländische SS and Finnish volunteers fought in the SS also. Danish volunteers joined the Norwegians serving in the Nordland Division and fought in Russia and Yugoslavia.

When Germany had invaded the Soviet Union in June 1941, the supply lines along which the logistical support would be transported were fixed to extend just over 300 miles along roads. This was thought to be the optimum range from the assembly points on the Soviet border where the points of attack originated. From the very beginning it was already recognised that the armoured columns would quickly out-pace the infantry on foot which would transport its own supply columns using horse-drawn transport.

It was calculated that motorised transport, Grosstransportraum, based on standard army trucks, along with those vehicles seized from defeated armies, would be able to complete the 425-mile round trip to locations such as Smolensk in six days, allowing for time to unload the vehicles. This would allow for a constant delivery of supplies to a division. That was based on paper calculations, which made sense to the planners, but such estimates did not make allowances for mechanical failure, servicing of vehicles, human fatigue and outside influences such as weather conditions and the column coming under enemy attack. By 1943, after two years of constant fighting, these supply routes were proving inadequate. By 1944 the supply system was on the point of collapse.

From the first days of the campaign in Russia the German transport fleet was forced to rely heavily on vehicles from many different sources, including trucks captured from France, Holland and Belgium in 1940. Civilian vehicles were commandeered, but these usually turned out to be more trouble than they were worth. Even with German operators, the rail system in Russia could not handle the weight of supplies and reinforcements. The Soviets had destroyed hundreds of miles of railway tracks and locomotives during their retreat. This placed greater strain on trucks. A fleet of 1,600 vehicles would be required to move a trainload of stores over 300 miles, but such levels of transportation were not available. German trains were not suitable for service in Russia because they had not been designed to operate in the sub-zero temperature conditions. For example, the steam pipes were outside away from the boiler where they would freeze rendering the train useless.

In August 1941 it had been recognised by the German army that it was deficient by 38,000 vehicles for its logistic needs. By 1943 in Russia, things were much worse with vehicles now worn out and deliveries of new trucks either not made or numbers much reduced. Congestion at railheads added to confusion and caused further delays. A turnaround time for unloading trains which should have been only three hours could sometimes take up to three days. These problems coming so early in the campaign were a foretaste of the worst which was yet to come. Losses of vehicles mounted, horses died in their thousands and fuel was always a problem. The number of replacement tanks and other vehicles dropped and there were many cases of gross incompetence as supplies were despatched to the wrong destination as the logistics lines failed under the strain. As the campaign progressed so the problems became compounded. No-one predicted just how bad things would become.

If transporting supplies in was difficult, then evacuating the wounded out from the front was another problem, bordering on the impossible as the casualty figures continued to rise and swamp the medical services. For example, a unit suffering 1,200 casualties in forty-eight hours was certain to overwhelm its medical units. Frostbite and non-battle illnesses added to the strain.

Russian partisan groups attacked motorised convoys, blew up railway tracks and generally disrupted the rear areas through which passed the logistics to support the army. The railways were being used to transport tanks, ammunition, artillery and troops to the front and these extended routes were particularly vulnerable. For example, in January 1943 some 397 attacks were recorded against railway targets which resulted in damage to 112 locomotives and bridges. Some of the bridges were particularly important such as the one spanning 330 yards over the Desna River on the Bryansk-Gomel railway line. To repair damage to bridges required specialist engineers and equipment along with materials such as replacement tracks, sleepers and points. In February 1943, the German General Directorate of Railways (East) reported 500 attacks. This rose to 1,045 incidents in May. In June there were 1,092 attacks against the railway and in July 1,460 incidents. In the rear of Army Group Centre, Russian partisans destroyed 44 bridges, 298 locomotives and 1,223 wagons and carriages so that movement by rail was widely disrupted. A soldier reported, 'With us trains move for one day and three days have to be spent repairing the track since the partisans blow everything up.' He continued by telling of a collision between a supply train and a troop train.

By 1942 the Germans had sustained losses of almost two million men killed, wounded or captured in Russia, a figure far greater than all their losses in all the other campaigns combined, including the debacle in North Africa. By January 1943, eighteen months since the start of Barbarossa, they were down to fewer than 500 operational combat tanks and were understrength by almost 500,000 men. They were receiving replacement vehicles and supplies were getting through but it was never enough. By contrast, the Russians quickly took advantage of their victory over the German army at Stalingrad and redeployed over 200,000 troops following the end of the fighting for the city. The Germans had first attacked Kharkov on 20 October 1941 and after four days of fighting captured the city. The Russians had not wasted any time and removed most of the important equipment and plant machinery from 70 major factories which filled 320 trains. That which they could not take was destroyed and as they withdrew they blew up the roads, bridges and railway tracks. During the Russian offensive from December through to February 1942 Kharkov remained in German hands. In May

1942, the Russians had detached troops from Izyum and Volchansk with the intention of encircling the city. German intelligence intercepted messages linked to the proposed attack and, being forewarned, fought it off.

The Russians were determined to recapture Kharkov and in preparation for the attack they poured in 500,000 troops to support the Veronezh-Kharkov offensive. They captured the city of Rostov on 14 February, with Voroshilovgrad being taken a day later. These successes were followed up with Kharkov being captured on 16 February 1943. By now, the city lay in ruins with nothing of any importance left. Most of the population had fled and around 230,000 had been killed. Many thousands more had been sent to work in German factories as forced labour, referred to as 'Ostarbeiter' (workers from the east). The Red Army had a force of over 346,000 troops which outnumbered the Germans by five to one. However, it would be a short-won victory.

On 7 March the Germans launched a counter-attack and a week later Kharkov was back in their hands. The fighting was intense, during which there were armoured engagements between Tiger I and T-34 tanks with the Germans benefitting from the support of self-propelled guns, including the StuG III, along with half-tracks such as the SdKfz 7 which towed the deadly 88mm anti-tank gun to claim more Russian tanks. By the end of the fighting the Russians had lost over 270,000 killed, wounded and captured but they had fought hard and in doing so inflicted 56% losses on the SS Panzer Corps. After the battle, Manstein, commanding Army Group South, claimed that they had destroyed or captured almost 1,200 tanks along with 3,000 pieces of artillery. In addition, the Russian Air Force lost almost 550 aircraft. This was a bitter blow for the Russians, coming so soon as it did after their great victory at Stalingrad. It showed the Russians that the German army was far from defeated.

After the battle the Russians held the line with a salient protruding into the German front line, encircling the industrial city of Kursk and stretching over 160 miles in width from Kharkov to Orel. A rail track ran north-south through the area along which supplies could be moved to points on the front. To Hitler, this was a totally unacceptable position. In the security and comfort of his headquarters looking at maps it all looked so simple to eliminate this salient. In some places the Russians had pushed the Germans back some 300 miles. This extended their supply lines and shortened the Germans' but even so, the German supply lines remained a mess, being attacked, as they were, by partisans in the rear and the regular army in the front, and attacked from the air by the Red Air Force.

For the Russians, this was not a problem because they were in their own country with a friendly local populace. Reporting on the war in Russia, the British journalist Alexander Werth, writing for *The Sunday Times*, sent an account of the movement of Russian supplies in the aftermath of Stalingrad: 'Horses, horses and still more horses blowing steam and with ice around their nostrils were wading through the deep snow, pulling guns and gun-carriages and large covered wagons; and hundreds of lorries with their headlights full on.' It was an image which would have been repeated all along the Eastern Front as the Red Army began to advance. Captain Nikolai Belov, later to be promoted to command the 142nd Rifle Regiment of the 5th Rifle Division, wrote, 'The weather and mud are dreadful. We face a winter amid forests and swamps. Today, we set off at 1000 [10am] and advanced about six kilometres in twenty-four hours. There is no ammunition. Rations are short because supplies have fallen behind. Many men are without boots.' Men stripped the dead of anything useful from their boots to their greatcoats. Ammunition and weapons were picked up and reused. On 5 May 1945 Lieutenant Colonel Belov was killed.

By mid-1943, after two years of war, the Red Army had been transformed from a fractured military force into a formidable fighting unit. The change had come at a high price, but the results achieved astounded those who remembered the early days of the war when everywhere the army was in full retreat. All that had changed after the German defeat at Stalingrad. The troops now knew they could stand and fight and, most importantly, win battles. Although strong in numbers and with better and newer weapons, the Red Army still had its weaknesses in some areas. One of these was its logistical supply lines which were often far from reliable.

One of the most senior Russian commanders in the field to recognise the importance of rebuilding the infrastructure of roads, bridges and railways was General Vasily Chuikov, who had commanded the 62nd Army at Stalingrad. With the Russian army now advancing, he knew how vital is was these routes be repaired to allow the movement of supplies to keep the army on the move. In 1944 he wrote, 'There was a mass of construction work to be done or redone in improved form, on highways, non-metalled roads, and on the railways. There were tens of thousands of tons of fuel to be brought up, millions of mortar bombs and shells and hundreds of millions of cartridges, and all the equipment and provisions needed to keep us in the field. And all these colossal quantities of stores had to be brought up as close as possible to the front line, to give us the necessary conditions for a breakthrough in depth and the gaining of broad scope for manoeuvre.'

The Red Army had begun to form tank armies by 1943, which was only possible due to increased production levels leaving the factories. In 1943, over 24,000 tanks, mostly T-34s, were produced. These new tank armies were composed of two tank corps with 500 tanks each, supported by mechanised corps for maintenance, repair and recovery. That was the theory at least. In reality it was a different matter. Heavy fighting meant that some tank armies could find themselves reduced to 250 tanks. But with a production rate of 2,000 tanks per month, deficiencies could soon be made good. Supplies from America and Britain, especially supplies of tanks such as Sherman and Valentines, added to the armoured units. These tank armies could move rapidly and there are examples where they could cover 250 miles in three days. In 1944, the Red Army would deploy 2.5 million men to spearhead its summer offensives which were supported by 5,000 tanks. Mechanised tank brigades were also formed, comprising three battalions each with 650 men to give a total strength of 1,950 men. To keep such a unit on the move it was provided with a fleet of around fifty trucks which were used mainly to transport supplies and tow artillery. These trucks could be American-built or Soviet-built, it did not much matter to the troops in the field, just as long as they had vehicles.

Another formation was the combined-arms army, comprising up to three rifle corps to give a nominal strength of 24,000 men, supported with 50 tanks and 25 self-propelled guns such as SU-76. Artillery strength was important and a corps could contain 1,000 guns and heavy mortars, rocket launchers and 4,500 trucks operated by 25,000 men. The combined-arms armies required over 3,000 tons of supplies each day when in contact with the enemy. This included 1,600 tons of ammunition, 550 tons of fuel, 1,000 tons of food and fodder for the horses. If the distance from the railhead was over seventy miles, the fleet of trucks assigned to transport the supplies to the unit might not be able to cope. As a result, the troops either went hungry or had their already meagre rations cut even further. Firing weapons would also be restricted and vehicles would be prevented from operating.

Hundreds of thousands of vehicles were supplied to Russia by America, but these deliveries took time to distribute to units. Russian factories were producing trucks which could be driven directly to units but there was always a demand for more vehicles. Units designated for the transport of logistics were created using a brigade of trucks comprising 18 battalions each with 100 trucks, giving a strength of 1,800 trucks, and these were assigned to supply each army. Vehicles included Russian-built GAZ-AA and ZIS trucks with 1.5- and 3-ton capacities. A rifle division might have 60 trucks to supply it along with 250 horse-drawn wagons, if it was fortunate, which gave a combined capacity of delivering up to 250 tons daily. Allowing for up to twenty per cent of the vehicle fleet to be incapacitated for repairs and maintenance there would always be a shortfall. Enemy action made things worse still. Russian soldiers learned to go without or scavenge anything they could. When German positions were overrun, foodstuffs which had been abandoned were eagerly seized, as were boots and warm clothing. Things were bad for the Russians, but for the Germans the lack of support was to prove catastrophic.

In 1943, the Red Army had 5.5 million men under arms and a reserve force of another million. In 1945, the strength of Russian forces would peak at over 20 million, more than that of America and Britain combined. All these units with millions of men and horses deployed along the Eastern Front had to be supplied. By 1943 the original pre-war system had been replaced and was better organised, but it was still far from being perfect. At least it worked after a fashion.

The Russians employed a method of supplying known as the 'push' system. This method entails the provision of supplies when demand is uncertain and the depots try to predict what might be needed. It does reduce wastage, but can leave an army lacking in certain areas. It can also result in confusion with the wrong ammunition being sent to the wrong location. In Russia it led to shortages at the front. Levels arriving at the supply depots were often far from sufficient and there was often a shortfall in fuel and ammunition which restricted the efficiency of the fighting units. Troops began to accept that something at least was better than nothing at all. The 'pull' method is used when demand for something is required in greater volumes and urgency above other stores. This places greater demand on the logistics supply lines which must respond to the shift. It does work, but only if supply can meet demands. This method failed the Germans most notably at Stalingrad.

The greatest problem the Russian logistic units faced was levels of transport whether rail, horse-drawn or motorised. The Red Air Force was strong but it lacked the resources to fly in supplies to keep an army operational. Motorised transport could deliver more and was not so prone to weather delays.

As the Germans retreated, they destroyed everything in their wake just as the Russians had done two years earlier. This destruction extended to railway tracks and locomotives and even the bridges which the Germans themselves had rebuilt to replace those destroyed by the Russians in 1941. The infrastructure and farmland producing food was reduced again with no chance of recovery, so that when the Russian army advanced it found nothing. Engineering battalions were formed to begin the replacement of facilities. Special railway repair brigades, with workforces of 3,000 men, were formed. They also repaired bridges and were deployed to each front of the army.

In mid–April 1943, Hitler set about formulating plans to eliminate the Kursk salient. The plan was named Operation Zitadelle. For the coming battle, almost one million men were assembled. Supporting them would be 10,000 pieces of artillery and 2,700 tanks, which represented around sixty-three per cent of German armoured forces in Russia. Air support would be provided by 1,800 aircraft. All of this required great preparation with fuel and ammunition being brought forward, vehicles being husbanded and troops massed, as well as food and fuel for cooking. The Germans hoped to keep the impending attack a secret, but the Russians discovered the plans because their spy network, known as the 'Lucy Ring', was keeping them informed and they set about making their own preparations.

Among the tanks being committed to the battle was the German army's latest design, the PzKw V or Panther. Weighing almost 45 tons and armed with a 75mm gun it made a formidable weapon. It could travel at 35mph which was faster than the Russian T-34 and the American-built M4 Sherman used by the Red Army. However, speed was not everything on the battlefield and the Russians would win by weight of numbers. The armaments minister, Albert Speer, wanted at least 300 vehicles built per month, but

German field kitchen of the type used to feed the troops in all theatres of war from France to Russia and Italy.

The Germans used heavy armour on the Eastern Front such as this example of a preserved Panzer IV with a 7.5cm gun.

The Panzer V, or Panther, with a 7.5cm gun surprised the Allies with its power. This preserved example shows how it would have been refuelled in the field.

The Panther proved to be a formidable tank and was among the last types to still be in service at the end of the war.

Panthers with their 7.5cm guns could engage and destroy most Allied tanks.

Allied bombing disrupted production and reduced this to half that figure. To counter this, the design was simplified and production figures rose to meet the figures demanded by Speer. In March 1945 380 Panthers were built, but at that late stage in the war there was scarcely enough fuel for the vehicles to operate. Also, finding enough trained crews for these vehicles would have been almost impossible. Around 6,000 Panthers were eventually produced, but this was fewer tanks than the Russians produced from 1943 onwards.

The Russians were deploying new vehicles into the field for the first time in readiness for the battle which commanders knew was coming. Among their new vehicles was the SU-122 tank based on the T-34 chassis. Despite mounting a 122mm gun it weighed only thirty tons. The larger SU-152 was the result of mounting a massive 152mm ML-20S gun onto a KV-1 chassis and was nicknamed the 'Zveroboy' (Beast Killer), capable of destroying heavyweight German tanks such as the Tiger, Panther and Ferdinand. Weighing 40 tons, the SU-152 carried twenty rounds of ammunition for its main gun, was served by a crew of five and had a top speed of 27mph. Russian troops could be reckless in their tactics when it came to tank hunting and infantrymen would often approach tanks to place demolition charges or mines directly on the vehicle to devastating effect. The tactic was suicidal but it achieved results. Tank crews had also changed their tactics. For example, in 1941, the range at which German tank crews engaged Russian tanks was around 500 yards and for Russian tank crews they engaged targets at 400 yards. During the battles of 1943 each side would demonstrate how their skills had improved, due to improvements in their tank gunnery and more powerful guns on tanks which allowed the range of engagement to be increased to over 1,000 yards.

The salient had a perimeter length of 360 miles and the Russians were determined to hold it at all costs. They busied themselves in preparing their defences which included laying massive minefields and erecting barbed wire obstacles. One minefield in the forward area contained more than 500,000 mines. They also dug more than 3,750 miles of trenches as anti-tank ditches. This defences included more than 9,300 command posts and 48,000 positions for the artillery to use as fire bases. The troop concentrations were formed into two main 'fronts' with a third in reserve. In the north was the Central Front commanded by General Rokossovsky. In the south, the Voronezh Front was deployed under the command of General Vatutin. Between them these two fronts had 1.3 million men with 20,000 pieces of artillery and 3,500 tanks with air support provided by some 2,650 aircraft. The reserve force, known as the Steppe Front, commanded by General Ivan Koniev, lay further south, just outside the southern edge of the salient, close to the city of Belgorod, with a strength of 500,000 troops, with vehicles and guns.

As with the Germans, this force had to be assembled in secrecy but it had to be supplied with food, fuel and ammunition in huge amounts. Everything was set for the coming battle and all that remained was the order to commence. Overall command rested with Marshal Georgi Zhukov, who would later write that he 'proposed to wear down the enemy in defence operations, knock out his tanks and then bring in fresh reserves, launch a general offensive and finish off his main grouping.'

At this stage in the war, both the Western allies and the Russians had encountered the formidable Tiger tank in battle which had caused them to rethink their respective tactics concerning tank fighting. The first Tiger I tanks had entered service with the 1st Platoon of the 502nd schwere (heavy) Panzerabteilung and sent into action in the area of Leningrad. Ever since Germany began its rearmament programme in earnest in the mid-1930s, the military had been considering designs for heavy tanks. In 1937 one of the suggestions proposed the idea that a version of the 88mm anti-tank gun be mounted on a heavy hull and chassis to produce a tank capable of destroying any challengers before they came close enough to open fire with any effect. Unfortunately for the German army the whole heavy tank programme kept changing direction and the requirements governing the final design of the tank kept being changed for no apparent reason. This led to delays and wasted materials and factory space being occupied. In 1942 a step in the right direction came when the armaments manufacturing company of Henschel was awarded the contract to produce the design of heavy tank on which all quarters agreed was the right one. The project was given the specification VK 4501, and when it appeared it was like nothing else ever deployed before on the battlefield. It was given the official designation of SdKfz 181, but the name Tiger became the identifying title to ally and enemy alike.

The Tiger's armour protection varied from only 25mm in less vulnerable areas, such as the rear engine deck, to 100mm over the frontal portion of the hull and turret and the gun mantlet where it was 110mm thick which almost guaranteed its survival on the battlefield. The best an Allied anti-tank gunner could hope for was to disable the Tiger by hitting the track or the vulnerable engine area at the rear of the tank. It was used in all theatres of war from 1942 onwards and yet, despite its almost ubiquitous presence, only 1,357 vehicles were produced. This relatively low production number was down to the fact that it was a complicated design, with each vehicle requiring some 300,000 hours for assembly time.

It weighed 55 tons and could carry 92 rounds of ammunition for its 88mm gun. These could pierce 112mm of armour at ranges over 500 yards. It also had two MG 34 machine guns. It was powered by a Maybach HL 230 P45 V-12 water-cooled inline petrol engine which developed 700bhp at 3,000 rpm giving it a road speed of 23mph and cross-country speeds of around 12.5 mph. The price to be paid for all this was a greatly reduced operational road range of only 62 miles which was reduced even further when operating cross-country.

The German attack against the Kursk salient was scheduled to begin at 5.30 am on 5 July, starting with the usual artillery barrage. Hitler had given his authorisation on 1 July. What their intelligence forces could not tell them was the strength of the Russian forces facing them. The Lucy spy ring had got most of the details concerning the German attack correct except for the time it was due to start. The agents reported everything would begin at 3.30am, two hours earlier than planned.

The Russians decided to act first and unleashed a massive pre-emptive artillery barrage which began at 2.20am with 3,000 guns firing. Such was the intensity of the barrage that General Vatutin's artillery in the Voronezh Front fired almost half the ammunition supply allocated for the entire battle. The Germans endured this for just over an hour and then launched a series of infantry attacks beginning at 3.30am. The Russians had prepared a series of eight defensive lines up to 100 miles deep and laid mines at the rate of 2,200 anti-tank mines and 2,500 anti-personnel mines per mile. Rokossovsky commented: 'you could not have put one of Goering's medals between them.' The minefields were four times denser than at Stalingrad. German Engineers worked hard to clear the mines, which at one stage saw them removing 10,000 a day.

Even so, it was never enough and they were unable to clear the minefields for the following tanks to move through. The Russians had laid the mines to leave pathways through the minefields. The Germans identified these pathways by detecting the mines and marking the routes. The German tank commanders then followed them, but were led directly into the firing line of the Russian anti-tank gun positions.

The Russians had copied the German PaK Fronts which were designed to engage tanks with intense firepower. They had 6,000 anti-tank guns in these prepared positions, supported by 1,000 Katyusha rocket launchers and units of tanks. The Germans' tactics were now about to be used against them. They had hoped to penetrate the defences in a day but Russian resistance slowed them down to crawl. For three weeks, the fighting raged to become the largest tank battle ever fought in history.

Hitler knew that he must eliminate either the western Allies or the Russians if his armies were to stand any chance of winning the war. The Americans and British had launched Operation Husky, the landings on Sicily, just as the fighting around Kursk was growing in intensity. It was not a campaign which would knock the Western Allies out of the war. The so-called Materialschlacht or materiel war, which Hitler had hoped would win him the war, was now lost. If he still harboured any doubts about this, the landings on Sicily shattered them. He realised that after Sicily the Americans and British would invade Italy. It was news of these landings which caused him to divert men and equipment to Italy. After that, it would only be a question of time before they attacked mainland Europe. But the Russians were a more pressing question because they could simply batter their way forward and drive across Europe bringing all their supplies with them. This was one of the reasons which made him decide to attack Kursk. A victory here might just tip the balance on the Eastern Front back in his favour.

German preparations had seen them pour troops, trucks, tanks and artillery into a concentrated area in a build-up for the operation. In the north General Model had the 9th Army, XX and XXIII Corps, the XLVI, XLVII and XLI Panzer Corps and able to call in air support. In the south, Manstein's Army Group South had the 4th Panzer Army under Hoth with II SS and XLVIII Panzer Corps. Other armoured units took the number of AFVs deployed to 2,700, but General Guderian was concerned about the capability of some of these vehicles, especially the Panther, which was at the time unproven in battle. The 9th Army had over 100 Tiger I tanks and 66 of the Tiger variant known as the Brummbar which mounted a 150mm gun. These were also being committed to battle for the first time as SPGs (self-propelled guns).

The Germans had lost the element of surprise when the Russian artillery beat them to it by opening their barrage. Yet within an hour the first German infantry units were leaving their trenches and leading the way to force open routes for the tanks to follow. They were supported by an artillery barrage from their own guns which rivalled the intensity of the Russian guns. The action throughout the day was long and hard and the

Germans achieved a penetration of four to seven miles. The two German commanders were still separated and there was a long way to go before the Blitzkrieg pincers could meet and surround the Russians. The Panther tanks were not proving as battleworthy as was hoped and the tactic of 'Panzerkeil' (armoured wedge) designed to destroy the Russian anti-tank guns was not as successful as hoped for either. Fighting continued with the Russians withdrawing, which encouraged the Germans to move deeper forward, but they were moving into a trap.

Between 6 and 11 July it looked as though any doubts Hitler had about the operation were unfounded. Then, on 12 July, just outside the village of Prokhovka, a force of 800 Russian tanks, mainly T-34, attacked 450 German tanks. This was the Russian counter-attack, Operation Kutuzov, which had been initiated by the code word 'Steel'. By the time darkness fell there were more than 350 German tanks burning on the battlefield and around 10,000 men had been killed. Further losses to the German tanks had been caused by the minefields and a figure has been suggested that for every tank lost to Russian tanks or anti-tank guns two more were destroyed by mines. Russian losses are believed to have been comparable to German losses but they had more vehicles to replace those destroyed and a massive reserve of manpower to draw from. In view of this action, on 13 July Hitler ordered his commanders to begin breaking off Operation Citadel.

The Germans began a massive withdrawal across a frontage of 400 miles wide. In some places, they retreated over 200 miles before halting, from around August, to establish new defensive lines along the Dniepr River. The whole Battle of Kursk and fighting retreat cost the German army over 200,000 killed, wounded and captured. Around 720 armoured fighting vehicles of all types had been lost along with hundreds of pieces of artillery.

As the Germans retreated they left a trail of destruction. They herded up 350,000 cattle and killed 13,000 more. They transported over 250,000 tons of grain and destroyed a further one million. Factories, bridges, railways and anything else considered to be of use to the advancing Russians were destroyed and young Russian men of military age were rounded up to be taken for forced labour in the west. At Zaporozhye they destroyed the enormous hydro-electric dam on the Dniepr which provided electricity to the whole of the Ukraine region. The Russians would find nothing of any use. As they retreated, the Germans abandoned access to the rich metal deposits in the Ukraine which had been vital for the manufacture of weapons and ammunition.

During the fighting the Russians lost over 863,000 men killed, wounded and captured and more than 6,000 tanks and other fighting vehicles had been destroyed along with 5,244 pieces of artillery. By now the Russians were in a strong enough position to absorb these losses and even make good the deficiencies with replacements from factories geared up for production which were no longer being threatened by enemy action.

They were also using large numbers of tanks supplied by Britain and America and the 2,000 locomotives supplied were ten times the numbers built in Russian factories. In 1944 Russian factories produced 29,000 tanks of all types, 122,500 pieces of artillery and mortars, 40,300 aircraft of all types and 184 million shells, bombs and mines. Convoys from America and Britain were delivering thousands of tons of explosives along with food and other accessories, including more than 400,000 telephones. At the time of the Battle of Kursk the Russians had over 5.5 million trained and armed men under arms and their tank force stood at around 10,000 of all types, mainly the superb T-34, but they were just as likely to use American-built Sherman and Stuart tanks along with British-built Matildas and Valentines.

At the beginning of August 1943 the Russians had established a small bridgehead across the Dniepr River at Kanev, which allowed them to maintain pressure on Manstein's retreating army of 750,000 men. On 5 August the Russians managed to recapture the towns of Belgorod and Orel on the same day. The city of Kharkov, for which both sides had fought so hard, was finally recaptured on 23 August and, a month later, almost 500 hundred miles to the north, the city of Smolensk was liberated on 25 September.

By December the Russians had entered the Crimea and cut off the entire German 17th army of 65,000 men with all their equipment, weapons and vehicles. This was disastrous for the Germans in terms of losses of men and equipment. It was becoming apparent even to the ordinary soldier in his trench that the war in the east was a lost cause. For the Russians, these great victories were resounding news and raised morale. With each mile gained their supplies had to be transported that bit further, but it was all undertaken uncomplainingly because they were liberating Russian towns, villages and cities along the way and gaining back their own land.

After the Italo-German surrender in North Africa the Western Allies were planning their next move. One thing they were certain of was they had to get back into mainland Europe. But how was this to be achieved? It had already been decided at the Arcadia Conference between Churchill and Roosevelt in Washington that Germany would be treated as the priority enemy to be beaten at all costs. At Casablanca Churchill took the opportunity to persuade the Americans to start through Italy, 'the soft under belly of Europe'. In the event, the invasion of Europe by the back door would prove to be a 'tough old gut'.

The first step would be to make landings on the island of Sicily and from there the Allies could 'springboard' into mainland Europe. The Royal and US Navies had dominance of the Mediterranean, and the operation would receive air cover from Malta. Codenamed Operation Husky the Allies had done a thorough job of amassing intelligence concerning enemy dispositions on the island and even conceived an elaborate deception plan to fool the Germans into believing the Allies planned to attack through

Greece. When everything was in place, the invasion fleet, which included 6 battleships, 15 cruisers and 128 destroyers, set sail. The fleet of 5,000 aircraft outnumbered those available to the Germans by ten to one.

The operation had three aims. Firstly, it would secure the supply routes across the Mediterranean Sea. Secondly, it would cause the Germans to divert troops to the area and thereby relieve some pressure on the Russians. Thirdly, it would place more pressure on the Italians. Field Marshal Alan Brooke, Chief of Imperial General Staff, believed that 'the conquest of North Africa, so as to re-open the Mediterranean, [would] restore a million tons of shipping by avoiding the Cape route; then eliminate Italy, bring in Turkey, threaten southern Europe, and then liberate Europe. This plan, of course, depended on Russia holding on.' In the end, Turkey remained neutral until 8 February 1945 when it entered the war on the side of the Allies. There was no need to worry about Russia, which, for its part, staunchly held out.

For six months, the Allies made their preparations to build up the invasion force of 2,590 vessels required to transport and support the force of 180,000 troops along with 14,000 vehicles, 600 tanks and 1,800 pieces of artillery, along with fuel, ammunition, food and medical stores to make this the largest amphibious landing of the war to date. The British troops were the most battle experienced, having seen action in the North African campaign but most of the vehicles and supplies were provided by America. The Allies knew that facing them on Sicily there were 315,000 Italian and 50,000 German troops with more in reserve. In terms of manpower the Allies were outnumbered.

Italy had already lost over 200,000 men killed, wounded or captured during the North African campaign; on the Eastern Front there were 217,000 Italian troops fighting alongside the Germans; there were 580,000 Italian troops fighting in Yugoslavia and engaged in anti-partisan operations in the Balkans. The coming battle would be a testing time for Italy's loyalty as Germany's ally.

The island of Sicily measures 9,927 square miles and the mountainous terrain in the interior is made up largely of volcanic rock and indeed the island is dominated by the active Mount Etna volcano which rises to a height of more than 10,900 feet. The Allies planned to land on two separate beachheads, which combined presented a frontage of 100 miles. The American 7th Army under Patton made its first landings under cover of dark at around 2.45am at Licata where the Italian defenders soon surrendered. The Italian defenders at Gela, further east along the coast, were supported by Germans of the Herman Goering Division equipped with Tiger tanks. The warships in the bay provided covering fire and targeted the tanks. Along the south-west corner of the island the British 8th Army under Montgomery included some 26,000 Canadian troops, most of whom, like many of the American troops, were going into battle for the first time. Separate landings were planned and were to be mutually supportive.

Timings for the landings were crucial for the ships in the armada. They had to rendezvous precisely after some had sailed directly from ports in America; others had sailed from Scotland or from ports in North Africa or Malta.

The glider landings went terribly wrong, with 70 of the 134 gliders ending up in the sea having been released too early; the men drowned and all the equipment was lost. The parachute drops, with 3,000 men from the American 82nd Airborne Division and 1,600 from the British 1st Airborne Division, fared little better with men and equipment widely scattered. To replace these losses, Patton requested a further 2,000 men be parachuted in on 11/12 July. The Italians overreacted to the parachute drops and panicked, believing there to be 30,000 airborne troops landing.

After landing, the troops began to move inland with the Americans fanning out to the west while the British and Canadians battled their way northwards up the east side of the island.

The landing ships for tanks and infantry served well and a new vehicle was used: the DUKW, an amphibious truck known to the troops as the 'duck'.

A British design to produce an amphibious truck did not progress very far and the Japanese did not pursue the idea either. The German army produced a lightweight amphibious vehicle, the Schwimmwagen, but this was never intended to carry supplies.

Royal Engineers at Randazzo on Sicily having replaced the destroyed bridge to allow supplies to be moved.

Only the American army saw the practical use amphibious vehicles would have for the transportation of supplies and for that reason they requested a design which would be comparable to a standard truck.

The army got exactly what it wanted in an amphibious version of the GMC 'Jimmy' (also known as the 'deuce-and-a-half' from their weight of 2.5 tons). The letter D stood for the year 1942 when the first request for an initial order of 2,000 was posted. The letter U designated it as amphibious. The letters K and W denoted all-wheel drive and dual rear axles respectively. The DUKW was essentially a six-wheeled CCKW 353 truck fitted with a boat-like hull to make it amphibious, along with a rudder for steering and a propeller which was powered from the main engine. The vehicle was thus able to propel itself in water to a speed of 6mph and drive directly onto land where it could reach speeds of over 45mph.

The 8.7 ton DUKW had a range of 400 miles on land and in theory could go 50 miles afloat. It had a large rear cargo area which could take loads of up to 2.5 tons or 25 fully-equipped troops. In an emergency more troops or payload could be carried. The amphibious capability of the DUKW meant it could be loaded at sea from a supply ship and on reaching land drive straight to the delivery point. During Operation Husky, the landings were supported by 1,000 DUKWs with some 230 being used by the British army.

The first operational use of the DUKW had taken place in March 1943 when it was used to support the landings in New Caledonia where it delivered supplies direct to the shore.

During the Burma campaign, DUKWs were used as ferries to cross the Irrawaddy River and in 72 hours they transported 6,000 men and 200 vehicles across the great waterway. During the Normandy landings some 2,000 DUKWs are credited with having carried around forty per cent of all supplies ashore on D-Day itself. It is estimated that the fleet of DUKWs used by the British army ferried some 18 million tons of supplies ashore over a period of three months in support of the landings. An idea was trialled to fit a fireman's ladder to help scale cliffs, but it proved too unstable in rough conditions and the idea was dropped. Another idea was to mount rocket launchers, but this was not pursued. Ordinarily, the DUKW was not armed but some did have machine guns mounted for self-defence. By the end of the war some 21,147 had been built by the Yellow Truck and Coach Manufacturing Division of GMC based in Pontiac, Michigan.

During the campaign on Sicily some units showed themselves to be adept at roles which were not their primary function in battle. For example, the American Rangers units proved to be remarkably good at anti-tank tactics almost from the moment they landed. On 11 July units of the 1st and 4th Rangers found themselves being attacked by the Italian Gruppo Mobile using thirty-two captured French tanks at Gela. During close-quarter fighting the Rangers destroyed three of these tanks and made the others withdraw.

The DUKW served in all theatres of war as an amphibious truck to deliver supplies.

The DUKW was equally at home on dry land as it was in the water.

DUKWs transferred huge amounts of supplies to troops during the Normandy campaign.

DUKWs served in the Pacific theatre during the island hopping campaign.

The Germans now committed seventeen Tiger tanks of the Herman Goering Division to support the Italians in attacking the Rangers, who responded by managing to get some abandoned Italian anti-tank guns into action. Over the course of three days of fighting, the Rangers and the warships firing in their support, managed to destroy at least sixteen Tiger tanks, damaged others and forced the remainder to withdraw. Air raids by Italian and German bombers caused a temporary suspension in the unloading of supplies from American ships. The situation was stabilised and unloading recommenced.

The Americans then made rapid advance inland and by 18 July had reached a point about a third of the way across the island. Some American units commandeered horses from various points which were used for reconnaissance duties in the harsh terrain. Mules were also used to haul artillery and carry supplies to keep the advance moving. By 22 July they had captured the town of Palermo on the north coast and forces further east were moving along the coast road to capture San Stefano on the same day. The British were having a hard time of it as the Germans mounted stiff resistance and fought fierce rearguard actions. In fact, by 20 July the British had only reached the town of Enna in the centre of the island. Patton was anxious to hurry ahead as he captured the port town of Messina from where he could look across the Strait of Messina to the Italian mainland.

On 26 July, in a rare move, Hitler agreed to allow the island to be evacuated. Kesselring put General Hans-Valentin Hube in charge of organising plans. Hube had been one of the few officers who dared disagree with Hitler over the decision to abandon the 6th Army at Stalingrad. He organised a rearguard defence to slow the Allies while he organised the evacuation, and on 11 August and for the next six days the Germans and Italians crossed over the three-mile stretch of water to reach mainland Italy. In charge of the flotilla ferrying the men and equipment was Kapitän zur See Gustav Freiherr von Liebenstein, a highly capable and brave officer with many years of service. Using Hube's plan 40,000 German and over 60,000 Italian troops were evacuated, along with over 9,600 vehicles, 47 tanks, 94 pieces of artillery and more than 17,000 tons of ammunition. The Allies had broken the German codes which would have revealed details of the planned withdrawal. Equipped with such information they could have used their superior air and naval forces to prevent the operation. Yet, for some inexplicable reason no attack was made. Such failure allowed three German divisions in fighting order to evacuate in a masterstroke of what could be referred to as 'reverse logistics'. Instead of abandoning their equipment and supplies, the Germans took it with them.

Finally, on 17 August, after 38 days very difficult fighting, the Sicilian campaign was declared finished, by which time the Allies had killed or captured 132,000 Italians and 32,000 Germans. They had also captured 3,500 vehicles, mainly Italian, around 700 pieces of artillery and 70 tanks. The British had suffered 9,000 killed and wounded, with a further 11,000 men stricken with malaria, who, along with the battlefield casualties, had to receive medical treatment. The British also lost 41,000 tons of shipping including supplies. The American 7th Army had sustained 8,735 casualties.

The way ahead was now clear for the Allies to cross the Strait of Messina. It is only two miles across but was defended by some 150 guns with calibres up to 280mm.

Even before the campaign in Sicily had been concluded events were unfolding on mainland Italy which would have a profound effect on the Allies. On 24-25 July the Fascist Grand Council voted a massive no confidence in Mussolini as a wartime leader. In the evening of 25 July, he had an audience with King Victor Emmanuel of Italy who replaced him with Marshal Pietro Badoglio, thereby ending twenty-one years of Fascist dictatorship. Mussolini was led away under armed escort, effectively military arrest, to be held first in Podgora Barracks before more permanent arrangements could be made. Italy now found itself in an almost impossible position with some troops deserting, others remained fighting alongside their German allies, while others wanted to join the Anglo-American forces to fight the Germans.

The Allies, having built up their forces and supplies, crossed the Strait of Messina on 3 September in Operation Baytown. Naval bombardment and air support, along with the fact the Germans had withdrawn much of their artillery defending the coast in the area, meant that the Eighth Army under Montgomery landed virtually unopposed at Reggio di Calabria. The Germans, however, had destroyed bridges, roads, tunnels and rail tracks as they left, which would hamper the progress of the British who would have to clear the mess to allow them to move.

In 1943, Mussolini was arrested and Italy agreed on an armistice with the Allies. Some Italians still loyal to Mussolini continued to fight on with Germany.

Once ashore and consolidated, the British began moving inland following two axes of advance up the peninsular. The left flank moved up the west coast heading for Pizzo after which it would take the town of Auletta. The right flank headed east to make for the coastal town of Catanzaro. For six days, the column continued to move eastwards, following the coastal road, heading for the Taranto. It was here on the 9 September the right flank met up with elements of the British 1st Airborne Division which had been landed by the Royal Navy in an amphibious landing Operation Slapstick. With the harbour facilities at Taranto in their hands the Allies had a port through which they could land supplies to support their advance up the east coast of Italy.

There was no German resistance in the area and within 48 hours the British had moved east almost 50 miles to enter the coastal town of Brindisi with its port facilities. The Allies had an air base at Bizerta in Tunisia from where they could fly in supplies and evacuate wounded. They also had the harbour facilities at Bizerta from where small convoys could move heavier loads of supplies and vehicles up to Italy through Brindisi. Two weeks after the landings at Taranto, the British reached the coastal town of Bari with its harbour. Convoys could berth here to unload supplies to keep pace with the advance up the Italian east coast. By 27 December the British had advanced over 175 miles to reach the coastal town of Ortona, having broken through the eastern end of the 100-mile wide German defensive position known as the Gustav Line. Canadian troops broke through here on 28 December and pushed northwards deeper into Italy.

British 5.5-inch field gun in action in Italy. All shells had to be delivered by the RASC.

Montage showing the various duties completed by the British army in Italy.

Although the Germans were retreating it was a slow, hard process to push them back. They still had the ability to mount stiff resistance and even managed the occasional air raid. On 2 December one such air raid attacked the harbour at Bari where thirty ships were waiting to unload their supplies. They were still laden with cargo when German aircraft attacked, sinking 28 ships with the loss of over 30,000 tons of supplies. Three ships were later raised and their cargo was salvaged.

On 9 September, as the British were landing at Taranto, an Anglo-American amphibious force landed at Salerno. This was Operation Avalanche comprising a fleet of 450 vessels carrying 69,000 American troops with 20,000 vehicles commanded by General Mark Clark. The force was made up of mainly the US 5th Army with the British X Corps commanded by Lieutenant General Richard McCreery. The mood as they approached the Italian coast was one of optimism and Clark was hoping that things were going to be easy. After all Italy had capitulated six days earlier. He hoped to be in Naples by 14 September.

The landings placed the Americans almost 300 miles further up the coast from Reggio di Calabria. This left the British Eighth Army under Montgomery having to conduct a tough slogging match as they advanced up the plains and mountain passes.

The American landings were not entirely unexpected, because the Germans had been tracking their progress since they sailed from North Africa. Kesselring believed the landings would head for a point north of Naples, further along the coast and dispatched several divisions to that area. This left only one division to defend the coast at Salerno. Clark had refused both air cover and naval bombardment to support his landings, hoping he would achieve total surprise by landing under cover of darkness. As it turned out, Salerno was not the best landing place. As the American troops came ashore they were greeted by the Germans making announcements in English calling through loudspeakers. They taunted them with phrases such as, 'Come on in and give up. We have you covered.' Then the firing began from the heights overlooking the beaches.

The British landed after a short preliminary bombardment. Their reception committee amounted to relatively light fire and they moved to secure the port facilities at Salerno and take the towns of Maiori and Battipaglia. With the troops ashore, landing craft bringing the supplies began to approach the shore. The German artillery opened fire sinking many and inflicting a terrible toll on the men coming ashore. The Luftwaffe launched radio-controlled bombs and managed to sink an Allied transport vessel. By now, it was becoming obvious that the troops were in for a tough fight. Three days later, General Alexander, commanding 15th Army Group, relayed his assessment of the situation to General Brooke in London: 'I am not satisfied with the situation at [Operation] Avalanche. The build-up is slow and they are pinned down to a bridgehead which has not enough depth. Everything is being done to push follow-up units and material to them. I expect heavy German counter-attack to be imminent.'

On the same day as Alexander sent his message, Kesselring launched an attack against the American sector. Throughout the day and into the next the fighting continued. German tanks were only two miles from the beach and General Clark seriously considered evacuating the beachhead. The Americans drew up defensive lines and fought back. During one period of fighting the Americans fired 10,000 artillery shells and they held the line. The British Eighth Army under Montgomery were advancing up the east coast, but they were held up 125 miles away. The delay was caused by having to repair the bridges and clear the roads which the Germans had destroyed. This led to a shortage of material and bridging equipment all of which had to be brought forward. Eleven days after the landings, elements of the American Fifth Army which had advanced from the beachhead met up with the advance units of the British Eighth Army at Auletta. It would be another two weeks before the Allies could be sure they had the area secured and finally break out of the beachhead in force.

By 10 October, a full month after the landings at Salerno, the Allies managed to get 200,000 troops ashore along with 35,000 vehicles including tanks and 15,000 tons of supplies. Hitler reinforced Kesselring with two divisions sent down from north Italy. He also received a further 40,000 men who had been withdrawn from Sardinia and Corsica. With these additional troops the Germans made a fighting withdrawal northwards firstly behind the Barbara Line of defensive positions before establishing themselves on the formidable Gothic Line which stretched across the breadth of Italy, cutting the

Polish army moving a heavy field gun into position in Italy. The truck carries the crew and other vehicles would transport the ammunition.

British troops pass a Universal Bren Gun Carrier operating in the medical role to evacuate wounded, which has been destroyed in the fighting.

country in two and barring the Allies advance. As they went, the Germans continued to leave a trail of destruction behind them. Also, as in Russia, they took foodstuffs with them, including nearly all the livestock, which would be denied the Allies. This meant the civilians would be left to starve. It was a calculated tactic, because the Allies would also have to feed the population.

One Allied soldier remembered advancing towards these positions in November: 'We piled into trucks and drove through the rain… Dozens of 105mm howitzers and 155mm Long Toms and other breeds of howitzers were all round, firing day and night.' On the east coast of Italy the British Eighth Army penetrated the left flank of the Gothic Line and captured the town of Ortona on 27 December. In the west the Allies were facing the seemingly impossible task of capturing Monte Cassino.

On the other side of the world the war in the Pacific was largely being defined by naval engagements supported with aircraft and conducted over vast distances of the ocean. In May 1943, the Allies had agreed that the British would concentrate on the Mediterranean and India, while America took the lead in the Pacific. US Navy aircraft carriers, warships and submarines took a massive toll on Japanese supply ships taking troops and stores to the island garrisons across the Pacific region. In effect, what the US Navy was doing to the Japanese was what the submarines and surface raiders of the German Kriegsmarine had tried to do to the Allied supply routes across the Atlantic. The US Navy established a blockade around Japan.

During the period of the blockade the US Navy sank 1,300 vessels amounting to over six million tons of merchant shipping and warships amounting to more than 540,000 tons, which was greater than the entire German fleet at the beginning of the war. In 1944, submarines and aircraft cut Japan's oil imports by 75%, reducing them to only 305,000 tons. Overall, imports fell by 40 per cent meaning the civilian population of more than 70 million would have to become increasingly self-sufficient in food production. Also there were power cuts as coal for power stations ran short. Towards the end of the war there were hardly any Japanese vessels left sailing. In 1945 the Japanese had 11,000 aircraft, but without fuel they were unable to fly.

On the larger islands, the Japanese established air bases. These islands were of special importance to the Americans. Not only would their capture deny the airfields to the Japanese, thereby preventing them from attacking American ships, but also they could use them to operate their own aircraft so they could provide air support to their own operations.

In April 1944 no time was wasted after the American landings on the northern coast of New Guinea and engineers set about creating a logistics centre at Hollandia. On observing the progress of the work, Lieutenant General Robert Eichelberger wrote, 'Where once I had seen only a few native villages and an expanse of primeval forest, a city of 140,000 men took occupancy'. The port facilities here grew and more supplies were delivered daily. From this point, other convoys set sail to continue the island-hopping campaign. One of these would be the armada of 100 ships transporting 40,000 men and all their equipment to attack the island of Moratai in September 1944.

Each island taken would have to be consolidated and, where possible, engineers and specialist units such as the 'Seabees' would build airfields. Aircraft from them could support the island-hopping strategy, whereby forces would advance stage by stage capturing one island at a time, in an inexorable move towards the Japanese homeland. Smaller islands which posed no immediate threat would be bypassed leaving the Japanese garrison to 'wither on the vine'. With no food or medical facilities, these garrisons would become increasingly weaker, so that when the time came they would surrender without a fight.

The first of these operations had proved a success with Guadalcanal recaptured at the end of 1942. This island had an airfield. The Japanese had evacuated the last of their troops in an operation lasting between 1 and 8 February. This was the first American victory but it proved they could successfully assault these island garrisons across the Pacific. This victory was underlined by the capture of New Georgia in the Solomon Islands between 21 June and 25 August and followed up by the landings on New Guinea on 29-30 August. On the eastern tip of Papua the town of Taupota with its port facilities served as the landing point for much of the supplies and other stores for the 1st Division of the US Marines. LSTs (Landing Ships Tank) were used to transport supplies. Each could carry up to forty tons in addition to tanks.

The Americans ended the year of 1943 by making a series of landings on islands forming the Tarawa Atoll in the Gilbert Islands, which lay 700 miles from the nearest operational base from where aircraft could operate. An invading force of 35,000 men, including 18,000 US Marines and 6,000 vehicles of all types, was assembled in readiness. To transport the men a fleet of 200 vessels assembled to ferry 6,000 vehicles of all types, including Sherman tanks, and 117,000 tons of supplies. The landings by men of the 2nd and 8th Marine Division took place on 20 November following a series of preparatory naval bombardments and air raids. 3,000 tons of bombs were dropped in 2½ hours on the island of Betio which measured only 1.5 miles by half a mile. The Japanese garrison had constructed an airfield on this small strip of land and built a series of coastal defences.

At the nearby island of Maikin, not much larger than Betio, the 27th Infantry Division landed with 6,470 men to attack a Japanese garrison of some 800 mixed troops which included labourers and Koreans, supported with a few light tanks. For two days the fighting raged here at the end of which 395 of the garrison had been killed and 100 Koreans taken prisoner. The Americans had lost just 66 killed and 152 wounded, but the escort carrier USS *Liscome* was sunk by a Japanese submarine resulting in 697 of the crew being killed. On 23 November the commander Major General Ralph Smith sent a message: 'Maikin taken'.

In taking the Tarawa Atoll, the Americans lost 2,700 killed and 4,200 wounded. The Japanese lost 4,690 killed. During the fighting the radio operators transmitted messages calling, 'Imperative you get all types of ammunition to all landing parties immediately.' Others were heard shouting above the din of battle, 'land ammunition, water, rations and medical support.' Men risked their lives to carry supplies to where they were most needed, which seemed to be everywhere.

With the island secure, earthmoving equipment could be landed so that construction companies, including the Seabees, could prepare an airfield. From two airfields on Betio and Maikin bombers could operate to cover the next landing assault. The narrow beaches and coral reefs around the islands made it treacherous to deliver supplies to support the operations of the airfields, but it was not impossible and the capture of the islands put the Americans one step closer to the Japanese main islands. It would be a long, slow, hard-fought process to grind down the Japanese, but now it had started the campaign would roll onwards. The battle for Tarawa underlined the need for good logistics and the importance of reliable transportation across the thousands of miles of the Pacific Ocean.

One soldier wrote of some of the difficulties faced by the troops during the island hopping campaign: 'Even under the best conditions, the unloading phase of a landing operation is a hot, rugged chore. With high surf pounding against a narrow strip of jungle undergrowth, with a set deadline of daylight hours, and under the scorching heat of a South Sea November sun, the job was an exhausting nightmare. Working parties were punching with every last ounce of blood to get ammunition, oil, supplies, vehicles, rations and water out of the boats and above the high-water line. Shore party commanders were frantically trying to find a few square feet of dump space and discovering nothing but swamp all along the beach. Seabees and engineers were racking their brains and bodies in a desperate effort to construct any kind of road to high ground where vehicles could be parked, oil stored and ammunition stacked. But there wasn't any high ground for thousands of yards – only a few scattered small islands of semi-inundated land surrounded by a stinking mire. And hour after hour boats roared in to the beach jammed with supplies.' This was just his own experience and observations, but he could have been witnessing any of the landings which had to be made.

Chapter 12

The Campaigns of 1944

A s 1944 began the Allies were in the ascendency, but in each country the leaders knew that the war was far from over. In both the west and east, they had scored victories against the German army. In North Africa Hitler's armies had been routed and the remnants rounded up as prisoners of war. These tens of thousands of men would be transported to prison camps across Britain and some would end up in camps in Canada. The landings in Sicily and the invasion of Italy had led to the capitulation of Italy. In Russia, the Red Army was gaining ground forcing back the German army along a massive front. The siege around Leningrad was continuing, but the population was holding on and with some supplies reaching them, they knew they were not forgotten. Hitler was still waging war on two main fronts and must have known that soon he would have a third front to contend with when the British and Americans launched their attack against Europe.

From February 1943 until March 1944, the combined USAAF 8th and 9th Air Forces had flown 107,001 sorties, dropping 92,500 tons of bombs for the loss of 1,500 aircraft, mainly B-17 and B-24 bombers. They also accounted for the destruction of 5,300 aircraft. The 8th Air Force by the end of the war had lost 11,687 aircraft for 1,034,052 sorties and destroyed almost 20,500 enemy aircraft. The 9th Air Force had flown mainly in support of operations in the Mediterranean theatre. From the time of its establishment on 16 October 1943 until the end of the war its crews had flown 659,513 sorties dropping 582,701 tons of bombs. They had destroyed 9,497 aircraft for a loss of 6,731 of its own. Such bombing operations hampered the German movements in the field and shattered supply lines, they also destroyed factories producing weapons, trucks ammunition and fuel production plants.

Across the occupied countries, the Germans made use of the factories in the industrialised centres, especially France which had an advanced heavy industry such as the steel plant of Creusot-Loire. The factories of Renault which had produced cars and trucks before the war, as well as tanks for the French army, were seized and their facilities used to produce vehicles for the German army. The head of the company, Louis Renault, tried to refuse to produce tanks for the German army, but the company still ended up making tank turrets and building trucks. News of this was passed to British Intelligence by the French Resistance network and the factory at Billancourt was bombed by the RAF in March 1942. The factory was rebuilt and in

April 1943 it was bombed by the USAAF. It remained a target, being bombed again in September 1943.

The company of Citroën, founded by André Citroën, had begun by producing weapons for the French army during the First World War. In 1919, it diversified and began building cars and then trucks. This made it another important factory to be exploited by the Germans for their war machine. During the occupation, Pierre-Jules Boulanger, president of the company, refused to meet directly with German representatives. Instead, he used intermediaries to communicate with the likes of Ferdinand Porsche, the tank designer. Boulanger organised 'go-slow' actions to reduce production levels which could be explained better than all-out strike action. Subtle acts of sabotage were used, such as the tactic of putting the indicator mark in the wrong place on the oil dipstick to give the wrong reading. This simple ruse resulted in engines seizing up for lack of oil.

To solve its transportation crisis, the German army commandeered any vehicle in occupied Europe, such as this preserved example of a heavy-duty French-built Renault truck.

In occupied countries, resistance movements were established to harass the forces of occupation and provide information to the British. This information was used to build up a picture of enemy dispositions and their strengths. To assist these resistance groups in their work, the British sent around 600 male and 50 female SOE agents into France, Holland and Belgium. Between 1943 and 1944 over 24,000 supporting flights were completed to France alone, delivering 26,555 tons of weapons, equipment and other supplies to the resistance groups. In the same period 554 tons and 484 tons of supplies were delivered to resistance groups in Holland and Belgium respectively. Also, as incredible as it might seem, one ton was delivered to resistance units in Germany. The USAAF 8th Air Force made deliveries and in one period dropped over 400 tons, including explosives, ammunition, fuel and medical supplies to French Resistance fighters. In Italy, after the country's capitulation in 1943, a resistance movement was formed with around 150,000 members fighting a guerrilla war against the Germans as they retreated northwards.

In Holland, the Dutch resistance organised strikes on the railways in 1941 and again in 1943. The Dutch refusal to cooperate with the occupying German forces was greater than in any other occupied country. In Denmark and Belgium some strike action was organised, but overall it did little to affect the German army's ability to fight the war, largely because they were not as industrially developed as France. Instead, these countries were used to supply food and coal and provide forced labour to work in German factories.

The people of Britain, although not under enemy occupation, had endured bombings and the rationing of food, clothing and petrol. They were living off such foods as powdered egg, dried milk, Spam and snook. The workers in the factories and coalmines were on the point of exhaustion following long hours and everything was in short supply. The face of the workers shown in the newspapers and the newsreels in the cinemas was one of cheeriness and good humour. The reality was much different and there were strikes in factories across Britain, which, while not having an adverse effect on war production, reminded 'the powers that be' there was a limit to human endurance. In 1943, a series of strike actions had beset factories. In one London-based factory producing fuselage parts for Halifax bombers the workforce went on strike. At the Rolls-Royce factory in Glasgow, which was producing engines for aircraft, 16,000 workers went on strike. In the docks, such as Liverpool, London and Bristol, where supplies were arriving on convoys from America, there were strikes and walkouts.

The number of days lost in Britain in 1939 due to strike action was 1.3 million. In 1940, during the most crucial phase of the war when the country was on its own, over 9 million working days were lost due to strikes. The figures for 1941 to 1945 were 10 million, 15.3 million, 18 million, 39.3 million and 28.5 million days. America also suffered strike actions, but in Russian such action would have been unpatriotic and not tolerated. The Russian factories benefitted from almost one million prisoners sent to work in steel foundries and assembly lines. They were unskilled labourers but they could still contribute. In Germany, it would have been unthinkable for factory workers to go on strike. The consequences for doing so would have been immediate prison or concentration camp.

Since late 1942 the Western Allies had concentrated on building up their forces and by 1943 an average of 750,000 tons of supplies were arriving in Britain each month in preparation for the invasion of Europe. By the beginning of 1944 that had reached two million tons. Most of this was for military purposes, but some of the commodities were for domestic consumption. To handle and distribute all this the American army established an administrative force of 31,500 officers and 350,000 men to deliver it to depots around the country. In addition, there were tens of thousands of trucks and tanks arriving, along with thousands of tons of oil and fuel. A fleet of trucks operated constantly to move everything to where it would be needed by the various units.

Hundreds of thousands of American troops had to be shipped across the Atlantic and to transport them the military planners turned to the fast ocean-going passenger liners which were requisitioned for the task. Ships from the commercial lines such as Cunard and White Star were used. Even French ships were commandeered, such as the *Île de France*, which carried logistic supplies at first and later in the war transported troops.

Men from a unit of the US 2nd Armoured Division 'Hell on Wheels' in the UK. They had already seen service in North Africa and were training for Normandy in 1943-44.

Typical GI based in the UK as the build-up for the invasion of Europe continued.

The 79,000-ton SS *Normandie*, another French vessel, had been impounded in America in 1940 and later renamed the USS *Lafayette*. In 1942, while she was in the process of being converted to troop-carrying duties she caught fire and capsized on the Hudson River. Hundreds of other types of ship were used on the convoys runs, including 220 known as 'Limited Capacity'. The 45,000-ton *Aquitania* of the White Star Line would eventually sail 500,000 miles and carry over 400,000 troops around the world.

All the ships used for this purpose were painted grey, to reduce their profile, including the RMS *Queen Elizabeth* and her sister ship the RMS *Queen Mary*, which was nicknamed the 'Grey Ghost'. Both these vessels, along with other liners, were conscripted for the duration. The 82,000-ton *Queen Mary* could carry 15,000 troops on each trans-Atlantic crossing, at 28.5 knots; once she carried 16,000.

Convoys bringing troops, supplies and vehicles across the Atlantic had to brave the elements and battle U-Boats.

The American army brought over vast numbers of vehicles to the UK, such as this (preserved) Dodge WC4 truck.

Heavy-duty trailers were used to transport bulk loads of food and other supplies.

Heavy-duty trailers transported loads which were bulky and heavy.

The 83,000-ton *Queen Elizabeth* is estimated to have transported some 750,000 troops and sailed 500,000 miles for the war effort. The arrival of American troops was hailed in the press as 'the friendly invasion'.

This was the time for those who properly understood logistics. General Brehon Burke Somervell, commanding the US Army Service Forces observed, 'Good logistics alone can win a war, bad logistics alone can lose it.' One only had to look at how the war in North Africa had developed. While the British benefitted from good supply lines and ample stocks of fuel and ammunition, the Germans had been conducting their war at the end of very precarious supply lines. The result was a British victory, even though it had taken some considerable time to achieve it. In 1943, the tide was also turning in Italy, if somewhat slowly. Nevertheless, it was obvious at that stage the Allies were winning due to superior logistics.

Brehon Somervell was a career soldier who graduated from West Point Military Academy near the top of his class in 1914. He was commissioned into the US Army Corps of Engineers and served on campaign during the Pancho Villa expedition along the Mexican border. Somervell was posted to France in 1917 where he served with distinction during the Meuse-Argonne offensive. He gained a reputation for getting things done and during the years between the wars he spent time overseeing various works. At one point, he was responsible for almost 500,000 men employed on hundreds of projects, including airports. One of the building designs which began construction under his supervision would become the Pentagon that was completed in 1943.

Somervell continued to stress how important it was to maintain good supply lines and educate those who did not know or understand how vital it was to the man in the field that he could rely on good support. Appointed head of Services of Supply, later renamed the Army Service Forces in March 1943, he was responsible for implementing the Army Supply Program. Earlier in his career, he had approached the question of managing logistics in a business-like manner and wrote how it could be applied. He reasoned, 'Successful management depends on five factors. The first factor is a precise understanding of the job to be done. The second is qualified and capable men in key positions. The third is a workable organization properly adapted to the job to be done. The fourth is a simple, direct system for carrying on the activities involved in the job. The fifth is a positive method for checking on the results. Given any three of these five, a business or agency can probably function with fair success. four of them operating together will result in much better than average efficiency. However, it requires all five to create the best management obtainable.'

When Somervell retired in 1946, Secretary of War Robert P. Patterson released a statement in which he praised his hard work and dedication during the war: 'In organizing and directing the worldwide supply lines on which our troops depended for their offensive power, General Somervell performed a service without parallel in military history. He was completely dedicated to the task of winning the war in the shortest possible time and with the smallest cost in America lives, and the energy and ability he applied to his task contributed in great measure to the force of our attack and the speed of our victory.'

Convoys from South America were bringing meat and grain from Argentina, Brazil and Uruguay which also had processing plants to tin meats on a vast scale. For example, the Uruguayan company of Fray Bentos exported 16 million tins of corned beef in 1943. This was used to feed not only the troops but also the civilian population of Britain.

Argentina broke off relations with Germany and declared war on 26 January 1944. The country produced vast amounts of beef and in 1944 supplied over 570,000 tons to the Allies. In addition, 600 Argentinians volunteered to serve with the RAF and Royal Canadian Air Force and 500 served with the Royal Navy. In 1944, Canada shipped three million tons of wheat to Britain, a four-fold increase from pre-war levels, while Australia and New Zealand sent 232,000 tons of dairy products, mainly cheese. Before the war, Britain had imported around 150,000 tons of eggs annually and in 1944 America sent 80,000 tons of dried eggs. To save weight and space on the merchant ships food was processed to make it compact and as light as possible. Beef had the bones removed and frozen while the process to remove the water content from eggs to produce the dried product reduced the weight by ninety per cent. Australia supplied its beef to the American military in the Pacific theatre as the armed forces of both countries cooperated in campaigns there.

The way in which the army of the United States of America expanded from its pre-war size of only 174,000 men in 1939, less than quarter the size of the Belgian army, to become the global force it did was one of the great miracles of the war. By 1941 it had 1.4 million men in the ranks; by 1945 that figure had swollen to eight million men and women serving in all theatres from Europe to the Middle East and the Far East. Combined with the other armed forces, the US Air Force, the Marine Corps and the US Navy, America would mobilise fifteen million men and women.

When the Second World War broke out in 1939 the US Army had only 300 light tanks in service, but because the country was not involved in the fighting this was believed to be sufficient for the country's needs at the time. However, three years later America had entered the war and the situation became very different. In the second half of 1942 alone, factories produced around 20,000 tanks of all types. This figure was increased by almost fifty per cent the following year when factories built 29,500 tanks. Between 1941 and 1945 America produced some 90,000 tanks.

The numbers of women entering the factories grew by 6.5 million during the war and at its peak in 1945 the female labour force had grown to 19,170,000 – 36.1% of the total labour force. One of these women was Rose Monroe, 22 years old from Pulaski County in Kentucky, who worked in a factory producing bombers in Michigan. 'Rosie the Riveter' became the face chosen for factory recruitment propaganda. There was also a drive to promote 'Women Ordnance Workers' or WOWs, producing ammunition. Any one of these could have become 'Wanda the Welder' or 'Lana the Lathe-turner'. Women were making an essential contribution to the Allied war effort. At one Ford factory producing trucks they employed 42,000 workers, mainly women, engaged on the assembly lines.

The inmates at San Quentin prison in California volunteered for war work and produced anti-submarine nets. Other inmates were used to build military roads, such as the road from San Diego harbour to March Airfield. In sharp contrast to all this patriotism, there were rare examples of corruption such as that uncovered at the US Cartridge Company of St Louis, where many hundreds of tons of ammunition were sent out to the military despite failing inspection and being declared defective.

Britain and its Commonwealth, including Canada, Australia, India and South Africa, had over 20 million factory workers, including more than 7.5 million women in the factories by 1943. Since the beginning of the war British women had been encouraged to enter the factories and posters appeared across the country with the extolling call, 'Women of Britain Come into the Factories,' showing the image of a female worker with arms stretched wide in a welcoming gesture.

In German factories, crisis threatened when more men were conscripted and the workforce fell from 25.5 million to around 13.5 million. German women were reluctant to enter factories although in 1939 they did represent over thirty-seven per cent of

Factories across Britain produced a range of equipment and vehicles for the war effort.

Women often worked shifts of up to twelve hours in factories.

the workforce, comparable to the figures in American factories. Foreign labourers were brought in from the occupied territories, 7.5 million from France, Belgium and Holland. Although some were experts they did not always produce the best results. Being reluctant and forced away from their families against their will, the quality of vehicles and armaments produced was inferior and often failed. The Germans were only able to keep factories in Hungary, Czechoslovakia and Poland in production by using forced labour taken from the industrialised centres in Russia and through the increasing use of slave labour from the concentration camps. It is estimated that around 1.3 million workers were obtained from the concentration camps. A further 3.3 million workers came from PoW camps, mainly Russian, and these groups combined made up around 20 per cent of the workforce. Millions died from ill treatment and from poor diets leading to starvation.

Foreign workers had to be housed, fed and their movements, as foreign nationals, had to be monitored. They posed a security threat which the police could not handle and troops had to be taken away from front line duties to serve as guards. If the Germans had handled the situation in a humane way by offering these people improved working conditions, better pay and accommodation, the return might have produced better dividends with better quality in production.

Thousands of troops were involved in the persecution of the Jewish population. Their transportation to concentration camps required hundreds of trains. These, in turn, required coal which was also needed to produce energy for the factories. Had Hitler and the likes of Goering, Himmler and Heydrich not persecuted and killed the Jews but instead employed them as a workforce, they would have proved invaluable. Among the millions seized and sent to ghettos there were thousands of skilled workers – carpenters, electricians, plumbers, cobblers, doctors, dentists, veterinarians and engineers – whose expertise could have been put to good use. Those without skills could have been employed as farm labourers to produce food. Instead, it suited Hitler's cause that these unfortunates should be sent to death camps. The fact that this act removed thousands of troops from the fighting front to act as guards could not have escaped Hitler's attention and yet the killings and deportations continued.

Since the first days of the war the Germans had had to cope with large numbers of prisoners of war. At first they came from Poland, then France, Belgium and Holland. Later, in 1941 in North Africa, they had to process thousands more PoWs, from Britain, Australia and New Zealand. An unfortunate incident occurred on 9 December 1942 when HM Submarine *Porpoise* torpedoed an Italian merchant ship called *Sebastiano Veniero*. What the captain could have not known was the ship was transferring 2,000 British PoWs. The badly damaged ship was beached to prevent it from sinking, but not before some 300 prisoners had been drowned. Canadians and Americans would join the count later and the Japanese victories in 1942 yielded up thousands more, including Dutch,

HM Submarine *Porpoise* torpedoed an Italian transport ship carrying British prisoners who had been captured in North Africa.

French, British and American, along with local military forces. These PoWs were sent to various camps where they were used as labour. The most notorious episode was the use of these prisoners to construct the Burma railway, stretching over 250 miles through dense jungle and ravines. The men were forced to work in the harshest of conditions with minimal rations, with many succumbing to tropical diseases. The railway was to be used for communications and transportation of supplies. Its completion came at a terrible cost in lives. Perhaps as many as 100,000 Asian labourers and 16,000 Allied PoWs died during its construction.

For Britain, the problem of PoWs began in a small way. At first, it was only the Luftwaffe air crews shot down during the Battle

Italian PoWs were kept in compounds across Britain and many were sent to America. They were employed as labourers on farms.

Italian PoWs were not a problem, unlike German prisoners, and did not pose a serious threat.

of Britain and these had not been a problem. One of the first of these was Helmut Ackenhausen, whose Junkers was shot down by Pilot Officer Eric Marrs of 152 Squadron over Porlock in North Devon. Ackenhausen had been on a photographic reconnaissance mission over Bristol when he was intercepted by Marrs in his Spitfire. The German pilot was taken prisoner by the local Home Guard and transferred to Minehead police station. After processing, Ackenhausen was sent to a PoW camp in Canada. The first large numbers of prisoners taken by the British to cause problems were Italians who surrendered in their tens of thousands in North Africa. These were processed and sent to PoW camps established in Wales, Scotland and in Somerset.

Conditions and treatment of prisoners varied. The 232,000 British and America troops captured by the Germans were kept in conditions that were harsh and food was rationed, and they suffered great hardship. The International Red Cross inspected the camps and distributed food parcels through its organisation network. One British PoW held by the Italians, Dan Billany, wrote of his experiences in the camp: 'It was just a matter of setting fire to a few twigs, and boiling the water for tea in a mess-tin or old can. Most of the Red Cross food was eaten cold from the tins, or perhaps you took it into the dining hut and put it in the watery Italian soup we got for lunch and dinner.' The Russian prisoners in German camps did not receive any Red Cross parcels and many thousands died from neglect and the appalling conditions they were kept in. British and American officers were not obliged to work but other ranks could be put to work which was frequently in factories, mines or clearing debris after air raids. Among the Allied PoWs held in camps in Germany and Poland around 8,348 died from a variety of causes, ranging from accidents and illness to being shot while trying to escape. The Russian PoWs held by the Germans were used as a labour force and their treatment was appalling. Germans taken prisoner by the Russians faced equally terrible conditions and many died in the labour camps and mines. It is estimated that only one in ten Germans taken prisoner on the Eastern Front ever returned home. The German and Italian PoWs sent to camps in America received the best treatment of all captives. Around 124,000 Germans and 50,000 Italians were transported to America.

The British army had considerable experience in handling logistics and had created a specialist unit which developed to become the Royal

Italian PoWs were not a problem, unlike German prisoners, and did not pose a serious threat.

This picture shows troops of the Italian army, which surrendered to the Allies in 1943.

Army Service Corps for the sole purpose of dealing with distribution of supplies. The regiment had served as the Army Service Corps (ASC) during the First World War, but in 1918 was granted the 'Royal' prefix to its title in recognition of the duties it had performed. Before the outbreak of the First World War the strength of the ASC was 500 officers and 6,000 other ranks. Four years later the ASC had swollen to 320,000 all ranks serving with some 165,000 vehicles. The regiment could trace its origins back to earlier transport units such as the Royal Waggon Corps in 1799 which then became known as the Royal Waggon Train between 1802 and 1823. During the Crimean War (1855-6) the unit was given the new title Land Transport Corps and then the Military Train between 1857 and 1869. In 1888, it finally became the Army Service Corps.

At the start of the war in 1939 there were only 10,000 men serving in the RASC but by 1945 there were some 135,000, supplying ammunition and stores to an army of almost three million men. It was planned that troops in the field would have supplies for two days 'within easy reach'. There would also be adequate emergency supplies. These had to be replaced when exhausted. It was a non-stop task to keep the army ready for operations. The RASC was also responsible for helping to transport the wounded from trains and hospital ships to hospitals in Britain.

Chapter 13

Vehicles and Guns

The American army developed special heavyweight transport vehicles which were used to carry tanks. All armies built a range of vehicles to move tanks (which could not be moved far along roads) and others to serve as recovery vehicles. One such design used by the American army was the heavy tank transporter known as the M25, nicknamed the 'Dragon Wagon'. The whole rig consisted of the M26 6x6 tractor unit, fitted with 18mm of armour plate to the front and 12mm of armour plate to the sides and rear of the driver's cab, towing the M15 trailer rated to carry loads up to forty tons. It was designed and developed in 1942 by the Knuckey Truck Company of San Francisco which had experience in designing heavy duty trucks for mining operations. The vehicle was built by the Pacific Car and Foundry Company of Renton in Washington, which designated it the TR-1, with the M15 trailer being built by the Detroit-based company of Fruehauf. Some 1,300 were built.

The M26 was rated to carry vehicles up to 44 tons although it could exceed that load capacity and frequently did. It could be used to transport supplies instead of vehicles and could carry 57 tons in an emergency. Fuel consumption was one mile per gallon. It was served by a crew of seven men to operate all the on-board equipment such as the front-mounted winch which was rated at 35,000 pounds and the two rear-mounted winches rated at 60,000 pounds. On board the vehicle was carried all the tools required to effect repairs in the field including oxyacetylene cutting equipment. Towards the end of the war a lighter, unarmoured, version known as the M26A1 was developed. The vehicle was never intended to go into battle but nevertheless it was armed with a single .50-inch calibre machine gun in case of emergency.

The British army was also developing specialist vehicles, forming new units to use them, and training drivers. For American vehicles, drivers had to get used to left-hand drive. Once mastered, half-tracks such as International and the versatile White M3 scout cars, became increasingly used by infantry battalions. The American-built half-track range was comparable in its versatility to its German counterpart range the SdKfz 251. Each had its own specific 'M' designation prefix: the mortar carrying vehicle was the M21, the anti-aircraft version equipped with quadruple-mounted .50-inch calibre machine guns was the M16 and the M14 and M3 versions were personnel carriers. Except for the M21 mortar carrier, these were all used by the British army.

The Americans developed two main types of mortar-carrying vehicle based on half-track designs and, although useful, neither was built in great numbers. Only around 110 models of the M21 mortar carrying version of the White half-track were built and perhaps only 600 vehicles of the similar M4A1 mortar carrier. The M21 and M4A1 mortar carriers were both based on the M3 half-track of which some 43,000 vehicles were built and served in various roles including self-propelled gun, anti-aircraft gun platform and communications vehicle. The White Motor Company built the prototype of the M21 in early 1943 as the T-19 and following successful trials it was standardised as the M21 Mortar Motor Carriage in July the same year. It was accepted into service in January 1944 and used during the 'Battle of the Bulge' in December. The M21 had a crew of six. Frames on the side allowed mines to be carried, so the crew could lay them as a defensive measure when in combat. The main weapon was the M1 81mm mortar which could be fired forward from the rear of the vehicle. Lockers either side of the hull carried 97 rounds of ammunition including smoke, illuminating and high explosive rounds. The mortar had a rate of fire of eighteen rounds per minute with a range of 3,300 yards. A .50-inch calibre machine gun was fitted on a pedestal mount to the rear of the vehicle. From there the firer could traverse through 360 degrees to provide all-round fire support. The vehicle was only lightly armoured up to a maximum of 13mm thickness. The open top of the vehicle could be covered by a canvas tarpaulin during inclement weather which could be thrown off quickly when going into action. Although only few in number, together with the more numerous M4A1 mortar carrier, these vehicles provided excellent mobile fire support to infantry units wherever required. They were equipped with a radio set to communicate where to deploy if needed.

As well as developing new heavier vehicle designs, British factories were producing new motorcycles and making modifications to improve older ones. Despatch riders were usually referred to as 'Don Rs'. Some were female from the Auxiliary Territorial Service (ATS). The army had been using machines such as the Ariel WMG 350cc since before the war, but after the retreat from Dunkirk it was decided to transfer those machines still in service to the RAF because the army required more powerful motorcycles. The new models included the 500cc BSA WD M20 design which entered service in 1942. When the Jeep came into service in sufficient numbers they replaced motorcycles because they were more versatile and had a larger carrying capacity. Motorcycles were still useful and many remained in service, such as the Matchless 350cc, and the James ML 125cc, nicknamed the 'Clockwork Mouse', used by the Airborne Divisions. These machines were small enough to be dropped by parachute or carried inside gliders.

As early as 1942, the British had considered forming a specialised armoured unit whose role would be to support an amphibious operation. The idea came about after the failure of tanks to get off the beach during the attack at Dieppe. A small-scale unit, known as the 79th Armoured Division, was formed for trials and, being experimental, it was possible to reorganise it and change its composition. In March 1943, just as it was on the point of being disbanded due to lack of equipment, Field Marshal Sir Alan Brooke, CIGS, intervened and suggested that the division be turned into a specialist unit to develop equipment and vehicles to deal with obstacles. In April 1943, the project was given new direction and, imbued with greater sense of importance, it was given the task of creating specialist armoured unit. That required a specialist in the field of armoured vehicles. The man chosen to command the new unit was Major General Sir Percy Hobart MC. After the First World War, he served in the Middle East where he had formed the unit which would become the 7th Armoured Division, 'The Desert Rats'. In 1940, Hobart had also seen service in France. At the time of his appointment to his new command he was not in the army, but serving in his local Home Guard unit.

Hobart assessed what was needed and came to a startling conclusion. Having looked at the German fortifications along the French coast he drew a comparison between them and the defences of a medieval castle. He knew how the armies of the Crusades had used special catapults and rams to batter at the walls to force a way through and ladders for troops to climb over the walls. Using this as a starting point, he would develop modern versions of these techniques and base them on tank chassis to produce specialist vehicles which could deal with certain difficulties on the battlefield, including the clearance of obstacles such as anti-tank walls and ditches, bunker emplacements and minefields. The 79th Armoured Division had originally been intended to serve as an ordinary unit equipped with a standard range of AFVs and tanks, but Hobart, who was strongly influenced by the writings of the military theorist Basil Liddell Hart, would transform it into a highly specialised unit. The way he saw it, the division would not fight as one formation but it would provide vehicles to support various units in the assault, the same way as engineer units already did.

One of the mainstays was the Churchill tank, introduced into service in 1941. The first two versions were armed with the 40mm 2-pounder main gun, which was proved inadequate; but it had good armour protection. When serving in North Africa the Mk III Churchill had been armed with a 6-pounder gun. It was Churchill tanks which had failed to get off the beach at Dieppe during Operation Jubilee in August 1942. Nevertheless, the Churchill proved ideal for the roles Hobart had in mind, which included a flamethrower version called the 'Crocodile' and another which could unload a tightly-bound roll of wooden staves, known as a fascine, which could be dropped into tank traps to fill the gap quickly and easily so that following vehicles could drive over the obstacle unimpeded. Another version was known as the 'Ark' which carried a length of bridging equipment which could be laid to span gaps and natural water obstacles and even propped up against anti-tank walls to allow troops to scale it. The 'Petard' Churchill tank was fitted with a spigot mortar to fire a powerful demolition charge of forty pounds to destroy obstacles such as machine gun posts and bunkers. The troops called the projectiles it fired 'Flying Dustbins' from their size and shape.

Mounted on Sherman tanks was the 'Crab', a rotating drum at the front of the vehicle fitted with heavy chains to beat a path through minefields and barbed wire obstacles in the same manner as the Matilda 'Scorpions' had done in North Africa. The 'Bobbin' was a massive reel of canvas matting which was carried on a drum mounted on a Churchill tank and designed to unroll in front of the vehicle as it advanced. This system allowed wheeled vehicles such as Jeeps and trucks carrying supplies to drive over soft sand without becoming bogged down. The 'Duplex Drive' was an amphibious tank based on the Sherman. A canvas screen was inflated by a cylinder of compressed air and kept rigid by a series of wooden slats. A propeller was fitted at the rear and operated by power take-off from the main drive shaft. The concept had been trialled on the Valentine but the Sherman had been chosen because it was more numerous in service and a modern design. Hundreds of these vehicles and many other designs were built and prepared in readiness for the D-Day landings at Normandy in June 1944. Some designs were quite simple, such as the Universal Bren Gun Carrier which was fitted with higher sides to cope with the deeper water. Another design based on the Bren Carrier was the 'Praying Mantis'. The idea was to mount a box-like structure, armed with two Bren guns, which could be elevated by rams so the gun could be fired over hedgerows. It was decided not

The British developed a range of specialist armoured vehicles for the Normandy campaign, such as this Centaur armed with a 95mm gun to destroy pillboxes.

to pursue this design. These vehicle designs of 79th Armoured Division would work well during the landings at Normandy, but there were some occasions when they failed due to misunderstanding how they should be used and misjudging their limitations.

During the war all armies came to realise that it was best to have a back-up vehicle to serve in a specialised role, in case of failure by the dedicated vehicle. The US Army developed a range of vehicles known as 'wreckers', fitted with crane jibs that could be used for vehicle recovery and lifting heavy loads. One type was the Diamond T 969 Wrecker truck. The vehicle was basically a standard truck body, as built by the Holmes Company, but was configured to the role of recovery truck. It was also used by the British and Canadian armies, who between them used around 6,420 by the end of the war.

The Diamond T 969 was heavy – 9.6 tons – but it had to be to deal with the heavy duties it was expected to cope with. Fitted with an 8.7-litre Hercules RXC engine, the front set of wheels were basic truck tyres with the two sets of rear axles fitted with double tyres. It was never intended for the vehicle to operate off-road but sometimes road conditions were bad and it could wade through water up to two feet deep. One in four vehicles were fitted with an M36 'race-ring' mounting on top of the cab so that a .50-inch calibre machine gun could be fitted to provide self-defence against low flying aircraft and as protection in case of attack by ground troops. Mounted on the rear of the

Other specialist armour for Normandy included bridge-laying versions of the Valentine tank which allowed vehicles to get off the landing beaches.

Not all designs were successful and this variant of a Bren Gun Carrier, called the Praying Mantis, did not enter service.

vehicle was a Holmes W-45 crane with a twin boom design, each one rated for a five-ton lift giving a combined lift capability of ten tons. This was useful for many duties, even to lift disabled aircraft onto trailers for removal. Many 969s were fitted with front-mounted winches which were useful for quick recovery of vehicles which had simply skidded off the road. The winch could haul damaged vehicles within reach of the on-board cranes. The vehicle could tow loads up to eleven tons, which meant it could cope with all but the heaviest armoured vehicles. The vehicle was equipped with a range of tools and equipment to enable maintenance in the field, including an air compressor.

Other designs of Wrecker truck were developed by the companies of Kenworth and Ward LaFrance which already had a pre-war reputation for providing specialist 6x6 trucks fitted with cranes which could be used for heavy recovery duties. From 1943 onwards this included a series of recovery trucks called the M1A1. Like other American-built trucks they would enter service with the British army and serve with the Light Aid Detachments of the Royal Electrical & Mechanical Engineers (REME) which used them in Italy and the Middle East. Between them Ward LaFrance and Kenworth produced 3,735 of the M1A1. It was operated by a two-man crew, driver and co-driver, and the vehicle was equipped for repairs in the field or to tow badly damaged vehicles back to a base workshop where there were the facilities to deal with them. Some

Wreckers towed trailer workshops which included cutting and welding equipment. The M1A1 Wrecker's massive weight of 15.5 tons helped with tackling heavy loads. The rear-mounted crane had a 9.75-ton rating and winches were fitted front and rear. The front winch had a rating of 13 US tons, the rear 22 US tons, making it suitable to recover most armoured vehicles and field guns. Along with the Diamond T 969 and the British vehicles they would provide the Allies with a fleet of recovery vehicles to keep the armies on the move.

Better equipment and specialist vehicles such as the Wreckers led to the development of another specialist recovery vehicle in late 1944. This was based on the Churchill Mk III tank and known as the ARV (Armoured Recovery Vehicle) Mk II. It was fitted with a winch rated to a 25-ton pull, a rear-mounted crane jib with a 15-ton lift capacity and a secondary jib mounted forward, which could be dismounted, with lift capacity of 7.5 tons. The Americans believed that on average 60 per cent of vehicles damaged in battle could be repaired using resources such as the field workshops. The British 21st Army Group in Europe believed that 30% of repairs were for battle damage, 70% were for mechanical failure. In one incident, a division lost 48 Sherman tanks damaged while negotiating a minefield; REME work parties recovered and repaired 32 of them and returned them to their unit within 48 hours. This represents a two-thirds recovery and repair rate, something which had never been thought possible in the early days of the war. Such capabilities had come about from lessons learnt during the North African campaign, during Operation Battleaxe in June 1941 when 135 Mk II Matilda tanks were overhauled in field workshops in 48 hours along with many other vehicles which were repaired and returned to their units to continue operating in the battle.

Vehicles used to tow artillery are known as prime movers and although this is their primary role they can always be used in other roles. For example, the vehicles used by the German army were operated only in this role but also proved themselves to be highly useful in a range of duties other than that for which they were originally intended. One of the most versatile of all these were the half-tracks, such as the SdKfz 251, which could be configured into no fewer than twenty-three separate roles. There were plans to extend this range with further designs, but the war ended before they could be developed. The Germans designed and developed their range of half-track vehicles in a variety of sizes and were considered important enough to be continuously produced throughout the war. Indeed, they were among some of the last vehicles still being built by German factories right up to the time of the surrender. Because of their adaptability to serve in any role they came to be regarded as the workhorses of the German army. They were used in all theatres of fighting and served in all the important campaigns.

Another important type of prime mover in the German army was the SdKfz 7. Development began in 1934, making it one of the first in the new range of specialist vehicles when Germany began its rearmament programme in earnest. It was designed in response to the army's need for an eight-ton half-track for towing artillery and transporting ammunition and the gun crew. The first model appeared in 1938 and during the war it was produced by three main companies: Krauss-Maffai, Borgward and Saurer. The SdKfz 7 was designated a 'Gepanzerte Zugkraftwagen', an armoured gun tractor, and became the main half-track prime mover of the German army to tow the 88mm gun and larger and heavier guns such as the 150mm calibre sFH18 howitzer. The first SdKfz 7 vehicles were issued to the Schwere Panzerjägerabteilungen (heavy anti-tank gun battalions) and used in the Polish campaign. The British army captured examples and these were returned to Britain for examination and evaluation. They impressed the inspectors so much so that in 1943 the Ministry of Supply asked Bedford and Morris to develop an improved version for the British army. These would be used for the same purposes as in the German army. It is understood that four prototypes were produced before the project was dropped.

The driver and co-driver were responsible for operating the vehicle and transporting either supplies or a gun crew for which seating was provided for up to ten men. A space behind the driver's position was provided for the storage of kit, weapons and personal items. The SdKfz 7 could be fitted with a soft canvas top which was erected during inclement weather, otherwise the vehicle was open-sided which allowed the crew to deploy quickly. Some vehicles were subjected to modifications made by engineers in the field who fitted armoured superstructures to the sides for protection, but this was never a standard feature. Only the driver's cab and engine compartment were fitted with armour protection, up to 8mm thickness. In the later stages of the war as Germany was facing a crisis of metal shortages, the SdKfz 7 was modified and wooden side frames were fitted which gave it a truck-like appearance.

The SdKfz 7 could tow loads of eight tons, and more in emergencies. Some vehicles were converted for recovery use and fitted with integral winches to improve this capacity. Torsion bars provided suspension to the track layout which comprised seven pairs of double wheels overlapping with the drive sprocket at the front on either side. From the desert wastes of North Africa to the sub-zero Steppes of Russia and all across Europe the SdKfz 7 served in the role of prime mover for artillery. The anti-aircraft gun platform vehicles were termed SdKfz 7/1 and SdKfz 7/2 and were armed with four 2cm FlaK 38 and a single FlaK 36 of 3.7cm calibre respectively. The SdKfz 7/1 was referred to as the 2cm Flakvierling 38 auf Fahrgestell Zugkraftwagen 8t.

The American army used wheeled trucks as prime movers, one design being the Mack NO produced by the North Carolina-based vehicle manufacturer Mack, which between 1941 and 1945 used its pre-war experience of building heavy trucks for the civilian market to supply a total of more than 35,000 trucks to the US Army. The company also built some for the British, Canadian and French armies, supplied under the Lend-Lease programme. These were mainly the 'N' series which made up almost

27,000 of that number. The 'NO' Series ran through 1 to 7 models. Some 2,053 'NO' 6x6 models were built up to 1945 with the Mack NO 7-yard (21 feet) two-ton vehicle being used for towing large pieces of artillery such as the heavy M1 155mm calibre Long Tom field gun capable of firing shells weighing over 90 pounds to a range of 14.5 miles. The Long Tom in its basic M1 version had a barrel length of 22.8 feet and was served by a crew of 14, who could be carried in the rear of the truck.

The Mack 7 was operated by a five-man crew and to help manoeuvre the Long Tom into and out of its firing positions a Gar Wood 5MB winch was fitted to the front with a 40,000-pound capacity. In the rear area a hoist was mounted and this was used to lift the trail arms of the Long Tom. The vehicle had a canvas cab and the cargo body was sometimes made from wood, but even so the Mack No 7 (G532) still weighed 30,000 pounds empty. It could carry loads of 10 tons and pull loads of 25 tons so the 30,600-pound load of the Long Tom was well within its capacity. For self-defence an M-36 race-ring mount for a .50-inch calibre machine gun was fitted over the roof of the driver's cab.

The US army also accepted into service a tracked prime mover known as the M4 High Speed Tractor (HST) built by the Allis-Chambers of Milwaukee. The first vehicles were built in 1942 with some 5,500 HSTs being produced. The HST was developed as a prime mover for the 90mm anti-aircraft gun, the 155mm Long Tom, the 8-inch howitzer and other large weapons. The vehicles were used in Italy and France where they were easily capable of hauling big guns through the mud. The HST weighed just over 14 tons, had a towing capacity of 17 tons and was fitted with winches which could pull loads of 13.4 tons. The HST was developed into three versions, none of which were armoured, the first being the basic M4. The M4C was used to carry the gun crews and spare ammunition and the suffix letter 'C' denoted crew compartment. The M4A1 version was fitted with wide suspension and ammunition was carried in containers which could be accessed from the sides and also the rear tailgate. Some vehicles were fitted with hoists to help in handling shells for the larger calibre guns. These vehicles allowed the artillery to be semi-independent from main supply routes and could be dispatched to collect their own supplies of ammunition.

The British army had its own equivalent of the Mack with the AEC Matador, a 7.5-ton recovery truck which could be used to recover vehicles but more commonly was used as an artillery tractor for the five-ton 5.5-inch calibre field gun. Some 11,000 of these were built. They were equipped with a winch rated at 5 tons with 250 feet of steel cable. In the artillery role, the Matador could be used to transport the entire gun crew and all their kit. A few Matadors were converted by fitting armour plate to them and others were fitted out as command posts, complete with map boards and desks.

Another British truck which could be fitted out for a range of tasks on the battlefield was the Retriever and some 6,500 were built by Leyland Motors. Originally produced in 1933 the vehicle was beginning to show its age by the time war broke out but nevertheless it was still serviceable and could be fitted out for use as a field workshop complete with breakdown gantry. Retrievers were also used to transport pontoon boats for river crossings and as mobile platforms for searchlights. Unarguably the most famous role for the Retriever was as the campaign caravan for General Montgomery.

Another prime mover used by the British army was known simply as the 'Quad'. When war broke out in September 1939 the Wolverhampton-based Guy Motor Company in Birmingham was already producing vehicles for the British army. Indeed the company had been supplying vehicles to the military since its foundation in 1914. One of the more modern designs was the 4x4 Field Artillery Tractor (FAT) which became the Guy Quad ANT, first unveiled in prototype form in 1937. It was designed specifically for use as the prime mover or tractor for the new 25-pounder field gun which was also just beginning to enter service. At the same time, the Morris Motor Company was producing a similar vehicle, known as the Commercial C8. As the rearmament programme increased, so demands for these specialist towing vehicles increased which led to Morris taking over production of the new FAT. Eventually the Quad would be built by other manufacturers and large numbers were produced by the General Motors plant in Canada. Wartime production of Quads was around 10,000 vehicles. The Quad had a distinctive shape with the rear portion from the roof dropping away in a marked manner. It was this feature which allowed the Germans to identify the vehicle and know when artillery was about to be directed against them for they had come to associate the shape of the vehicle with artillery. To counter this a canvas screen was developed to disguise the characteristic shape. The Quad was associated with the 25-pounder gun but it could also tow the 17-pounder anti-tank gun and the hybrid 17/25-pounder gun known as the 'Pheasant'. The Quad was produced in three variants, all of which were unarmoured. In addition to the tow hook for the gun and ammunition limber, the vehicle was fitted with a winch. The interior was cramped but the crew always managed to store their kit and personal weapons, even if it meant hanging excess baggage on the outside of the vehicle. It had seating for five men in addition to the drivers who served as crew for the 25-pounder. It pulled the ammunition limber and the 25-pounder which weighed almost 1.8 tons, and could cope with most cross-country conditions.

Once Britain had decided on a rearmament programme it followed through by completing the development of new weapons and vehicles for the army. The country's armaments industry was far from being over-burdened despite this and when war broke out there was still a lot of space on factory floors to produce more for the war effort. Most projects were not ready for service when the country went to war and some weapons would not enter service until many months or even years later. For example, the 5.5-inch gun/howitzer, development of which had started in the mid-1930s, did not enter service with the Royal Artillery until 1941. The first active theatre of operations for the new weapon was in North Africa in 1941.

Another example of this prevarication was the 6-Pounder anti-tank gun (57mm). This useful weapon was designed in 1940, but would not enter service until 1942 when it was used in North Africa for the first time. The weapon was also used by the American army who referred to it as the 57mm Gun M1. It could stand alone or be mounted in tanks, such as the Churchill Mk III or the Valentine from the Mk VIII to Mk X, to replace the light 40mm 2-pounder guns.

The 5.5-inch gun came about as the result of a requirement for a field gun with a calibre of at least five inches which could fire a shell weighing 100 pounds out to a range of over 16,000 yards (over 9 miles). Even though the standards for the new weapon had been agreed during development stages, changes were being made to it as late as 1939, which added to the delay in the weapon entering service. For example, there was debate over the calibre of 5.5 inches which led to further trials and evaluation in 1940. Once in service, though, the 5.5-inch gun became an important weapon in the British Army's arsenal. This can be judged from the fact that the guns deployed with the British 21 Army Group in Europe from June 1944 to May 1945 fired well over 2,600,000 rounds between them. With a production run of 5,000, the gun was also used by Polish, Indian, New Zealand, Canadian and Australian troops and saw service in North Africa and across Europe.

Britain did not follow the route taken by America or Germany and never developed half-tracks for towing artillery. It did conduct field trials with experimental designs, but beyond this the army relied almost entirely on wheeled vehicles such as the Quad and the Matador. The Quad had an enviable reliability on the battlefield in all theatres from the blazing heat of North Africa to the damp muddy fields of Europe and the humid tropics of the Far East.

German Jagdpanther SdKfz 173 armed with an 88mm gun.

Chapter 14

Italy 1943

In Italy at the beginning of 1944 the Allies found themselves facing a stalemate in some locations, while in others some progress had been made. The advance up the length of Italy was going agonisingly slowly. German cartoons compared the Allies unfavourably to snails. The tenacity of the Germans to hold defensive positions and extreme weather conditions combined to present both natural and man-made obstacles. This created a backlog of supplies; the problem was not too little but too much. The traffic on the roads moved slowly and supply routes became clogged.

For once, the Germans had been fortunate and were able to send some reinforcements when the garrisons were withdrawn from Corsica and Sardinia. Meanwhile, the Allies were having troops syphoned away to redeploy them in readiness for the invasion of Europe through France. Facing northwards along their lines of advance the Allies found themselves staring at the Germans as they stared back from their defensive positions along the Gustav Line. The Allies outnumbered the Germans three to one. It was an international effort including South Africans, Poles, Australians, Indians, French colonial troops (known as Goumiers), Americans, Canadians and British. All realised this would be a tough obstacle to break through. The Canadians had broken through at Ortona on 27 December, but to the troops further to the west in the line looking at Monte Cassino, rising from among the hills and rocks to dominate the surrounding area from its elevation of over 1,700 feet, it appeared a foreboding target. From their positions the Germans could see the length of the railway line. More importantly they could see the road known as Highway 6, which ran all the way to Rome seventy miles away. They would be able to direct artillery fire at anything that moved along the route. Monte Cassino, topped by the Benedictine monastery, would have to be taken.

The terrain was not suitable for tanks, even though the Allies had almost 2,000 armoured vehicles they could commit to the coming battle. Instead it would fall to the infantry, with artillery and massive air support, to fight the coming battle. Over the next four months, from mid-January to mid-May, four distinct battles would be fought before Monte Cassino was taken. In that time, the Gustav Line would be penetrated in several places to the south and north which would isolate the position but not capture it. The first attack was made on 17 January when General Mark Clark, commanding the American Fifth Army, ordered a two-pronged assault hoping to envelop Cassino. Some advances were made but after five days of fighting there was little to show for the effort. The attack would continue until 11 February when it was finally called off with very heavy casualties.

To help take the pressure off the front line, the Allies launched their plan to make an amphibious landing over fifty miles behind German lines at Anzio, which it was hoped would make the Germans divert troops away to respond to the attack. The Anglo-American operation, codenamed Shingle, was under the command of US Major General John Lucas whose forces included the US VI Corps. British intelligence, acting on information received, reported the landings would not be expected and therefore resistance would be very light. The operation was the idea of Winston Churchill, who wanted to 'tear the heart out of the Boche'. He had faith in the commanders and he believed in his plan. Mark Clark on the other hand thought the landings would be as bad as Salerno, if not worse. He knew the Germans held the town of Anzio and believed the attacking force faced a very real threat of a strong counterattack. Fearing the worst, he spoke to General Lucas and offered some words of advice, saying, 'Don't stick your neck out as I did at Salerno.' Lucas understood and quietly predicted, 'This is going to be worse than Gallipoli.' He had his orders: to 'advance on the Alban Hills'. He would take that literally to the word.

During the planning for this amphibious landing it was pointed out to Churchill that it would require ships and landing craft. It would also require troops and they, in turn, would need weapons, vehicles, supplies and air cover. There was one major problem: its planning and implementation would bring it into conflict with the planning for Normandy, which was only five months away. Normandy would have to have the priority because its planning was advanced. Now the moment was at hand they could not cancel or even delay the operation. The landings at Anzio would also have to proceed if the objective of drawing German troops away from the front were to succeed. If this happened, it would place them in the position of having to fight on two fronts. Germany was fighting two campaigns already on separate fronts – Italy and Russia – and having to provide supplies to each. The Allies in Europe had only Italy to supply but that was about to change. The war in the Pacific was being supplied and handled in its own way; the distance involved meant it did not interfere with the war in Europe.

Nevertheless, it was decided the landings at Anzio should go ahead. The assault force set sail from Naples on 21 January and headed for Anzio 150 miles further up the coast. It arrived off the coast at Anzio at 2am on the morning of 22 January, under cover of darkness. The fleet of 289 ships carrying a force of 40,000 men with 5,200 vehicles began to launch the landing craft for the run-in to the coast. The assault was divided into three beachheads and could rely on covering fire from a flotilla of 120 warships. No commander ever feels he has sufficient troops or resources for the battle ahead and so it was with Lucas. The landing ground was marshy and overlooked by elevations from where the Germans could bring fire to bear on the beachheads.

On the day of the landings the Allies consolidated their positions and by midnight had landed 36,000 troops and 3,200 vehicles, including the British 1st Division which managed to push two miles inland meeting very little in the way of opposition. The Americans had also moved inland to establish a defensive perimeter, for the cost of 154 killed, wounded and missing. The way to Rome appeared open, but Lucas, ever cautious, wanted to wait until his reinforcements had arrived with more tanks and vehicles, artillery and supplies before making a concerted breakout. The Germans responded quickly and Kesselring, commander-in-chief of German forces in Italy, ordered units from locations across Italy to move on Anzio. Within 48 hours he had 40,000 troops deployed in the area, putting them on a parity with the Allies hemmed inside the beachhead which now measured 16 miles wide and 7 miles deep. The Germans had the benefit of armour, self-propelled guns and supply lines to bring in more equipment.

The Allies continued to land at Anzio so that by 29 January there were 69,000 troops crammed into the beachhead with 508 pieces of artillery, 200 tanks and thousands of other vehicles. HMS *Boxer* operated in the role of landing ship tank (LST), having been specially adapted for the task by having loading doors fitted into the side of the hull and ramps fitted to the bows for unloading. She was armed with anti-aircraft guns and could transport 193 troops, 13 Churchill tanks and 27 trucks plus tons of stores and other equipment.

The Germans, by 29 January, had around 72,000 men in the area with armoured support. They were holding the vital Highway 7 which was the main road running south from Rome. With the arrival of the 14th Army commanded by General Eberhard von Mackensen the Germans had around 90,000 men with increased armoured support. They also had artillery support, including massive long-range weapons with calibres of 210mm and 240mm which could fire on the landing beaches. These guns would be joined in the bombardment by a particularly large gun of 280mm calibre capable of firing shells weighing 560 lbs from its position forty miles away. The Allies nicknamed this gun 'Anzio Annie'.

Despite the continued build-up on the beaches, which was becoming more and more congested as further troops and supplies were landed, Lucas still did nothing to break out of the beachhead. Each day six LSTs sailed from Naples to deliver 1,500 tons of food, fuel and ammunition which were loaded into fifty trucks to support the operation. The Alban Hills, that were to be his objective, lay twenty miles inland on the far side of the Highway 7 controlled by the Germans. He was taking too much time, much to the annoyance of his senior officers. Churchill commented, 'I had hoped we were hurling a wild cat onto the shore, but all we got was a stranded whale.' The two sides had been exchanging fire since 25 January, but the first real clash of forces came on 30 January when Lucas attempted his only serious attempt to break out. The attack was a two-pronged operation with the British initially making good progress in the direction of the town of Campoleone. The Americans, to their right, attacked Cisterna using the 1st Armoured Division, but it became a victim of minefields. The 1st, 3rd and 4th Battalions of the Rangers, formed into the 6615th Ranger Force, were caught in an ambush by German forces which included armour support. Despite being outnumbered and faced by heavier weapons the Rangers stubbornly fought on. After the battle only six men out of a force of 767 made it back to the beachhead. The British 2nd Battalion of the Sherwood Foresters were being badly assaulted and suffered seventy per cent casualties. Even with such high losses the Allies were resolved to hang on because having come this far, they were determined to remain in Italy.

The weather at times was atrocious with heavy rain washing away roads, river bursting their banks and extensive flooding. The mountainous terrain also caused delays and destroyed bridges which had to be repaired. Italy was turning out to be a 'tough old gut' rather than the 'soft underbelly of Europe' the optimists had hoped. The Germans were in retreat but the price being paid by the Allies for the victory was a high one. The rate of advance was painfully slow and every yard gained had to be fought for. Exactly how hard the fighting was can be measured in the expenditure of ammunition fired in battle. In the eleven months from 1 January to 30 November 1944 the British 8th Army needed at least nine million rounds of rifle ammunition each month. The 25-pounder field guns fired 10.1 million rounds in the period, which equated to one shell being fired every three seconds non-stop day and night for eleven months. The Germans could not begin to hope to reply in the same way and even the supply chain for the British Army would find itself hard-pressed to maintain supply to keep up with demand. At one stage, in late March 1944, General Alexander was forced to order his 25-pounders to fire only fifteen rounds per day. The medium guns, including the 5.5-inch calibre, were restricted to firing ten rounds per day to conserve stocks until supply problems were resolved, except when an attack was expected. By October the problems of supplying ammunition for the guns looked as though it was turning into a crisis equal to that experienced in the First World War with the 'shells scandal'. The situation became so bad, that in November even the crews of American guns were ordered to limit their rate of fire.

It was not just ammunition that was in short supply for the Allies. The wartime diary of the 78th Division reported how 'there was a shortage of socks, boots and battledress and every other kind of clothing'. Keeping the troops fed was a vital consideration, as the war diary of the 38 (Irish) Brigade in the 78th Division recorded: '…keeping the company cooks as far forward as possible so that we were supplied with a hot meal each day… a great boost to morale especially when we were wet and cold.' It continues with an entry concerning the Americans who were 'very envious of our [British] ration system of fresh food each day. They were fed on K rations, a package of dried food (biscuits, meat, cheese etc.). Each man was issued with a package each day. Our rations as far as I can remember originated from different countries. Biscuits (very hard) came from the UK, cheese from Canada, marmalade from South Africa... The cheese and marmalade went well together and helped soften the biscuits. Very occasionally we were issued with comp (composition) rations, high quality tinned food,...a great luxury if you could get hold of them but allegedly expensive to produce and therefore seldom seen...The Americans were impressed by our habit of shaving daily whenever... possible. Even if it were not possible to wash, a shave helped to freshen one up and keep alert. It could be a painful process when the only water available was in the nearest shellhole and very cold.'

At a later stage in the Italian campaign, in November 1944, the Allies were suffering ammunition shortages and while the Germans were in retreat they still had some 2,500 anti-aircraft guns in action. The Germans were still using the railway to transport a daily capacity of 24,000 tons of supplies in both directions, to the front and the rear. Electric and steam locomotives were used. Learning of this, the Allies commenced Operation Bingo, air-raids which were directed against destroying the power stations supplying the electric trains. Destroying these facilities reduced the capacity to some 6,000 tons daily which was carried on steam trains.

The Allies had landed in Sicily in July 1943 and fought a campaign up the length of mainland which lasted one year and ten months, when the Germans finally surrendered on 2 May 1945. By comparison, it took the Allies ten months fighting to cross western Europe after D-Day and reach Germany. Such was the level of resistance and difficulty of the terrain. All this, however, lay in the future.

In the meantime, fighting to capture Monte Cassino was still fierce and when the hoped-for breakout from Anzio did not materialise things did not improve. Finally, on 22 February, one month to the day after the landings at Anzio, Mark Clark had had enough with Lucas's inability to make headway and relieved him of his command. In his place came Major General Lucien Truscott Jr., who was a 'fighting' general and well-liked by the British. His reputation as an aggressive commander preceded him, but he was wise enough to realise that he had a tough battle ahead of him. A week earlier, on 15 February, the Allies had launched an air raid on Monte Cassino dropping 450 tons of bombs on the site in a bid to shift the Germans. It made no difference and the Germans continued to hold the ground, repulsing all attempts to take the heights. Another air raid was launched against the position a month later, on 15 March, with aircraft dropping 1,000 tons of bombs. Adding to this, artillery fired 195,000 shells. To keep the Allied troops supplied and artillery firing, ammunition had to be brought forward and the RASC supervised mules and their handlers from Cyprus. The mules would carry wounded troops on their return journeys. They proved vital in moving supplies along the narrow routes to reach the front. One officer from an artillery unit seeing men from the British 51st Highland Division questioned them saying he did not know they had mules. In response, the mule handler replied, 'Oh, the Gordons can handle anything, Sir; by tomorrow morning he'll have a Gordon cap badge on his belly.' In the hostile, rugged terrain it was the only way the stores could be transferred. Observing these columns from their elevated positions, the Germans incessantly targeted them with mortars.

Finally, on 13 May, Truscott had managed to sort out the mess at Anzio and was able to begin breaking out from the beachhead. It was not a simple task, given the congestion caused by the number of vehicles and men that had been arriving. At the Gustav Line the two sides were equally opposed with fourteen divisions each. The big difference was the Germans were suffering from lack of supplies and reinforcements. By 18 May, a breakout was being made from the beachhead and heading inland towards Highway 7 leading to Rome. On that day, Polish forces fought their way to the summit of Monte Cassino and succeeded in capturing the position. At one stage during the fighting the Polish troops received logistic support in a most unusual manner when some ammunition was uniquely carried forward with a bear. It came to be owned by Polish troops when they found an abandoned bear cub while they were serving in Persia (Iran) and adopted him as a mascot. They named him Wojtek (Warrior), issued him with military papers, and took him everywhere with the 22nd Artillery Supply Company, Polish II Corps. At Monte Cassino Wojtek was put to work carrying ammunition. The contribution the bear made in terms of carrying supplies was but small, but in terms of morale, he did wonders. Wojtek survived the war and was retired to Scotland where he lived until December 1963.

The Allies had already managed to penetrate the Gustav Line at several points before the battles for Monte Cassino and the breakthroughs continued to advance towards the next line of German defensive positions known as the Hitler Line. Five days after the breakout from the beachhead, Truscott with 36th Division had advanced past Cisterna and Campoleone moving along two lines of advance. On 26 May, troops from the Anzio beachhead met up with units of those who had fought at Monte Cassino. The way to the Italian capital lay ahead. Mark Clark finally entered Rome on 4 June but the Allies had no intention of allowing such a prize to distract them from maintaining the pressure on the retreating enemy. In the space of twelve days they pushed the Germans back more than ninety miles. This was a great improvement from the first days of the Italian campaign when progress was crawling. The Allies had anticipated being in Rome by Christmas 1943. Clark's entry was six months behind schedule.

The Hitler Line was an interim position onto which German troops could consolidate and reform. It was never intended as a long-term defensive position as the Gustav Line had been. The Germans created a series of other similar defences, such as the 'Caesar Line'. These positions allowed the German army to fall back in good order, taking much of its supplies and weaponry to remain a cohesive fighting force. All the time

Polish troops prepare ammunition for a 5.5-inch field gun in Italy.

falling back, the pace at which the Germans withdrew began to slow until finally they reached the 200-mile-wide 'Gothic Line', which had been under construction since the Allies landed on Sicily in July 1943. German engineers and forced labourers built anti-tank obstacles, minefields and belts of barbed wire which extended up to ten miles deep in some places. Fortified defences included turrets removed from tanks which were either damaged or had no fuel to operate. These were mounted in concrete foundations to provide makeshift pillboxes complete with the tank guns. Almost 2,400 machine gun positions, 479 artillery positions, 100 steel-lined shelters and miles of tunnels and trenches for the infantry defenders were built into the Gothic Line.

Kesselring was satisfied with the progress being made in preparing the positions along the Gothic Line. Each day it was becoming stronger and more troops arriving. The Allies bided their time to build up their resources for what they knew would be a tough battle ahead. In a period of fifteen days, the Allies had moved 80,000 vehicles and artillery along with the US 5th Army and eight divisions from the British 8th Army. They also had overwhelming air superiority. All the while, probing attacks and limited operations had been made against the German defences to test their strength and weakness, but no attack in strength had been made. Finally, on 12 September, preparations were complete and Mark Clark ordered an attack along a thirty-mile stretch of the line. Kesselring noted he had a 'terrible feeling that the whole thing is beginning to slide'. The Allies maintained the pressure and took San Fortunato.

Polish troops fought in North Africa and Italy where they captured the strategically important position of Monte Cassino.

Polish troops in Italy firing an American 155mm 'Long Tom' field gun.

The town of Rimini was also captured but only after being subjected to a combined artillery bombardment of almost 1.5 million shells. By late October, Clark was deep into north Italy and holding secure positions. Winter was setting in and bringing with it bad weather conditions which destroyed roads. The Germans had fallen back in good order, leaving the Allies to hold the ground they had gained. Throughout the winter there would be limited operations until 21 April 1945 when the Allies finally broke through into the Po Valley. On 29 April, German commanders in the field signed an unconditional surrender, effectively ending the campaign in Italy.

These gains had allowed the Allies to establish airfields in northern Italy from where they could step up their air raids against German oil production in Romania, in continuation of Operation Pointblank. In May, the USAAF had dropped over 5,000 tons of bombs on the Romanian oil fields. Despite the attacks, they still managed to produce 156,000 tons of aviation fuel. In June, the Allies targeted more oil installations and dropped 17,700 tons of bombs which succeeded in reducing aviation fuel production to 52,000 tons. Throughout July the pressure was increased with almost 21,500 tons of bombs dropped on oil installations and output of aviation fuel plummeted to 17,000 tons. In January 1945, by now having lost the Romanian oilfields, the level of aviation fuel produced in Germany was negligible and two months later in March, nothing was produced. In the same period the raids were having the same effect on fuel stocks for the army. In March 1945, Germany produced 39,000 tons of non-aviation fuel, much of it synthetic. Production of diesel oil fell from 100,000 tons in March 1944 to 39,000 tons in March 1945. The once-mighty German war machine, on the ground and in the air, was being brought to a halt for lack of fuel.

Chapter 15

Kettenkrad and Kübelwagen

At this stage in the war the Allies had encountered a wide range of German vehicles, not all of which were equipped for fighting. One handy vehicle was an unusual half-track design called the Kleines Kettenkrad (little chain cycle). This handy vehicle, developed during the mid-1930s and built by the NSU and Stoewer Company, was the HK101 but given the official designation of SdKfz 2. Introduced into service in 1939, it was intended that the Kettenkrad would serve as a utility vehicle capable of operating in a variety of roles, including liaison and communications. Weighing only 1.5 tons it could tow loads of about half a ton or up to four tons in extreme circumstances. This capability made it suitable for transporting ammunition or medical supplies in a trailer. It was also used for towing light anti-tank guns, Nebelwerfer rocket launchers or recoilless guns. The vehicle, which could reach road speeds up to 50mph, was based on a small tracked unit to which was fitted the front half of a motorcycle. The driver's position was fitted with a motorcycle saddle and was steered through the front wheel by means of motorcycle handlebars which were linked to the transmission to control the differential movements of the tracks.

The original HK 101 was only in service between 1939 and 1940, after which an improved version was introduced in 1941, designated the HK 102, which was slightly larger but still called SdKfz 2. It was the HK 102 version which gave service throughout the rest of the war. There were two radiators mounted between the driver and the two passengers it carried in rear facing seats, through which cooling air was drawn. Warm air from the engine could be ducted towards the driver, which was useful in Russia where temperatures could plunge. The SdKfz 2 Kettenkrad was a design of vehicle unique to the German army. Around 8,345 Kettenkrads were built and they served throughout the war in all theatres with all branches of the army.

When Hitler repudiated the Treaty of Versailles he ordered vehicle manufacturers to begin production of trucks and cars which would have a military application as well as civilian use. One of these manufacturing companies was owned by Ferdinand Porsche, whom Hitler approached to develop a 'Volkswagen' or 'People's Car' which would be inexpensive and easy to manufacture. The design that started as a mass-produced family vehicle, with some modifications proved to be suited as the basic vehicle for military use. During the rearmament programme of the mid-1930s, the German motor industry underwent a radical change to reduce development and production costs. For

The Germans produced a range of specialist vehicles such as the Kettenkrad which could be used in liaison duties and for laying telephone cables.

example, four companies, Audi, DKW, Horch and Wanderer, combined to form the Auto Union AG in November 1931 with the government of the Weimar Republic providing financial backing. Two years later, by which time Hitler and the Nazi Party were in power, more money was invested into developing the motor industry. The amount continued to increase and between 1933 and 1935, investment more than doubled from five million marks to eleven million, with around thirty-six companies producing vehicles.

After Germany and Austria were unified with the Anschluss in 1938, Hitler pressed for more territorial gains and by the end of the year had taken over Czechoslovakia with its huge manufacturing base and the capacity to produce all types of motor vehicles. There were now over 100 different types of truck being produced, 55 various types of cars and 150 forms of motorcycle. It was obvious that streamlining was necessary and this number was reduced to create a more efficient industry. The number of truck designs was reduced so that only 19 types were produced. The different types of cars were reduced to 30 types, one of which would be Ferdinand Porsche's Volkswagen. It was a radical move but it reduced waste and introduced a range of commonality in parts.

Before war broke out the main vehicle in service with the army was the Type 62 car which was already being used in a range of liaison roles. Following experiences during the Polish campaign in 1939, the army asked for a more refined vehicle with better off-road capabilities. This resulted in the Type 82 or 'Kübelwagen' (bucket-seat car). Trials to develop variations were conducted, and not all were successful. Those which were developed and entered service included an ambulance version, a light supply vehicle, the Type 82/1, which was a radio vehicle with three seats, and the Type 82/7 which served as a command car. Production of the Type 82 commenced in February 1940 and continued until 1945 by which time almost 50,500 vehicles had been built. With an operational range of over 320 miles it lent itself to a range of duties. It could be equipped with radios and used in liaison duties, or it could carry wounded and deliver light supplies such as medical stores, making it the German army's equivalent to the Jeep. Like the Jeep, the windscreen could be folded down. The vehicle was highly successful in service, especially in Russia, because being air-cooled there was no radiator to freeze. It was a very basic vehicle with basic driving controls. It weighed 0.65 tons in its basic form but weights varied according to the role and the version. For example, the Type 276 Schlepperfahrzeug (tractor), produced in 1944, was fitted with a tow hook which allowed it to tow the 3.7cm calibre PaK35/36 anti-tank gun and carry the gun crew and ammunition.

Another light liaison vehicle to emerge from the restructured motor industry and enter service with the German army, albeit rather late, was the Volkswagen Schwimmwagen. More than 15,500 were built between 1941 and 1944 and they served in all theatres of the war. The Schwimmwagen used many of the same automotive and electrical systems as the Kübelwagen and the Type 87 command car. Initially it was intended that the vehicle would serve as a replacement for motorcycle combinations and indeed the term Kradschutzen Ersatzwagen (motorcycle troops replacement vehicle) was given to the first production models.

The Kübelwagen was a multi-purpose vehicle used for liaison and light transport.

Prior to the development of this vehicle, the German army had never really seen a need for light amphibious vehicles. An earlier design called the Trippel did inspire some interest but was never built in the same numbers as the Volkswagen vehicle. The Schwimmwagen was a 4x4 and entered service with the German army and Waffen SS units who deployed it to units across Europe and into Russia where its fording capabilities made it valuable in crossing the many rivers. The body was made of an all-welded design known as a unitised structure and there were no doors for the obvious reason that they would have compromised the water-tight design. The front end of the vehicle had a sharp incline which permitted it to be driven directly into the water smoothly and to exit most river banks. It weighed less than one ton and while it could be armed with a machine gun, it did not always carry armament.

For propulsion in the water it was fitted with a triple-bladed propeller which was stored upright when driving on roads and manually lowered only on entering water. Power take-off came from the engine crankshaft. The propeller provided forward motion only and the driver turned the steering wheel to turn the front wheels to guide the vehicle in the direction required, the same as driving on the road. If the vehicle had to reverse in the water then paddles were provided for this purpose. The propeller design meant the Schwimmwagen could never be used to tow trailers because a tow hook would have got in the way, so it was restricted to liaison duties. In an emergency, however, it could be used to evacuate wounded.

Chapter 16

German use of foreign manpower

A t the beginning of 1944 Germany had 320 divisions either engaged in fighting or serving as forces of occupation. Across Holland, France, Belgium and the Channel Islands there were fifty divisions. The greatest proportion were fighting in Russia, where 206 divisions were engaged across a massive frontage and at the end of a very tenuous supply line stretching for hundreds of miles. In Italy and the Balkans there were 22 and 24 divisions respectively, leaving the remaining 18 divisions deployed in Norway and Denmark. Such dispositions fighting on two fronts, Italy and Russia, with the possibility of a third opening any time soon with the Allied invasion of Europe, all had to be supplied with ammunition, food, fuel and medical supplies, and wounded evacuated. The age of the replacement troops was getting younger and the German army sought recruits from the occupied countries to serve in in the ranks. Some had already joined the Waffen SS divisions to fight in Russia, now it was the turn of the field army to entice recruits. Tempted by the prospect of food or to avoid enforced labour in factories, there were young men who joined.

In Holland between 20,000 and 25,000 served in the army, with thousands more coming from France and Belgium. From Norway around 50,000 men served either in military or paramilitary units. The number of volunteers from Russia were possibly as many as 1.5 million and these were posted to various locations, including France, where they were referred to as 'Ost Battalions'. Some of these were used to help in the movement of supplies and were known as either 'Ivans' or 'Hiwis', short for 'Hilfswillige' (volunteer helpers). Their presence allowed the German army to free up trained German soldiers to serve in combat units, leaving these Russians to work under supervision. They also served as a labour force for road building and construction of defences. The fighting ability of those sent to combat units was always in doubt but they were better than nothing. More than 18,000 volunteers came from Spain to form the Azul (blue) Division which was sent to serve in Russia. After suffering crippling losses of almost 13,000 casualties, the division was withdrawn from frontline duties in October 1943.

As well as having these volunteer forces from occupied states, Hitler benefitted from troops in the armies of allied states. These states included Romania, Bulgaria and Hungary. Finland was friendly towards Hitler, but the Finnish army was mainly committed to supporting the siege against Leningrad. Before the war, Germany, Italy and Japan signed the so-called Tripartite Pact or Pact of Steel which lasted until 1943, when Mussolini was arrested. Only Italy and Germany had deployed troops together to fight in the same theatre of operations, in North Africa and Greece. This left Japan to fight on its own on the opposite side of the world.

In November 1940, Hitler gained Romania as an ally when Prime Minister Antonescu signed a pact with Germany. Even before that, as early as September, there had been some 18,000 German troops based in Romania to act as 'advisors' to instruct and train the Romania army. When Germany attacked Russia in 1941, Romanian troops had taken part in the campaign, even though they were inadequately prepared, with little or nothing in the way of transport. They advanced on foot or horseback and losses soon mounted to reach 130,000. In November 1942, the army lost a further 20,000 men in the Crimea. The Romanian army, despite its losses, remained committed and Hitler's largest military ally with almost 270,000 men in Russia. Hungary had already allied itself to Germany even before war broke out, later taking part in several operations, including the attack against Yugoslavia in April 1941.

The Hungarian army had a pre-war strength of 80,000 which made it a corps-strength force. It was old-fashioned in composition, with artillery being largely horse-drawn and formed around cavalry, but still having around 200 armoured vehicles, including light tanks, and infantry with bicycles. From July 1941, Hungarian troops advanced 750 miles into Russia and sustained heavy losses in the process. Over 26,000 men were killed and wounded, over 1,000 trucks were also lost and 90% of its armoured vehicles. Six months later the force had returned to the capital Budapest where it was re-equipped and reformed. Some troops were assigned to construction or support service duties, others were deployed back to Russia. They had very little in the way of supplies and reserve forces and hardly any winter clothing. When the Russians attacked in January 1943 the Hungarian army suffered 148,000 casualties. After such a mauling, they were retained for rear area duties under German supervision in roles such as supply and labour. As late as February 1945, there were still 215,000 Hungarian troops serving, of which 20% were employed on labour duties. The garrison in Budapest was starving and resorted to eating all 25,000 of its horses and even the animals in the zoo – out of 2,500 only 14 were left. By this time, the German army had seventy-three weakened divisions and, in the absence of air support and lacking supplies, it was on the verge of collapse.

If Hungary and Bulgaria were stalwart German allies, Bulgaria would turn out to be a burden. Originally, the country had not been Hitler's ally and only became committed to Germany after the attack against Russia. The army was equipped with obsolete equipment and mostly used horses for transportation. Like its other allies, Germany had to provide weapons, equipment, tanks and supplies including fuel, food and ammunition. This placed additional strain on the resources. These allies of Germany provided what they could, such as uniforms, but they lacked the industrial capacity to fight independently. Only Finland had resources to provide for itself, with Germany providing tanks. The Finnish army mobilised 400,000 men in 1941 in the so-called 'War of Continuation' against the Russians, but limited itself to operations north of the Karelian Isthmus and the siege of Leningrad. By May 1944, the strength of the Finnish army had dwindled to 270,000, 1,900 pieces of artillery and 800 tanks, and it was facing shortages of aircraft and supplies. Throughout the war, it remained a well-trained and well-equipped force, and on 19 September 1944 the country signed an Armistice with Russia.

Finland had been Germany's ally and participated in the siege of Leningrad, but it withdrew from the war in late 1944 and later joined on Russia's side against Hitler.

Chapter 17

D-Day

The Allies with General Mark Clark had entered Rome on 4 June 1944. On that day in England, decisions were being debated concerning the orders to launch the operation which would affect the entire course of the war in Europe. The Supreme Allied Commander, General 'Ike' Eisenhower, had had to postpone the operation due to bad weather. Briefings continued at Southwick House, just outside Portsmouth in Hampshire where much of the planning had taken place. It was at one of these briefings that the RAF meteorologist, Group Captain James Stagg, reported to Eisenhower that he saw a break in the weather which would allow it to go ahead. It was Stagg's earlier weather report about a storm which had led to the operation being postponed. Now the forecast was good. The word to launch the invasion of Europe would be given. On 5 June ships were moored at their berths in ports all along the south coast of England and up the west coast to Wales. They were waiting for the signal to set sail to rendezvous in darkness in the middle of the English Channel at a point codenamed 'Piccadilly Circus'. An elaborate deception plan known as Fortitude South had led the Germans to believe the invasion would be directed against the Pas de Calais coast, the shortest crossing point between England and France. The deception had been created by a force called First US Army Group (FUSAG) which did not exist beyond some vehicles pouring out radio signals. The Allies had made their plans carefully. They knew that the Pas de Calais area was heavily defended and Brittany was too far away, which only left the Normandy coast as a credible landing point. For many months, the Allies had been building up a detailed picture of the landing points where their invasion force, larger than anything before seen, would go ashore. The build-up for the invasion had begun in 1943 and by 1944 had turned Britain into one gigantic airfield and a series of vehicle parks all over the place.

In 1944, Britain had been at war for five years and everyone knew what it was to make sacrifices for the war effort. People had learned how to cope and adapted to each new situation. Rationing seemed to get worse with each passing year. Now, the arrival of these extra troops placed an even greater strain on the island nation which was having to find room for these millions of men. It also had to find space to grow extra food. The troops needed training grounds and depots to store all the supplies.

Part of the problem of where to put the troops, vehicles and so much equipment was solved by requisitioning country estates such as Lupton House in Devon, which was taken over by the US Army in 1943 and designated as Camp K6 in Marshalling Area K in readiness for D-Day. The site could accommodate 2,500 troops and 350 vehicles. The troops sent here soon settled into a training routine in the surrounding area. In the grounds of the house they dug 'blast' trenches to use as shelters in the event of an air raid. In the event, the site was never attacked. Another estate taken over was Saltram Park, also in Devon, where the American army based elements of the US IV Infantry Division. Units included the 75th Medical Battalion (Armoured) 858 Quartermaster Fumigation & Bath, Company M, Detachment M, and the 4059 Quartermaster Service Corps 389 Engineer General Service Regiment, 2nd Battalion, Company D. These were some of the many support units which would be needed when the army landed in Europe. Littlecote House near Reading was used to base some of the troops from the 101st Airborne Division and in the grounds more vehicles were parked.

Country lanes and roads, fields and sports grounds were all used to disperse tanks, artillery and vehicles, preferably under trees to prevent them from being spotted by German reconnaissance aircraft. In fact, so much equipment was now in the country that comedians of the day said that if it was not for all the barrage balloons Britain would sink.

The GIs caused quite a stir across the whole of the community, young and old, male and female alike. Young boys enjoyed the thrill of seeing these new troops with their

Saltram House estate in Devon, England, where the grounds were used as a camp for American troops in the build-up for Normandy.

Southwick House, just outside Portsmouth in Hampshire, England, where Operation Overlord was planned and conducted.

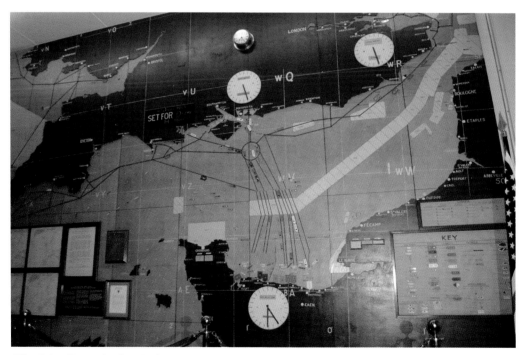

The Map Room in Southwick House, showing the large-scale detail used during the Normandy Campaign.

Saltram House estate in Devon.

strange accents and endless supplies of chocolate. The young women took to these fit, good-looking young men for different reasons. The older members of the community blessed and cursed them in equal measure, for their politeness but, at the same time, brashness. The Americans had a lot to learn when it came to understanding the ways of their Allies. They had to learn to drive on the left-hand side of the road which, to them, was the wrong side. Things would go back to normal for them, driving on the right-hand side of the road, when they went into Europe. There was a language problem too. They had to come to terms with British phrases for everyday things, such as petrol for which they used the term 'gas' from gasoline. In the villages, especially in the West Country, these young men had to get used to pubs (bars) which sold local beer and cider, which could be surprisingly intoxicating. At the peak, the number of US troops in Britain would reach almost two million, with more undergoing training in America. Specialist troops, such as the Seabees, US Naval Construction Battalions, also began to arrive. In September 1943, a Seabee unit arrived at Salcombe in Devon to establish an amphibious base. They were followed in October by more troops and moved to nearby Dartmouth, where they established Amphibious Forces Training Center No XI. Numbers built up to reach 3,684, of which more than half were accommodated in the Royal Naval College. The remainder lived in huts, specially built, and tents in the grounds of the college. Over 400 men were billeted with civilians in the town. The

In the grounds of Saltram estate, the American army engineers built special service bays such as this for the maintenance of vehicles.

Littlecote House, near Newbury in Berkshire, where elements of the 101st Airborne Division were camped during training in the lead up to D-Day.

numbers at Salcombe reached almost 2,000, outnumbering the local civilian population by 2 to 1. The Salcombe Hotel was requisitioned along with sixty other properties, and huts, known as Quonset (the American version of the British Nissen hut but larger), were built just outside the town. Some derelict houses were demolished which allowed the Seabees to build slipways into the harbour, so vehicles could be loaded onto landing craft. The St Elmo Hotel was taken over for use as a hospital and the Cliff House guesthouse became part of the cookhouse. This was only one of many locations to be taken over by the Friendly Invasion.

With so much available from its American Ally, British factories reduced their output in some areas. For example, tank production was almost halved from the 8,600 built in 1942 down to just 4,600 in 1944. In terms of artillery, Britain produced 43,000 guns but in 1944 this was down to 16,000 weapons. By the end of the war, America had supplied 47% of armoured vehicles, including tanks, used by the British army and Commonwealth and Dominion forces. American small arms, mainly machine guns, accounted for 21% of weapons used by the British army. Even so, Britain absorbed only 11.5% of total US military production. Around 5% of US food production was sent to Britain, made up of tinned goods and dried foods such as eggs, milk and potatoes.

Floor space in British factories was now freed up to convert the new specialist armour for the invasion of Europe. Smalls arms and ammunition were items whose

Royal Navy planners organising protection for convoys carrying supplies.

Once ashore on any beach, the Seabees would begin to operate as seen here with this restored crane.

Once ashore on any beach, the Seabees would begin to operate as seen here with this restored crane.

The crane jib was mounted on a vehicle chassis for mobility.

The crane jib from a different angle.

The Dodge WC52 'Weapons Carrier' was a versatile vehicle, capable of transporting supplies or carrying troops.

British trucks were loaded with ammunition and other stores as the build-up for Normandy advanced.

The Bedford OY truck was a standard vehicle for the British army, used to transport supplies and troops.

American trucks such as the GMC were shipped across to the UK in their thousands ready for Normandy.

American troops at Dunkeswell in Devon queue to buy personal items from the stores.

output was increased. Shipyards were still building vessels for convoy duties and warships to protect them. Aircraft production was increased, mainly the heavy Lancaster bombers which were being used to destroy Germany's factories and railway centres. Large numbers of workers were employed on the construction of the modular artificial harbours which would support the invasion of Europe. Known as 'Mulberry' harbours their construction would require a workforce of over 55,000 men, involve 300 companies in the building of the main structures with a further 250 companies engaged in other roles. The two harbours each required hundreds of thousands of tons of concrete and ballast and thousands of tons of steel reinforcing rods. The modular parts known as 'Phoenix' caissons alone absorbed over 170,000 tons of concrete and almost 50,000 tons of steel reinforcement bars. The parts were constructed at locations around Britain's coast and made ready to be towed over when ready.

American troops brought all manner of equipment and vehicles with them, some of which were specialist for their particular role. One type of armoured vehicle which began to arrive in readiness for the invasion was the category known as Tank Destroyer. The Americans would come to make good use of these powerful vehicles when they engaged the heavier German tanks such as the Panther and Tiger in the battles across Europe. One design of tank destroyer which earned a good reputation for dependability was the M18 Hellcat. Development of this vehicle had not been without its fair share of problems. Originally it had been planned to arm the new tank destroyer

Two British soldiers, typical of the men who fought in Italy and Europe.

Landing Craft Tank as used on D-Day to land armoured vehicles, along with stores and supplies.

with a 37mm gun, but following the poor performance of this weapon which had been observed in combat on the M3 Stuart Light Tanks in North Africa, it was decided to fit a larger weapon. The development programme was designated T49 Gun Motor Carriage. The Tank Destroyer Command suggested increasing the calibre of the gun to 76mm, and so the M1A1, or one of the variants, was mounted for which forty-five rounds were carried. Six pilot vehicles were made for which trials were successfully conducted and rewarded with favourable comments. The new M1A1 76mm gun demonstrated its effectiveness by penetrating more than 100mm of armour plate. The Army Service Forces were impressed and placed an order for 1,000 vehicles. By February 1944, as the final plans were being drawn up for the D-Day invasion and the build-up of equipment continued, the new design was officially designated the M18 Tank Destroyer with the name 'Hellcat'. With a top speed of 55 mph, it was one of the fastest vehicles of its type in the war. During the Normandy Campaign, it proved to be the ideal ambush vehicle capable of being manoeuvred into position to catch enemy tanks unawares. By October 1944, the production of the M18 Hellcat was over 2,000 vehicles

Lighter vehicles such as the Jeep became a familiar sight on the roads across Britain and these were joined by the heavy, powerful military motorcycles built by Harley Davidson, the most widely used type being the Model 50 WLA, used for duties such as convoy escort, traffic control, liaison roles and despatch riders. The 50 WLA could ford water obstacles up to sixteen inches deep and panniers or saddlebags were fitted over the rear wheel for carrying various items of kit. A holster for the rider's personal weapon was fitted by the front wheel for easy reach.

It was in 1903 that two friends, William S. Harley and Arthur Davidson, both motorcycle enthusiasts, established the company which bore their names in Milwaukee in Wisconsin. Their machines soon gained a reputation so that by 1916 the US military were using them for patrol duties during the Mexican Border War. When America entered the First World War in 1917 Harley-Davidson supplied the military with 15,000 machines. Between the wars the company still supplied motorcycles to the military, but in reduced numbers. When America entered the war in 1941 it was only natural that Harley-Davidson should supply motorcycles to the army. This was the 740cc WL design which was given a suffix letter 'A' to denote Army and while the US Navy also used the motorcycles, it was the army which used the greatest numbers of the 90,000 machines supplied. Harley-Davidson also built machines for the Canadian army, known as 43 WLC, and 30,000 for the Soviet Union which were supplied under the Lend-Lease Act from 1941.

Training grounds were established at locations around Britain so that troops could practise in preparation for the invasion of Europe. Some locations were for firing practice and driver training and amphibious assaults were conducted on beaches such as Slapton Sands in Devon. The US 175th Infantry Regiment, which would later distinguish itself in the Normandy Campaign, trained there. Some locations were sufficiently remote to permit realistic training with live firing exercises, including artillery and mortar firing. One such location was Saunton Sands in North Devon, where beach assaults were conducted. What the men involved in these exercises did not know at the time was that the terrain here was almost identical to the beaches they would land on at Normandy. Other locations were found which also bore a striking similarity to those which the Allies would face in France. For example, US Rangers trained with Royal Marine Commandos on the cliffs in Swanage Bay, Dorset, where the chalky rock face resembled the feature at Pointe du Hoc which the Rangers would have to climb to attack a gun battery. The British 2nd Battalion Oxfordshire and Buckinghamshire Light Infantry, glider-borne troops of the 6th Airborne Division which would assault and capture the bridge across the Orne Canal at Bénouville, practiced on bridges across the Exeter Ship Canal at Countess Wear in Devon.

On Friday, 17 December 1943, American forces in Italy won a decisive victory over German forces at the Battle of San Pietro. Some 1,200 miles to the west, back in England, the population of Tyneham, a tiny village in Dorset, were making their contribution to the Allied war effort by vacating their houses for the military to use for training. The village of Tyneham, with a population on only 225, some of whom had relatives fighting in the armed forces, lay in an area which was already being used as a training ground by the military. Part of the area included the Lulworth firing ranges which had been used by the army since 1917. It was decided to expand these ranges but to do so, the village of Tyneham would have to be evacuated. In November 1943, the households were given twenty-eight days notice to leave the area. The amount of land gained by requisitioning the village was small, but in vacating the area the military now had 7,000 acres of uninterrupted training ground which was perfect for tanks and artillery. The people packed their belongings and left their properties, some of which had been their homes for generations.

They were not alone. Castlemartin in Wales and Imber in Wiltshire were requisitioned. In Devon, residents were leaving their homes in the villages of Blackanton, Chillington, East Allington, Sherford, Slapton, Stokenham, Strete and Torcross. At Inkpen near Reading British airborne forces practised on a specially constructed site to gain experience attacking the gun position they would assault for real during the Normandy landings. For five months, one major exercise after another was conducted, culminating in a final training exercise which was scheduled to last for eight days.

On the night of 27/28 May 1944, a convoy of several vessels set sail from Plymouth and headed towards Slapton Sands in Lyme Bay where there were training grounds. This was the opening phase of Exercise Tiger, designed to practise all aspects of amphibious landings involving vehicles and infantry. By chance a group of German Schnellboote (torpedo boats), operating from their base in Cherbourg, were engaged on a patrol in the middle of the English Channel. They heard the noise of the ships' engines and proceeded to intercept the convoy. In the dark, the German boats fired torpedoes, several of which hit vessels in the group. Two LSTs were damaged and two were sunk. A total of 749 soldiers and sailors were killed and many vehicles were lost including Sherman duple-drive (DD) 'swimming' tanks which had been specially developed for the invasion. The incident, coming barely a week before the Invasion of France, was kept secret in case it upset morale.

The incident did not affect the decision to mount Operation Overlord. The Allies had learned valuable lessons from the disastrous operation at Dieppe in 1942, and they had also learned from successful operations, such as the landings in North Africa, Sicily, Salerno and Anzio. Raids by commandos against the French coast and intelligence received from French Resistance groups helped the Allies build up a comprehensive intelligence picture of German defences and dispositions. One such raid was the operation against the radar station at Bruneval on the French coast on 27/28 February 1942. It was a resounding success and rendered up vital details regarding German developments in radar technology.

The artificial 'Mulberry' harbours had to be towed across to the landing beaches in sections where they would be assembled to allow vehicles and supplies to be taken ashore to support the troops. These massive structures had been built because previous operations, such as the landing on Sicily and Salerno, had shown how vital it was to have port facilities to unload supplies to maintain the offensive. In the case of Mulberry, there would be two such harbours, each equipped with roadways which floated up and down with the tide to permit unloading to continue regardless of the state of the tide. The 'A' Mulberry was the American harbour to support the landings on Omaha beachhead. The British or 'B' harbour would be built at Arromanches to support the landings at Gold Beach, and would also supply logistics to the other beachheads, the Canadians at Juno and the British at Sword, further east. The operation was the largest, most complex ever undertaken by the Allies during the war.

Finally, after many months of planning, in the early hours of the morning 6 June 1944, an armada of 5,000 vessels of all types took up their positions off the Normandy coast and prepared to land 160,000 troops at five separate beachheads. It was planned that the landings would be made at different times due to the state of the tide along the coast. Some were designated as LSIs (landing ships infantry) and others with bows that opened to permit vehicles to be driven out were called LSTs (landing ships tank) which the Royal Navy nicknamed 'large slow targets'.

During the night of 5/6 June 24,500 British and American airborne troops had been landed by parachute or glider to capture or destroy strategic targets such as bridges. These airborne troops became scattered over a wide area and lost a great deal of their equipment. The American airborne units lost 30% of their men and 70% of their equipment during the drops.

The first of the amphibious landings over the beaches were made following a massive naval bombardment and air support from 8,000 aircraft. The troops had been given specific targets they were designated to capture by nightfall, including the city of Caen, but this was not achieved and only a few objectives were taken on the first day.

At the end of the first day of Operation Overlord the Allies managed to land some 150,000 troops. Of the five separate beachheads, only the western flank of the Canadian beach, Juno, would succeed in linking up with the eastern flank of the British beach, codenamed Gold. The other three beaches, the British at Sword, and the American landings, codenamed Omaha and Utah, would not link up properly for some days to come. At Sword, 29,000 troops landed and incurred 630 casualties killed and wounded. At Gold and Juno, 25,000 and 21,500 troops were landed and sustained 413 and 925 casualties. At Utah, the beach furthest west, the Americans landed 23,250 and suffered only 210 killed and wounded, the lightest casualty level of the beaches. At Omaha, 34,250 men landed in successive assault waves but stronger German resistance resulted in 3,880 killed and wounded, more than the other four beaches combined. To the west of the landing beaches the two American Airborne Divisions, the 82nd and 101st, dropped 13,500 men between them and suffered almost 2,500 casualties. To the east, the British 6th Airborne Division dropped around 6,000 men by parachute and glider landings, sustaining some 1,200 killed and wounded. Casualty rates, though high, were much lower than expected. The landings were the first phase of the operation; the second phase would be hold the ground gained. The third phase would be the break out.

At Omaha Beach, the landing craft bringing the troops ashore had been launched twelve miles out to sea and the thirty-two DD Sherman tanks designated to support the landings were launched over three miles from the beach, a distance they were never designed to cover. They became caught in a cross-current and twenty-seven sank. The Americans had refused the support of specialist vehicles from the 79th Armoured Division, which could have assisted in getting the troops off the beach and breached obstacles such as barbed wire and minefields. At the end of the first day's fighting, the Omaha beachhead was secure, but in a very weak condition with troops having penetrated only two miles inland. It had been planned to have 2,400 tons of supplies for the troops, but due to the fierce fighting leading to delays, this was reduced to only 100 tons.

At Utah Beach, things went much better. The first assault wave of troops had drifted over one mile to the east of their designated landing point, which caused some confusion over identifying where they were. Once the problem was sorted, all other assault troops landed in the same vicinity. It would turn out to be a lucky mistake, resulting in the lightest casualty rate of all the beaches. But problems were also encountered here and the landings began to fall behind schedule. Two days after the landings, 32,000 men of a planned 39,722 had been landed and only 3,200 vehicles out of a planned 4,732 were ashore. It was the reduced level of supplies which was giving the greatest cause for concern, with only 2,500 tons landed out of a planned 7,000 tons. This shortfall was noticed and steps were taken to remedy it. Later in the campaign, Utah Beach would become more important than the planners could have predicted. It was here that French General Leclerc landed with his 2nd Armoured Division and the US 3rd Army, commanded by General Patton, landed here also. Eventually, the numbers of troops and vehicles and supplies coming ashore here would be staggering.

The landings had been made with an incoming tide which the Allies had used to their advantage to help them avoid some of the obstacles. On Juno beachhead, the Canadians waited until 7.35am, ten minutes later than the British landings at neighbouring Sword Beach, in order that the tide could help them over a rocky reef just off shore. They began to move off the beach relatively quickly and capture their objectives such as the village of Bernières-sur-Mer. Along the landing area so many vehicles were coming ashore that it became congested and the movement area reduced by a quarter which threatened to bring operations to a halt. Gradually, the impending mess was sorted out by the beach masters and traffic controllers who got things moving off the beach. The landings here were supported by DD tanks and other specialist vehicles of the 79th Armoured Division. At some points the DD tanks were landed 'dry', which is to say, they were not launched at sea but brought directly to the beaches and driven ashore.

The problem of supplying fresh water was partly solved by using tankers such as this to transport it in bulk.

Juno Beachhead managed to link up with the flank of Gold Beach to the west and extend the frontage. There was no such luck with Sword Beach to the east which left a gap between the eastern flank of Juno and the western flank of the British Sword beachhead. The Germans noticed this and the 21st Panzer Division mounted an attack to exploit the situation. However, the anti-tank gunners opened fire to drive back the tanks and the infantry troops opened fire on the German infantry. Each man carried, in addition to his ammunition and spare clothing, sufficient food to sustain him for a period of twenty-four hours. This included biscuits, tinned food, tea, chocolate and other items which could be eaten quickly without much preparation. They also carried small heaters with blocks of solid fuel to boil water to make hot drinks. Each man carried a water bottle but it was not sufficient as thirst set in.

Indeed, supplies of fresh drinking water became an increasing problem for the Allies as more troops were landed. The problem was partly resolved in the small village of Hermanville-sur-Mer, in the Sword Beach sector, where the Royal Engineers installed pipework for thirty taps along the presbytery wall outside the aptly-named Puits de la Mare Saint-Pierre (wells of St Peter). Between 6 June, when the taps were first in use, until 1 July, 1,540,000 gallons of water would be dispensed for troops and for the twelve field hospitals established around the village where the wounded were being treated. In the days following the landing more stores were landed and the RE and RASC established a fuel and ammunition dump just south of the village of Hermanville-la-Brèche, which lay on the coast. By 13 June this stockpile included 400 tons of ammunition and 100,000 gallons of fuel and vehicles were arriving to collect stores and supplies for distribution. On that day, the Luftwaffe mounted one of its infrequent air raids and caught the British by surprise. The pilots in the low-level attack dropped several bombs hitting the supplies which detonated in a massive explosion. In overall terms, the loss was relatively minor compared to the levels of supplies being landed daily and was soon replaced.

Among the armada of warships and landing craft were hundreds of other vessels which had been pressed into service and converted for use. Cross-Channel train-carrying ferries which had rails mounted on their decks were used to transport locomotives and wagons which would carry supplies. Engineers repaired damaged railway track. Around 400 barges from riverways such as the Thames were converted to become Landing Barges. These were employed in a variety of roles, including Landing Barge Oil and Landing Barge Water: LBO and LBW. There were some equipped with anti-aircraft guns, some with repair workshops. Several were configured to the role of Landing Barge Kitchen. One of these was known among the troops as 'Micky's Fish and Chip Bar' and served up 1,000 hot meals on D-Day itself. The hot meals provided by the LBKs were not for the men on shore but to feed the crews working on the landing craft bringing the supplies ashore; in effect, to feed the men who were feeding the men. Each LBK had a crew of 25, of which 13 were cooks, and each could provide up to 700 hot meals a day.

The crews of some vehicles carried their own supply of fresh water in cans strapped to the outside.

The troops on Sword, Juno, Gold and Omaha beaches advanced inland, fanning out and moving south. On Utah, things were more complicated. Here, as they moved inland, the 90th Division under the command of General Eugene Landrum was ordered to turn west and advance to cut across the base of the Cherbourg Peninsular. The manoeuvre would isolate the Germans in that area but in turn it also meant that an enemy force would be left in the rear of the advancing Americans as they moved south. This threat was something that had to be eliminated. Unfortunately Landrum was not inspiring his men who were being mauled by German units. He had served in administration posts in the First World War and although he had proven himself an effective organiser he had never held a real field command. Landrum was replaced by General Manton Sprague Eddy. He was given the task to isolate the Cherbourg Peninsula and by 15 June he had advanced to capture Pont l'Abbé, St Saveur-le-Vicomte and Barnville to reach the west coast, thereby effectively cutting off the German 77th, 243rd and 709th Divisions in the north. Eddy had seen extensive service in North Africa and had taken part in the fighting at Kasserine Pass in 1943.

General Lawton Collins with VII Corps provided cover to the south with airborne troops and the 91st Division advanced towards Cherbourg. To undertake the manoeuvre the 9th Division had had to complete a full 180 degrees turnaround with the 4th Division commanded by General Barton on the right and the 79th Division under General Wyche on the left. It was a masterful manoeuvre and one which had never been attempted in the middle of a battle on such a scale. General Bradley later wrote, 'Within 22 hours he [Eddy] was expected to turn a force of 20,000 troops a full 90 degrees towards Cherbourg, evacuate sick and wounded, lay wire, recce the ground, establish his boundaries, issue orders, relocate his ammunition and supply dumps, and then jump off in a fresh attack on a front nine miles wide.' Eddy was up to the task and when the order to advance was given everything was in place. The port at Cherbourg was captured on 15 July by the US VII Corps commanded by Collins, but such was the destruction to its facilities that it was not open to handle deliveries until 29 September.

After D-Day came elements of the SAS, which would eventually have a strength of 2,000 men, to operate behind enemy lines using heavily-armed Jeeps. In six months between June and November 1944, they sustained 300 casualties but inflicted far greater losses on the Germans out of all proportion to the strength of the unit. The SAS operations were supported by air drops flown by 38 Group of the RAF which flew 780 delivery missions. Of these, 600 were successful and 180 had to be aborted for various reasons. These missions delivered 10,370 canisters and replacement vehicles and at least two 6-pounder anti-tank guns. The brigade killed and captured over 12,500 Germans and destroyed 740 vehicles of all types along with several trains. They also destroyed railway tracks at 164 points which hampered the German army's ability to resupply units. Destruction of locomotives and wagons not only hampered the resupply lines it meant that reinforcements could not be moved in and the wounded could not be evacuated. In the first half of September 1944, one SAS group managed to kill 500 Germans, destroy 95 vehicles, a train and around 100,000 gallons of fuel. The SAS would radio back the location of supply dumps for the RAF to bomb. An offshoot of the SAS was the Raiding Support Regiment (RSR) which also made use of the versatility of the Jeep. During operations in Greece this unit attacked German supply lines by destroying 17 bridges, 5 trains and blowing up 18 railway lines as well as destroying stocks of logistics essential to supporting the German war effort.

On 7 June, the first parts of the massive Mulberry harbours were brought into place and the construction of the whole operation was undertaken by a workforce involving thousands of engineers. Each section had been towed over from locations around the English coast – Portland, the Thames Estuary, Selsey and Dungeness. Over the following days sections were towed into position and sunk in place to be joined up to form the structure of the Mulberry harbour. It was planned to use them to bring 7,000 tons of supplies ashore per day each by D+4 or 10 June. By D+8 they were unloading 12,000 tons of supplies a day, and the British Mulberry at Arromanches allowed 16,000 troops to be brought ashore. At the American Mulberry harbour 20,000 troops were being landed and by D+11, or 17 June, 22,000 tons of supplies were being brought ashore being driven directly from ships on trucks and DUKWs which could drive inland to supply depots.

The next day, 18 June, just as the last parts of the Mulberry harbours were being put in place, a powerful storm, the worst in forty years, blew up along the Normandy coast. On 19 June it was battering the harbours and damaging or destroying around 100 landing craft at the American Mulberry which was declared irreparable but it was still used. The storm continued for almost a week, during which time about 850 other vessels were destroyed or damaged along the landing area, but troops and supplies were still landed at slightly reduced levels. After the storm, repairs were completed and the British Mulberry was put back into service.

The Mulberry harbours were only intended to be used for 100 days or until a deep-water port was captured, but this would not be achieved until the port of Antwerp in Belgium was captured several months later, meaning that all supplies to support the Allied advance had to be brought over the Utah beachhead and through the British Mulberry harbour at Arromanches. Between 6 June and 31 October, the British managed to land 236,358 vehicles of all types, using the Mulberry harbours and other port facilities, along with 964,703 troops.

On D-Day itself the British task force transported 63,000 gallons of fuel as a reserve stock. One week later stocks of fuel had increased to one million gallons. Planners were estimating that around 1,000 tons of fuel per day (298 gallons in a ton) would be required to keep the vehicles moving and a further 700 tons for aircraft operating from airfields in France. The Allies were delivering fuel in tankers which pumped supplies ashore at smaller port facilities such as Port-en-Bessin and Sainte-Honorine-des-Pertes, in an operation codenamed Tombola. The ships were able to pump 600 tons an hour. In the planning for D-Day a system was devised whereby an underwater pipeline would be laid through which fuel would be pumped from England to depots in France. Being underwater it was safe from being damaged by enemy action. It was given the secret codename of Pipeline Under the Ocean or PLUTO. The first pipes covered seventy miles from Shanklin on the Isle of Wight to Cherbourg and this was joined by other pipes as the Allies moved eastwards. Eventually there would be four pipes laid between Shanklin and Cherbourg. To the east another series of fuel pipes, codenamed DUMBO were laid across Romney Marsh to Dungeness in Kent from where they snaked across the seabed to Ambleteuse in France.

Much had been promised of the system and much was expected of it, but at first it was something of a disappointment. Between June and October 1944 it was delivering

Fuel was essential and had to be delivered round the clock.

Containers for fuel were loaded for delivery right to the fighting units at the front.

Compressor vehicles like this supplied air to power tools and pumps for fuel.

Recreated scene showing how part of the supply depot may have looked.

a mere 5,500 gallons per day, a pathetic 0.16% of the Allied fuel consumption for the period. Delivery levels increased and by January 1945 around 300 tons (90,000 gallons) was being pumped through PLUTO and DUMBO each day. When levels increased to 3,000 tons per day by March 1945 the Allies were using far more than that. By the time the system was achieving levels of 4,000 tons (1.2 million gallons) per day the war in Europe was virtually finished. By the time the war ended in May 1945, PLUTO had delivered a total of 172 million gallons of fuel. The capture of the port at Cherbourg should have helped the situation of landing supplies, but the Germans had destroyed the facilities. Looking ahead long-term, Eisenhower realised the importance of the port of Antwerp early in the Normandy campaign and had written to General George Marshall to highlight the problem of supply: 'Until we get Antwerp we are always going to be operating on a shoestring.' Things were not quite that bad, but there certainly were shortages.

As the Allies moved eastwards they captured further ports along the French coast, each of which in its own way helped relieve some of the burden on the Mulberry harbours. The Germans had deployed 100,000 troops to defend the Channel ports, but still they were captured one by one. Dieppe port was captured on 1 September. Within a week it was operational and receiving thousands of tons of stores daily. In his memoirs, *Operation Victory*, Major General Sir Francis de Guingand, who served

Fuel was essential for the Allies and it was stockpiled in any available space.

as Chief of Staff to 21st Army Group between 1944 and 1945, states that Dieppe was handling more than 6,000 tons of supplies daily by the end of September; records agree. The next port to be captured was Le Havre on 12 September, which became operational on 9 October, allowing an additional 3,650 tons per day to be handled. The ports at Boulogne and Calais were captured on 22 and 30 September, becoming operational in October and November. Boulogne could handle 11,000 tons of supplies each day. Things were improving, but yet more was needed. Indeed the combined ports never handled the amount needed to meet demand. Calais was closest to Dover for resupplies, but it was used mainly to handle arriving troops and to evacuate the wounded. The port at Dunkirk, which had been vital to the British and French in June 1940, was defended by 10,000 Germans with ample stocks of ammunition, food and other supplies. The Allies advanced to encircle the town and its port facilities and on 15 September had isolated the garrison. For eight months, the Allies had the area under siege. The garrison did not surrender until the last day of the war, 8 May 1945.

In the days after the landings in Normandy, the Germans continued to mount stiff resistance against the Allies. But it was never sufficient to prevent them landing troops, vehicles and supplies. During the first forty-eight hours of the battle the Allies landed 1,500 tanks across the beaches, the same number the Germans would lose during the entire Normandy campaign.

Hitler now faced having to fight a war on three fronts; Italy, Russia and now France. The German army was being squeezed by armies which between them had more than 20,000 tanks and thousands more AFVs and SPGs. Supporting them, each of these armies had vast fleets of trucks to haul supplies and artillery. The Allies had unrestricted access to oil for fuel while Germany was running out and having to resort to other means of obtaining fuel for the tanks and trucks. Germany had vast reserves of coal to fuel the factories and scientists developed a method of extracting synthetic oil from the coal to keep the vehicles moving. In 1938 Germany had been producing around 3.8 million barrels of synthetic oil annually but by 1944 this had been increased to 12 million. From January 1944, processing plants were refining 159,000 tons of synthetic oil each month which was distributed for a range of uses but mainly for the military. The fuel crisis deepened as the war continued to go against Germany and by November 1944 it was reported that the army 'had become virtually immobile because of the fuel shortage.' In December 1944, synthetic fuel production dropped to 26,000 tons per month as Allied bombing disrupted production and distribution.

It was all very well the factories still producing vehicles and tanks and ammunition and guns but without fuel to power them and no crews to drive them they were completely useless. Between the shortage of fuel and the effects of the bombing campaign the required levels of supplies could not get through to the front-line units. For Hitler, the war had entered a stage of attrition and it was only a question of time before the armed forces ran out of everything from troops to trucks and could no longer fight. It would take time for such a situation to develop and time was something the Allies had. Even so, it would be in their interest to finish the war sooner rather than later. In preparation for the invasion of France the Allies began a programme of bombing bridges, railway depots and roads, the damage and destruction of which would disrupt lines of supply. At the beginning of 1944 it was believed there were some 2,000 locomotives in operation in France of which it is thought around 1,500 were destroyed in the air attacks and the rail capacity was reduced to only some forty per cent of its former capability. To make good these losses the Allies brought replacement locomotives with them. The US Army, who was used to using its national railways for moving tanks and artillery over long distances from its factories to its ports, would bring 7,570 locomotives into service in Europe for its own use.

At the time of the Allies landing in France, Rommel was absent in Germany where he had met Hitler to ask him to release more armour for the defence of Normandy because he believed that was where the invasion would land. On being informed of the attack, Rommel immediately hurried back to take charge of the situation. Even when told of the strength of the attack, Hitler remained adamant that the divisions in the Pas de Calais region would remain where they were. He was convinced the landings at Normandy were a diversionary attack and the main assault would come at the Pas de Calais. His decision would prove crucial to the German army and advantageous to the Allies. It had been Montgomery's intention to draw as much German armour as possible onto his Anglo-Canadian beachheads to give the Americans some respite. His tactics worked and the Americans only had to face a fraction of the German armoured units; but they would encounter strong resistance as they moved inland into the Bocage.

The Bocage comprised farmers' fields fringed by tall, dense hedgerows which made ideal camouflage for tanks and for anti-tank guns. To get the better of these obstacles Sergeant Curtis Culin serving with the 102nd Cavalry Reconnaissance devised an attachment which could be fitted to the front of tanks to rip through the hedgerows. He suggested that metal girders which had been used as obstacles by the Germans be cut up and welded to form 'teeth-like' frames which could be mounted on the front of tanks. The conversion could be made in the field using equipment and material to hand so there was no delay. The idea was an instant success and the device was referred to as the 'Culin Cutter'. It was mounted on the M4 Sherman or the M5 Honey.

The M5 Honey design was taken directly from the earlier M3 Honey and was so apparent in the style that the only real difference was the M5 was built using welded construction while the earlier M3 was built using rivets. Production of the M5 Stuart Light Tank commenced in March 1942 on the Cadillac assembly line in Detroit. There were several variants produced which were not very different from each other. The main armament was a 37mm gun for which 123 rounds were carried including high explosive, armour-piercing and canister which could be used against infantry and soft-skinned vehicles. Its top speed was 40mph, its weight less than 15 tons, and vertical obstacles up to two feet in height were not a problem for it. One .30-inch machine gun was mounted co-axially in the turret, a second was fitted in a ball mounting in the bow and a third dismountable machine gun could be fitted to the roof of the turret. The M5 was used in combat for the first time during Operation Torch and they were deployed to the Pacific where they proved ideal for combat on the smaller islands.

The Culin Cutter was fitted to the front of tanks to plough through hedgerows in France. It was a very successful 'in-field' modification.

During amphibious landings, such as the Normandy landings, some were fitted with extensions to their exhaust for deep water wading. Three other variants were also built including the Command Vehicle which lacked a turret and was armed with only a .50-inch machine gun. The M5 'Dozer' had a blade for moving earth fitted to the front and also lacked a turret. The M8 Howitzer Motor Carriage was armed with a 75mm howitzer, for which forty-six rounds were carried, which was used to provide fire support. In all, some 1,800 of these were built and used in action in Europe with the remainder serving in Italy and the Pacific.

The Normandy campaign took a huge toll on the manpower of the German army. At one point in the battle Rommel received only 6,000 men to replace more than 29,000 men lost. Equipment and vehicles were also being lost at an alarming rate and could not be easily replaced. With aerial domination, the Allies ruled the skies and anything seen moving northwards along the roads was immediately attacked. Truck convoys bringing up supplies, armoured vehicles and even horse-drawn wagons were bombed and shot up. The bombing had destroyed roads and bridges rendering the movement of troops even more difficult. With supplies running low and fewer supplies getting through than needed, the Germans conducted a fighting withdrawal. But there were startling moments when they could and did regroup to attack.

Rommel's men were fighting hard actions often in the face of overwhelming odds. Tank commanders proved audacious opponents, sometimes mounting swift, hard-hitting attacks which took the Allies by surprise. One such took place on 13 June on the outskirts of the village of Villers-Bocage. Leading the attack was SS-Obersturmführer Michael Wittmann serving with the Schwere SS Panzerabteilung 101 (heavy tank battalion). He was a veteran of the Russian Front where his personal score was eighty-eight enemy tanks destroyed and numerous other vehicles. On that fateful day in Normandy, Wittmann was in his Tiger when he came across a column of vehicles of 22nd Armoured Brigade of the 7th Armoured Division parked up and not fully alert.

The British vehicle crews were taking advantage of the lull in the fighting to prepare a hot drink and have something to eat, when Wittmann, in company with other tanks, opened fire. The attack lasted less than fifteen minutes. When they withdrew, they left behind a trail of destruction which included Cromwell tanks destroyed, a Sherman

The mighty Tiger tank, armed with an 88mm main gun, was feared by the Allies. This example, in the collection at the Tank Museum at Bovington, is the only operational vehicle of its type in the world.

Firefly, three M5 Honeys, two observation tanks, and several other vehicles including half-tracks. His attack was only ended when his tank was knocked out by a 6-pounder anti-tank gun; Wittmann escaped on foot. In all he had destroyed 25 Allied tanks and 28 other armoured vehicles.

Stalin, who had been pressing the Western allies to launch a 'Second Front' by attacking Europe, welcomed the news of the Normandy landings with caution and only agreed to telling the Russian people over a week after the landings had taken place just in case they failed.

Towards the end of June, the Allies had achieved two phases of the invasion by breaking in and holding on to the gains they had made. Now they had to break out and Montgomery had plans to do just that. Patton, who did not arrive in France until 6 July, would be part of the breakout. On 26 June Montgomery ordered the start of Operation Epsom which was to penetrate to the west of the city of Caen. Four days later after encountering fierce opposition the attack was called off with 4,000 casualties, but they had inflicted at least 3,000 casualties on the Germans and destroyed 126 tanks. Montgomery made his next attempt to break out on 18 July by ordering Operation Goodwood to attack east of Caen, for which he had more than 1,100 tanks available. Again the Germans mounted fierce resistance and destroyed or seriously damaged 400 tanks and inflicted 4,000 casualties. The Germans sustained high losses in the fighting which included more than 2,500 taken prisoner and 100 tanks destroyed by the time attack was suspended on 20 June. Over to the west the Americans were planning their own operation, Cobra, which began on 25 July with the support of 2,451 tanks and tank destroyers. Facing them the Germans had deployed 190 tanks and assault guns including the Surmgeschutz III, known as the StuG III, which, being a specialised vehicle, was given the Sonderkraftfahrzeug title of SdKfz142.

The StuG III was developed between 1935 and 1936 following the specifications as laid down by the German Army Weapons Department. Daimler-Benz was responsible for providing the chassis which was based on the design used on the Panzer III tank. The engine was a Maybach HL 120 TRM V-12 water-cooled petrol engine, of the same type as fitted to the Models E to N of the Panzer III. Some versions were armed with the long-barrelled StuK40/L48 of 7.5cm calibre, others with the short-barrelled StuK 37 L/24 of 7.5cm calibre, for which 44 rounds were carried. As an assault gun the new vehicle was a departure from conventional tank design lacking, as it did, a turret and upper superstructure. The StuG III had a reduced silhouette because the gun was mounted so low down in the hull. The overall height was kept down to nine feet and six inches, making it one of the lowest vehicles in the war. Production did not begin in earnest until July 1940. Deliveries were slow at first but once production was up and running factories built over 9,400 between 1940 and 1944. Units equipped with the StuG III recorded 20,000 enemy tanks destroyed using this one type of vehicle alone.

By the time Operation Cobra was concluded on 31 July the Germans had lost 100 tanks in the fighting along with more than 250 other types of AFV. The Allies were becoming more secure each day and, although progress was slow, they were getting stronger with more fresh troops and reinforcements which allowed them to push the enemy back. They were fortunate to capture intact three bridges at Avranches which the Germans had failed to destroy, thereby giving them a route across the River Sée. Allied aircraft added to the destruction of German armoured units as they moved on roads during daylight, such as the Panzer Lehr which was rendered 70 per cent ineffective and virtually finished as a fighting force. Between 6 and 8 August the Germans mounted a bold counter-attack codenamed Operation Luttich, aimed at Mortain, but after initial gains the attack faltered. On the day Luttich was halted the Germans suffered a blow to morale when their tank ace Michael Wittmann was killed. During Operation Totalise his battalion was engaged by a squadron of Sherman Fireflys from the 1st Northamptonshire Yeomanry of 33rd Armoured Brigade. In an area around the woods near Delle de la Roque, a Firefly opened fire with its 17-pounder and destroyed Wittmann's tank and at least two other Tigers.

German resistance was slowly crumbling and by this stage they were receiving almost no reinforcements, but they were still fighting. Fighting had moved inland and to the east where the Allies were engaging other powerful German tanks including the Panzer V.

British tanks move inland after the landing at Normandy.

The Stuart Mk.5 M3A3 tank served across Europe in 1944-45.

The Stuart was a useful, light design which could operate in the reconnaissance role.

Used by all Allied armies, including the French, the Stuart was a versatile vehicle.

Known as the Panther with the designation SdKfz 171, armed with the 75mm gun and weighing 44.8 tons, the Panther had become feared by Russian tank crews and now, here in Normandy, it was giving the Allies an equally difficult time. It had been developed specifically to combat the Russian T-34 and between 1942 and 1945 5,508 were built, which was more than four times the number of Tigers produced. The first models had not proved reliable, being overweight and underpowered, and of the 200 deployed at Kursk 160 were out of action due to mechanical failure. Even when repaired and sent back into action they were not improved and at the end of the battle only forty-three were still effective. In Normandy, it was the Panther's powerful gun and the thickness of its armour, up to 100mm, which gave them a true edge over the Allies. But even so, it was the Tiger which was most feared by tank crews, along with the powerful 88mm anti-tank gun.

In one engagement near the town of St Lambert, on 14 August, a solitary Panther engaged a group of fourteen Sherman tanks from the Canadian South Alberta Regiment as they approached the town. The leading tank was destroyed and the Canadians, commanded by Major David Currie, decided to withdraw and adopt a different tactic. The following morning, the aptly-named Lieutenant G.G. Armour led a section of his men to attack the tank. They took it by surprise and finding the hatch open Lieutenant Armour dropped a grenade inside, killing the crew and disabling the tank.

On the same day, over 700 miles away to the south, the Allies were making their amphibious landings in the South of France in Operation Dragoon. The invasion fleet comprised almost 1,000 vessels, supplied by five navies, from France, Australia, Greece, America and Britain, including 466 landing craft. This was a mainly Franco-American army that would eventually build up to a force of 200,000 men, landed at points along the coast such as St Tropez and St Raphael. The Germans had to defend 400 miles of coastline from Menton to Cerbère, and the 19th Army had been stripped of units to send north towards Normandy, so resistance to the landings was relatively light. The Luftwaffe had just 60 aircraft to engage the Allied air force of 2,100, which including heavy bombers and 216 aircraft operating from carriers in the Mediterranean. In support of the landings, these aircraft flew 4,250 sorties to bomb positions and supply lines. The Allied armada, known as the Western Task Force, fired a bombardment of 50,000 shells to pound the German defences.

In preparing for the operation, the Allies had had to take men, tanks and artillery out of the campaign in Italy. They had also had to take supplies out and allocate them to the logistic lines for Operation Dragoon. It had proved a calculated risk and by the end of the first day's fighting the Allies had landed 60,000 troops, 6,000 vehicles, 50,000 tons of supplies and captured around 1,000 Germans all for the low cost of 320 men killed. With this second invasion of France the Germans were fighting a war on two fronts in the same country. These two invasions in western Europe meant Hitler's forces were now engaged on *four* fronts and the logistical support required could never hope to keep all of them adequately supplied. As in the north, the Allies' advance was successful in pushing the Germans inland. As in the north, the Germans demonstrated their ability to consolidate and the fighting intensified. Ten days after the Dragoon landings, Hitler, in a rare move, ordered General Blaskowitz to fall back to positions from where he could counter-attack. Blaskowitz retreated as ordered, but he never mounted an attack.

Three weeks after the Dragoon landings, the French and Americans were deep into France and had secured intact the port facilities at Toulon and Marseilles. The capture of these installations meant the Allies could unload 17,000 tons of supplies each day.

The Germans retreated northwards up the Rhône valley and managed to avoid being trapped by the US Seventh Army, commanded by Lieutenant Alexander Patch, due to the actions of the 11th Panzer Division which kept the route northwards open to allow the army to escape. By 16 September, the Franco-American forces had pushed eastwards to the border of Italy. The French First Army, under the capable leadership of General de Lattre de Tassigny, and the American Seventh Army moved around the western border of neutral Switzerland and headed north, all the while forcing the Germans back.

In the area between Belfort, Épinal and Vittel, the American Seventh Army and French First Army linked up with the American Third Army. France was now cut in two. The fighting had cost the Allies 13,000 killed and wounded but 79,000 Germans had been killed, wounded or taken prisoner. The Allies had destroyed or captured vast amounts of heavy equipment and supplies. The Germans were retreating eastwards but to the west, behind Allied lines, there were still strong pockets of potential resistance. One by one these too fell, such as St Malo which surrendered on 17 August. This was followed by Brest a month later.

This still left 30,000 men of the 319 Division in the Channel Islands under the command of Lieutenant General von Schmettow. These were true fortresses in every sense of the word, but now, being isolated, the garrison could not be resupplied. The civilian population was over 70,000 and the problem of feeding everybody would become the main priority. Unsupported and with no prospect of relief the commander held fast, sitting behind the concrete bunkers and weapons which ringed them in. Churchill declared, 'let them rot'. But in condemning them to their fate, he was also condemning the civilian population, who were British subjects. The Allies continued with their liberation of Europe, but the Channel Islands were not entirely forgotten.

In England thousands of beds had been prepared at dozens of hospitals in readiness to receive the wounded coming back from France. Medical staff in France would have already treated the wounded in casualty clearing stations but they had to be evacuated from the battle area. They were put into ambulances such as the American WC 54 or the British-built Austin K2Y, nicknamed 'Katy' by the troops and Royal Army Medical Corps staff who drove them.

More than 13,000 of these useful ambulances were built between 1939 and 1945 and served in all theatres. They were capable of 50 mph and were designed to carry four stretcher cases or ten seated or 'walking' wounded under normal conditions, but one exceptional account reports a Katy carrying twenty-seven wounded during the North African campaign.

In September 1938, as part of the preparations for war, the British army formed a female unit called the Auxiliary Territorial Service (ATS). It was not an entirely new idea because the Women's Auxiliary Army Corps had been created in 1917 with women serving as clerks, cooks and telephonists (disbanded in 1921). Now there was a pressing need for service personnel to fill these roles once again and even branch out into other duties. By 1940, there were 65,000 women serving in the ATS and by the end of the war this figure was almost 200,000. The women served in mixed batteries of anti-aircraft defence units, thousands trained as drivers and some were used as despatch riders. Among these women in the ATS were Winston Churchill's daughter, Mary, and Princess Elizabeth, the eldest daughter of King George VI and future queen of Great Britain. These, and many other women, qualified as drivers on the K2Y ambulance.

In America, a volunteer medical unit known as the 'Rochambelles' was raised by Florence Conrad. The women were formed into a medical company of the 13th Medical

It was essential to build airfields from where fighters could operate and transport aircraft could land to fly in supplies and evacuate the wounded. Engineers are seen here building an airstrip in France.

American engineers serviced vehicles and other equipment round the clock.

Battalion attached to the 2nd Armoured Division and served across Europe from 1944 to 1945. In 1943, they had served in North Africa and drove Dodge WC54 ambulances.

By 29 August 1944 the Allies had landed a total of one million troops ashore along with 332,654 vehicles of all types from motorcycles to tanks, and 1.5 million tons of supplies. By late 1944 the Allies had increased this to 2.5 million men in the European theatre along with 500,000 vehicles and four million tons of supplies. The Australian war correspondent Reginald 'Chester' Wilmot, who later became a military historian, wrote of the build-up: 'In the first seven weeks, one and a half million men were transported across the Channel with all their arms, equipment and supplies, an unparalleled achievement. While the Germans were reinforcing Normandy with 20 divisions, the Allies landed 36 plus a vast number of supporting troops, air squadrons and service units.'

Once established and secure, more engineer units were landed along with their heavy earthmoving equipment. These units built airfields for aircraft to fly in supplies and evacuate the wounded. In the American sector 50 airfields were constructed and the British built a further 31 to handle cargo planes and fighters. Bombers, with their long range, could operate from airfields in Britain.

The strength of a British division at the time was around 18,000 men, of which only one third represented riflemen engaging the enemy directly. If one includes the

British troops advance across France in the breakout from Normandy.

Some of the French villages and towns were very badly damaged in the fighting and bulldozers were used to clear the mess.

The Royal Artillery firing a 5.5-inch field gun in the Odon Valley in France during the advance. The stock of shells shows how well prepared they were for the operation.

firepower provided by armoured units and artillery attached to the division this level increases 65.3% of the divisional strength used to fight the enemy. The remaining 29.7% comprised support units including signals and medical staff.

As they began heading inland, the Allied armies required 800,000 gallons of petrol each day. With 28 divisions deployed to the front, each requiring 750 tons of stores every day, including food and ammunition, the figure was 21,000 tons in total. It became apparent to the military planners that the amount of collateral damage caused to the road and railway infrastructure by strategic bombing were causing a problem in keeping the armies supplied. Bombing the French railway system had been necessary to hamper the Germans moving reinforcements and supplies forward but now, as the Allies were chasing the retreating Germans, they were facing the same problem which had been caused by their own air forces. They were now a victim of a problem that was their own making. The Dutch-born military historian Martin van Creveld in his 1977 book *Supplying War* wrote, 'No less than 1600 lorries were needed to equal the capacity of just one double-tracked railway line.' The French roads had anyway never been built to withstand this weight of traffic, plus they had been severely damaged in the fighting. Another problem was mines. The engineer units had to work round the clock to repair the roads and put them back into serviceable condition.

The speed of the German army's retreat across France drew on the Allied commanders and foremost of these was Patton. Urging his men to advance fast meant that his supplies could not be moved forward quick enough to keep pace. Normal methods were not proving up to the task and something had to be done. Patton believed that 'The officer who doesn't know his communications and supply as well as his tactics is totally useless.'

The solution was devised by Major General Frank A. Ross, the US Army's transportation chief, who on 25 August emerged from an emergency meeting lasting thirty-six hours, during which the problem had been discussed. His idea was to create a specialist transport unit using 6,000 vehicles in 132 truck companies capable of carrying 12,000 tons of supplies each day. It was to be called the 'Red Ball Express' and its name would become a byword for resupply. Given Patton's tactics and speed of advance it was as though the Red Ball Express was created specifically for his form of warfare.

In his book *For Want of a Nail: The Influence of Logistics on War*, Hawthorne Daniel wrote, 'The highways in France are usually good, but are ordinarily not excessively wide. The needs of the rapidly advancing armies, consequently, promptly put the greatest possible demands upon them. To ease this strain, main highways leading to the front were set aside very early in the advance as "one way" roads from which all civil and local military traffic were barred. Tens of thousands of truckloads of supplies were pushed forward over these one-way roads in a constant stream of traffic. Reaching the supply dumps in the forward areas, the trucks unloaded and returned empty to Arromanches,

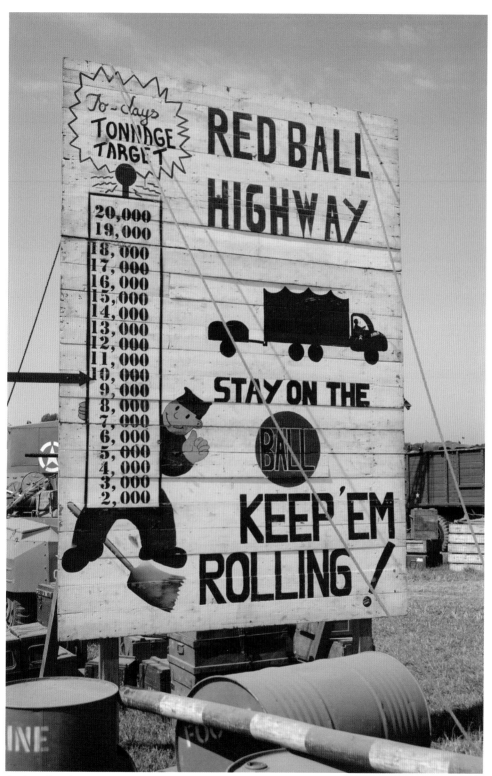

A signboard typical of the day's achievements of the Red Ball Express.

Cherbourg and the lesser landing places by way of other one way highways. Even the French railroads were, to some degree, operated similarly, with loaded trains moving forward almost nose to tail.' This was written in 1948, only four years after the extraordinary achievements of the Red Ball. At the stage in the war when the Red Ball Express was in operation, the subject of logistical supply was better understood than it had been four years previously in 1940. Even so, it was still a learning process for those involved and never more than in this innovative solution to a problem in the field.

The man put in charge was Colonel Loren Albert Ayers, nicknamed 'Little Patton'. He organised the drivers, of which three-quarters were African-Americans, into pairs to each truck. The vehicles would be driven at 25mph with a minimum gap of sixty yards between vehicles to avoid strafing by German aircraft. Each driver would take a break of ten minutes an hour to prevent falling asleep at the wheel. At least that was the theory, but drivers, knowing the importance of their task, often went without rest and some would go on to clock up 20,000 miles during the operation. The vehicles were organised into small convoy groups of five trucks escorted by a jeep at the front and another at the rear. No overtaking would be allowed. Each vehicle carried a red disc or 'Red Ball' to denote its duty and the drivers followed routes marked with similar red discs. Another theory in the operation was that the trucks were officially regulated to a top speed of 25mph. This was ignored and mechanics modified the vehicles to allow speeds of almost 60mph. The slogan of the unit was 'Push 'em up there!' Each

These restored trucks show how vehicles used on the Red Ball Express were packed to full capacity.

American-built GMC trucks such as these restored examples were standard vehicles used by the Red Ball Express.

day hundreds of vehicles engaged in the operation were being serviced and repaired at depots along the route. Trucks were driven day and night, drivers were exhausted but kept going, tyres were shredded by the debris of war littering the roads and eventually the whole enterprise would use 30,000 trucks to keep the supply lines operational.

The term Red Ball Express was derived from the US Santa Fe Railway which in 1892 had established the system for the fast delivery of freight. It was the only way planners could see of solving the problem of delivering supplies. By August 1944 the one-way system ran from St Lô in Normandy to Versailles just outside Paris. There the vehicles branched either north to Soissons to supply the US First Army commanded by General Courtney Hodges or to the south towards Sommesous to supply the US Third Army under Patton, which on its own required 380,000 gallons of fuel daily. The system proved itself by supplying almost 500,000 tons of materiel in just over eleven weeks. In one twelve-day period between 25 August and 6 September the Red Ball Express delivered more than 81,500 tons of supplies by which time the route extended some 300 miles. The drivers were reckless in delivering their cargoes and infantry marching on the roads risked being run down by the trucks passing non-stop. As one British soldier commented, the only way to avoid them was to 'not only get off the road but climb a tree'. The vehicles themselves consumed 250,000 gallons of fuel each day but the army had to be kept moving.

The most commonly-used trucks in the Red Ball convoy system were CCKW, built by GMC, and known by the troops as either the 'Deuce-and-a-half' or the 'Jimmy'. They were capable of carrying payloads of up to 2.5 tons but in reality many were greatly overloaded due to the emergency of battle. All could tow trailers and some were also developed for specialist roles such as the 750-gallon capacity fuel tanker or the 700-gallon capacity water tanker. Others were converted to be used in bomb disposal, medical support, fire trucks, and the DUKW was developed from the CCKW design. There were two basic types of these 6x6 trucks, the Short Wheel Base 352 and the Long Wheel Base 353 and either the closed cab or open cab versions. The CCKW lettering designated the year 1941 (C), conventional cab (C), all-wheel drive (K) and tandem rear axles (K). Between 1941 and 1945 General Motors produced over 562,000 of these trucks and other manufacturers increased the production figure to more than 812,000 vehicles. Some Jimmys had provision for a .50 calibre machine gun to be mounted above the cab roof.

The route being followed by the British 21st Army Group, commanded by Montgomery, was considerably shorter but they were hit by a shortage of supplies when the fleet of 1,400 Austin 4x4 K-5 trucks, capable of transporting 800 tons of supplies per day, had to be taken out of service because they had been fitted with the wrong parts which resulted in gearbox failure. The British army averted a crisis by organising a supply system called the Red Lion Express, operated on a similar basis to the American system. There was never a problem over a shortage of vehicles because the Allies could replace their losses from the huge stockpile of American equipment which had been arriving in Britain since 1942.

At this stage in the war an infantry division had a strength of almost 13,000 troops and supporting them were a comprehensive group of technical services including engineers, signals, ordnance, medical and transportation. These support units could number as many as 50,000 men employed in moving up to 1,600 tons of supplies each day just to keep the division moving and in fighting order.

In 1944, an armoured division had 3 tank companies within its structure, each with 4 companies of 18 tanks, to give a combined strength of 236 tanks. In addition, there were hundreds of other vehicles to tow artillery, armoured scout cars and trucks to transport supplies and ammunition and carry the troops. It was estimated that a single Sherman tank could use up to 8,000 gallons of fuel each week in combat. When an entire US Armoured Division was on the move it required 60,000 gallons of fuel a day. One quartermaster serving with the US 3rd Armoured Division calculated that it took 125,000 gallons of fuel for the whole division to move 100 yards. Fuel consumption would increase dramatically when vehicles were operating in cross country conditions. Vehicles carried their own fuel cans and trucks brought up additional supplies. Bulk fuel transportation was carried in vehicles such as the M-25 fuel tanker which could carry 16,000 gallons.

On 20 August, the British and Americans finally linked up at Chambois just south-west of Falaise to where many Germans had managed to escape on foot. In their wake they left behind the debris of an army in full retreat. It was reminiscent of the retreat by the French and British armies to Dunkirk four years earlier and just like that army the Germans had abandoned all their heavy equipment, tanks, artillery and trucks because they were out of fuel or mechanically unserviceable. Faced with a shortage of transportation the Germans resorted to horses, which in many cases they commandeered from farms.

Five days later Paris was liberated and the Normandy campaign over. The city had been prepared for destruction but the commandant, Major General Dietrich von Choltitz, declared it an open city to prevent destructive fighting. The Normandy campaign had cost the Germans 500,000 men killed, wounded or captured, and 1,500 tanks had been lost along with 3,500 guns and 20,000 other vehicles. The Allies had lost almost 210,000 killed, missing and wounded and in terms of materiel the losses were great but they could be replaced.

Paris was free at last after four years of occupation, but the military garrison had to be supplied as they established hospitals within the environs for the treatment of wounded. To support this influx required 2,400 tons of supplies to be delivered daily by a fleet of military trucks until the railway network was repaired and operational.

On the Eastern Front the Russians had been biding their time and building up their resources in readiness for a series of massive offensives. All the while they had been engaging the Germans to prevent them from guessing that anything was in the offing. News of the Allies' landings in Normandy was delayed until 14 June because Stalin wanted to be sure the attack was a success. Finally, on 22 June, exactly three years to the day when Germany had attacked, the Russians launched an offensive on an unprecedented scale. This was Operation Bagration. For the Russians, 1944 would become known as the 'Year of Ten Victories'.

At the end of 1943, the Russians had 6.5 million troops in the field to face down Germany's forces of 4.5 million men, which included its allied troops. With 5,600 tanks of all types they had more than twice the number available to the Germans. The Red Air Force outnumbered the Luftwaffe by a factor of almost 3:1 and in terms of artillery, which Stalin referred to as the 'God of War', the Red Army had 90,000 guns and mortars compared to the German army's 54,000 pieces of artillery.

The prelude to the first of these started on 14 January 1944 when the Russians unleashed a massive artillery barrage lasting just over an hour, during which time they fired 100,000 shells against the German forces investing the city of Leningrad. The following day an even more intensive barrage by 3,000 guns lasting 105 minutes poured out 200,000 shells. The Germans were shattered and left with no response. The full weight of the Russian attack now went in with the 42nd Army in the van. They were stalled when faced by German artillery but still managed to advance. Two days later, they had penetrated five miles into the German positions, forcing Field Marshal Georg von Küchler to ask permission to withdraw. Hitler ordered him to hold on. Küchler, realising the futility of this, decided to pull back anyway and twelve days later the Russians had cleared away the last German positions. The city was finally relieved after a siege lasting 890 days and, wasting no time, supplies were poured into the 600,000 survivors.

Planning for this onslaught had started in November 1943, with the Russians using barges on the waterways to move hundreds of thousands of troops and their equipment into position. The plan was to lay siege to the Germans who were, in turn, laying siege to Leningrad. The Germans, 100 miles south of the city, had identified that the Russians were planning an attack, but believed it would be localised. The full weight of the attack was made with a force of 375,000 men, including the Second Shock Army, and produced results far quicker than they could have ever expected. The success and the speed with which it was completed illustrated just how weakened the Germans had become.

In November 1943, the German army was enduring its third winter of the war on the Eastern Front. Conditions were terrible with little chance of any improvement. Lack of clothing, no food and with fuel and ammunition in short supply, it was a desperate time for the troops who were by now exhausted. Those who could remember the first winter in 1941, if there were any veterans left from that time, could see how matters had deteriorated. Things had come full circle from 1941, when von Bock had commanded Army Group Centre during Operation Barbarossa.

Field Marshal Fedor von Bock had served in the Polish campaign and in France in 1940. He had been relieved of his command by Hitler in July 1942 and was never appointed to hold a senior command for the rest of the war. He had been one of the most senior officers to recognise the problems posed to the German army's supply lines by the extreme winter conditions in Russia. He realised how vital logistics were and the difficulties faced by the support troops in trying to move the supplies forward. In December 1941 he had written, 'The reason why it is doubtful whether the units can hold a new, unprepared defensive line is clear – because of the shortage of fuel and because of the icy roads I am not getting my motorized units back; I am not even getting my horse-drawn artillery back because the horses cannot manage the weather. Today, for example, the 267th Division had to leave its artillery behind. There is therefore a grave danger that as we retreat we may reach new positions, but without artillery. On the other hand an order to stand and fight would induce in me the fear lest the soldiers would, somewhere or the other, retreat without orders.' Two years later, nothing had changed.

On another part of the front the Russians attacked the German positions at Korsun, where 60,000 troops were holding out, despite being surrounded and cut off, with no prospect of being relieved. Their armoured vehicles were low on fuel were forced to crawl slowly over the ice in sub-zero conditions to conserve what precious fuel reserves they did have. The position, measuring twenty miles wide, was referred to as the 'Korsun Pocket'. Inside the defensive ring supplies were moved to locations using horse-drawn sledges and carried by men. Casualties were mounting and everything was running out. The Luftwaffe tried to supply the group by air lift but it was useless. In a period of five days the Luftwaffe lost forty-four Ju52 transport aircraft to Russian anti-aircraft guns as they flew in to drop provisions. On 11 February elements of the III Panzer Corps managed to break through the besieging Russian lines from the direction of Lysyanka. In the early hours of 17 February, the defenders began their breakout to link up with III Panzer Corps. The operation was discovered and attacked. The remaining vehicles were destroyed in the fighting, horse transportation was lost and it became a question of every man for himself. The Korsun Pocket had been pinched out, not that it would have posed any threat to the Russian rear areas. Around 30,000 men managed to escape but they had to abandon all their equipment.

All along the Eastern Front the German army was in retreat, despite exhortations that it must stand and fight. Hitler made gestures by sacking generals and field marshals, but it made no difference. Those Germans taken prisoner were put to work clearing away the debris of battle and removing ammunition and wrecked vehicles which littered the path of retreat.

The Ju52 'Iron Annie' was the standard transport aircraft for the Luftwaffe and for airborne troops. Around 4,845 were built.

The Russians continued to advance at all points along the front, pushing towards Romania, Poland and Norway. Sevastopol was evacuated by the Germans within a week of being attacked. The movement was being repeated all along the Eastern Front as the German army tried in vain to save itself.

In the face of such strong attacks being pressed home with determination, Hitler must have realised that it was only a question of time before the whole Eastern Front collapsed. On 23 August, Romania surrendered and two days later joined the war on the side of Russia. After Italy's surrender in 1943, Hitler had now lost the second of his former allies. On 26 August, Bulgaria announced its decision that it was abandoning Hitler. Ten days later, on 5 September, Bulgaria declared war against Germany. This was the third of Germany's allies to turn against it. Two weeks later, this news was followed by the announcement that Finland had signed an armistice in Moscow on 19 September. Three days later, Russian troops captured the Estonian capital city of Tallinn, while further south they crossed the border into Yugoslavia. To add insult to injury, Finnish troops now rejoined the war but this time fighting against their former German allies. Russian troops attacked Hungary and Czechoslovakia on 5 October, leading to heavy fighting and Hungary seeking an armistice on 16 October. The armistice would be ratified on 20 January 1945, formally breaking the alliance between Hungary and Germany.

Germany had been supplying weapons, fuel and equipment to these former allies including tanks, as used by the German army. They had fought together against Russia on the Eastern Front and supplying them had placed added pressure not only on German resources, but also on their supply lines. Being released from the pressure to provide for Germany's allies meant the factories could now concentrate on just supplying its own army. The supply lines would become much simpler to operate too. Faced with massive offensives approaching Germany from the east and west, Hitler, in an act of desperation to stave off what even he must have known was the inevitable, announced the raising of the Volkssturm, made up of men aged 16 to 60 years of age who would become the defenders of Germany (about whom more later). His allies having quit, Hitler was now faced with a huge drop in manpower. Volkssturm would work in the factories and be called out to deal with any crisis, such as supplying ammunition to the anti-aircraft guns.

In June 1944 the Russians' supply lines became increasingly extended as they continued to advance westwards. This was what the Germans had experienced three years earlier as they advanced on Moscow, Stalingrad and Leningrad. Following the German defeat at Kursk in July 1943, General Manstein pronounced that 'the initiatives in the Eastern Theatre of war [had] finally passed to the Russians.' But unlike the German army which was always short of supplies, the Russians had plenty of supplies which included material, vehicles and food from Britain and America. The Russians also had the manpower and, now that the Germans were in retreat with no chance of returning to reconquer territories, they had time.

While the Western Allies were continuing to move in from Belgium and the Netherlands the Russians maintained their pressure from the east, by adding the capture of Latvia and Estonia to their list of Ten Victories for the year of 1944. The Russians poured 450,000 troops into Finland along with 800 tanks and massive air support. Finland did not go down without a fight. Between 26 June and 13 August 1944 Finnish troops fought a tough battle against Russian troops at Ilomantsi, during which their artillery fired 36,000 shells against the Russians' 10,000 shells. One reason for the imbalance was because Finnish troops were disrupting the Russian supply lines preventing ammunition and equipment from getting through. Hitler had sensed for some time that Finland might be considering withdrawing from the war, and the German army set about making plans accordingly. In September, the 20th Mountain Army evacuated more than 4,000 non-essential troops and over 3,300 casualties through the ports of Oulu, Kemi and Tornio on the Gulf of Bothnia. A total of 42,144 tons of stores were also ordered to be removed through these ports but some of the ships only sailed as far as neighbouring Sweden which was neutral and some 13,064 tons were lost in this way. A larger stockpile of 106,000 tons of ammunition, medical supplies and stores were destroyed to prevent them being captured by the Soviets when there were not enough ships to remove their cargoes. Germany was now fighting on its own, apart from some volunteers still serving in SS Divisions and a few other units.

In their preparations for Bagration the Russians concentrated their build-up in the region of Minsk, an area held by German Army Group Centre, part of which included assembling an artillery force of 285 guns per mile. When they opened fire at first light on 22 June, the massed ranks of some 4,000 tanks supported by SU–122 assault guns rumbled forward. The Russians forces numbered some 1.2 million men in 166 divisions, with 80,000 Polish troops, making them over ten times greater than the strength of the Anglo-American invasion at Normandy. The Russians had enjoyed the benefit of not having to mount an amphibious assault, and the numerical superiority of the army would be overpowering. Hitler had dispatched 48 infantry divisions and three panzer divisions to protect the Romania oilfields, leaving just 500,000 men to face the Russian onslaught across a frontage of 650 miles.

The German position was a salient, so their forward lines were exposed to attack from three side sides: north, south and centre. Within three days the Germans had lost 20,000 killed and 10,000 captured along with all their equipment and vehicles. As on other fronts and in similar situations Hitler refused to allow trapped groups of men to fight their way out. By 28 June, the Russians had advanced almost one hundred miles, destroying 13 divisions and killing or capturing 200,000 in the process. The prisoners would be sent to the rear where they were added to the labour force clearing away the debris of battle and burying the dead. Marshal Zhukov, Soviet Supreme Command, wrote his impression of the battle: 'Fires broke out on the battlefield. Dozens of vehicles and tanks were in flames; fuel and lubricant dumps...' Operation Bagration began to be wound up on 19 August, by which time the Red Army had inflicted 350,000 casualties on the Germans. The Russians eventually committed 2.3 million troops to the two-month offensive, which was supported by 2,715 tanks, 1,355 assault guns, 24,363 pieces of artillery and fleets of trucks to bring supplies forward. After the battle the Germans were left with just 118 tanks, 377 assault guns and 2,589 pieces of artillery. By the time the last of the fighting ended on 29 August, the Germans had lost 2,957 tanks and assault guns and 2,447 pieces of artillery and had only 33 divisions to face 133 Russian divisions.

The Russian army had entered the war with a massive tank force calculated to be 24,000 vehicles strong, most of which had turned out to be obsolete and no match for the modern German tanks. The tactics used by the tank commanders were out-dated and they never stood a chance against the massed forces of the Panzer Divisions. Following one defeat after another the Russians finally managed to stabilise their positions and the hundreds of relocated factories began to produce more modern designs in large numbers.

In the early engagements, the Russians had used vehicles such as the 7.8-ton T-26 Light Tank and the 13.6-ton BT-7 Fast Tank, capable of speeds up to 46mph on roads, both armed with the 45mm calibre gun. These served in many battles along with other AFVs such as the T-40 Amphibious Tank, the T-70 Light Tank and the BA-64 Armoured Car. These were fast, but they lacked armour and the guns were not sufficiently powerful to hit back at the German tanks. The heavier tanks, such as the KV-1 and KV-2, armed with 76.2mm guns could hit back but they were slow. These were replaced by new, more powerful tanks, the first of which was the T-34, and it was these which were available for the defence of Moscow in late 1941. The chassis of these vehicles would also serve as the basis for SPG designs. The Tankograd factory alone produced 13,500 KV tanks. One of the SPG designs based on the KV-1 chassis was the ISU-122, armed with a 122mm gun, which later led to an even heavier version armed with a 155mm gun. These were used at Kursk in 1943 and later in the fighting in the streets of Berlin in April 1945. The smaller SU-76 SPG entered service in 1943 and was armed with a 76.2mm gun. Like other vehicles of this type it went through a series of variant designs including anti-aircraft versions and by the end of the war some 12,600 had been built.

The Russian tank factories also produced the 29.1-ton SU-85, which first appeared in 1943, followed by the heavier 31.1-ton SU-100 a year later. The titles of these vehicles came from the calibre of their guns. These innovative designs forced the Germans to build more powerful tanks, tank destroyers and develop heavier anti-tank guns. Together with the T-34 tank, they helped swing the balance of armoured power in Russia's favour.

The T-34 would come to form the backbone of the Russian tank forces. By 1941 2,810 had been built and when deployed in the defence of Moscow its appearance shocked the Germans. It basic version weighed around 28 tons and was armed with the M40 76.2mm gun. Served by a crew of four the T-34 was committed to battle along all sectors of the front. It was developed into a flamethrower, a clearer of mines, and a layer of bridges. Later variants were fitted with a more powerful 85mm gun and long-range fuel tanks to extend the operational range to 220 miles. It carried 77 rounds for its 76.2mm gun or 55 rounds for the 85mm. The T-34/85 version began production in 1943 and by the end of the war 11,000 had been built.

The Russians also developed a rocket artillery system called the Katyusha (Little Kate) which was used extensively by the Russian army and developed into several versions being mounted on vehicles such as the ZIS or GAZ trucks for mobility. They were built in calibres ranging from 82mm to 300mm and their range varied accordingly. Depending on the calibre of the rocket the system could fire 12 or 16 rounds in a matter of seconds. The M31 300mm version fired thirty-six rockets from rail launchers on the rear of the transporting truck to saturate an area and whole batteries could pulverise enemy positions.

By September, the Western Allies had advanced 300 miles from their landing beaches in Normandy and had built up to forty-seven divisions numbering around two million men. At some points units were advancing so fast they were outstripping the pace with which the supply lines could maintain contact. Things were running short and troops were resorting to using stocks of food and fuel captured from the Germans. There were instances where troops 'hijacked' convoys and redirected them to their own units.

Royal Marines would play an important role during the Normandy invasion. They were trained to march for discipline.

Chapter 18

Market Garden

The Normandy campaign was still fresh in the minds of all who fought in the battles across France and as the Allies crossed into Belgium Montgomery proposed a new plan which he was sure would help win the war by the end of the year. His plan was a simple one in principle but in practice it was complicated, relying on too many 'ifs and buts' and made no allowance for unforeseen complications. The idea was to make a powerful thrust along a narrow front into the Ruhr, the heartland of German war production. He believed that if these facilities were seized the country could not fight. Then, once the Allies had penetrated the area they would be able to swing round the northern flank of the Siegfried Line protecting Germany's border.

In 1944, the Ruhr produced almost one third of Germany's hard coal required to power the factories, which, in turn, produced more than 30 per cent of all steel needed for weapons and tanks. The German army in the field was reeling under the weight of attack on three fronts, but it was still being supplied with arms, ammunition and equipment. Factories in the Ruhr between July and November 1944 turned out a prodigious amount of weaponry: one million rifles, 51,000 machine guns, 5,000 antitank guns, 11,000 mortars, 9,700 pieces of artillery and 1.5 million tons of ammunition. It was a target worth eliminating. The German army had shown the Allies how it could still turn and fight. Its armoured divisions were by now only a fraction of what they had been four years earlier, but new powerful weapons in its armoury such as the Hetzer ('Baiter') tank destroyer, also known as the Panzerjäger 38(t) or SdKfz 138, showed what its industrial resources could produce. The vehicle arrived late in the war and was issued to the defensive anti-tank units serving with infantry divisions which had requested that suitable weapons be made available to them to engage superior Russian armour. In view of such examples, Montgomery's scheme made perfect sense.

After meeting with initial reluctance Montgomery's plans were finally approved and given the code name Operation Market Garden. His idea was to land 34,600 airborne troops, complete with 1,736 vehicles, 263 pieces of artillery and supported with 3,342 tons of supplies, behind German lines to seize vital bridges which would allow British armoured divisions to race down a corridor, crossing the rivers, to secure the area. On 17 September, men from the American 101st Airborne Division took off from bases in England and were flown in daylight to drop zones in the area around Eindhoven to secure the bridges. Likewise, the American 82nd Airborne Division took off from bases to capture bridges further along the route at Nijmegen. The British 1st Airborne Division was given the task of landing around the town of Arnhem to seize and hold the bridge over the River Rhine. Between them these three divisions would hold open the route along which British XXX Corps, with 50,000 men and 23,000 vehicles, would fight its way to link up all the bridges, which, in turn would hold open the door, as it were, for the British 21st Army Group to thrust into the Ruhr. The airborne flotilla included parachute troops carried in C-47 Dakota aircraft with gliders carrying the heavy equipment and supplies which included anti-tank guns, motorcycles and Jeeps.

The Germans were still in full retreat and, so the British thought, in a state of disarray. The British also believed that in such a disorganised state they would not be expecting such a daring, indeed reckless, assault. Ten days before the operation, Dutch Resistance relayed warnings that the SS II Panzer Corps, 15,000 men and 250 tanks, had been moved into the area of Arnhem with the purpose of refitting their vehicles. The news was ignored, which would become a costly mistake.

At 2.35pm on 17 September, the leading elements of XXX Corps set off from Neerpelt up the Eindhoven road to begin covering the sixty-mile route to Arnhem, flanked by XII Corps and VIII Corps to the left and right to provide support. By that time around 20,000 troops had already landed in their drop zones, or landing zones in the case of gliders, along with over 500 vehicles, mainly jeeps, and 330 pieces of artillery.

The American-built C-47 'Dakota' was the Allies' principal transport aircraft and over 10,000 were built.

The road was very narrow and elevated which presented the vehicles in silhouette, making them easy targets for German anti-tank guns. Within twenty minutes of setting out the column was being fired on and lost nine tanks in two minutes by enemy fire. Self-contained with artillery, engineers and signals, XXX Corps with the Guards Armoured Division was experienced having seen action in Tunisia, Sicily and had fought all the way from the beaches at Normandy. Unfortunately, the nature of the terrain over which they were passing, known as polder, was too soft to bear the weight of tanks which prevented the tanks from spreading out. The British armour was constrained to the roadway. They would continue to be pounded as they advanced up the only route. The airborne drops experienced a series of complications leading to troops and their equipment being widely scattered.

The Germans realised that these airborne troops were only lightly armed and not properly equipped to deal with heavy armour. Reacting to the landings, especially those at Arnhem, the Germans brought in tanks and other armoured vehicles from SS II Panzer Corps to bear on the British forces and began to surround the parachute troops. Delayed in its advance, XXX Corps fell behind schedule and did not reach Eindhoven until the following day where they were informed that the bridge over the Son River was destroyed. The 101st Airborne Division had secured their area but there was fighting to hold off the German Fifteenth Army. Specialist equipment with Royal Engineers was driven forward and a Bailey bridge was built over the river. This was just one of many hundreds of Bailey bridges built across Europe to replace those destroyed by the Germans. This remarkable design, by engineer Donald Bailey in 1940, could support loads of seventy tons.

During the campaign in Europe the Allies built 2,498 bridges with a combined length of 48 miles in total. This included 759 assault bridges, 1,738 Bailey bridges and other 'fixed' types. They were used to span major rivers (the Moselle was spanned five times), smaller rivers and to replace either railway bridges or to cross other natural obstacles.

On 19 September, two days behind schedule, XXX Corps continued its advance towards the 101st Airborne Division at Nijmegen, reaching the bridge at the Grave river. By now, XXX Corps had taken such a battering that the troops were calling the route 'Hell's Highway' and with good cause. With every passing hour, the advance was falling behind schedule. At Nijmegen, Major General James Gavin, commanding the 82nd Airborne Division, decided to pre-empt the arrival of XXX Corps and try to capture the bridge across the Waal River. The plan called to attack it from both ends at once. To do so would require boats to get the across to the far side of the river to attack. Unfortunately, they had no boats and so a message was sent requesting they be delivered. This caused additional delays as they were brought forward along the narrow road now littered with abandoned vehicles. Meanwhile, the men of 1st Airborne Division at Arnhem were fighting desperately against tanks and being squeezed in at all points. Supply drops were being made by RAF aircraft but the Germans had overrun most of the drop zones and, most importantly, on the first day of the landings SS-Hauptsturmführer Schleffer, the intelligence officer with the 9th SS-Panzer Division, captured a British officer who had in his possession instructions for marking the drops zones along with ground marker panels, coloured flares and smoke markers. With these in German hands the RAF could be coaxed into dropping supplies in the wrong place without ever realising their mistake.

German anti-aircraft guns were taking a toll on supply aircraft and were even firing on parachute troops as they descended. In one drop of 1,914 men, 36 were killed by ground fire and several became entangled with one another. A scheduled delivery by 31 Stirling aircraft dropped 80 tons of supplies but only 12 tons were in the right drop zone. With British ground marker panels now in their possession the Germans could lay out the markers to deceive the transport aircraft. On 19 September, the second day of the operation, 63 Dakota aircraft and 101 Stirling bombers flew over Arnhem to deliver 390 tons of supplies. The deception worked and the Germans reaped the harvest of 369 tons of the delivery. The result was being repeated elsewhere.

It was not as though the Germans were desperate for the supplies, they had ample stocks of food and ammunition before the landings, but by denying them to the British they were winning the battle. Hauptsturmführer Sepp Krafft of the SS Panzergrenadier Depot and Reserve Battalion 16 recalled: 'Increased fighter-plane activity always indicated a new drop over a particular sector, and because we had captured ground signs and white flare ammunition, we succeeded in deceiving the enemy to drop supplies in our lines, which he usually did.'

Accompanying the British troops in Arnhem was the BBC war correspondent Stanley Maxted from Canada who prepared a recording for broadcast on 20 September 1944. He was there to report first-hand on the operation and tell the civilian listeners in England how well things were going. The recording he made were his observations of an air drop of supplies:

> *Just a few minutes ago the fighter cover showed up and right behind them came those lovely supply planes which you can hear up above us now. Yesterday and this morning our supplies came and were dropped in the wrong place. The enemy got them, but now these planes have come over and they've dropped them right dead over us…Everybody is cheering and clapping, and they just can't give vent to their feelings…All those bundles and parachuted packages and ammunition are coming down here all around us, through the trees, bouncing on the ground. The men are running out to get them, and you have no idea what this means to us to see this ammunition and food coming down where the men can get it. They're such fighters, if they can get the stuff to fight with.*

His report was only partially correct. On the day he made the recording, 22 September, less than half the intended 386 tons dropped to British troops were recovered for use.

But, of course, the British public did not want to know how badly things were going, but how brave the troops were. Maxted's recording was not broadcast until a week after he made it, by which time Operation Market Garden was finished.

SS-Officer Cadet Rudolf Lindemann recalled: 'We watched the supply drops every afternoon, when they were expected at about 1600 [4pm]. Having found the key to signal the aircraft using panels, we would start setting these out at about 1600 hours every afternoon. The aircraft always dropped on to the signs. We always had sufficient supplies – the British did not get anything.' The Germans had captured so many British weapons and ammunition, they were using them against the men they were intended to supply. After the fighting stopped, Obersturmbannführer Walter Harzer, chief staff officer with 9 SS Panzer Division, said, 'It was the cheapest battle we ever fought. We had free food, cigarettes and ammunition.'

Market Garden was an operation which according to plans should have lasted only three or four days until XXX Corps reached Arnhem. Its failure to do so meant the men at Arnhem were forced to fight against overwhelming odds for ten days until the survivors were given the order to get out as best they could. The German defences were too strong and the badly battered XXX Corps found it almost impossible to reach Arnhem. The bridges captured by the American airborne divisions were secure but at Arnhem the position was evacuated and of the almost 10,000 men who went into Arnhem 2,163 escaped, 1,440 were killed, with the remaining 5,354, including wounded, being taken prisoner. The effort had cost the Allies 88 tanks plus trucks and others AFVs. The Germans had lost between 6,315 and 13,300 killed, wounded or captured. They had also lost around thirty tanks and SPGs destroyed by anti-tank guns and PIATs. Some of these were ageing French tanks such as the Char B1 bis, which had been captured in 1940 and now, after four years, had been put into frontline service and used in battle. The operation had involved 20,190 men parachuted in and 13,781 men landed by 491 gliders along with 5,230 tons of supplies, 1,927 vehicles and 568 pieces of artillery. Market Garden had been a bold plan and its failure left the Allies with the disappointing prospect of having to fight through another winter. It also proved that the German army still had plenty of fight left and there was still a long way to go before it was beaten in the field.

Most of the tanks and other armoured vehicles produced by British companies dated from the period of rearmament just before the outbreak of war. Between 1940 and 1941, the British army had lost many vehicles during the fighting in France in 1940 and the North Africa campaign in 1941. Those surviving vehicles were showing signs of age after hard driving and battling. With the Lend-Lease Act in 1941, American-built vehicles began to arrive to make up for the shortfalls in armoured vehicles and take the pressure of what was in service. Initially, the British army greatly benefitted from three of these designs, the M3 Honey, the M3 Grant Lee and the M4 Sherman, which would be battle tested by the British army before America entered the war. These vehicles were being produced in quantity and by 1944, along with some British designs, such as the Churchill and Cromwell, there were sufficient numbers to allow some to be turned over to specialised battlefield roles to equip the 79th Armoured Division in readiness for the invasion of Europe. In the later stages of the European campaign through Belgium, Holland and into Germany, the range of light British armoured vehicles proved themselves in many actions.

For example the Dingo, a compact vehicle capable of 55mph, proved extremely useful in the reconnaissance role. It had five forward gears and five reverse gears to maintain speed in all situations and with an operational range of 200 miles it was ideal for extended operations in the scouting role. The crew comprised a driver and commander who, between them, operated the little vehicle which was usually armed with a single Bren Gun although some were armed with a Boys anti-tank rifle and others with Vickers 'K' machine guns. It was protected by armour up to 30mm thick which was sufficient against some small arms fire but its light weight and low ground clearance of around 200mm left it vulnerable to mines. As a design, the Dingo dated back to 1937, originating from specifications for a new scout car placed before the Coventry-based company of Alvis by the Mechanisation Board. The request was met with a speedy response and Alvis produced a prototype 4x4 Dingo armed with a single Bren Gun. At the time, the Bren Gun was just beginning to enter service with the British army.

By coincidence, at the same time as Alvis was undertaking this development work, two other manufacturers were developing their own separate designs for vehicles to operate in the role of scout car. The first was Birmingham Small Arms, BSA, whose vehicle was also a two-man design armed with a Bren gun. The other was Morris Commercial Cars, which, although interesting enough, did not match either the Alvis or BSA vehicles. During 1938, a series of trials was conducted between the vehicles and it was decided that after some modifications the BSA design would be the vehicle for the British army. At this time, BSA was in the process of being acquired by Daimler and so it was that when the vehicle went into production in 1939, under a design team of engineers headed by Sidney Shellard, it was known as Car, Scout, Daimler Mk I or Dingo for short which was the name applied to the Alvis design. By the end of the war the vehicle had been produced in five different marks with a total of 6,626 being built, which is an incredible number considering the original order placed in 1939 had been for only 172 vehicles.

The first version was the Mark I which was fitted with 4x4 steering and a sliding roof. The tyres were of the run-flat type but still allowed for a smooth ride. This was followed by the Mark IA which had a folding roof and improved suspension. The Mark IB appeared with a reversed engine cooling fan, but in almost every other aspect differed very little from the original version. The Mark II Dingo was fitted with slightly different radiator grilles and the 4x4 steering was replaced by front wheel steering, which made it easier for inexperienced drivers to control. The final version was the Mark III which had a waterproof engine but lacked overhead cover. The compact design still allowed for a good range of storage lockers to be provided to stow tools, personal kit and a small cooker for the crew to heat food and make hot drinks when operating ahead in the scouting role. In the desert, sand channels were carried to help recover the vehicle if it became bogged down in the sand. The Dingo did remarkably well throughout the war and proved itself to be a most resilient vehicle from the early engagements in France in 1940 to North Africa, to the beaches of Normandy in 1944 and in Italy.

Another scout car design was the Humber, which entered service in 1942 and was not too dissimilar to the Daimler Dingo, but was slightly larger and heavier. The company of Rootes built over 4,100 scout cars in two variants, both of which proved popular with crews. The first vehicles were known as the Mark I, of which some 1,698 were built, and were followed by the Mark II, which differed by having an improved transmission. Humber Scout Cars were used by the Guards Armoured Division, Canadian troops, the 1st Czechoslovakian Armoured Brigade and the Polish II Corps, the last two of which were fighting with the Allies as free forces in exile. The 11th Armoured Division with its distinctive emblem of a black bull on a yellow background, landed on the beaches at Normandy a week after the initial assault and was involved in the Goodwood and Epsom 'breakout' operations around the city of Caen as the British army forced its way inland. The 11th Armoured Division used the Humber Scout Car and later saw action during the Battle of the Bulge in December 1944 when they fought German units on the Maas in weather conditions which, according to the historian Charles Whiting, 'would have undermined the morale of any but the staunchest soldiers'.

The Humber Scout Car was normally served by a crew of two, the driver and commander, but provision was made for a third person inside the small vehicle. This was usually someone serving in the role of forward observation officer (FOO) directing artillery fire. To keep in contact with other units and relay details back to the artillery positions the vehicle was fitted with a No 19 radio set. It had a top speed of 60mph and a maximum operational range of 200 miles which was impressive and comparable to the Dingo, and it had heavy-duty tyres for good cross-country capability. The Mark I vehicles used components from existing Humber designs such as the Light Reconnaissance Car (see below), which helped with early production somewhat. It had a ground clearance of ten inches, could scale vertical obstacles twelve inches high and ford water three feet deep.

The armament was often a single .303 Bren Gun mounted on the roof and fitted with a special Parrish-Lakeman mounting which permitted it to be fired from within the vehicle. This mounting resembled the handlebars of a bicycle, with the trigger mechanism being operated in a method not dissimilar to applying the brake lever on a bicycle. The Bren Gun in this case was modified to be fitted with a drum magazine holding 100 rounds which was more than three times the capacity of the standard magazine and meant that the man firing it did not have to expose himself to reload so often. This allowed the vehicle to engage infantry in the open but beyond that it had to rely on speed and manoeuvrability to extricate itself from any unexpected situation which might arise. An alternative armament layout was to fit a pair of Bren Guns mounted side by side on the roof. A thousand rounds could be stored in the vehicle and because it was a standard .303 rifle round it was easily resupplied. The Humber Scout Car weighed 2.4 tons and was protected by armour up to 14mm thick with an open top and unarmoured floor. The hull was well angled to deflect light projectiles and the crew accessed through hatches in the roof or by a single door on the left-hand side.

The terms Scout Car and Armoured Car described exactly what roles these vehicles served in, but the British army came up with another term, the Light Reconnaissance Car (LRC), which was just another form of repeating what was already in service. The Canadians produced a design known as the 'Otter' for this role, but the British army would take into service two principal designs. The first was the Humber Light Reconnaissance Car, of which 3,600 would be produced in four different marks. The second type was a design built by Morris. The first version of the Humber LRC was naturally termed the Mk I and entered service in 1940. It was nicknamed the 'Ironside 1' and with the engine housing extending forward it resembled an old-fashioned armoured car from an earlier age, an impression which was added to by the small turret sitting atop the vehicle housing. It gave road speeds up to 50mph and with an operational range of 250 miles they were ideally suited to drive members of the British War Cabinet. The turret had a full 360-degree traverse capability for all-round defensive fire. The armament was usually a Bren gun but some versions were armed with the heavier Boys anti-tank rifle. The Mark III and IIIA, both of which entered service in 1942, had four-wheel drive and some extra observation slits. A crew of three operated the Humber LRC and it would have been very cramped with all the personal kit to be stored, food, personal weapons and the radio equipment. Its main role was to use the No. 19 radio set to transmit observations back to the main force and try to avoid being engaged by the enemy. It had 10mm of armour, well sloped, and a smoke grenade launcher could be used to screen the vehicle's movements for short periods. Some LRCs had their turrets removed and served in the Forward Observation Officer (FOO) role for the Royal Artillery and others were used by the Royal Engineers. The Royal Air Force Regiment used the Humber LRC to provide airfield defence duties after D-Day as they advanced across France and Belgium.

The second type of LRC to be used was the Morris which entered service in 1942 and was deployed to units in Tunisia and Italy. Later they would be used in the Allied advance across Europe. They were never intended to replace other reconnaissance vehicles, such as the Humber or Daimler scout cars, but rather to supplement them, first within the Reconnaissance Corps and then, when this unit was absorbed, with the Royal Armoured Corps. The Royal Air Force Regiment used around 200 Morris LRCs for patrolling forward airfields after the Normandy landings and for security at other bases. Some Polish units used the vehicle for reconnaissance duties too. Around 2,290 Morris LRCs were built. The first version was built by the Nuffield Group and was fitted with armour 8 to 14mm thick. It was two-wheel drive and had a top speed of 50mph. It had an elongated rear deck area and a rather stubby bow-fronted appearance with a short glacis plate. The crew of three sat in line abreast with the driver's position in the middle. This allowed the man to his left to operate the radio and fire the Boys rifle, and the man to the right to operate the Bren Gun mounted in the turret. (The Boys anti-tank rifle by 1942 had little if any value against armoured vehicles, but it could still be used against light trucks. It weighed 36 lbs and measured 63.5 inches in length, so was probably best used mounted in a vehicle. It fired a steel-cored armour-piercing bullet with a muzzle velocity of 3,250 fps which could penetrate 20mm of armour at ranges of 500 yards.) The front of the turret had a long vertical opening and veterans who operated the vehicle felt vulnerable to this because they believed the opening allowed bullets to enter. The position for the Boys rifle had a pair of hinged covers which could be folded down to give some overhead protection against shell splinters. The underside of the Morris LRC Mark I was flat and free from any protuberances and a good ground clearance made it suitable for cross-country operations. The front wheels were equipped with large coiled springs to provide independent suspension. A variant of the Mark I, the OP, was fitted with a pair of range-finders and used for spotting fall of shot for artillery batteries. The radio operator would relay changes to be made direct to the gun positions to engage enemy targets. In response to demand, the Mark II was fitted with four-wheel drive in 1943. After the Normandy landings the RAF Regiment moved forward with their Morris LRCs around Bretteville and they were involved with Operation Goodwood, the breakout action south-east of Caen on 18 July 1944.

German engineers and tank designers continued to produce a range of new vehicles to meet the ever-changing situation on the three battle fronts. Some were completely new designs while others were either combination of two types to make the use of parts from ageing vehicle designs, or a modification to produce a variant from an old design. The chassis of the 38 (t) tank, with its the Christie-type suspension, which gave good road speeds but had very poor cross-country performance, was an example of this. Its deficiencies were more than compensated for by the fact that it had excellent manoeuvrability. Unfortunately, by 1943, although it had performed well during the early campaigns of the war, it was approaching the end of its useful service life. Against the more powerful Russian tanks such the T-34 it could not compete. Rather than phase the vehicle completely from service it was decided to use the chassis to form the basis of a series of alternative fighting vehicles, one of which was the Marder III self-propelled gun armed with a 75mm gun. Between April 1942 and May 1944 2,812 such vehicles were built using redundant 38 (t) chassis to produce a weapon system which had a road speed of 25 mph and an operational range of 118 miles. The 38 (t) chassis was so versatile that it was used in a whole range of specialised roles including recovery, ammunition supply, self-propelled guns and tank destroyers.

In March 1943, General Guderian, now in his capacity as Inspector of Armoured Units, suggested the development of a light tank destroyer which could be used to break up enemy armoured formations. On his proposal, all available 38 (t) chassis were given over to the production of tank destroyers. The result was the Hetzer, a light, but extremely well armoured and effective tank destroyer specifically intended for use with the defensive anti-tank units of infantry divisions. From April 1944 to May 1945, 2,584 Hetzers were built, which gives an indication of the degree of urgency placed in producing the vehicle. The company of BMM in Prague served as the controlling firm with Skoda producing all the automotive parts for the vehicle. The final design as it appeared was a low profile, being only six feet and five inches in height, with well sloped armour up to 60mm thick. The main armament was the specialised 75mm PAK 39 L/48. The mantlet had a distinctive shape which was referred to as 'saukopfblende' because it was thought to resemble the nose of a pig. The Hetzer could engage targets out to almost 2,000 yards which made it deadly against a range of Allied tanks including the Sherman and T–34s. It was armed with a single MG34 or MG42 machine gun and the firer was protected by a small shield. The Hetzer served successfully in all theatres of operation after its introduction, but was particularly effective on the Russian Front. Before the war ended plans were in place to produce 1,000 Hetzers per month, but even with the best engineering skills, with diminishing resources it is unlikely that could have happened. At least 20 Hetzers were converted to the Flammpanzer, a flame throwing version ready for Battle of the Bulge in December 1944. From a tank containing 154 gallons of fuel it could project flame for 87.5 seconds to a range of 65 yards. The recovery version was known as the Bergepanzer of which 64 vehicles were produced entering service from October 1944.

As winter approached in late 1944, the Allies had advanced hundreds of miles across Europe from the beachheads in Normandy, but they still lacked the proper port facilities to unload the supplies necessary to maintain the advance. Everything had to be transported over 300 miles by road from ports such as Cherbourg. Each Allied division required a minimum of 520 tons of supplies each day if they were to keep at levels of combat readiness. To move this mountain of supplies the Allies had around 450,000 trucks being driven day and night. For the most part these were American 'Jimmys' and British Bedford and Morris trucks, but there were also 15,000 trucks which had long distance capabilities for exceptionally heavy loads and to move replacement tanks to the front. Even so, the drivers were finding it difficult to keep up with the advancing armies and Montgomery's 21st Army Group which should have been receiving 12,000 tons of supplies per day was having only 6,000 tons delivered. To supplement this shortfall 1,000 tons per day was airlifted but still it was not enough. The Allies had put German PoWs to work repairing the railway network and roads, but the damage was great and making the routes good would take time.

The problem of moving supplies forward was partially alleviated when the deep-water port of Antwerp, lying fifty miles inland from the coast, was captured by the British 11th Armoured Division on 5 September. The surrounding areas approaching the port from the sea had to be cleared before ships could sail into the port. The fighting to capture Antwerp cost the allies 12,873 casualties but they had captured over 41,000 prisoners

German PoWs being led into captivity past a Sherman tank.

By August 1944, the German army in France was in retreat and leaving a trail of detritus in its wake. Seen here among the wreckage is a destroyed Panther tank and other vehicles.

and seized stocks of weapons. The Germans had been able to evacuate some troops and remove heavy weapons and vehicles. Over a period of 16 days they managed to withdraw 65,000 troops, 225 pieces of artillery, 750 trucks and 1,000 horses to prevent them being captured by the Allies. These resources were used in other areas across Holland and the Albert Canal where General Jodl ordered a new front to be established to be 'held at all costs'. Eisenhower understood what its capture would mean to the continuance of the Allied advance and proclaimed, 'I insist upon the importance of Antwerp…I am prepared to give you everything for the capture of the approaches to Antwerp.'

The Allies captured the port of Ostend on 9 September but it was badly damaged. Urgent repairs were completed on 28 September, but it was still only capable of handling 5,000 tons of supplies per day.

At Antwerp the Allies would be able to unload 40,000 tons of supplies each day which would eliminate the need to transport everything long distance, but the Germans still held the area around the approaches to the port and these had to be cleared out. The supplies were there but they could not be delivered in quantity which meant a slowing down of the Allied advance which, in turn, gave the Germans time to regroup and reorganise. Referring to the delay in capturing the port of Antwerp, the historian Jacques Mordal estimated, 'Allowing for 40,000 tons a day, the two months lost represented materiel amounting to 2,400,000 tons which, if supplied at the time required, would certainly have cost the Allies fewer disappointments in October.'

Crews of vehicles would load crates of ammunition and items for personal comfort. The cases were all wooden and so could be burned for firewood if necessary.

Food and ammunition were priorities for a vehicle crew.

This restored example of an M3 half-tracks show how a crew might have stacked it with all the necessities.

Perhaps over-laden, but this restored M3 half-track shows how a crew could be prepared for anything.

The Western Allies continued to advance but heavy rain hampered them. Roads which had been damaged and weakened by the weight of military traffic were washed away. German units were fighting rearguard actions which delayed the Allies but finally they pushed into the area of the Scheldt estuary covering the entrance to the port of Antwerp and cleared it of the enemy. On 28 November the first convoy arrived to unload cargo. Supplies could now be brought close to the front line and replacement vehicles driven directly to where they were needed along with reinforcements.

To the south, in the mountainous region of the Vosges, the French First Army under the command of General de Lattre de Tassigny, completely equipped with American-built weapons, uniforms, and vehicles including the M8 Armoured Car, was advancing in company with the American Seventh Army under Major General Alexander Patch. They were closing in to trap the Germans in what would become known as the 'Colmar Pocket' close to the Swiss border. When the fighting finally ended there in February 1945 the French had lost 13,390 killed and wounded and the Americans 8,000 casualties. According to some sources the Germans lost 38,500 killed, wounded and captured and those who escaped abandoned 55 AFVs and 66 pieces of artillery.

By mid-December 1944, the Western Allies had broken through the once much-vaunted 'Westwall', referred to as the 'Siegfried Line' by the Allies, and crossed the German border in several places. The onset of winter slowed everything down on both sides, or so it seemed. On the side of the Allies, there was very little movement and over in German-held territory there was nothing to give cause for concern. In fact, military intelligence concluded that the Germans were not in a position to mount any serious offensive. Around the densely-wooded area of the Ardennes Forest, widely considered to be impassable by tanks, 83,000 largely inexperienced men of the American 1st Army, commanded by General Hodges, were looking forward to Christmas. The area was quiet and patrols reported nothing unusual apart from some isolated exchanges of gunfire. Suddenly at 5.30am on the morning of 16 December Germany artillery opened fire with such intensity that it threw the Americans into disarray. The Germans had planned a parachute drop, which would have added to the confusion, but it was abandoned when the trucks taking the troops to their aircraft ran out of fuel. This was Operation Wacht am Rhein (Watch on the Rhine) which had been in the planning since October and Hitler was hoping it would push the Allies back.

Two main considerations had been given priority during the planning phase of the operation and these were fuel and ammunition. The manpower could be pulled from various quarters, but it would be logistics which would decide the outcome. As early as October, Hitler and other the generals agreed that stocks of at least 4.5 million gallons of fuel would be required for the opening phases and to start the operation. Vehicles of all descriptions were husbanded and fifty ammunition trains would be made available to support the attack. Hitler ordered that anything that could be used as a means of transport was to be used, even horse-drawn wagons, and charged Himmler to see to it that over 2,000 horses were provided for the 7th Army.

On 28 October deliveries of fuel were beginning to arrive in the assembly areas where it was stockpiled in great secrecy. At the time, the German army facing the Western Allies was using 172,000 gallons of fuel each day and there was pressure to release some of these stockpiles for immediate use by the fighting units. By mid-December less than half the amount of fuel required had been delivered which threatened to delay the start date of the operation. The problem was caused by Allied bombing which was destroying the rail network. As the start date approached, 3.17 million gallons had been delivered, with a further 2.8 million gallons promised. This would exceed the estimates and give a reasonable reserve for at least four days. There were additional delays in preparations caused by slow deliveries in ammunition due to lack of transportation. Nevertheless, Hitler remained confident the offensive would succeed and was adamant about the start date of the operation.

The attack was launched across a sixty-mile front, extending from Monschau in the north to Echternach in the south. It was supported by 275,000 troops, many with considerable combat experience, along with 1,900 pieces of artillery and 950 tanks and other AFVS. Opposing them were six divisions with 394 pieces of artillery and 420 tanks and AFVs. The Germans had been redeploying troops and moving equipment since September and by 15 December some 1,500 troop trains had moved units into the area along with 500 supply trains bringing in stores. Hitler allocated 100 trains just for the movement of ammunition. The officer given the responsibility of arranging this vast undertaking was Generalmajor Alfred Toppe. Eventually some 145,000 tons of ammunition was stockpiled for the coming operation but fuel, or rather the shortage of it, would remain the critical factor.

The Germans advanced quickly and were in danger of becoming a victim of their own success. Moving so many vehicles was never going to be easy and at one point a traffic jam of 100 tanks built up. As the crews waited for the road to be cleared the tanks kept their engines running, all the time using fuel.

Committed to the operation was the formidable Jagdpanther, a powerful tank destroyer armed with the 88mm gun capable of destroying targets up to 3,000 metres away in ideal conditions. The first production models of the vehicle had been built in February 1944 with the first units entering service with 559th and 654th Panzerjägerabteilungen (tank hunting battalions) in June 1944. Many Jagdpanthers were deployed to the Russian Front, where they were used against T-34 tanks and other heavy vehicles and SPGs. These tank destroyers were operated within a separate heavy anti-tank battalion on a Panzer Division. The Jagdpanther had inflicted severe losses against Allied armoured units in the later stages of the Normandy campaign. During one engagement in July

1944 three Jagdpanthers destroyed eleven tanks in only minutes before a squadron of Churchill tanks arrived, destroying two and causing the third to withdraw.

The Jagdpanther served on the Russian Front and the last units would still be in action as the fighting fell back to the outskirts of Berlin in the final stages of the war. In December 1944 the Germans had concentrated numbers of the Jagdpanther together in the Ardennes, but with fuel shortages and no air cover to protect them against Allied air strikes they were hampered, but not before giving good account of themselves in action. The Jagdpanther was developed using the Panther as a starting point with the hull and chassis being kept and a new superstructure built on to the bodywork. The engine remained the same, which is to say a petrol-driven water-cooled Maybach HL P30 V-12 which developed 700bhp at 3000rpm to produce road speeds of 29 mph and cross-country speeds of 15mph. A wooden mock-up was prepared in October 1943 and the prototype was ready for inspection by Hitler in December the same year. Satisfied with the results, production of the new tank destroyer was approved and designated as the Jagdpanther SdKfz 173 with the contract being awarded to the company of MIAG in January 1944 with the order to produce 150 new vehicles per month. The company of MNH also began production in November 1944, but at such a late stage in the war the monthly output of the new vehicle would never reach anywhere near the stipulated monthly production figures. In fact, by the time production ceased in March 1945 only 382 vehicles had been produced, with 72 vehicles being produced in January, just four months before the war ended.

The Americans began to fall back in disarray under the weight of the attack, but it was not total panic and pockets of resistance were established such as the town of Bastogne where men of the 101st Airborne Division held out against everything sent to attack them. The American 9th Armoured and 4th Infantry Divisions also held their ground during the first two days of the operation and such resistance led the Germans to exercise caution. For six days, the Kampfgruppe Peiper with 110 tanks tried to force its way forward and eventually succeeded in capturing the town of Stavelot. Approaching the Trois Ponts (three bridges) spanning the rivers Amblève and Salm they were destroyed, bringing the advance to a halt.

The Allies had total air supremacy with sufficient fighters to escort transport planes and protect them against attack by German fighters. However, bad weather prevented them from flying and fighting on the ground intensified. On 21 December, there was a break in the weather and making use of this to their advantage the Allies flew in support to the defenders at Bastogne, who by now were surrounded. A force of 961 Dakotas and 61 gliders delivered 850 tons of desperately-needed supplies, especially ammunition and medical equipment. Patton with the 3rd Army moved northwards to attack the left flank of the salient which was forming due to the nature of the Germans' attack. Over a period of five days, between 18 and 23 December, six divisions with 133,000 vehicles of all types were kept on the move. Operating on a 'round-the-clock' basis 37 truck companies moved more than 43,000 tons of supplies and 18,910 tons of ammunition, all in support of Patton's advance. At the height of the battle, Patton was given a report covering various aspects of the fighting, including the state of logistical support: 'Third Army service installations are exceptionally well situated at the present time to support continuation of the attack. Our stores in these installations are being improved daily. Our rail net in this area is excellent. The present supply situation within the army is good. It has been geared to support the attack and if Communications Zone can continue to put supplies within reach of Army, we can continue. Presently we have a strong Signal communications network, well placed and in operation.' This last part involved laying almost 20,000 miles of wire. It was all good news for Patton.

The Germans had been hoping to use captured stocks of fuel to keep their vehicles moving but destroyed bridges slowed them and prevented them reaching these vital stocks. They did seize a stockpile of fuel at Bullingen but they missed the huge store of some 2.5 million gallons at Francorchamps which would have made up for the shortfall in their initial plans. Realising how important the fuel dumps were to the Germans, the Americans began to destroy them. One of these contained a stock of 120,000 gallons and its destruction no doubt prevented the Germans from completing aspects of the attack.

Slowly the front began to stabilise and the Americans began to deal with the Germans such as at Remonville, where Patton's forces captured the town. By 26 December Patton had linked up with Bastogne where the paratroopers of the 101st Airborne Division had used Bazooka shoulder-fired rocket launchers to destroy several tanks. By now, the German attack was becoming a spent force, having used up the last reserves of fuel and ammunition. The weather began to clear and Allied aircraft could fly air support missions which destroyed German vehicles as they moved. The operation had cost the Americans and British 7,000 killed, 33,400 wounded and 21,000 taken prisoner or missing. The fighting had also cost them 700 tanks and other AFVs destroyed or damaged. For the Germans it was disastrous with 120,000 men killed, wounded or captured. They had lost 1,600 aircraft, 600 tanks and 6,000 other AFVs and trucks.

Over a period of five days during the battle, pilots of the American XIX Tactical Air Command claimed the destruction of 3,200 vehicles, 293 tanks and other armoured vehicles, 57 pieces of artillery, 42 locomotives, 1,800 railway trucks, eleven bridges, five ammunition dumps, 234 buildings being used by the Germans, 52 aircraft either destroyed or damaged and the railway track system cut in 106 places.

Logistical support had proved vital throughout the operation which American troops called the Battle of the Bulge after the salient caused by the attack. The expenditure of ammunition was massive. For example, between 1 and 8 January 1945, during the last days of the fighting, American artillery fired over 400,000 rounds. By comparison the American First Army had fired 300,000 rounds of 105mm and 155mm calibre in six months from D-Day to the Battle of the Bulge. Air supply was possible and Dakota aircraft dropped 60,000 packs of K-rations, 15,000 gallons of petrol, 2,000 rifle grenades and 5,500 mortar rounds to units of the 4th and 87th Divisions holding positions around the town of Prum. During its time fighting across Europe, almost 1.25 million tons of supplies had been despatched to the Third Army which had, in turn, transported almost 2.2 million tons of supplies within its zone. The XIX Tactical Air Command had been busy, as its operations record shows, by destroying an enormous amount of materiel to deny it to the enemy, including aircraft, trucks, armoured vehicles, trains and various military installations, along with 3,237 factories destroyed, 285 bridges and 220 supply dumps.

Over the next three months the Western Allies would maintain a steady but relentless pressure, all the time pushing the Germans back. On the Eastern Front, the Russians approached the end of 1944 content in holding positions in eastern Poland with a front line extending from the Baltic Coast in Lithuania in the north and running down the Czechoslovakian border in the south. They would continue to hold these positions, which extended for over 750 miles, for six months before making their next move. The time was spent building up their reserves, stockpiling fuel, ammunition and other supplies. In the centre lay the First Belorussian Front under the command of Marshal Zhukov, to his left was the First Ukrainian Front with 2.2 million men commanded by Marshal Ivan Koniev. In the north on Zhukov's right flank was the Second and Third Belorussian Fronts with 1.6 million men. Facing this massive force was German Army Group Centre with only 400,000 troops. Army Group A commanded by General Josef Harpe was outnumbered at every level including tanks at the scale of 7 to 1. It was a question of time before the Russian army began to roll forward and senior officers realised this. Hitler ensconced in his bunker in Berlin was moving armies which now only existed in strength on his maps.

Chapter 19

Island Hopping in the Pacific

O n the other side of the world, the war in the Far East and the across the Pacific Ocean, the war was going in favour of the Allies. Whereas most of the fighting in the west was conducted on land, the fighting in the east involved fighting on land and over vast distances of water. On land the British were fighting down from the Indian border and moving south along with the America contribution from the direction of China. The island hopping campaign had been going well for the Americans, since their landings on Guadalcanal in 1942, but it was taking a toll on manpower and placing a strain on resources. On 30 June 1943, the Americans devised a plan called Operation Cartwheel which involved advancing across the Pacific Ocean in two huge thrusts. In the north, the Central Pacific Area, Admiral Chester Nimitz would be in command of the US Pacific Fleet, which in 1943 consisted of seven battleships, ten aircraft carriers, and scores of other types such as cruisers and destroyers. All the while it was growing in strength. This force would operate in the deep water advancing to the Philippine Islands before moving on to the Japanese home islands where it would reinforce the blockade cutting off resources vital to the Japanese war effort.

To the south, the area designated as the South-West Pacific Area, General Douglas MacArthur, would advance towards the Philippines, a move which he believed would push the Japanese away from the oil fields of Indonesia and the rubber plantations of Malaya, which would deny them two vital resources necessary to its war effort. Since the beginning of 1943, the Allies had been scoring successes against Japanese supply routes across the Pacific, such as the destruction of the convoy to resupply the garrison on New Guinea. On 5 January 1943, American and Australian ships and aircraft intercepted a Japanese convoy of eight cargo ships with an escort of eight destroyers. The attack was completed with the sinking of all eight cargo ships which were carrying troops, fuel and medical supplies, along with four destroyers. The loss would have severe implications for the Japanese on New Guinea.

The crescent-shaped island of Kwajalein, in the Marshall Islands archipelago, 2.5 miles in length and less than half a mile in width, had a garrison of 5,000, but despite its otherwise insignificance this was one island which could not be bypassed and left to 'wither on the vine'. It had to be captured because it had an airfield on it from where Japanese aircraft could attack shipping and provide air support. The 7th US Infantry Division landed on 31 January 1944 and for four days fought a fierce battle. It cost them 142 killed and 845 wounded. After the fighting finished on 4 February, only 49 Japanese were taken prisoner, representing a 99 per cent loss among the garrison as they fought to retain the island. The marines had benefitted because, for the first time, they were supported by aircraft flying from bases on Tarawa. The whole of the Marshall Islands had to be cleared to eliminate the Japanese navy from operating in the region of Truk and the operation was given to Rear Admiral Marc A. Mitscher, commanding Task Force 58 with twelve aircraft carriers and a full complement of 700 aircraft. The next target was the island of Eniwetok which was attacked on 17 February and finally secured six days later. The Americans had lost 258 killed and 568 wounded and out of a garrison of 2,741 only 64 were taken prisoner. This represented a mortality rate of ninety-seven per cent and another demonstration of the Japanese fanaticism which the Americans realised they would increasingly face as they advanced.

The island of Saipan in the Mariana Islands could not have been more different from the islands previously attacked by the Americans. It was mountainous and the garrison defending it numbered some 30,000 troops. The Japanese had constructed two main airfields on it and there were several port facilities around its coast to allow supplies to be delivered. This was not a coral and sand atoll in the vein of Eniwetok or Betio, this was a well-supplied garrison with artillery and armoured support and aircraft.

On 15 June, the assault waves of landing craft left the main fleet to make their landings on the west coast. They were supported by a naval bombardment and had air cover. Within twenty minutes around 8,000 marines from the 2nd and 4th US Marine Divisions were ashore and fighting fiercely to get off the beach. They were followed by another wave of 18,000 troops. Fighting across the island was intense and lasted for over three weeks, with supplies having to be hauled up ravines and mountains. The fighting ended on 9 July and left the Americans with 3,426 killed and 10,364 wounded out of a force of 72,000 men committed to taking the island. The Japanese lost 29,000 killed and only 921 taken prisoner. The port facilities allowed supplies to be landed and the wounded evacuated, but most importantly they had captured the air bases. The island lay only 1,300 miles from the Japanese home islands, which put them in range of the heavy B-29 bombers which could operate from Saipan. These aircraft would bomb factories, military installations and oil supplies to reinforce the naval blockade around the islands.

Twelve days after Saipan had been secured, the next island in the Mariana atoll to be attacked by American troops was Guam, measuring around 28 by 8 miles. The first landings were put ashore on 21 July. The island had been in Japanese hands since they captured it on 10 December 1941, only three days after the attack against Pearl Harbor. In the more than thirty months of their occupation, the garrison of over 18,500 had built defences and there were port installations through which supplies could be landed to support them. They had artillery and armoured support to face the attacking

Americans who would commit 59,400 marines to the battle along with dozens of tanks in support. For almost three weeks the Americans continued to battle against stiff Japanese resistance. On Guadalcanal, there had not been a problem getting the supplies of water, food, ammunition and fuel ashore. The problem there was getting it from the beach to the forward positions. Here on Guam, every stage of resupply was a nightmare. Firstly, getting the supplies ashore was not easy because of the coral reefs; but they were overcome and deliveries were made to the shore. The problems mounted as they advanced along the island and all the supplies had to be hauled forward. Finally, on 10 August it was all over. The Americans had lost 1,777 killed and 5,798 wounded. The Japanese had lost 18,337 killed and only 1,250 were taken prisoner.

Each island was being fiercely contested, but each one taken meant more security and improved operational bases for the advancing Americans. Neighbouring Tinian was captured by 2nd and 4th US Marines on 9 July and units of the Seabees began to set about constructing an airfield on the island. Eventually some 15,000 Seabees would construct six airstrips, each measuring 7,900 feet in length from which B-29 bombers could operate against Japan. Accommodation for 50,000 men was also built and the island became the busiest airfield base in the Pacific during the war. It was from here that B-29 bombers would fly the missions to drop the atomic bombs on the cities of Hiroshima and Nagasaki on 6 and 8 August 1945 which would bring an end to the war.

The next stepping stone to receive the attention of the Americans in their island hopping campaign was the archipelago of the Palau Islands and in particular Peleliu, being the largest and most important. This was attacked on 15 September by the 1st Marine Division, with armoured support from the 1st and 710th Tank Battalions with Sherman tanks. Capturing these islands would be the perfect location from where they could launch the invasion to recapture the Philippines. Once again, it was Mitscher's Task Force 58 which provided the naval bombardment. By now his fleet had increased to sixteen aircraft carriers. The ships, including the USS *New Jersey*, opened fire as the first wave of marines approached the shore. Between the time of the first landings until 27 November, the Americans would land 47,561 men on the island to wrest it from the Japanese garrison of 10,900. The Japanese had seventeen tanks and artillery to provide fire support and aircraft could operate from the airfield.

Japanese tanks were largely obsolete designs by European standards but some development to improve them was undertaken such as the amphibious 11-ton Type 2 Kamisha, while the Imperial Japanese Navy experimented with the 26-ton Kachisha amphibious tank. By and large, though, the Japanese remained committed to what they had in service and preferred to improve armour and fit heavier guns such as the Type 97. The Japanese tank force was never involved in campaigns or battles to the same degree as in Russia or Europe. On islands where there was no opposition they were used as mobile machine gun posts. On the mainland in China and in Malaya they were used in 'penny packet' formations usually in support of infantry. In 1944, Japanese industry produced 400 tanks and in 1945 this figure was a mere 141, such was the desperate state of raw material supplies, especially metal.

Allied armoured units in the early part of the war in the Far East were restricted by the terrain and the dense jungle which confined vehicles to moving along defined routes which left them open to ambush tactics with anti-tank guns, a strategy at which the Japanese were extremely good.

Peleliu was less than nine miles in length and barely two miles across at its widest point, into which the Japanese had built defensive strongpoints. The wide bays made natural anchorages and in its time there the garrison had built up its supplies of ammunition and food. The US Marines would have to fight for every inch of the hot and barren island. As the fighting intensified and the heat increased, water became a priority. Supplies were transported in old oil cans which made it taste foul. One marine recalled, 'By the fourth day there were as many casualties from heat prostration as from wounds.' Another remembered, 'The terrain was abominable. Sharp coral cut our shoes and clothing…there were many tunnels.' These tunnels were old mining works from before the war and the Japanese made use of them. Everything the marines needed, from ammunition to food, had to be carried forward and the wounded were evacuated the same way. They would be taken out to the ships of Task Force 58, where medical staff treated them. Fortunately, the naval bombardment, which included some 2,500 shells and 800 tons of bombs, had destroyed the Japanese aircraft.

Day after day the battle raged as the Japanese resisted at all points. Finally, the marines got the upper hand and on 27 November, after more than two months continuous fighting, the island was in their hands. They had suffered 2,336 men killed and 8,450 wounded. The Japanese had sustained 10,695 killed with all tanks and artillery destroyed. Only 200 prisoners were taken, mostly foreign labourers brought to the island to work on the defences. The remainder were listed as 'missing' and had probably been incinerated by the flamethrowers. After the war, it was calculated that it took over 1,500 rounds of ammunition to kill each Japanese defender. There is no figure for the Japanese expenditure of ammunition during the fighting, but it is recorded that the Americans fired 13.32 million rounds of .30-inch calibre rifle and machine gun ammunition, 1.52 million rounds of .45-calibre (used in pistols and Thompson sub-machine guns), 693,657 rounds of .50-calibre bullets, threw 118,262 hand grenades and fired approximately 150,000 mortar rounds. All of this had to be taken in the ships to the island along with everything else, including fuel and ammunition for the Sherman tanks which supported the battle.

Even while the battle on Peleliu was raging, almost 1,000 miles away to the west, General Douglas MacArthur arrived back in the Philippine Islands, setting foot on Leyte on 22 October. He was fulfilling the promise he made to the Filipino people that he would return. Indeed, later in the afternoon he broadcast on the radio, 'People of the Philippines, I have returned!' He continued by appealing to them, 'Rally to me! … For your home and hearths, strike! In the name of the sacred dead, strike! … Let no heart be faint. Let every arm be steeled. The guidance of Divine God points the way. Follow in his name to the Holy Grail of righteous victory.' All stirring stuff. The Japanese still had 350,000 men defending the islands and there was a long way still to go before they were liberated. The archipelago of the Philippines consisted of some 7,000 islands and would be an extremely difficult task to tackle, not only for the fighting man but also for those involved in keeping them supplied.

Two days earlier, the first troops from Sixth Army had waded ashore at around 10am to quickly secure a beachhead some four miles wide, as the last salvoes of the naval bombardment supporting the landings were being fired. This amphibious landing was so well organised that within an hour of the landings heavy vehicles, including tanks, were being driven along with supplies. Over the next ten weeks the fighting would become fierce and the Japanese resisted at every turn. The Americans would commit 200,000 men to the battle against the Japanese garrison of 65,000 men supported with tanks and artillery. It would not be a one-sided battle all in the Americans' favour – on 11 December, the Japanese managed to land 34,000 reinforcements and over 9,000 tons of supplies through the port at Ormoc. This was after they had lost substantial amounts to American air strikes against the convoy. The Americans were supported in moving their supplies by hundreds of Filipino civilians who volunteered to help in any way they could. When the fighting was concluded, the Americans had sustained 3,504 killed and 12,000 wounded. Japanese casualties, as usual, were frighteningly high with 49,000 killed, and the net result weakened their force considerably across the island group.

While the fighting was developing on land, two great fleets of warships were approaching one another for a decisive battle in the Leyte Gulf. On 23 October, the first opening shots of what would become the largest naval battle were exchanged by a fleet of 63 Japanese warships and those of the combined US Third and Seventh Fleets, commanded by Admiral William Halsey and Vice Admiral Thomas Kincaid, numbering almost 800 vessels of all types, including troopships carrying reinforcements for the fighting on Leyte. Over the next two days the naval forces attacked one another, but the advantage was always in favour of the American fleet. At the end of the engagement the Japanese had lost almost 300,000 tons of ships, including 4 aircraft carriers, 19 cruisers and destroyers and support ships. The American Navy now had control of the seas and skies.

Chapter 20

1945 and the End Approaches

T he Battle of the Bulge was still being fought in the Ardennes when the Germans made their next move. On 28 December 1944, at his Adlerhorst (Eagle's Nest) headquarters, Hitler addressed an assembly of field commanders to appraise them of his latest plan 'Nordwind' (Operation North Wind): 'This attack has a very clear objective, namely the destruction of the enemy forces. There is not a matter of prestige involved here. It is a matter of destroying and exterminating the enemy forces wherever we find them.' At this stage in the war, German troops did not have to look far to find the enemy, either Russian or Western Allies. The attack would be launched on 31 December and be directed against the American Seventh Army and the French First Army in the Vosges.

The aim was to break through to attack the Allies as they were strung out along a frontage of almost seventy miles. Commanding the attack was Generaloberst Johannes Blaskowitz with Army Group G. Results began to be achieved almost immediately as the 125 Regiment of the 21st Panzer Division threatened the American supply lines. The Seventh Army had been weakened when it had been ordered to release troops to move north to support the Battle of the Bulge. The fighting continued for three weeks, during which time the troops were returned from the Ardennes to bolster their original units.

By 21 January 1945, the Germans were running out of ammunition, fuel for vehicles and other supplies. The battle continued for a further four days and was a tough contest, but in the end it did not achieve the results Hitler had intended. In just over three weeks of fighting the Seventh Army alone inflicted 23,000 casualties and captured almost 6,000 prisoners for a cost to themselves of 11,600 killed and wounded. The French had 295,000 troops in the area along with 125,000 Americans and the final casualty count for them was 29,000 American and 2,000 French. It was another demonstration how the Germans still had fighting spirit, but lacking supplies they could not sustain an attack of this scale for any duration.

Over on the Eastern Front on the morning of 12 January 1945, the Russian artillery opened fire with such intensity the Germans were forced to fall back. General Joseph Harpe was stunned because no-one had foreseen this attack. In fact, the Russians launched it less than a week after Stalin had received a message from Winston Churchill asking that the Russian army do something to try and take pressure off the situation in the Ardennes. Stalin's reply was that the Allies could 'Rest assured we shall do all in our power to support the valiant forces of our Allies.' The result of the attack was that within five days the 1st Ukrainian Front had advanced 100 miles across a front of 160 miles. Two days later, the Russians were approaching Warsaw. Maintaining the pressure the Germans were all but cleared out of Poland by the end of the month, leaving only a garrison holding out at Poznan. This would finally surrender on 23 February.

Mass panic set in among the German civilians living in the area and they began to flee westwards, blocking the roads in scenes reminiscent of Poland in 1939 and France in 1940. Evacuations by ship were organised and Russian submarines sank several of them. The worst incident was the *Wilhelm Gustloff* which was sunk on 30 January laden with almost 8,000 refugees of which only 964 were saved. By 31 January, Zhukov had reached the Oder River near the town of Kustrin, having advanced his entire front 300 miles in less than three weeks. According to estimates drawn up by Field Marshal von Manstein, the Russian army comprised 527 infantry divisions, 43 artillery divisions 302 tank and mechanised brigades, with some 13,400 armoured vehicles and a total of 5,300,000 troops. Facing such an overwhelming force the Germans had 164 divisions with a manpower level of 1,800,000 troops. There was nothing they could do except conduct a fighting retreat, all the while abandoning vehicles for lack of fuel and leaving their artillery behind because there were no vehicles to pull the guns.

In October 1944, Hitler had ordered the raising of a new military force known as the Volkssturm (Peoples' Guard) to provide manpower for the forthcoming defence of Germany. It would be formed using men aged between 16 to 60 years of age who were not otherwise already serving in the military. Ordinary members of this force were known as Volkssturmmänner or privates. Each district would be responsible for recruiting members and the average strength of a Volkssturm battalion was around 642 men commanded by a Bataillonsführer, a rank comparable to a major. Within this

German PaK43 8.8cm anti-tank gun being towed on the Eastern Front in Russia.

German troops fought desperately against determined Russian troops as they were pushed back.

structure there were unit formations which were termed company, platoon and squad, commanded by a Kompanieführer (captain), Zugführer (lieutenant) and Gruppenführer (corporal). These titles gave it the semblance of being a proper military unit.

By now, at this late stage in the war, uniforms were in short supply and although some standard items such as caps and jackets were issued to members of units, most men of the Volkssturm wore their own civilian clothes as if they were going to work.

German SdKfz 124 Wespe (Wasp) self-propelled gun on the move in Russia. Horses serve as transport animals to carry ammunition.

Feeding horses was essential and here German troops are engaged in harvesting fodder.

Recreated scene showing how a field workshop might have looked in the German army.

Weapons were also in short supply and members were supplied with weapons ranging from captured enemy types to obsolete weapons left over from the First War, rifles, machine guns and anything else. A few units were fortunate enough to be issued with K98 standard service rifles and even Panzerfaust anti-tank weapons which could destroy tanks at close range and it was hoped that with these it might be possible to slow down the advancing Soviet T-34s.

The one official piece of uniform was the regulation armband which bore the title 'Deutscher Volkssturm Wehrmacht' in the national colours of Nazi Germany, usually worn on the left arm.

These men had better training in handling weapons than factory workers who had received only rudimentary instruction in weapons and tactics, and Hitler decreed that they should come under the command of the army: 'Experience in the East has shown that Volkssturm, emergency and reserve units have little fighting value when left to themselves, and can be quickly destroyed. The fighting value of these units, which are for the most part strong in numbers, but weak in the armaments required for modern battle, is immeasurably higher when they go into action with troops of the regular army in the field. I, therefore, order: where Volkssturm emergency, and reserve units are available, together with regular units, in any battle sector, mixed battle-groups (brigades) will be formed under unified command, so as to give the Volkssturm emergency, and reserve units stiffening and support.'

The intention was to raise a reserve force of six million men who could be thrown into the defence of Germany against the Soviet Army advancing from the east and the Anglo–American armies from the west, but it was never realised. Senior ranking Nazis such as Goebbels and Himmler urged these men to fight through propaganda. Despite the age limit being placed on recruits, men over 60 and boys as young as 11 or 12 saw it as their duty to join the ranks. Serving the ranks were veterans from the First World War and amputees from other campaigns. The fighting capability of such a disparate mixture of old men and young boys was doubtful but although some ran away, many stood and fought.

As the Russians closed in around Berlin in April 1945, there were perhaps as many as 100 battalions of Volkssturm within the boundaries of the city. They fought in other areas as well but theirs was a lost cause against battle-hardened veterans, who were better trained and equipped with modern weapons. Thousands of Volkssturm were wounded and taken prisoner and it is believed that perhaps as many as 175,000 were killed. The Volkssturm could be considered as being comparable to Britain's Home Guard, but while this was never put to the test in battle, Hitler used the Volkssturm in front line areas, where they joined troops facing a Soviet force of over 2.5 million supported with tanks, artillery and aircraft.

Just how poorly equipped and ill-prepared the Volkssturm were comes from a member taken prisoner by Canadian troops who told his captors how there were '400 men in my battalion and we were ordered to go into the line in our civilian clothes. I told the local Party Leader that I could not accept the responsibility of leading men into battle without uniforms. Just before commitment the unit was given 180 Danish rifles, but there was no ammunition. We also had four machine guns and 100 anti-tank bazookas (Panzerfaust). None of the men had received any training in firing a machine gun, and they were all afraid of handling the anti-tank weapon. Although my men were quite ready to help their country, they refused to go into battle without uniforms and without training. What can a Volkssturm do with a rifle without ammunition! The men went home. That was the only thing they could do.' It was a brave effort, but, in the end, it was a wasted effort consuming the lives of men and resources.

In the west, the Allies had 46 infantry divisions, 20 armoured divisions and four airborne divisions, a total of 70 divisions in all, which would be joined by a further 15 reinforcement divisions by May 1945. On 8 February 1945, XXX Corps with 200,000 men and 35,000 vehicles, including the Guards Armoured Division and the 15th Scottish, began to move forward. Montgomery had been planning for this as early as October 1944 and been carefully husbanding his resources which included stockpiling 250,000 tons of supplies and equipment and assembling a support force of 59,000 engineers to build bridges, repair roads and keep the supplies moving. The Germans had flooded the plains and vehicles soon became bogged down. One observer noted of the 15th Scottish, 'There was already too much traffic on this one road and it was impossible to deploy across the country owing to the boggy ground. The arrival of this extra division caused one of the worst traffic jams of the whole war.' This was the start of Operation Veritable, the advance to the Rhine and the break into the heartland of Germany's war production. Lying in Montgomery's way was the city of Cleeves, which the RAF bombed to reduce the possibility of any resistance. Around 786 aircraft dropped 2,700 tons of bombs and destroyed 90 per cent of the city. Firepower on the ground was providing support with 1,300 pieces of artillery firing 60,000 tons of ammunition.

The RAF and USAAF mounted further bombing operations to support the advance and destroy further the infrastructure supporting Germany's war effort. One target was the city of Dresden which had been identified as having hundreds of factories, rail and communications centres for troop movements and a workforce of around 50,000. Between 13 and 15 February, four massive raids in which 4,000 tons of bombs were dropped, succeeded in destroying 23 per cent of the industrial capacity and 56 per cent of non-industrial buildings along with civilian residences. At the time the attack was controversial, but thought necessary.

As the British 21st Army Group was advancing in the north, the Americans in the south were keeping up pressure with US 6th and 12th Armies pushing forward and capturing intact the bridge over the Rhine at Remagen on 7 March. German engineers had tried to demolish the bridge but it had proved stronger than they thought and it survived the explosion, albeit weakened. It would stand for another ten days until it finally collapsed, being targeted by German artillery and attacked by aircraft. The collapse came after the Americans had moved 25,000 men, vehicles and supplies across the river. To replace the bridge engineers used 30,000 tons of equipment to build pontoon and Bailey bridges across the river.

Between 20 and 22 March the RAF and USAAF flew around 16,000 sorties in support of ground operations and dropped 49,500 tons of bombs on targets from supply dumps to troop positions. Montgomery finally crossed the Rhein on 23 March. The skies were dominated by Allied aircraft which meant that friendly traffic could move in daylight to deliver supplies in a continuous convoy system while intercepting anything the Germans moved. One pilot remembered attacking German vehicles moving on the roads: 'I…decided to bomb first on the curve in the road. I dropped my two wing bombs on the curve, tore big holes in the road and knocked out six trucks. This stopped the whole column deader than a duck. Then we really went to work: bombed and strafed the column of tanks, half-tracks, cargo-trucks and horse-drawn vehicles over an area of about five miles.' The city of Berlin lay miles away, but it was not scheduled for attack by the Western Allies. It had already been agreed that that task would be left to the Russians.

The following day, the Allies launched Operation Varsity, an airlift to transport troops over the Rhine. Aircraft began to take off from airbases in England and France and flew to the rendezvous point over Brussels before turning north-east for the Rhine dropping zones. The airlift included 541 transport aircraft for airborne troops along with a further 1,050 troop-carriers towing 1,350 gliders. The US 17th Airborne Division transported 9,387 in 836 C-47 Dakotas, 72 C-46 Commando transports and more than 900 Waco CG-4A gliders. The British 6th Airborne Division was made up of 7,220 personnel flown in using 42 Douglas C-54 and 752 C-47 Dakota transport aircraft, as well as 420 Airspeed Horsa and General Aircraft Hamilcar gliders. The British glider airlift included 342 Jeeps, 348 trailers, 3 gun-trailers, 7 Locust light tanks, 14 lorries, 2 bulldozers, 11 carriers, 19 cars of 5cwt, 59 light motorcycles, 127 heavy motorcycles, 68 bicycles, 20 field cycles, 378 panniers, 53 handcarts, 10 mortars of 4.2 inch calibre, 2 75mm guns, 50 6-pounder anti-tank guns, 12 17-pounder anti-tank guns, and two 25-pounder field guns. Bomber aircraft such as Liberators dropped other supplies and air cover was provided by more than 1,200 Mustang and Thunderbolt fighters which could also attack ground targets including German supply lines.

The Hamilcar glider could carry troops, supplies or vehicles and was used in operations such as Market Garden and Varsity.

Hamilcar glider seen here in flight, tow-rope still attached.

Hamilcar glider being towed by an RAF Lancaster bomber.

Hamilcar glider being loaded with a Locust light tank, showing its capacity to lift vehicles.

When airborne, the fleet of aircraft extended more than 200 miles and took 2 hours and 37 minutes to pass any given point. It was protected by some 2,153 Allied fighters from the US Ninth Air Force and the Royal Air Force. The combination of the two divisions in one lift made this the largest single-day airborne drop in history. At 10 am British and American troops belonging to the 6th and 17th Airborne Divisions began landing on German soil, some thirteen hours after the Allied ground assault began. The Rhine crossing was observed by the war correspondent Wynford Vaughan-Thomas: 'All the way from the river bank, the roads are full of new troops moving up and infantry marching through the dust, and the farmhouses being taken over as headquarter, ration dumps being set up in the fields…all the signs of the army moving in, in a big way.'

On 23 March, as Montgomery was crossing the Rhine, Patton distributed an open letter to the Third Army and the XIX Tactical Air Command. The men had 'wrested 6,484 square miles of territory from the enemy. You have taken 3,072 cities, towns and villages…You have captured 140,112 enemy soldiers, and have killed or wounded an additional 99,000, thereby eliminating practically all of the German 7th and 1st Armies.' Patton had famously said, 'No bastard ever won a war by dying for his country. He won it by making the other poor dumb bastard die for his country.' In this letter, Patton was evidently making a reference to this. He finishes off by expressing his 'heartfelt admiration and thanks for what you have done, and remember that your assault crossing over the Rhine at 2200 hours last night assures you of even greater glory to come.' Patton had also said, 'Don't tell people how to do things, tell them what to do and let them surprise you with the results.' They had done all he had said, and much more besides, in just over seven weeks of combat. He expresses his gratitude to XIX Tactical Air Command: 'from the air, the peerless fighter-bombers kept up a relentless round-the-clock attack on the disorganized enemy.' Although he does not make any mention of the logistic support which allowed all this happen, he no doubt realised it all the same knowing full well that the 'campaign was only made possible by your disciplined valor, unswerving devotion to duty, coupled with the unparalleled audacity and speed of your advance on the ground.' Such momentum could only be maintained by logistical support.

As late as April 1945, much of Holland still lay under German occupation and the food situation was growing increasingly desperate for the three million Dutch civilians. In one of the most incredible incidents of the war, an armistice was arranged in which Allied aircraft would be allowed to drop food supplies to Dutch civilians and the Germans would not fire on the aircraft. British Operation Manna and American

Dutch Resistance fighters of the 'Flushing Division' march past in a liberation parade in 1945.

The town of Eindhoven in Holland is finally liberated.

Operation Chowhound dropped 11,000 tons of food between 29 April and 7 May. On 2 May, 200 trucks were permitted to pass unmolested through German lines to make further deliveries of food. There was no such good fortune for the Channel Islands, isolated since June 1944, where the military garrison and civilians were existing on meagre rations. No deliveries were arranged even though the civilians were British

After the German surrender on Guernsey in the Channel Islands on 8 May 1945, the British wasted no time in removing the German garrison and bringing in supplies for the civilian population.

The clear-up operation was not without its risks, as here with a truck which has veered off the road above the harbour at St Helier on Jersey in the Channel Islands.

German war materiel is loaded onto a German Siebel ferry in St Helier Harbour, ready to be taken out to sea for disposal.

This French FT-17 Renault tank was used on Guernsey by the German occupying force.

citizens. A raiding party had managed to steal an entire cargo ship laden with coal from France after the Allied landing and the last food shipment from France had been in July 1944 before the fall of Brest.

In January 1945, weekly rations were less than two ounces of fat, 1.5 ounces of meat and vegetables around seven pounds per week, but these could not be guaranteed. The Red Cross arranged for deliveries of food parcels transported from Portugal on the SS *Vega*. Five such deliveries were made with 460,000 food parcels for the more than 80,000 civilian population between Guernsey and Jersey. The garrison of 30,000 troops had to make their own arrangements for food, which did go further now that it did not have to be shared with the civilians. Guernsey would be liberated on 8 May followed by Jersey the next day. Clearing the islands of war material would require the removal of 50,000 tons of ammunition along with hundreds of thousands of weapons. The indigenous herds of cattle were decimated and other livestock had been almost wiped out.

On the Eastern Front, the Russians were making plans for the final assault on Germany. The scale of the logistical build-up for the attack on Berlin was immense. Zhukov noted, 'The nature of the operation required a steady stream of ammunition from front depots to the troops, bypassing the intermediate links such as army and divisional depots. The railway line was converted to the Russian gauge and ammunition was brought up almost to the very bank of the Oder. To picture the scale of these transport operations it suffices to say that if the trains used to carry these supplies were stretched out buffer to buffer they would have extended over a distance exceeding 1200 kilometres.'

The gauge of railway used across western Europe was standardised on a track width of 4′8½″. This meant that German locomotives could operate on French and Belgian tracks. However the standard gauge for railway tracks in Russia was slightly wider at five feet. On the Eastern Front when the Russians retreated, destroying the railways as they went, German army engineers repaired the lines and laid them to western standard which allowed them to use their own rolling stock or that captured from France or other occupied countries. When the Russians advanced, they were faced with the same problems as the Germans who destroyed rolling stock and ripped up the tracks in their retreat. As they advanced further and invaded Germany, the Russians used whole armies of engineers to repair roads, build bridges and repair the railway track, which was laid to the Russian five-foot gauge which was the most expedient solution to the problem, because it fitted their locomotives.

The First Belorussian Army had 125 combat engineering battalions attached to it and these built 136 bridges for the advance and constructed command posts and bunkers in the thousands. The attack on Berlin would involve 85,000 trucks and 10,000 other vehicles to tow the artillery. A total of seven million shells were stockpiled and it was believed that over one million would be fired in the opening phase of the attack.

A fleet of 2,450 train wagons moved 1.23 million shells, totalling some 98,000 tons, forward in readiness.

The Russians and the Americans had made direct contact with one another at Torgau on the River Elbe on 25 April, but fighting was still raging. The Russians and Western allies had liberated the death camps at Auschwitz, Belsen and others. Humanitarian aid had to be transported in. Patton headed into Czechoslovakia and American troops had crossed the northern border of Austria at several places. The days when German artillery could fire 50,000 tons of ammunition and continue to fight after having lost 25,000 men, as happened in capturing Sevastopol in July 1942, were long gone, but Hitler still believed his army could pull back from the brink of defeat. In a desperate measure he appointed Himmler, head of the SS and with no formal military training at any level, to command Army Group Vistula in the north. The Russians were now only forty miles from Berlin and Hitler responded by ordering operations to be conducted in the south by understrength units lacking in supplies, which only served to cost the army more troops lost and tanks destroyed.

Further pressure was exerted by the Russians as Zhukov ordered the 1st Belorussian Front forward, crossing the Oder and advancing six miles across a front thirty miles wide. This force, together with the 2nd Belorussian and 1st Ukrainian Fronts, now threatened Berlin directly. Fighting slowed the Russian advance down somewhat as

The Russian advance of 1944 was spearheaded by the T-34 tank.

The British army crossed the Rhine in 1945 at several places. Here vehicles, including Matadors, cross the river using a pontoon bridge.

the Germans put up a concerted defence, but it was only prolonging the inevitable. The Russians scheduled the final push for 16 April and the 2nd Belorussian Front was ordered north to deal with the German 3rd Panzer Army. This still left Zhukov with 2.5 million men, 41,000 pieces of artillery, 6,250 tanks and AFVs, with air support from 7,500 aircraft. The Germans had 700,000 men, 9,000 pieces of artillery and 1,500 tanks and AFVs. The Volkssturm comprising of old men and the Hitler Youth added another 70,000 men. The best they could hope would be to slow the Russian advance.

Zhukov began the final assault with a massive bombardment from artillery positioned at the rate of one gun every 13 feet along a front stretching over 55 miles. By 25 April

Once across the Rhine, the Allies continued to advance into Germany, as seen here with British troops supported by Sherman tanks.

the city had been encircled by the pincers of the 1st Belorussian Front to the north and the 1st Ukrainian Front in the south. It was a strategy reminiscent of the vast encircling movements which had led to the Russian victory over the German army at Stalingrad in January 1943. Hitler appointed General Karl Weidling, commanding the remnants of the LVI Panzer Corps, in charge of defending Berlin. By now, all Weidling had left in his own unit were some 1,500 men and 60 tanks. Berlin was ringed by a series of anti-tank ditches, dug by a labour force which included civilian men and women, but these and other obstacles did not pose a problem for the Russians as they advanced. On 21 April indeed, the Russians had already broken into the suburbs of the city and street fighting had broken out. Tanks are not suited to fighting in urban conditions, but the Russians pushed them in anyway to deal with last remaining German vehicles. They were joined by artillery units firing their SPGs at buildings at point blank range, causing them to collapse on the defenders. In the Reichstag, the parliament building, over 5,000 troops fortified their position.

On 28 April, Himmler attempted to make one of the most extraordinary deals of the war when, with Count Bernadotte of Sweden, he tried to exchange Jews for trucks. He told Count Bernadotte that he was prepared to release 100,000 Jews from concentration camps in return for 10,000 trucks from the Americans. Exactly what he intended to use so many vehicles for at such a late stage in the war can only be guessed at. Furthermore, what he proposed to use as fuel given there was nothing in Germany for a fleet of vehicles this size was anyone's guess. In the end, nothing came of the talks. Day by day the Russians continued to press in on all sides, reducing the Germans' pockets of resistance.

Air Chief Marshal Arthur Tedder with Soviet General Sokolovsky in a meeting of Allied leaders on 7 May 1945.

On 30 April Hitler committed suicide in his headquarters bunker in Berlin, just as the Russians made their attack against the Reichstag. For two days they fought from room to room and floor by floor killing half the defending force. In Italy the Germans finally surrendered and on 5 May German forces in Denmark surrendered. Fighting across Berlin continued for almost a further week as diehard units continued to resist. Gradually these last small pockets of resistance surrendered. It was finally over and the cost had been the lives of 100,000 defenders. The 8 May was declared VE Day (Victory Europe Day) and the end of the war was proclaimed.

When the German army had gone to war in 1939 there had been 328 tanks to a division, by 1943 that number was reduced to 73, and by the time of Germany's surrender, only 54. There was no fuel to move them and very little ammunition. The once-great military machine no longer had any fight left in it. The cost to the army was 3.25 million killed and two million wounded out of a total of ten million servicemen and women mobilised. Before the war, Germany had a population of over 79 million of which two million had been killed in air raids.

Captured German trucks being used to take German PoWs into captivity.

Chapter 21

Burma

The fighting on the mainland in Burma would develop its own unique set of problems concerning resupply because of the distances involved and the difficult terrain. The troops on the ground could only carry so much with them, either as individuals or on mules. To maintain their operational status these men had to be resupplied by air drops. This was something which the Germans had tried with mixed results. With the Allies, it would be different because their air power was in the ascendancy and became the dominant force in the region.

For example, during the Imphal and Kohima battles the British Chindit forces were kept supplied by the 3rd Tactical Air Force of the RAF which flew hundreds of missions and covered many thousands of miles during a period of four months in early 1944. At one point during the battle for Kohima, when some 15,000 British and Indian troops were surrounded by the Japanese and cut off, these men were supplied by air drops. Each day 400 tons of supplies were dispatched by a fleet of 130 aircraft flown by RAF and USAAF pilots. The aircraft came from eight squadrons of Dakotas bolstered by a force of twenty C46 Curtiss Commandos. The Japanese could not match this. In a period of four months between January and April 1944, Troop Carrier Command delivered 69,000 tons of supplies to the Imphal-Kohima area, an average of 575 tons per day. This was what the Germans had wanted at Stalingrad to keep a much larger force supplied, but they failed. With better aircraft and in greater numbers, the Allies could meet the challenge.

Japanese supply lines were mainly road and track with mules to deliver ammunition and food. It was never enough and amounted to only a fraction of what the troops needed. It was but a trickle compared to what the Allies could deliver to their troops. Japanese and Allied troops alike carried heavy loads with them. Typically, a man on patrol in the jungle carried a personal load weighing up to sixty pounds, comprising mainly ammunition and about two pounds of food which included biscuits, cheese, dried fruit and tea. This could be supplemented by bartering with villagers living in the jungle who could supply fresh fruit and possibly eggs or meat. However it was aircraft, such as the Dakota or the Commando C46 with an operational range of 3,000 miles which could transport nearly seven tons of cargo or forty troops, which made the massive difference to Allied troops on the ground. These aircraft could also evacuate thirty wounded men as stretcher cases when operating from airfields. One of these

The cost to US airmen in the Pacific was high. Here, a wounded gunner is lifted from the turret of his badly-damaged Grumman 'Avenger' torpedo-bomber.

airfields was established at Sinzweya where the British had a massive supply dump and administrative area operated by Royal Army Ordnance Corps, RASC, Royal Corps of Transport and Royal Army Medical Corps. Nearby was the Ngakyedauk (nicknamed 'Okeydoke' by the troops) Pass. It was along this route that General William Slim said passed 'the vehicles, stores and equipment for the 7th Division'.

During their operations, the Chindits lost 17,000 mules and pack ponies. These had to be replaced and were usually flown in by air. It is estimated that between 1944 and the end of the war the Allies used 23,600 mules for transport, along with more than 6,700 horses. These animals had been used with success during the Italian campaign and in North Africa and were proving invaluable in the Far East. Major Frank Turner was a mule transport officer with Wingate's second expedition and he remembered mules as being unpredictable, but very useful animals. Fodder for the mules had to be delivered by airdrops but they had a fondness for eating green bamboo. Frank Turner recalled how this diet caused the animals to develop diarrhoea which attracted the flies. If an animal became lame it was of no use and had to be shot. Frank Turner said, 'I would despatch that mule, having transferred his load if it was an important one, such as a radio set. Our chaps would have mule steaks that night if we could have a fire. I shot the mule, no one else in the whole brigade was allowed to do it. I did it with my revolver.' Brigadier 'Mad Mike' Calvert had mules in his unit during the first Chindit expedition and remembered with great affection one animal which the men called 'Mable'. They looked after her and came to see her as some a kind of mascot and could not bring themselves to even consider the possibility of eating her, even though they were hungry. Brigadier Calvert became convinced that if anything had happened to Mable the troops' morale would have dropped. Mable survived the rigors of jungle warfare and returned safely to India.

The Japanese were finding it difficult to resupply their troops and air drops were impossible due to the Allies having air supremacy. On its own, the RAF flew in one million gallons of fuel, 6,250 tons of supplies including food, ammunition and medical equipment along with 12,000 replacement troops and evacuating 13,000 casualties. That was only part of the overall total to support operations in Burma. Between 1943 and 1945 the combined efforts of the Allied air forces flew some 650,000 tons of supplies into airstrips which had been carved out deep in the jungle. They also flew in 315,000 men and evacuated 110,000 casualties all of which kept the campaign moving. In addition to problems with air supply, the Japanese were now finding that the local civilian population, who once saw them as liberators from European colonialism, were turning against them and refusing to provide food.

In Burma, the Japanese had the potential to recruit some 200,000 men who were in the Burma Independence Army which had sprung up on the outbreak of war in the Far East. However, their harsh treatment by the Japanese reduced this number to 50,000 and ultimately, being unreliable, proved to be of limited military. The Burmese wore what uniforms they had and used a mixture of captured weaponry or supplied by the Japanese. The Japanese also, like the Germans, recruited some troops from PoW camps, such as the 40,000 Indian troops who were formed into the Indian National Army. They enlisted to get better treatment and improved conditions. The large majority deserted when deployed and made their way back to British-held areas. Smaller groups engaged in sabotage duties to disrupt the supply lines such as the railway system. Of the Indian troops who did fight, such as the 7,000 men of the 1st Division, taking part in the battles of Imphal, Kohima and the Arakan between January and June 1944, only 2,600 survived.

Sir Robert Thompson, who in February 1943 was serving as a flight lieutenant in the RAF and attached to the Chindits as a liaison officer, wrote about air supply drops to various units: 'This air supply became so efficient that the troops relied on it completely. You could run yourself down to one day's rations or less, you could go a day almost without rations and know perfectly well that if you demanded a supply drop at 10.00pm one night in a particular area of the jungle or in a paddy field alongside you knew you were going to get it.' This was only possible after the Allies had recovered and went on the offensive with air superiority. In the first months of the war in the Far East the Japanese had mastery of the air, and resupply, even if the troops had not been retreating, would have been almost impossible. The only problem lay in delivering fresh, clean drinking water. This commodity was essential in preventing illness among the troops on the ground. There was plenty of water to be accessed, but most of it was contaminated by parasites. Marine Frazer West, serving on Bougainville Island, remembered the lack of fresh water: '...bad diarrhea – bad water...you can develop diarrhea real quick.' Air drops of clean, fresh water were necessary on occasion to prevent such troubles, and especially to prevent dysentery. Unfortunately, not all air crews were trained or experienced in how to deliver water and much was lost when dropped from the air.

On 13 November 1943, the first elements of a newly-created American unit arrived in Delhi, India, with the mission of providing air support to the Allied forces fighting the Japanese in Burma. This new unit was commanded by Lieutenant Colonel Philip Cochran who had been given permission to raise the force known as the No 1 Air Commando Force (ACF). Among his force of aircraft were 25 transport planes, 12 medium bombers, 30 fighter-bombers, 100 light aircraft and 225 gliders. In three months, Cochran was ready to lead the unit's first bombing mission against Japanese communications routes and supply lines in northern Burma on 3 February 1944. The unit could also provide air supply drops to Allied units using parachute and glider.

US Marines fighting on Bougainville with support from Sherman tanks.

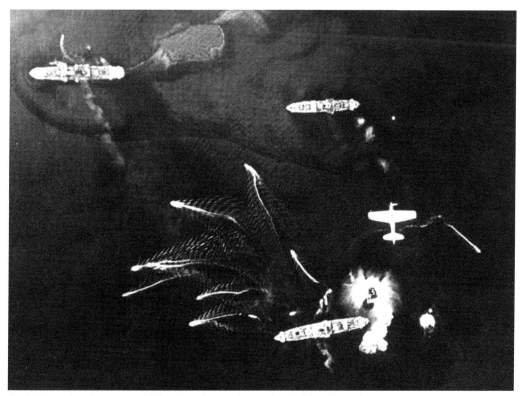

Aerial view showing an amphibious landing underway in the island hopping campaign. It is being shelled by the Japanese as the landing craft head towards the shore.

Parachutes used in supply drops were traditionally made from silk which was lightweight and strong but it was expensive. After drops into the jungle very few parachutes were recovered for further use and the silk material was usually abandoned. This created a problem of providing replacement parachutes. A British army officer, Major Alfred Snellings, searched around Indian factories to try to find an alternative to silk. He discovered a solution in Calcutta where factories had developed a material using jute which could be used for parachute canopies. It was discovered that the material, which would be called 'parajute', was 85 per cent as efficient as silk which was acceptable when delivering supplies such as ammunition, food and weapons. However, when it came to deliveries of more fragile supplies such as replacement radios, medical equipment and troops, the traditional silk parachute was used because of its better qualities. Jute had a long history of being processed to make material for sacks but mostly for the manufacture of rope. During the First World War, Britain had grown around 18,000 tons annually to make textile material for covering aircraft, but this amount was dwarfed by the crop grown in India where conditions were ideal for its cultivation. The local workforce was sufficiently large to process it into other material suitable for a wide range of purposes, such as harnesses for mules and horses.

In March 1944, No 1 ACF was called on to supply the Chindits who had established the bases known as Piccadilly and Broadway 200 miles behind Japanese lines in the Irrawaddy Valley. The Japanese had advanced across the River Chindwin and were threatening Allied bases in Imphal and Kohima. In that month, the ACF used gliders to fly in 539 reinforcements and deliver by airdrop 13 tons of supplies for the Chindits. Also in that month, a 4,700-foot airstrip had been created at Broadway which allowed No 1 ACF to land supplies and evacuate the sick and wounded. The first arrivals were 6 Dakotas which landed in daylight followed by a further 67 aircraft which flew in during the night to deliver more reinforcements and heavy equipment. Admiral Lord Mountbatten, Supreme Commander of South-East Asia Command, wrote, '…it was not just a question of auxiliary air supply, because ninety-six per cent of our supplies to the Fourteenth Army went by air.'

By contrast the Japanese were finding it extremely difficult to bring their resupplies forward and at one point during the campaign the artillery of the 31st Division of 15th Army had stocks of only 100 to 150 rounds per gun. The artillery of the 33rd Division, on the other hand, had stocks of 1,000 rounds per gun. Forces under Lieutenant General

Australian and British troops land with tanks in Burma.

Renya Mutaguchi were expecting 48,000 tons of supplies from Singapore but by the end of January 1944 less than half that amount had been delivered. It had been planned to transport 3,000 tons of supplies each day but lack of aircraft meant that only 400 tons on average was being delivered, most of it coming overland carried on mules. Japanese soldiers obtained mules and even elephants from the larger villages which could haul guns for the artillery, but elephants were slow, ponderous beasts and depending on conditions could only manage to travel at one mile an hour. To try to preserve what stock he had, Mutaguchi ordered that supplies be dispersed and hidden in jungle. Allied aircraft located these caches and destroyed them. The Japanese believed they lost 20 per cent of their supplies through such air strikes. To supplement these losses, the Japanese used stocks of food and ammunition captured from the British.

The fighting at Kohima and Imphal cost the Japanese 30,000 killed and 25,000 wounded out of a force of 85,000 men committed to the fighting. In terms of other irreplaceable losses, all vehicles, including all tanks, had been destroyed and all animal transportation was killed. The survivors faced starvation and further depletion due to tropical diseases as they withdrew. The Japanese war correspondent Shizuo Maruyama wrote, 'We had no ammunition, no food, no clothes, no guns…the men were barefoot and ragged and threw away everything except canes to help them walk…all they had to keep them going was grass and water…. . At Kohima we were starved and then crushed.'

One of the supply routes across the area was known as the Burma Road. Stretching 712 miles, it had been built in 1937/8 by a workforce of 250,000 Chinese labourers. It ran from Lashio in Burma to Kunming in China and was the main route along which America could send supplies to support the Chinese Nationalist Army of General Chiang Kai-shek in the war against Japan which had invaded in 1937. An article in the *Manchester Guardian* on 2 February 1941 stated that every day some 5,000 trucks used the route to transport 30,000 tons of supplies. Whether it was this item, which may have been reported to army intelligence in Tokyo, that prompted the Japanese to attack the route is not clear, but when the Japanese captured Lashio on 29 April 1942 they cut the road and held it until 3 May 1945 when they were finally pushed back.

An additional 400-mile section of this vital supply route would become known as the Ledo Road. Construction began in late 1942 and involved 17,000 American engineers, 50,000 Indian labourers and thousands more Chinese. Some doubted whether it would ever be any use, but it did prove valuable in allowing vast quantities of supplies to be moved to the troops fighting the Japanese. Work progressed to improve the railway track between Allahabad and Assam, so that by October 1944 it was carrying 4,400 tons of supplies each day. Fuel was being piped across 275 miles from Bombay to Bhusawal and the port facilities at Calcutta and Chittagong were greatly improved and enlarged.

Between March 1941 and October 1945, America would send Chiang Kai-shek military and medical aid to the value of $631,509,000 and in return no real cohesive force would emerge, even though in 1942 there were 3.8 million men in Chiang's army. When supplies amounting to 40,000 tons of weapons, ammunition and other equipment was delivered by air to Myitkyina, the Chinese Nationalist Army there still made little difference to the situation. Indeed, much of these deliveries were stolen before they could be distributed to the troops.

Once air routes had been established and protective air cover provided, No 1 ACF flew in more supplies and troops for the Chindits with an average of 100 flights each night. The fighter cover of the ACF comprising Mustangs intercepted Japanese aircraft and ground troops moving in to attack Broadway. The operations during the month had resulted in the Chindits destroying 50 aircraft, 38 supply depots, several ammunition dumps, 4 trains and 8 bridges all of which reduced the Japanese ability to supply their troops and thereby restricted their ability to fight. A second airstrip was carved out of the jungle at Broadway and during the course of one week the RAF flew 650 night sorties with Dakotas and gliders to deliver 9,000 reinforcement troops to the Chindits, 1,350 transport animals, 250 tons of stores, a battery of light anti-aircraft guns and another battery of 25-pounder field guns into the heart of Japanese-held Burma. The ACF also delivered 223 tons of supplies and evacuated 1,200 sick and wounded.

British supply drop at East Kaladan to support operations against the Japanese.

The Japanese army deployed 620,000 troops to China and to support the Chinese troops engaged against this force the Americans established the Air Transport Command (ATC) with units of the 10th Air Force flying missions to deliver supplies. The American pilots were based in Assam and flew a route which took them over the Himalayas – the pilots called it 'flying the hump'. To fly the 700-mile route the pilots operated from airfields in India to reach depots such as Yunnanyi and Kunming in south-west China. They had to cope with severe weather conditions and were constantly exposed to attack by Japanese fighters. In 1942, the ATC were using C-46 and C-47 transport aircraft and the C-87, a transport conversion created from B-24 bombers. This fleet of aircraft was initially able to transport 3,700 tons of supplies per month but by late 1944 this figure had risen ten-fold to exceed 35,000 tons per month. Each aircraft could carry a cargo of four to five tons but each one could only complete one round trip daily. The route remained operational for almost three years and losses were high. During 1943 the ATC lost 468 aircraft. As well as supplying Chinese forces, the aircraft of the ATC joined with the RAF as it continued to deliver supplies to the Chindits.

In the face of such levels of resupply the Japanese could not hope to compete. They continued to rely heavily on their manpower who fought just as fanatically and suicidally as on the Pacific islands – but as the war continued this resource was dwindling. They used horses and mules, as did the Allies, but not in the same numbers. The Japanese did not treat their animals very well and the 15th and 33rd Divisions lost some 5,000 animals due to lack of food, wounds and disease.

The Chindits, while having the support of superior air power with the capacity to deliver huge amounts of supplies, were frugal when it came to food. The troops developed a taste for rice and tried adding different flavours to make it interesting. Flight Lieutenant Robert Thompson of the RAF noted: 'the troops had to learn to be mobile in the jungle and to live on fairly tight rations. I certainly think that the two things from my point of view that I felt the need of most were hot sweet tea and rice. I got used to rice as the bulk food. You could make it up into something more palatable even if you were only adding curry powder to it or chocolate or melted cheese or something to make a hot evening meal. We could never have done those type of operations on what I would call normal rations. One, you couldn't have carried them. Secondly, I don't think that troops in those sort of circumstances need them. If you are fit before you go in [to the jungle] and well fed then you can manage two or three months on very light rations. You know you're going to be well fed again when you come out and you have, I think, a better stamina if you go in a bit too well fed. I always used to think that one didn't go into a thing like this like a Derby winner. You went into it with quite a bit of fat on you because that's part of what you were living on while you were in there.'

Chapter 22

Iwo Jima and Okinawa

The 'island hopping' campaign was continuing and gaining momentum with each success. This was a purely American campaign. Landings had been made in 1942 which were followed up throughout 1943 and 1944, inflicting further defeats on the Japanese. On 9 January 1945, American troops landed on Luzon in the Philippine Islands where the Japanese had 275,000 troops. The numbers looked impressive, but they had little in the way of supplies or reinforcements. The American victory at Leyte Gulf had seen to that with the destruction of the Japanese navy. The man behind the success to clear out Luzon was General Eichelberger, who had graduated from West Point in 1909 and seen service in Panama, the Mexican Expedition and the First World War. In 1940, he had instituted changes in the training programme to better prepare troops for the war in which he knew America would inevitably become involved.

After Pearl Harbor, Eichelberger applied for an active command and was appointed to the 77th Infantry Division. Six months later, in June 1942, he was asked to organise a demonstration of troops to a group of visiting dignitaries, including Winston Churchill. His organisational skill impressed the whole group and he was given the task of preparing the amphibious landings in North Africa. He did not take part in the landings however, and was transferred instead to Australia in August 1942, where he established a rigorous training regime. When troops were sent to Buna, he went with them and shared in their hardships. In January 1944, he was given command of the amphibious landings at Hansa Bay on New Guinea. Stores were being unloaded but left exposed on the beach. A lone Japanese aircraft flew overhead and strafed the fuel dump which ignited and destroyed 60 per cent of the ammunition stocks. In August he was given command of the US Eighth Army and assumed operations on Leyte Island in December. In January 1945, the Eighth Army moved to Luzon where it conducted 14 major amphibious operations to clear the Japanese out of the islands, along with another 24 smaller operations. Deliveries of supplies continued to improve and reached a record 90,000 tons per week within two months.

The next island to be targeted was the tiny volcanic rock measuring eight square miles called Iwo Jima, lying only 600 miles from the home islands of Japan. The commander of the garrison was Lieutenant General Tadamichi Kuribayashi, who had over 21,000 troops supported with 23 tanks, 438 pieces of artillery, 33 naval guns, 69 anti-tank guns and 300 anti-aircraft guns. The troops had machine guns, rifles, mortars and all the other equipment associated with infantry units. They had also had plenty of time to prepare their defences which included excavating eleven miles of tunnels which interconnected with caves, pillboxes and trenches, all well protected. For all their preparations, though, they were not adequately supplied. The garrison had only been receiving a trickle of the supplies they required due to American control of the waters which intercepted convoys. As a result, the garrison on Iwo Jima had only 60 per cent of the ammunition stocks required and food and fuel for four months. There were three airfields on the island but their aircraft were outclassed and outnumbered by the Americans'.

Once the island had been chosen as the target, the Americans began to bombard it. For seventy-six days prior to the landing, Iwo Jima was subjected to intense bombing from aircraft and naval gunfire. The Japanese retreated into the caves and tunnels for shelter, where they had 550 barrels of fuel for generators to provide light and power for the radio sets. On 19 February, around 9am, the first wave of about 8,000 American troops waded ashore and began to stumble up the black volcanic sand. At first they believed the bombardment had done the job because there was no enemy fire. The marines from the 4th and 5th Divisions advanced about 300 yards in from the beach, where the first vehicles were being landed along with supplies. That was when the Japanese unleashed a devastating fire and inflicted heavy casualties.

As successive waves of landing craft from the Fifth Fleet of 500 ships approached the shore they were fired on by Japanese artillery. The troops were ashore and now the struggle to move inland began in earnest. The Japanese held every foot of ground and the marines had to fight all the way. More vehicles were brought ashore, including the earthmoving equipment needed by the Seabees to repair and improve the airfields as they were captured. The airfields would allow B-29 bombers to fly missions against factories and military installations in Japan. A workforce of some 18,000 Seabees was landed.

Between 19 February and 26 March, 110,000 troops, including marines, army and support troops, would be committed to the battle. With no chance of relief or reinforcements, the Japanese fought on with suicidal fanaticism. The Americans, with numerical superiority on land, naval domination of the waters around the island and air supremacy, were still faced with a determined enemy. Two weeks after the landings, the first American aircraft were using the airfields. These were bombers returning from raids over mainland Japan which had developed engine trouble. Being able to land on Iwo Jima saved them from being lost.

By the time the island was declared secure, the Americans had lost 6,821 killed and 19,217 wounded. The Japanese had lost around 18,000 killed and only 216 taken prisoner. The remaining 3,000 hid out until they were eliminated by American patrols.

The battle for the island was summed up by General Holland Smith, one of the most successful planners of amphibious operations, who called it 'the toughest we've run into in 168 years'. He went on to say, 'When the capture of an enemy position is necessary to winning a war it is not within our province to evaluate the cost in money, time, equipment, or most of all, in human life. We are told what our objective is to be and we approach the job.'

On 1 April, as the last mopping-up patrols were being completed on Iwo Jima, 850 miles away directly west another, even larger, amphibious landing was preparing to land on Okinawa. This was Operation Iceberg, supported by an armada of 1,500 ships, including 430 landing craft and assault ships, 40 escort carriers with aircraft, 18 battleships, and 200 destroyers. This was three times the size of the fleet supporting the landings on Iwo Jima. For the preliminary barrage to break up the defences on Okinawa it was estimated that the naval artillery would have to fire almost 250,000 rounds of ammunition of all calibres before the first wave of the invasion was launched. In addition, around 35,000 rockets would be fired and aircraft would drop 44,000 bombs. The strength of the defending force was estimated to be between 55,000 and 65,000 troops along with 200 pieces of artillery. The ships in the fleet carried 27,000 tons of anti-aircraft ammunition to defend against *kamikaze* air attacks which the Japanese had used against the fleet at Iwo Jima. Pre-invasion estimates believed there would be a high casualty rate with American losses in the region of 75,000 killed, wounded and missing. Such estimates did not sit well with planners, but they had a job to do and to complete it, such facts had to be faced.

During the period of the island hopping campaign, invasion fleets had been growing in size and strength. Keeping the troops well supplied was a matter of course, but supplying so many ships at sea was highly specialist. To support the huge fleets assembled to mount the amphibious operations over the vast distances a comprehensive method of supplying the ships at sea had to be devised. The Central Pacific Drive conducted by Admiral Nimitz, initially based in Hawaii, would be supplied by mobile service squadrons which had been created to follow the fleet and keep it supplied as it moved forward. The most important of these units would be Service Squadron 10, with its headquarters at Majuro Atoll in the Marshall Islands, some 2,000 miles west of Hawaii.

This unit consisted of many different types of vessel to suit specific tasks: light barges or tenders which would be used to transfer supplies short distances to the larger ships, ammunition barges, hospital ships, and fuel tankers. The role of these ships would become increasingly important the further the distances to be covered. Escort carriers – light aircraft carriers carrying a complement of around forty-five aircraft – provided protection against air attack and acted as ferries to resupply the aircraft lost by the larger carriers.

After the defeat of the Japanese fleet at the Battle of Leyte Gulf in October 1944, Service Squadron 10 moved to Eniwetok in the Marshall Islands. From here it moved 1,400 miles south-west to Ulithi Atoll, from where it could support operations in the Philippines. A series of redundant fuel tankers were formed together to create a floating oil terminal to refuel ships. This was at the edge of the operational zone and to better provide the fleet formation a new supply unit known as the 'At Sea Logistics Service Group' was created which could ferry supplies and aircraft from Ulithi to the ships in the fleet. It was a simple solution to a monumental task and it kept the fleet on the move to support the amphibious landings.

The pre-invasion bombardment of Okinawa lasted a full week after which the initial landings were made without any opposition. The troops quickly established a beachhead eight miles wide extending inland for two miles. On the island, General Mitsuru Ushijima had 106,000 troops, 27 tanks, 743 pieces of artillery and 1,400 aircraft. The garrison was much stronger than had been calculated by American planners. Ushijima had been reassured by Tokyo that *kamikaze* suicide attacks would sink the American ships and leave them unsupported and without supplies.

American forces were much stronger with 183,000 combat troops, which would increase to 250,000, supported by 800 M4 Sherman tanks which easily outclassed Japanese armour. The Americans also had artillery superiority and dominated the skies

Part of an American convoy sailing during Operation Cartwheel to invade the Pacific islands. Every ship was loaded with troops, supplies and vehicles.

Scene on Okinawa showing the mountain of fuel drums used to keep the army on the move. Oil had been vital throughout the war.

and water around the island. The promised *kamikaze* attacks, along with warships, did sink 12 destroyers and 15 amphibious ships and damaged a further 386 other ships, but they did not inflict a level of damage which would have affected the operation. The American force had 750,000 tons of supplies and, with a well-established logistical supply route, it could be replenished.

The Japanese inaction to the landings was the calm before the storm which would last for over eleven weeks, during which time the fighting would reach levels of ferocity never before encountered on any of the other landings. At the commencement of operations, the weather had been fine, but as the weeks passed it began to rain with an intensity which turned the ground to mud. The tracks across the island, which measured seventy miles by seven, became impassable for vehicles, including tanks. The only vehicles which could move were the amphibious tractors (amtracs) and DUKWs and these were used to transport supplies. The Japanese launched suicidal charges against American positions and fought to the last man when holding defensive positions. The fighting ended on 22 June by which time the Japanese had lost 110,000 killed along with all their tanks and equipment. The Americans had lost 20,000 killed, 55,162 wounded, 700 aircraft and 225 tanks. It was an indicator of what lay ahead should the homeland islands of Japan, which lay only 340 miles away, be invaded.

Despite its losses, the combined strength of Japan's armed forces still numbered five million men. Of its 11,000 aircraft, few could be flown because of lack of fuel. Between 1941 and 1945 over 1,100 merchant ships of over 500 tons had been sunk which crippled the Japanese military machine. Operation Olympic, the invasion of Japan, was planned for December 1945. Meanwhile, B-29 heavy bombers were ranging across Japan attacking factories such as the Nakajima aero-engine plant, the Imperial Iron and Steel Works at Yawata, and the port installations. On 14 July, aircraft operating from carriers flew almost 1,400 sorties during which they sank and 20 merchant and 11 warships. Japan was being pounded relentlessly and still it would not surrender. Then, on 6 August, a B-29 dropped a single bomb of a new design which wiped out the city of Hiroshima with its supply bases, shipyards and factories. The blast killed at least 75,000 people and injured a further 68,000. This was the atomic bomb, unarguably the greatest secret weapon of the war. Three days later, another was dropped on Nagasaki with similar results. In the wake of this, the Japanese had no option but to surrender, which they did on 15 August. The war was over.

The fighting had finished, but the dismantling of Hitler's war machine would take time and some Japanese garrisons resisted until September 1945. Humanitarian aid was dispatched and the programme for resettlement of the millions of displaced persons was begun. The victims of the Nazi campaign to exterminate the Jews of Europe had to be treated, and slave labour workers returned home, some after more than four years of being separated from their families. Gradually the world returned to normality, and the process was greatly helped by the logistical support systems which had been developed for the military.

Today, modern armies around the world have a better logistical service than could have ever been imagined and it has only been made possible by the methods implemented during the Second World War. Armies today have helicopters and transport aircraft with heavy-lift capability which can support operations anywhere in the world. For over 2,000 years, logistics have been the 'silent partner' in military operations. This expertise which has been built up can be used just as easily for humanitarian aid following natural disasters as well as providing for the military forces. Many soldiers and civilians today can be thankful for the development of logistics.

Bibliography

Arnold-Forster, Mark, *The World at War*, William Collins, Sons & Co, London, 1973.

Bacon, Admiral Sir Reginald, et al (ed): *Warfare Today*, Odhams Press, London.

Barker, A.J., *Japanese Army Handbook 1939-1945*, Ian Allan, Surrey, 1979.

Beevor, Antony, *Stalingrad*, Penguin, London, 1999.

Brereton, J.M., *The Horse in War*, David & Charles, Devon, 1976.

Campbell, Christy, *The World War II Fact Book*, Futura, London, 1986. Chamberlain, Peter and Doyle, Hilary, *Encyclopedia of German Tanks of World War Two*, Arms & Armour, London, 1999.

Chandler, David, *The Art of Warfare on Land*, Penguin, London, 2000.

Davies, W.J.K., *German Army Handbook 1939-1945*, Ian Allan, Surrey, 1973. Deighton, Len, *Blitzkrieg*, Jonathan Cape, London, 1969.

Dyer, Gwynne, *War*, Guild Publishing, London, 1986.

Evans, Martin Marix, *Retreat, Hell! We Just Got Here! The American Expeditionary Force in France 1917-1918*, Osprey, Oxford, 1998.

Fletcher, David, et al, *Tiger Tank*, Haynes, Somerset, 2011.

Forty, George, *US Tanks of World War II*, Blandford Press, Dorset, 1983.

Foss, Christopher F. et al., *Tanks and Fighting Vehicles*, Salamander Books, London, 1977.

Georgano, G.N., *World War Two Military Vehicles*, Osprey, Oxford, 1994.

Hawks, Ellison, Captain R.A., *Britain's Wonderful Fighting Forces*, Odhams, London.

Jukes, Geoffrey, *Kursk the Clash of Armour*, MacDonal & Co, London, 1968.

Keane, Fergal, *Road of Bones*, Harper, London, 2010.

Macksey, Kenneth and Batchelor, John H., *Tank Warfare, A History of the Armoured Fighting Vehicle*, Military Book Society, London, 1970.

Macksey, Kenneth, *Panzer Division, The Mailed Fist*, MacDonald & Co, London, 1968.

Macksey, Kenneth, *The Guinness History of Land Warfare*, Guinness Superlatives, Middlesex, 1973.

Macksey, Kenneth et al, *The Guinness Book of Tank Facts & Feats*, Guinness Superlatives, London, 1976.

Morris, Eric, *Tanks, Tank Weaponry and Warfare*, Octopus, London, 1975.

Perrett, Bryan, *Knights of the Black Cross*, Grafton Books, London, 1990.

Perrett, Bryan, *Tank Warfare, Arms & Armour*, London, 1990.

Quarrie, Bruce, *Lightning Death, The Story of the Waffen SS*, Patrick Stephens Ltd, Somerset, 1991.

Rutherford, Ward, *Kasserine Baptism of Fire*, MacDonal & Co, London, 1970.

Smithers, A.J., *A New Excalibur*, Grafton Books, London, 1988.

Smurthwaite, David et al., *Against All Odds*, National Army Museum, London, 1989.

Sutherland, Jonathan, *World War II Tanks and AFVs*, Airlife, Shrewsbury, 2002.

Swaab, Jack, *Field of Fire*, Sutton Publishing Ltd, Stroud, 2005.

Townshend, Charles (ed.), *The Oxford Illustrated History of Modern War*, OUP, 1997.

Ware, Pat, *Military Jeep*, Haynes, Somerset, 2010.

Ware, Pat, *Sherman Tank*, Haynes, Somerset, 2012.

White, B.T., *Tanks and Other Armoured Fighting Vehicles of the World*, Blandford Press, Dorset, 1975.

Winter, Denis, *Death's Men; Soldiers of the Great War*, Penguin, London, 1979.

Winter, J.M, *The Experience of World War I*, Equinox, Oxford 1988.

Index